Battle Hardened

BATTLE
HARDENED

AN INFANTRY OFFICER'S HARROWING JOURNEY FROM D-DAY TO VE DAY

CRAIG S. CHAPMAN

REGNERY
HISTORY

Regnery History™ is a trademark of Salem Communications Holding Corporation; Regnery® is a registered trademark of Salem Communications Holding Corporation

Cataloging-in-Publication data on file with the Library of Congress

ISBN 978-1-62157-657-0
e-book ISBN 978-1-62157-708-9

Published in the United States by
Regnery History
An Imprint of Regnery Publishing
A Division of Salem Media Group
300 New Jersey Ave NW
Washington, DC 20001
www.RegneryHistory.com

Manufactured in the United States of America

10 9 8 7 6 5 4 3 2 1

Books are available in quantity for promotional or premium use. For information on discounts and terms, please visit our website: www.Regnery.com.

To Bill and Beth, and other couples like them, who bore the terrible burdens of global war, then went on to live their lives with love and grace—we needed you then.

CONTENTS

LIST OF MAPS

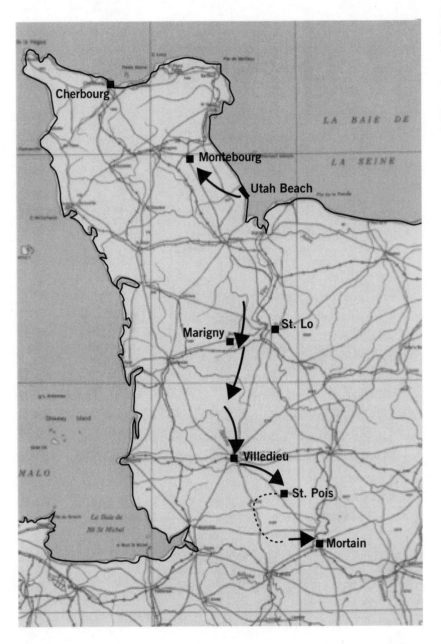

Map A

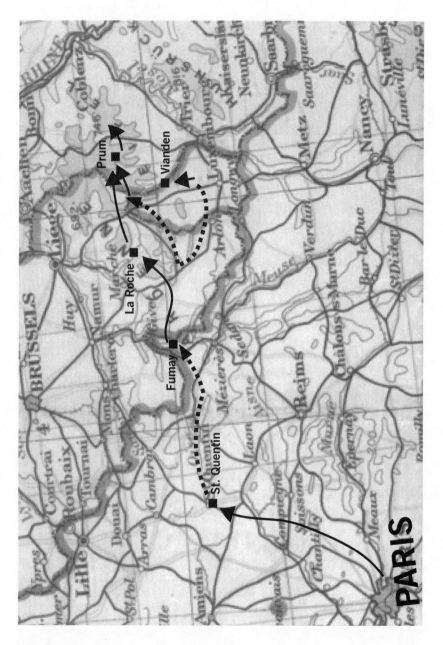

Map B

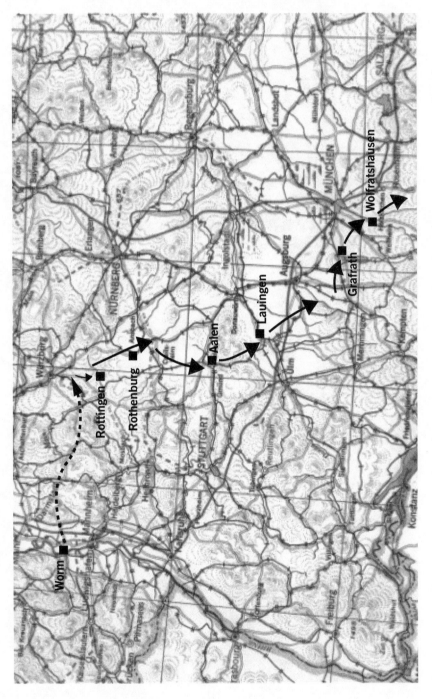

Map C

MAP ICON LEGEND

Unit Symbol:

Unit Size

Unit Identity

Parent Unit

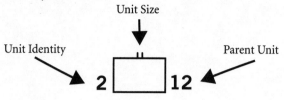

Unit Type:

American:

Infantry   Armor   Combined   Tank   Medical
                         Arms   Destroyer

German:

Volksgrenadier   Panzer   Panzergrenadier

Unit Size:

Symbol	Organization	Strength
XX	Division	~13,000
III	Regiment	~3,300
II	Battalion	894
I	Company	194
•••	Platoon	36 in MG Plt or 60 in Mortar Plt
••	Section	15-17

Miscellaneous Icons:

Mortar   88mm *Flak*   German   Pillboxes   Tank
Ditch   Gun   Position

LIST OF ILLUSTRATIONS

GLOSSARY

Terms and military organizations from non-English speaking nations have been italicized (e.g. *Panzerfaust* and *Second SS Panzer Division*) but not foreign place names (e.g. Villedieu les Poeles).

A&P	Ammunition and Pioneer Platoon—part of a rifle battalion headquarters company
AAR	After Action Report
Alpenfestung	Alpine Fortress—rumored German National Redoubt
AT	Anti-Tank
BAR	M1918A2 Browning Automatic Rifle
Bn	Battalion
CCA/B/R	Combat Command—regiment-sized unit in an armored division
CP	Command Post

CT	Combat Team—usually a regiment with attached tank, tank destroyer, and/or engineer units
DP	Displaced Person
FDC	Fire Direction Center—artillery team that plots fire missions then passes azimuth and elevation settings to the guns
FFI	French Forces of the Interior—organized elements of the French Resistance
FPL	Final Protective Line—a preset fire line of last resort for machine guns in a defensive position
FM	Field Manual—Army training publication
FO	Forward Observer
G-1/S-1	Personnel staff officer—division/regiment or battalion level
G-2/S-2	Intelligence staff officer—division/regiment or battalion level
G-3/S-3	Operations staff officer—division/regiment or battalion level
G-4/S-4	Logistical staff officer—division/regiment or battalion level
G-O-T	Gun–Observer–Target, abbreviation for fire control techniques to align guns on an observed target
HE	High Explosive
HQ	Headquarters
I&R	Intelligence & Reconnaissance—rifle regiment's platoon of scouts
IP	Initial Point—the spot where a march begins
Kampfgruppe	German ad hoc tactical force equivalent to an American task force
KIA	Killed In Action
LCI	Landing Craft Infantry—cross-channel vessel for personnel

LCM	Landing Craft Medium—assault boat
LCVP	Landing Craft Vehicle Personnel—assault boat, also called Higgins Boats
LD	Line of Departure—the designated line where an attack begins
LST	Landing Ship Tank—cross-channel vessel for heavy equipment
Luftwaffe	German Air Force
Mils	A precise angular measurement used by artillery and mortars that divides a circle into 6400 mils, in lieu of 360 degrees
MLR	Main Line of Resistance—the front-line trace of a defense, normally behind security outposts
MP	Military Police
Nebelwerfer	German multiple rocket launcher system
OB West	*Oberbefehlshaber West*—German high command on the Western Front
OCS	Officer Candidate School
OKW	*Oberkommando der Wehrmacht*—German armed forces command
OP	Observation Post
Panzerfaust	German hand-held anti-tank rocket launcher
Panzergrenadier	German infantryman within a larger armored unit
PT	Physical Training
PW	Prisoner of War
QE	Quadrant Elevation—elevation setting on a crew-served weapon
ROTC	Reserve Officer Training Corps
SHAEF	Supreme Headquarters Allied Expeditionary Force
SS	*Schutzstaffel*—German units comprised of Nazi loyalists
TD	Tank Destroyer

TF	Task Force—ad hoc force of combined arms elements
TO&E	Table of Organization & Equipment—an inventory of the personnel and equipment authorized in an army unit
TOT	Time-On-Target—an artillery fire mission combining the massed, simultaneous fires of multiple battalions against a single target
Volksgrenadier	German infantryman
Wehrkraftzersetzung	German laws to punish acts of "undermining the war effort"
Wehrmacht	German armed forces
WP	White Phosphorous—a special chemical mortar munition that dispersed smoke on a target
XO	Executive Officer

PROLOGUE

This book relates the World War II experiences of an American soldier, William Paul Chapman, husband of Beth Hartley Chapman and father to myself and my brothers Bruce, Brian, and Dean. I drew the story of his service from published accounts, archives, letters, and the stories he told family members over many years. All of his immediate family and several of his grandchildren have contributed anecdotes. Nearly all his reminiscences have been recalled by more than one family member.

Between June 6, 1944 and May 8, 1945, Bill Chapman spent seven months fighting across Northern Europe and four months convalescing while assigned to the 2nd Battalion, 12th Infantry Regiment of the 4th Infantry Division. He served the entire campaign in an infantry company, the most hazardous duty in the Army. Out of the battalion's original thirty-five officers who landed on Utah Beach, only he and three others remained by VE Day. Except for the most recently assigned lieutenants, virtually every one of the 180 officers who served in the battalion since

D-Day had been a casualty, accounting for the battalion's 514 percent turnover rate among its officers. Thirty-eight officers—more than a full complement for an infantry battalion—were killed or died of wounds.[1]

Bill earned a Silver Star and two Purple Hearts and witnessed the two biggest events in the 12th Infantry's history: the landing on D-Day and the liberation of Paris. He started fighting as a Second Lieutenant assigned to a mortar section, rose to command a rifle company, and ended the war as Battalion Operations Officer (S-3). His battalion commander called him one of the three best soldiers he had served with. Not bad for someone the Army rejected before and after the war.[2]

Although his war record did not make him famous, Bill's story provides compelling testimony to the brutal actions endured by the Allied infantrymen who defeated the Nazi war machine. Combining the regiment's extensive operational history and Bill's personal perspective allows me to tell a story of war at the small-unit level that reveals much of the best and worst of human nature: courage, brutality, cleverness, anguish, determination, callousness, and mercy. What Bill saw, what he and his comrades suffered, and what they accomplished deserve our remembrance, if only to underline the price of victory paid by the men who achieved it. The operations of the 4th Infantry Division and the 12th Infantry Regiment in World War II are well-documented but not well-known. Somehow the Ivy Division (a nickname that plays on the unit's Roman numerals: IV) missed the limelight. The desperate fight at Omaha Beach overshadowed its landing at Utah Beach. The Air Corps' bombing during Operation Cobra earned credit for the breakout in Normandy while the division's breaching of the German defense—and maintaining that breach—often gets overlooked. Charles de Gaulle proclaimed that Paris had been freed by the French people and the French Army, ignoring the 12th Infantry's role in the city's liberation. During the Battle of the Bulge, the siege of the 101st Airborne Division in Bastogne—and Patton's drive to relieve it—stole the headlines from the 12th Infantry's heroic defense of Luxembourg. The race to Berlin in the last month of the war eclipsed the 4th Infantry Division's drive across Franconia and Bavaria. Yet, the Ivy Division had persisted through some of the war's most intense combat, suffering the highest number of casualties among all American divisions during the Northern European Campaign, third most for the entire war.

I hope this history of Bill Chapman's wartime experiences illuminates not just what the regiment and division accomplished, but also the everyday existence of the men who fought on the front line, face-to-face with a desperate enemy. When we can see them as individuals, instead of bodies of non-descript GIs, we gain a greater appreciation for their sacrifices.

As carefully as possible, I matched my father's war stories in place and time with recorded historical events. The movements and battles of his unit provided context and meaning to his personal recollections just as his experiences added perspective to the historical record. Not all of Bill Chapman's recollections could be pinned to a specific time or place. In these instances, I inserted the story at a place in the narrative that best served to illustrate a tactical situation but alerted the reader in endnotes that the narrative does not imply that the recollection happened on a specific date or site. For the sake of the story, I've added some dialogue. Most of these quotes are paraphrases, a few are exact, but all closely match the words Bill used to describe conversations that took place. Some of the descriptions of crew-served weapons in action have been inferred by the tactical situation and Army doctrine for machine gun and mortar platoons. I included these in order to explain how the infantry fought, not necessarily what they did during a specific battle. The book can best be described as a narrative history of an infantry battalion in the thick of one of the most significant campaigns of the war, as seen through the eyes of a company officer.

Sadly, Bill Chapman died on April 9, 2002, without ever writing down what he so often related verbally. Friends and family often asked, even begged, him to put his war memories to paper. He refused. On a couple of occasions, he contributed a paragraph or two when Milwaukee newspapers ran a story about D-Day, but he balked at the idea of recording his wartime adventures. Bill never explained this reluctance. Most people assume that writing about what he saw would awaken too many dark memories. However, he was not too traumatized to talk about the war. He could recount a battle without becoming maudlin or distraught. At the same time, he was neither withdrawn nor emotionless. Whatever held him back, it was not a lack of writing ability. After the war, he earned a Master's Degree in Thermal Engineering from Purdue University and went on to a career as a highly respected engineer. He held nearly every post and garnered almost every award offered by the American Society of Heating Refrigerating and Air-Conditioning Engineers (ASHRAE). He rose the corporate ladder to become a senior vice president of a Fortune 500 company. Even after he retired, Bill continued to serve the community as the volunteer executive director of Discovery World, Milwaukee's museum of science and industry. Bill Chapman wrote numerous professional articles and speeches that demonstrated a vibrant intellect and a great command of the English language.

Humility may explain some of his reticence. Bill never liked to call attention to himself. In his mind, achievements should speak for themselves. He performed many notable, even heroic, acts during the months he spent fighting but so did many others, some of whom did not live to tell about it. Writing about what he did in the war may have seemed presumptuous.

His professional success and a happy home life likely disinclined Bill from writing about the war. It was something in his past, while he was more concerned about the life he was living. He seldom, if ever, brought up the subject of war. His battle experiences usually came up in discussions of other related topics or to illustrate a point. A war movie or an article about one of his battles could prompt him to describe something he had gone through. He kept his medals in the attic until his wife, Beth, put them on display—forty years later. He never joined the American Legion or VFW. The only memorial he attended was the fiftieth anniversary of D-Day, when he served as a representative of the 4th Infantry Division at Utah Beach. Even then Beth had to pressure him to go. In short, Bill Chapman did not want the war to define his life.

One time, my brother Dean and I pressed him about recording his war stories. After considerable effort, he finally agreed. He only made a half-hearted attempt. When I complained, he took offense and insisted that I write the stories, given that I had heard them enough times. In all my life, this was the only time I saw my father fail at anything. I gave up all hope of getting him to write down his wartime experiences.

Perhaps he was right. His stories were destined to be told by someone else. This book honestly describes Bill Chapman's battlefield accomplishments and notes his brave conduct, something that would have made him uncomfortable. At the same time, it does not overlook his flaws. With the help of family members, published accounts, and military archives, I weaved his experiences into the story of the few thousand men of the 2nd Battalion, 12th Infantry Regiment, 4th Infantry Division. The pages that follow retrace their footsteps across France, Belgium, Luxembourg, and Germany from D-Day to VE Day.

Craig S. Chapman

CHAPTER ONE

PREPARING FOR WAR

April 16, 1945, Steinsfeld, Bavaria

Gut check time—First Lieutenant Bill Chapman watched American artillery hammer Steinsfeld, his company's objective. He checked his watch. The barrage would lift soon. Once it did Bill would personally lead E Company's attack into the small town. The young company commander looked at his troops positioned behind the crest of the rounded swell that overlooked the German village. They all looked nervous. *Why wouldn't they be?*

E Company had advanced against Steinsfeld the previous afternoon and ran into a buzz saw of machine gun fire with green tracers from MG 42s crisscrossing the gentle slopes of the shallow valley surrounding it. The battalion commander, Lieutenant Colonel John Gorn, yanked E Company back from its attack before it lost too many men, preferring to make a more deliberate attack the next morning. Then came the bad news—Gorn tapped E Company to lead the battalion's attack on April 16 over the same ground. The rest of the battalion would follow behind them and pass through Steinsfeld to exploit their penetration. Gorn attached a platoon of tanks to E Company, but Bill and his riflemen would have to attack across terrain that offered no concealment.

When Bill briefed his subordinates about the upcoming operation, they all voiced opposition to the attack plan. Steinsfeld was too heavily defended for a single company to take, they said. The attack would constitute a senseless waste of lives with slight prospect of success. Bill faced his toughest decision of the entire war. The men did not want to attack but E Company had orders to tackle Steinsfeld on its own and Bill stood by them. He refused to go back to Colonel Gorn to beg off the mission, as the lieutenants asked. He ordered the attack to proceed as planned.

Watching the shells toss dirt and debris into the smoke-clogged atmosphere, Bill felt the chill of anticipation. He knew he would have to abide with the consequences of his decision, possibly the death of some of his men or his own. He accepted that when he volunteered for the infantry two years earlier, despite having an engineering degree in his pocket. At the time, he wanted to prove his mettle in battle—he had long since done that. Now he had command of a rifle company because he had that rare mix of courage, quick wits, and battle-hardened experience to handle combat command.

Another time check revealed that the artillery prep had almost finished. The moment had arrived. Bill wanted to get his men as close to the town as possible once the artillery lifted so they could pounce before the enemy machine gunners could react. Bill rose to his feet and motioned to the lead platoon leader to start the advance. He stepped forward setting the example for his men. After taking a couple dozen paces toward the impacting artillery rounds, he looked back to check the movement of his troops. All he saw behind him was one very frightened radio operator.

★

With no Junker or samurai class, how does America produce its combat leaders, the ones who shoulder both the burdens of command and the trauma of battle? If it has no equestrian order, where does it find warriors prepared to lead the nation's youth into mortal combat? In this case, the answer came not from "the playing fields of Eton" but the crowded city lots of California's East Bay.

William Paul Chapman—Bill to those who knew him—was born October 19, 1919 in Oakland, California to William Porteus Chapman and Lucy Agnes (McCarthy) Chapman. The elder William wanted his son to be his namesake but Lucy changed the middle name to Paul because, as she told her husband, she did not want her son to be known as "Junior." The reality was that she detested her mother-in-law and could not bear the thought of her son carrying the Porteus family name. Lucy picked the name Paul because she admired a cute little boy with that name who played in a local theater.[1]

Bill's paternal grandfather, Charles Chapman, worked as a carpenter, and Lucy's father painted houses in San Francisco until the 1906 earthquake wiped out his business. Despite these modest beginnings, Bill's immediate family fared well during the Roaring Twenties and Great Depression. His father joined the Oakland Fire Department the year after Bill's birth. The steady job and Lucy's frugal ways saw them through lean times. On his off-duty days, William used the carpentry skills he had learned from his father to supplement the family's income by managing some rental property. As the 1930s progressed and the country suffered economically, the Chapman family moved up to nicer homes in neighborhoods just across Foothills Boulevard from Oakland's Fruitvale district.

William, Lucy, and Bill formed a very tight-knit nuclear family, mostly because of Lucy's attitudes about relationships. She believed that friends and acquaintances should be held at arm's length—relatives even farther. Both parents' extended families lived within the East Bay but they might as well have been in separate states for all the interaction Bill had with them. William's twin brother had to visit him at the firehouse to keep him up on the rest of the family. This led to some embarrassment for Bill. When he enrolled in junior high, he noticed a cute girl in his class. After school, he went out of his way to follow the girl home. Bill later told his father about the girl and where she lived. William burst out laughing. "That's your cousin, Gladys."

As soon as Bill was old enough, he helped his father maintain the apartment buildings they rented. He grew up operating the drill press, table saw, and other power tools his father kept in their household shop. First hand exposure to woodworking, plumbing, and electrical repairs served him well. He learned the skills to build and repair household fixtures, working beside his father. He also came to appreciate the deliberate way his father went about building furniture by hand. When a craftsman used the right tools and followed proper techniques, he learned, the outcome always turned out better. Despite his handiness and family background in carpentry, Bill never considered a career as a craftsman. His ambitions ran in another direction.

Even as a little boy, Bill dreamt about wearing a uniform. His mother often said, "A man always looks better in a uniform." Bill's father wore a fireman's uniform to work for years. Lucy's eldest brother, Jack, served with the Oakland Police Department before he was killed in the line of duty. Military service ran in the family, too. Lucy's father, Timothy, ran away from home at fifteen to fight in the Civil War. Bill's paternal grandfather, Charles Chapman, won an appointment to West Point in the 1870s but had to pass on the opportunity when he contracted "brain fever." Charles's grandfather, Nathaniel Chapman, fought in the Revolutionary War, serving in the Massachusetts Continental Line and the Commander-In-Chief's Guards at places that had become part of American folklore: Bunker Hill, Saratoga, and Valley Forge.

Besides the family's background, the rise of Fascism, Communism, and Japanese imperialism in the 1930s directed Bill toward a military career. Long before Pearl Harbor, he felt certain that America would be pulled into a world war and that he would fight in it. The biggest question on his mind was whether or not he could face the dangers of combat. Bill had great respect for his father, who confronted hazard when fighting fires. The calm, gentle strength the elder William demonstrated every day seems to have prompted him to wonder if he, too, had the courage to stand up when duty called. His wartime letters to his wife revealed a deep personal motivation to prove his worth in battle.

Bill showed early promise and excelled at school, especially in math. With his disciplined approach to problem solving, subjects like algebra, trigonometry, and calculus came easily to him. He breezed through his high school math classes with perfect marks. In four years of advanced math, Bill never got a single incorrect answer on a test, quiz, or homework assignment. Years later, one of his math teachers included Bill's name, among other distinguished engineers and mathematicians, on a published roster of the finest students he ever taught during his career in the Oakland School District.

Bill's academic ability made him college material, and he had one college picked out—the United States Military Academy. West Point stood above all other institutions of higher learning in Bill's mind. Steeped in traditions of duty, honor, and country, West Point had produced many American giants: Lee, Grant, Sherman, and Pershing. The boy from California focused his dreams and aspirations on attending the Academy then pursuing a career as an Army officer.

Bill applied to his congressman for an appointment but lost out to the nephew of a West Point instructor. He did not let that setback stop him. After he graduated from high school in 1937, Bill enrolled at the University of California, Berkeley but dropped out after one semester to enlist in a one-year West Point prep school that the Coast Artillery Corps ran at Fort Scott in San Francisco. There, he devoted twelve months to prepare for the academy's rigorous entrance requirements. The young man learned a lot about the Army in that year. The veteran enlisted men had found a comfortable way of life within the structured environment, and they had an intense pride in being soldiers. At the post's weekly dress parade, each man showed up with an immaculate uniform and stood at attention like a marble statue. "Stick your chest out!" they said. "Burst your buttons!" Following their example, Bill learned how to present himself as a soldier and share *esprit de corps*.[2]

Bill advanced into the final selection process for a regular Army appointment to West Point's Class of 1943. He passed the academic and physical entrance requirements with flying colors. The last step in the process was an appearance before an officer who would evaluate the candidate's military bearing. In front of this officer, Bill felt confident. His spit-shined shoes and ramrod stature presented the classic image of a cadet. Just as the inspection was about to conclude, the officer leaned in toward his face.

"How long have you had that twitch?" he asked.

"Sir, what twitch?"

"The one on your cheek."

"Sir, I don't have a twitch."

"Yes, you do. I can see it."

At this point Bill assumed the officer was testing him. "Sir, I do not have a twitch."

"Don't tell me you don't have a twitch. You're just denying it to cover up your nervous condition."

"Sir, I don't know anything about any twitch."

"You're lying."

"I am not! How dare you accuse me of lying!"

The officer abruptly ended the inspection and quashed Bill's application, remarking that the twitch might distract the troops. In fairness to the officer, Bill did have a twitch in his cheek. He never saw it because it only appeared when he blinked. A slight vibration in his left cheek could be seen on rare occasions, so minor that members of his immediate family recalled seeing it only once or twice over the years. The idea that this miniscule physical anomaly might "distract the troops" seemed absurd but it was enough to deny his appointment to the U.S. Military Academy.

In spite of the arbitrary and insulting denial of his appointment, Bill never let this episode diminish his admiration and respect for the Academy. He remained a lifelong fan of West Point. The incident did have another important consequence, however—it fueled his desire to prove himself in battle and vindicate his worth as a soldier.

Bill re-entered the engineering program at UC Berkeley in January 1940. The college education did not come free of charge like West Point, so he worked several jobs to pay his way through school.[3]

Even with the part-time jobs, he kept up a stellar academic record. Among his courses, Bill enjoyed surveying the most. The professor assigned the aspiring engineers problems to map out parts of campus. Bill and his fellow students peered through their scopes, held stadia rods, and pulled measuring tape around the Berkeley buildings and commons. All of this would stand Bill in good stead during his future duties in Europe.

Bill's performance in his engineering classes caught the notice of Dr. Frank Hutchinson, an assistant professor specializing in thermal engineering. He recruited Bill and a few other students to perform heat-loss calculations on a research project. The tedious problems tied up the research assistants until Bill found a "completely valid" shortcut to the calculations. Bill's inventiveness helped the professor fulfill his research contract on time. Hutchinson pegged Bill as a student with real potential, and he made a point of keeping tabs on him.[4]

While he was studious, Bill was no bookworm. He enjoyed the typical life of an undergraduate, though his lack of money precluded joining any of the social fraternities on campus. He sat in the card section during football games, flashing messages to the crowd and rooting for the Golden Bears. He also treated himself to an occasional social event. At an Independence Day dance in 1942, he met a tall, thin coed from the San Joaquin Valley, Beth Hartley, and they dated throughout his senior year.

The war in Europe had already started by the time Bill returned to Berkeley. All the talk of isolationism and staying out of European squabbles did not change Bill's long-held assumption that America would eventually be drawn into a global conflict. He enrolled in ROTC (See Glossary) as soon as he returned to college. Bill was well on the way to his degree and a commission when the Japanese attacked Pearl Harbor. The country's need for young men altered the Berkeley curriculum and the university put ROTC and engineering students through accelerated course work. Bill and his classmates graduated in January 1943, six months ahead of schedule, then promptly left for military training camps.

Because of the compressed ROTC course, the graduates did not receive commissions. Instead, the Army dispatched them to branch specific Officer Candidate Schools (OCS). With a mechanical engineering degree, Bill was a logical candidate for the venerable Corps of Engineers. Yet, in his heart, he still had to prove that he could perform well in the army's most dangerous branch—the Infantry. The Army granted his wish, sending him to Fort Benning, Georgia and an OCS course that combined infantry training with basic instruction for officers.[5]

Before he shipped out, Bill said goodbye to Beth. Although they both felt committed to each other, Bill ruled out any whirlwind marriage. He knew the dangers that lay ahead and did not want to saddle her with life as a war widow. He even made Beth promise that if he got lonely and later asked her to marry in a weak moment that she would be strong enough to refuse. With that promise secured, he left Berkeley for his home in Oakland.

Bill's parents accompanied him to the airport in San Francisco to see him off. Lucy pulled him aside in the terminal and suggested that he might not want to kiss his father goodbye, as he normally did. She feared it might look awkward for a man in uniform.

Bill gave her a stern look. "I don't care. I will kiss my father." At the gate, he made a point of kissing both Lucy and William. After many tears and best wishes, Bill climbed the steps up to the plane. He turned around before boarding to get one last look at his parents on the tarmac. Gazing down at them, Bill got the eerie impression that he would not see this sight again. He did not know what to make of the feeling but he shook it off and went to his seat. That sensation would come back to haunt him when he learned to appreciate what this uneasiness meant.

Fort Benning, home to the U.S. Army's Infantry School, hummed with activity in the spring of 1943. Bill's OCS class occupied barracks in the Harmony Church area of the post. He wrote to Beth about his eclectic group of classmates. "We have a representative fraction of the U.S. population. One of the men here was a burlesque agent (also booked the strippers for conventions and stag parties). Another fellow was a reporter, another a sports writer then there is our pro wrestler."[6]

With experience in the Coast Artillery and ROTC, Bill readily adapted to OCS. "I thank my stars for my year in the Army. Picked up a few tricks that are coming in handy." He already knew the basic officer requirements, and infantry tactics came naturally to him. Bill had a different reaction to the physical training (PT). "This course is as tough as a boot," he told Beth. He especially disliked the obstacle course. "We ran the G. D. thing 5 times—twice Sat."[7]

One of the poetically inclined candidates captured some of the curriculum and spirit of the OCS experience in a clever ditty.

Notebook, pencil, alidade
Fish on Friday, lemonade
Name plates, open lockers, gigs,
Pacing course, and other rigs

"Action here," and "Watch my tracer,"
GT pencil, no eraser:
Armor piercing, up three clicks,
Bullet guide, and burst of six.

QE, azimuth, range, deflection,
HE light, and mil correction:
"Out of action," "Fire at will,"
Assembly point on Turner Hill.

Practice, dummy, fragmentation,
Trigger, tripper, demonstration;
"C for dinner," unionalls,
37, four-man hauls.

Double apron, booby traps,
Situation on your maps;
Blitz-course, duck-walk, Lewisite,
60 mortar, M-1 sight.
Benning Bulletin, Daily News,
Saturday morning's up turned shoes;
Plenty action, lots of noise,
That's the Benning School for Boys.[8]

Bill also encountered some uncomfortable things about Army life, like the time he walked into a latrine and found a sign directing men with "VD" to use a certain stall. Oakland had plenty of tough neighborhoods but Phenix City, Alabama, located across the Chattahoochee River from the post, was almost totally devoted to vice. The small town had tripled in size since the army built Fort Benning in 1918, and most of that growth came from gambling and prostitution. The post commanders put most of the establishments in Phenix City off limits but the troops still found ways to blow their money on illicit thrills.

During the weeks sweating under the Georgia pines, Bill's thoughts kept turning back to Beth. The time apart convinced him that he wanted to spend the rest of his life with her. He wrote home to tell her that he had changed his mind about a wartime marriage. "I want to throw all the logic and reason to the four winds. I want to marry you." She told him "no," just as she had promised. It took another exchange of letters before Bill convinced her that he had a true change of heart and was not proposing just because he was lonely.[9]

Bill and Beth arranged to marry after his planned commissioning date of June 21. Their plans hinged on Bill earning his gold bars. The Army paid second lieutenants just enough for a young couple to support themselves. Their anxiety rose as the course neared completion. The Infantry School did not post class standings and the candidates stayed in the dark about their commissions. The Army sent failed candidates straight into the ranks as privates. Bill's tension peaked a week before his class's scheduled graduation when he learned about a candidate in the preceding class. "Today just 20 minutes before graduation a man was told he was not going to graduate... In 6 ½ days I will know how I stand."[10]

Bill passed. He immediately telegraphed the good news to Beth. She hopped on a plane to head East. She got as far as El Paso before getting bumped by higher priority passengers and finished the rest of the trip by train. Because Bill had to report to his new post without missing any duty, the couple looked for the closest state where they could marry without a waiting period. That turned out to be South Carolina. Both arrived in Greenville, South Carolina on June 26, 1943. The couple went to the Buncombe County Methodist Church where they met Rev. Rhett Turnipseed, the presiding bishop of the Methodist Southern Synod, who kindly performed the ceremony. At the end, he turned to Bill and said, "She's all yours."[11]

The Army assigned 2nd Lieutenant Chapman to Camp Wheeler outside of Macon, Georgia. In urgent need of living quarters, Bill went into Macon knocking on doors to see if anyone had spare rooms to let. He discovered a lieutenant at one large house who needed another tenant to help cover the monthly rent. Bill and Beth thought they had lucked out until a new general arrived on post. The general took a fancy to the same house. When he learned that two of his lieutenants had prior rights to rent the place, he fixed the problem by transferring them.

Bill's transfer took him to Camp Blanding, Florida and the 63rd Infantry Division. Beth took an apartment in nearby Jacksonville, Florida to stay close to her husband. Bill's aptitude with math led to an assignment training mortar sections. He teamed up with an old sergeant who knew all the tricks and techniques of handling mortars but didn't have the foggiest idea of how the mortars could hit their targets. The college-educated officer and the experienced non-com paired nicely. Bill could explain the geometry for aligning the tubes, calculating the trajectory of the rounds and the formulas for adjusting fire. The old sergeant showed the men how to set up the tubes, fire the rounds, and care for the equipment. The sergeant often expressed his appreciation to the green lieutenant. "Sir, you sure know your stuff. If you teach those azimuths, deflections and firing tables, I can take care of the rest."

Part of the training regimen focused on whipping the new soldiers into better physical condition. In 1942–43 the Army discovered that millions of young men who had joined its ranks were in lousy shape. Unlike the farm boys accustomed to daily physical labor that filled the Army in earlier conflicts, the soldiers of World War II tended to come from cities and suburbs where they held jobs that required little exercise. Bill led his platoon in daily PT. He had never excelled as an athlete but months spent at Fort Benning had already conditioned him. He started the PT sessions with calisthenics, including pushups. After demonstrating the exercise, he put the platoon through the repetitions. None of the men could perform even the minimal number of pushups while he completed twenty-five with ease. After a week, some of the men were completing twenty-five repetitions, too. Bill increased the number to thirty-five. Before long the whole platoon was competing against him. Every day they cheered on the best enlisted man to see if someone could finally catch up to the lieutenant. The PT program worked. The men shaped up in a month.

Bill and Beth had to adjust to life in Dixie where summertime felt very different from the dry, temperate climate of California. The humid conditions bred a lot more bugs, for instance. Bill and another young officer learned that when they went off post from Camp Blanding one afternoon to visit a nearby town. As the soldiers walked down its main street near dusk, they noticed that every civilian had cleared the sidewalks and gone indoors. The confused soldiers thought the citizens resented their presence. They stood by themselves on the sidewalk until a huge cloud of mosquitoes swarmed them. Swatting and cursing, they ducked into a shop for shelter. One of the locals inside the store explained that the mosquitoes arrived around the same time each night, and most people in town knew when to get inside.

According to regulations, every soldier had to qualify with the M1 rifle. Bill's company commander told him to run the qualification range and get the entire company to meet the minimum score. Most troops had no difficulty qualifying but the commander also wanted to exempt soldiers who would seldom handle a weapon—cooks, clerks, and others—from qualifying. Regulations required that each soldier turn in a target sheet with a satisfactory score, so Bill and a couple other men shot extra targets then signed them for the exempt troops. The heat of the day and the shock of absorbing the recoil of several hundred rifle shots left Bill feeling punchy by the time he finished. He spent that night with Beth in Jacksonville. As he slept, he started dreaming about leading a convoy of trucks. In his dream, he was looking down at the trucks instead of being at ground level. He waved and shouted but the trucks did not seem to react to his commands. Beth woke up to find Bill leaning out the window of their apartment and waving his hands. It took her several seconds to realize that he was still asleep. She managed to wake him and lead him back to bed but the incident made her very uneasy. For the rest of the war, Beth could not shake the image of Bill rising from his foxhole in the middle of the night, stumbling around in his sleep and getting shot.

The Army transferred the 63rd Infantry Division to Camp Van Dorn, Mississippi in the fall of 1943, and Beth moved to an apartment in Baton Rouge, Louisiana. In early November 1943, a call went out for volunteers to serve in Europe. Anxious to get in the war, Bill signed up along with several other soldiers from the division.

Bill had other reasons for volunteering. He wanted to control where and against whom he fought. Like many other white Americans on the West Coast, Bill harbored a personal distaste for Asians. Furthermore, the alien culture of the Japanese and their brutal methods of warfare offended Bill's sensibilities. Some of his attitude came from personal experience growing up in Oakland, but he had absorbed a lot from his mother. There was hardly any group, ethnicity, or race that Lucy didn't disdain. Despite his surname and his father's ancestry, Bill even harbored ill views of the British. Bill also saw Germany as the main enemy and felt more comfortable fighting in the European Theater where, he believed, he would understand the enemy he would fight.

When Bill received orders to depart for overseas duty, he wrote home to tell his parents that he had requested a combat assignment and soon would be heading overseas. The orders allotted him some leave, so he and Beth traveled to New York to visit Beth's sister, Marie.

Bill's letter to his parents arrived on November 8, 1943. His father, William, had the day off but was out of the house when the mail arrived. Lucy opened the letter and immediately became distraught to learn that her only child had drawn a frontline infantry assignment. When her husband returned, he found Lucy on the couch weeping. He did his best to comfort her but she was inconsolable. Finally, he said, "Lucy, I'd lay my life down to bring our boy back."

Through her tears Lucy shushed him. "Don't ever say that."[12]

A fire alarm sounded a short while later. William stepped out his front door to see a massive column of black smoke boiling skyward just a few blocks away. The fire had started in a military warehouse storing a huge stockpile of tires that burned with searing heat and thick fumes. Lucy begged him not to go. It was his day off, she reminded him, but William would not sit at home while a five-alarm fire raged within sight of his house. Wearing just his street clothes, Bill's father joined a fire crew already on the scene. He grabbed a hose to contain the flames then collapsed, felled by a massive heart attack. He died before an ambulance could get him to the hospital.

Bill received a telegram in New York that gave him the sad news. He wrangled emergency leave and flew back to Oakland in time for his father's funeral. While on leave, he missed the convoy taking the rest of the troops from Camp Van Dorn overseas.

Bill rejoined Beth in New York after the funeral. A couple weeks later, the Army ordered him to report to Fort Meade, Maryland. The couple shared a sad, tearful farewell in Baltimore before Beth returned to California, beginning a long period of anxious separation.

At Fort Meade, Bill received new orders sending him to Camp Myles Standish in Taunton, Massachusetts. Bill frittered away the month of December at the camp. He had to supervise a group of enlisted men who, like himself, awaited further orders. He spent his days hiking with the enlisted men to keep them in shape and his nights censoring their mail. The latter task often amused the young lieutenant. "One of the men gave an excellent, but obscene, description of Betty Grable's ___, ____, and ____." The Army alerted Bill and several others for movement on Christmas Eve. Then a screw-up in the orders forced Bill to stay. His bags shipped without him. He wrote to Beth but security prevented him from telling her where he was, so he did not receive her letters. More than anything else, the forced idleness frustrated him. On New Year's Day, he wrote, "Oh God, will I ever leave this hole?"[13]

CHAPTER TWO

ENGLAND

Bill finally got a berth on a Liberty Ship, the SS *Henry W. Grady*, that sailed from Boston on January 8, 1944. The ship initially headed to New York where the crew loaded eight P-51s as deck cargo. From there, Bill fired off a letter to Beth, alerting her to his deployment.[1]

A large convoy, sailing with an escort of warships, picked up the *Grady* on its way out of New York harbor. As the only soldier on board, Bill had complete run of the ship. With nothing to do and no one to report to, he decided to grow a beard. The ship's captain, an old salt who kept a tight rein on his crew, did not take to the young officer's whiskers. A couple weeks out, he pointed to Bill's beard and said, "You know, Lieutenant, I have a wife at home who pees through something that looks like that." Bill shaved that night.

Although the convoy did not run into any U-Boats, it did encounter a gale that, at one point, caused the *Grady* to roll 40 degrees Bill proudly told Beth that he did not get sick, despite the rolling sea. He would tell a different story about seasickness in a few months.

The convoy arrived in England on January 28. As a replacement infantry officer, the Army scheduled him to fill a slot in one of the divisions already in England but before they sent him to a unit someone noticed he had a degree in mechanical engineering. The massive pre-invasion influx of troops, vehicles, and equipment already strained England's facilities. The Army needed engineers to oversee construction of infrastructure all over England. The theater personnel office snatched up the young lieutenant to design and supervise a building project. Sensing he had an advantageous bargaining position, Bill made a suggestion. He would perform the engineering work provided the replacement depot—aka, the "repple-depple"—would afterward assign him to a top-notch unit that would see action soon. He wanted a combat position, just like many other hard-charging young officers, but he wanted to serve in a first-class unit that knew its business. HQ agreed.[2]

He drew an assignment to build new camp facilities at Whittington Barracks outside Lichfield, Staffordshire. Bill jumped into the work. Drawing on his engineering education, he sketched the layout for the barracks, road system, and utilities. "Sure do like my new job...I never did like doing nothing at all—accomplishment gives me satisfaction." Plans in hand, Bill went to the site and surveyed the property. He laid out where each building would be erected and planned the road and drainage system. As soon as he finished with the blueprints, Bill ordered materials and issued work orders to the construction teams.[3]

Bill did see one potential problem. Because of the topography, he had to lay a sewer line across part of an English country club's golf course, including some of the greens. Bill had earned spending money as a young man by working as a caddy, so he appreciated the care that went into maintaining the greens. He went to the course superintendent at the country club to warn him about the upcoming construction, thinking the club might dig up the sod beforehand.

The course superintendent immediately objected. Bill explained that the construction job was a military necessity. He suggested that the club take up its sod while it had the chance. Instead of following Bill's sound advice, the superintendent called for help.

The next day a British engineer officer, who bore a striking resemblance to the movie caricature of Colonel Blimp, approached Bill at the construction site. "See here, Lieutenant, you can't just dig up the greens on this golf course," he said.

"Yes, I can. I have orders to build this camp and that includes putting drainage pipes across your golf course. I only told the superintendent about it because I thought he'd want to dig up his sod. You can replace the greens once the sewer is in."

"We'll see about that. I intend to make a few calls to stop this nonsense."

"You better hurry. We'll have the trench dug by the end of the day."

The officer scoffed. "It'll take you days to dig a sewer line. By that time, I'll have your orders countermanded." Apparently, he thought the Americans would dig the trench with shovels.

"Not with the right equipment. I have a crew coming in today."

The British engineer stomped off.

Just as Bill promised, the American construction engineers showed up with excavators and dug up the country club's greens in one afternoon. By the time the British engineer returned, the sewer pipe was in and covered over with dirt.

The British were amazed at how quickly Americans got things done. Bill was equally amazed that a British engineer would still depend on manual labor. The incident did not improve Bill's opinion of the English people. He wrote to Beth, "You know how I felt about the English before I left...Too bad such nice countryside is wasted on these people." Clearly, some of Lucy's Irish attitudes had passed on to her son.[4]

Bill spent February and half of March doing engineer work. He enjoyed supervising a crew of 130 men and getting something accomplished. The project and Bill's performance pleased the Army. The engineer company commander went so far as to ask him to transfer into his unit. Bill declined. "The work is fine but the infantry is my outfit and there I stay."[5]

Bill informed the 10th Replacement Depot once he finished the project and asked them to honor their part of the bargain. The "repple-depple" reneged. "They told me yesterday that I never should have come here—it was all a mistake. Now I'll go to the pool that I should have gone to in Jan. I had to count to 100 when I heard that." Now that Bill had earned a reputation as someone who could get things done, the classification officer offered him a position in a training command. Many officers would have been delighted with such a posting but Bill turned it down. He explained to Beth, "It is a soft job, absolutely safe, plenty of time off and nice quarters but you know how I feel about combat."[6]

Bill had run afoul of the Army's practice for assigning officers. Unlike the German Army that prized infantry leaders, the U.S. Army tended to place highly educated officers and men in the "technical branches," such as the Engineer, Signal and Quartermaster Corps, or the more mechanized combat arms, such as Armor and Field Artillery. The infantry got the leftovers. Military historian S. L. A. Marshall observed the negative effect this policy had on the Army. "[A]s the new army took shape the infantry became relatively the most slighted of all branches." The replacement depot recognized Bill as a well-educated professional and followed normal policy to steer him into a role in which he could apply his education directly.[7]

The young lieutenant argued his case with the personnel office. After an hour-long debate, the classification officer gave in and assigned Bill to the 12th Infantry Regiment of the 4th Infantry Division. On March 27, 1944, Bill joined the regiment at its training camp near Exeter in Devon. He explained his reasoning for pursuing the infantry assignment to Beth. "I needed this test for my own conscience."[8]

The 12th Infantry, a Regular Army regiment, traced its lineage back to the War of 1812. Disbanded after that conflict, the Army reconstituted it in 1861, and it had fought in every major conflict since the Civil War. The current commander, a 1926 West Point graduate, Colonel Russell "Red" Reeder, had already earned a reputation within Army circles as the author of a study on combat in the Pacific, *Fighting on Guadalcanal.*[9]

The 4th Infantry Division also had a distinguished record. One of its commanding generals from the First World War, Major General John Hines, succeeded Pershing as Chief of Staff of the U.S. Army. The current division commander, Maj. Gen. Raymond Barton, a 1912 West Point graduate, was described by the famous war correspondent, Ernie Pyle, as "a fatherly, kindly, thoughtful, good soldier." Noted British military historian B. H. Liddell Hart called Barton "refreshingly open-minded." Bill knew at once that he had joined the type of hard-core unit he longed for. What he did not realize, at the time, was he could not have found a unit scheduled for combat any sooner.[10]

The regiment slotted Bill in Company H of the 2nd Battalion. The company occupied quarters in the city of Exmouth where the River Exe enters the English Channel. H Company served as the battalion's heavy weapons company, responsible for supporting the battalion's three rifle companies (E, F, and G) with mortars and heavy machine guns. A lanky officer from Charleston, South Carolina, 1st Lieutenant Tallie Crocker, commanded the company.[11]

Given Bill's experience at Camps Blanding and Van Dorn, Crocker gave him responsibility for one of the company's 81mm mortar sections, reporting to 1st Lt. William Slaymaker, the mortar platoon leader. The sixty-man platoon was split into three sections. Each section had two mortar squads and was led by a junior lieutenant. Theoretically, the platoon's organization allowed one mortar section to fire in support of each of the battalion's three rifle companies. In practice, the heavy mortars usually massed fire to support the battalion commander's overall fire plan. Having three separate sections did enable the mortar platoon to move forward, a section at a time, during an advance while having tubes available for immediate calls for fire.[12] (See Fig. 1)

The M1 81mm mortar could fire a seven-pound projectile out to a maximum range of three kilometers. On impact, the mortar round could kill or wound exposed personnel within a 23-meter bursting radius, delivering nearly as much punch as the old French 75mm (*soixante-quinze*) artillery guns of World War I.

The high trajectory of the mortar rounds allowed them to hit targets that might be hiding "in defilade"—that is, behind walls, trenches, or hills—and they could sustain a high rate of fire (eighteen rounds per minute). This responsiveness and potential volume of fire made the mortars

BATTLE HARDENED

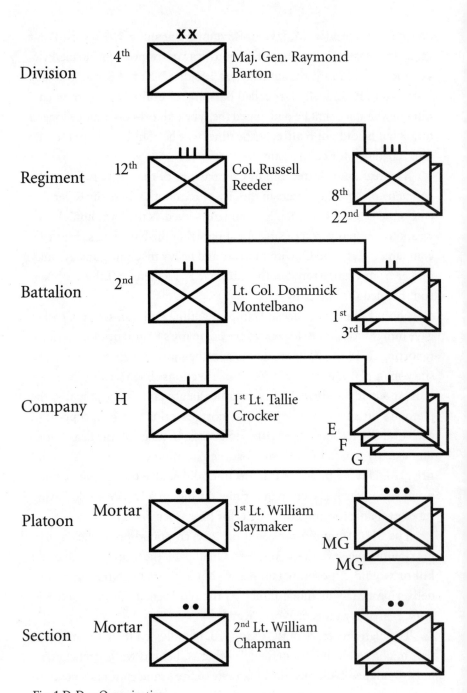

Division	4th	Maj. Gen. Raymond Barton
Regiment	12th	Col. Russell Reeder — 8th, 22nd
Battalion	2nd	Lt. Col. Dominick Montelbano — 1st, 3rd
Company	H	1st Lt. Tallie Crocker — E, F, G
Platoon	Mortar	1st Lt. William Slaymaker — MG, MG
Section	Mortar	2nd Lt. William Chapman

Fig. 1 D-Day Organization

invaluable when the battalion needed to repel an enemy infantry assault or suppress dug-in weapons. Because the mortar platoons were under their direct control, battalion commanders tended to think of them as their own "hip pocket artillery."[13]

The 12th Infantry Regiment concentrated on tactical training at scattered sites in Devon. Bill ran his section through repetitive exercises, setting up and aligning the mortars. The section sergeant and gunners operated the aiming circle and sights to lay the section while the mortar squads practiced handling the munitions and plunking the rounds down the tubes. The crews soon honed their skills to a fine edge. Bill proudly watched his mortar squads fire nine rounds into the air before the first one impacted. "Received some congratulations...I feel relieved at the outcome of our two-day problem."[14]

Setting up and firing the mortars was one thing, training the men in fire control was quite another. In the process of fire control, the mortar platoon's observers called in an initial azimuth (that is, direction) and distance from the guns to the targets. The sections calculated the proper charge for the rounds and adjusted the correct deflection and elevation settings for the mortar tubes. "To be sharp with fire control a man should have knowledge of trigonometry," Bill said. Yet, many of the men had trouble handling fractions much less advanced mathematics. The platoon's officers and most of the non-coms had the experience necessary to manage fire control but Bill worried about the junior enlisted men. "It is disappointing to know that when your key men go you must rely on men who won't try more due to [the] impossibility of promotion."[15]

The Army field manual taught observers to direct mortar fire by positioning themselves and the guns on a straight gun-observer-target (G-O-T) line. To achieve this, once an observer spotted a target he set up an alidade, basically a stake with a straight edge mounted on the top. The observer aligned the alidade with the target then turned around to direct where the mortars should set up. Using the alidade and a compass, the observer established an initial fire direction for the guns. To ensure greater accuracy, mortar, machine gun, and artillery units expressed angles in mils, a more precise measure than degrees (6400 mils versus

360 degrees). At a distance of 1,000 meters, a deviation of 1 yard or meter created an angle roughly equal to one mil. The observers adjusted fire onto the targets by spotting the impact of the rounds and determining the angle of deviation from the target, aided by a reticle in their binoculars. After correcting for the difference in range between the observer and the guns, the observers gave adjustments to the guns, for example: "Right 50 [yards], add 100 [yards]."[16]

This method of fire control, more suited to open country, did not account for the terrain or the enemy American infantry would face in Europe. Doctrine held that observers would be able to give their commands by voice or hand-and-arm signals, which meant they had to be close enough to be heard and/or seen by their section. Fighting in the dense thickets of Normandy while dodging enemy fire, the observers learned to acquire targets anywhere they could see and survive rather than worry about establishing a neat G-O-T line. The Army did train observers how to calculate the direction of fire when their observation posts (OPs) were outside the G-T line but it involved more math and

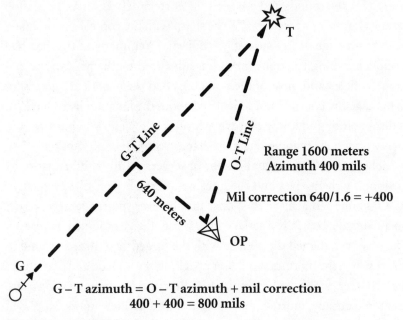

Fig. 2 Compass – Mil Method

estimation. Bill's observers relied on either the "parallel-line" or the "compass-mil" method to call fire orders to the guns in these situations. Both methods challenged the mental faculties of the observer, especially under fire. The Army duly noted that "the ability of the observer is the most vital single factor in the effective delivery of fire."[17] (See Fig. 2)

After crew training, H Company participated in platoon and company field exercises at Huxham Brake and Harpford Commons. The mortar and machine gun platoons from H Company learned how to keep up with the rifle companies in the offense and coordinate fire plans with them in the defense.[18]

On April 14, the overall ground force commander for the invasion, General Sir Bernard Law Montgomery, visited the regiment. The entire unit formed on a cold, soggy morning to hear the famous commander who had defeated the brilliant commander of Germany's *Afrika Korps*, General Erwin Rommel. Standing on the hood of a jeep, wearing his familiar beret and a warm overcoat, Montgomery looked over the assembly of more than three thousand troops. He commented that he wanted to see the faces of the men, so Colonel Reeder ordered everyone to remove their helmets. While the drizzle pattered on the heads of the assembled soldiers, Montgomery warmed into his topic of how important it was to defeat the "Hun." The references to Huns irritated Bill. He worried how well men with such names as Fischbach, Pfeffer, Reithner, and Stolzenbach would take the general's comments. Montgomery's self-promotion and disparagement of the Germans failed to inspire the troops, who concentrated more on the rainwater trickling down their backs. By the time he finished his speech, Bill and many of the men shared the opinion that "Monty" was an egotistical bastard.[19]

To add realism to pre-invasion training, in late April, the 4th Infantry Division participated in Exercise Tiger, a mock invasion of Slapton Sands on the Devon coast, complete with naval gunfire, beach assaults, and convoy operations. The regiment performed its part of the mission well. Tossed around on the Channel waves, the men transferred from their Landing Craft Infantry (LCI) to the smaller Landing Craft Mechanized (LCM) and Landing Craft Vehicle, Personnel (LCVP or Higgins Boats) that landed them on the beach. The infantrymen then charged across the pebbled beach, drove off a simulated enemy force, and headed inland. Over the next couple of days, the 12th Infantry practiced tactical maneuvers in a mock battle. Bill gained more confidence in the regiment's proficiency. "From what I've seen this last week I <u>know</u> we will come out all right in this war. Our men are excellent soldiers and extremely tough."[20]

While the ground exercise proceeded smoothly, the naval convoy suffered a disaster. German E-boats (the rough equivalent of the U.S. Navy's PT boats), sallying from Cherbourg, slipped through the naval screen, and caught nine Landing Ship Tanks (LSTs) carrying specialist engineer units as they entered Lyme Bay. The E-boats sank two LSTs and damaged two others. Almost eight hundred men were killed or went missing, including ten officers who had been briefed about the upcoming invasion. The ten missing officers caused an operational security panic, and the Navy patrolled the Channel for days looking for survivors. After this sobering event, the Army and the Navy untangled the convoy security lapses to prevent a similar tragedy during the real invasion.[21]

As the invasion date neared, visitors came by to see the Ivy Division in Exeter. Lieutenant General Omar Bradley, commander of the First U.S. Army, addressed the division's officers. The audience took note when the general closed his remarks by saying, "I'll see you on the beaches."[22]

Bill had a visit from Beth's older brother, 1st Lt. Howard Hartley, who had just completed his fiftieth bombing mission with his B-26 squadron. Bomber crews normally earned a rotation back to the States after fifty missions but Howard and most of his crew volunteered to stay on for ten more missions because of the approaching invasion. After agreeing to fly the extra missions, Howard went on a short leave. He decided to stop in to see Bill on May 13. Howard stayed for two full days in Exmouth, even though Bill's duties prevented him from showing him a good time. The two officers spent Bill's spare time talking about "everything." This would be the only time the two men would meet. Howard's B-26 flew two missions on D-Day to knock out

German gun emplacements that threatened the Utah Beach landings. The bombing skills of the B-26 crews played an important role in the Allied success at Utah Beach, in contrast to the ineffective attacks by heavy bombers against Omaha Beach defenses. Eight days after D-Day, Howard and his crew were shot down and killed over St. Peravy la Colombe, France. He was flying his sixtieth mission.[23]

In May, the final preparations for the invasion began in earnest. Besides their battlefield training, the troops started combat loading vehicles and waterproofing their equipment. The regiment departed Exmouth for a marshaling area in Plymouth on May 16. The 2nd Battalion occupied an old British army barracks in the seaport town. Once inside the marshaling area, all contact with the civilian population ceased and security details ensured that the men stayed confined. The troops saw maps of their objective areas and mockups of the landing site on the Cotentin Peninsula—Utah Beach. They received special 1:25,000 maps with detailed overprints of known German defensive positions. The maps displayed artillery batteries, gun emplacements, wire entanglements, and individual machine gun positions that the regiment would face.[24]

Rehearsals and briefings concentrated on specific missions for the terrain where they would fight. The command shared aerial reconnaissance photos of the beach and small towns they would pass through. Once the division secured the beaches and the routes to the interior, the plan called for it to attack to the north to capture Cherbourg, a port city that would become a critical logistical facility.

The photos also showed that the Germans had flooded the low-lying terrain behind Utah Beach, inundating several square kilometers. That meant the division would need to cross water-laden farmland and secure the causeways leading from the beach to the interior. The division commander, General Barton, had special concerns about the 12th Infantry's advance from the beach. He pulled Colonel Reeder aside. "You may land and discover the causeways leading inland clogged by traffic," Barton said. "In this case it may be best to wade the lake so you may get into your zone of advance without delay." He went on to warn Reeder that the Germans had plowed deep furrows in the low-lying terrain before flooding it to create sumps that could drown men crossing the area on foot.[25]

The 2nd Battalion, commanded by Brooklyn native Lieutenant Colonel Dominick Montelbano, would land on the Uncle Red sector of the beach, then march straight up causeway #3 to higher ground. Sharing the details of the invasion plans and the tactical missions helped boost morale and gave the men even more confidence. "You can take it from me these men are really tops and deserve plenty of credit. Theirs is the drudgery, but by God they take it like true men...All in all our outfit is damn good and incredibly tough." Bill would later comment that his men had reached the highest degree of combat readiness of any unit he had ever seen.[26]

Bill and his peers did not see the major shortcomings in the division's training program. Beating the heavily armed and mechanized German army would require a well-coordinated combined force of armor, infantry, and artillery. The Ivy Division's riflemen knew how to fight as infantrymen, but they were not given any training alongside tanks. Even at the doctrinal level, the Army's tactics fell short on infantry-tank operations. The infantry battalion field manual only devoted two pages to fighting with tanks and appeared mostly concerned about separating their avenues of approach to avoid running over the riflemen. Months later American tanks would drive into battle draped with infantrymen but the U.S. First Army in 1944 had yet to learn the critical skills of fighting as a combined arms team. Those lessons would come the hard way, after heavy losses in France.[27]

Bill and his fellow soldiers felt upbeat and proud to be part of the largest seaborne invasion in history. They had the mission to crack the "Atlantic Wall" and break Nazi Germany's hold on Western Europe. By now Bill, his men, the 4th Infantry Division, and the entire free world were anxious to launch the invasion of France and open a second front against the Germans. Allies and Axis, friends and foes, combatants and civilians had spent months anticipating the American, British, and Canadian assault against Hitler's Atlantic Wall.

As the day of the invasion neared, Bill wrote more frequently to Beth, sometimes twice a day. He mostly used V Mail to get news back home more quickly. The War Department worked out a system that allowed a deployed soldier to write a letter on a standard "V Mail" sheet. The postal clerks then photographed the page and, along with hundreds of other letters, copied it onto a microfilm reel that was sent via air to the States. Once the reels arrived, War Department clerks printed the individual V Mails and mailed them to the soldiers' loved ones.

Bill could not say anything about the upcoming operation because the censors would black out all sensitive information. He mostly wrote about how much he missed her. Beth noticed something else in his letters—the strain was getting to Bill. He even admitted to "a certain grimness and cynical attitude I find creeping in." The intense workload and worry about the upcoming battles naturally put a lot of emotional pressure on Bill but that was not the source of his anxiety. He felt more concerned about the young wife he had left back in California. His old fears of leaving her a war widow weighed on his mind. Bill felt guilty that Beth risked a lifetime of sorrow to serve as his emotional crutch. Another, even bigger issue, frayed Bill's emotions. The closer the invasion got, the sooner he would have to answer the question of his ability to stand up in combat.[28]

On June 2, the order came to start loading the landing craft in Plymouth Harbor. The invasion would take place on June 5. Bill Chapman's path to the battlefield was about to end—and his long and dangerous fight home was about to begin.[29]

CHAPTER THREE

D-DAY

On June 3, the men of H Company, 2nd Battalion, 12th Infantry crammed into one of the thirteen LCIs in Plymouth Harbor, the same port Sir Francis Drake had sortied from to engage the Spanish Armada. Once the regiment completed embarkation, the LCIs cleared the port and slipped out to the English Channel on the evening of June 3. In the Channel, they joined the LSTs transporting the regiment's vehicles and heavy equipment and, with them, sought temporary shelter in bays and coves along twenty-five miles of the rugged shoreline between Salcombe and Torquay. Thousands of similar vessels, each packed with men and materiel, huddled near shore across the southern English coast and waited for their respective convoys to form. One of the men in the Intelligence and Reconnaissance (I&R) Platoon, Carmen D'Avino, occupied himself painting watercolors of the peaceful, verdant Devon coast where the sea had sheared off the gently rolling farmland into a crag-bound shore.[1]

On June 4, gale-force winds whipped the sea into a boiling chop, and pelted the ships anchored offshore with rain. The severe weather made an invasion on June 5 impossible. However, meteorologists on Eisenhower's staff felt confident enough about a possible break in the bad weather to recommend that the operation be postponed rather than cancelled outright.

Bill and his men spent June 4 trying to stay dry as their ship bobbed up and down. The constant jostling nauseated the troops, and a few started throwing up. More followed. Soon the stench of vomit thickened so much that everyone succumbed to the heaves. Topside or below deck, no one could escape the smell. If a man put anything into his stomach, it wound up on the deck a short time later.

As night fell, the troops tried to sleep off the seasickness. If they were going to be miserable, they might as well rest while retching. Bill wedged himself into a space on one of the decks and managed to doze off. He awoke the next morning to the sight of his boots floating. *My God! We've sprung a leak!* Bill jerked himself upright, and franticly looked around to see what had happened. It took him a moment to realize that his boots were floating in vomit, not seawater. A second later the ship rolled, and the tide of spew swept to the other side.

In the mid-afternoon of June 5, word flashed to the invasion fleet. Supreme Headquarters Allied Expeditionary Force (SHAEF) had made its decision. "D-Day is June 6. H-Hour is 0630." The escorting warships started to organize the convoys. The packed LCIs formed up in Lyme Bay under the direction of Rear Admiral Don P. Moon in USS *Bayfield*. For the men, the knowledge that their shipboard ordeal was coming to an end helped offset any fear they had of the approaching battle.[2]

The 4th Infantry Division and the rest of the force set to attack Utah Beach formed Force U. The ships steamed due east in twelve long columns that stretched to the darkening horizon. South of Weymouth, Force U joined the Omaha Beach convoy (Force O) to form the Western Task Force. Under cover of darkness, the long line of ships passed through the German minefields following lanes cleared by minesweepers. They steamed into their designated assault areas shortly before dawn.[3]

Looking out from their LCIs in the pre-dawn twilight, the men could see ships in every direction. The invasion fleet seemed to fill the entire English Channel. "A water spectacle more breath taking and awe inspiring than any of us had dared to imagine greeted our eyes. There were battleships and cruisers, destroyers and gunboats, corvettes and landing craft of all sizes, service ships, hospital ships, tug boats, dispatch boats, coast guard rescue cutters and miscellaneous vessels of every description. There were tankers full of high-test gasoline, LCIs full of seasick infantrymen, LSTs full of tanks and trucks."[4]

Around 0550 hours (H–40 Minutes), the pre-invasion aerial and naval bombardment began. Several hundred B-26 medium bombers rained bombs on German gun emplacements within range of Utah Beach. Battleships and cruisers of the Western Task Force lobbed 14", 8", and 6" shells at the German defenses behind the beaches. Destroyers and rocket ships drenched the coastal defenses with even more suppressive fire. The bombardment was short, fierce, and successful. German gun batteries up and down the Cotentin Peninsula remained mostly silent as the first waves hit Utah Beach. At the actual landing site near la Madeleine, the main German strongpoint had taken several hits that befuddled the defenders.[5]

The 4th Infantry Division's 8th Infantry Regiment landed at 0630 hours, followed by the 22nd Infantry, then the Twelfth. Despite the safe passage to the beach, both the primary and secondary control vessels for Utah Beach were lost, one to a mine, the other to mechanical trouble. Without the radar on these vessels to guide them, the landing craft of the initial waves drifted almost a mile south of the intended objective and hit the beach at la Madeleine. Instead of having two causeways (Exits 3 and 4) leading from the beach to the interior, the landing site had only one road over the inundated area (Exit 2).

The news was not all bad. The 8th Infantry landed at a weakly defended stretch of the beach, and the troops quickly overwhelmed the defenders. The Assistant Division Commander, Brigadier General Theodore Roosevelt Jr., had landed with the first wave and conferred with the battalion commanders on the beach. They debated whether to bring the succeeding waves to la Madeleine or shift them to the designated objective. Roosevelt reflected for a moment then announced, "We'll start the invasion from right here!"[6]

The 12th Infantry's convoy arrived off Utah Beach around 1030 hours. Men craned their necks to get a glimpse of the French coast, but they could see only a murky shore clouded by mist and dust. Countless barrage balloons floated above the gloomy horizon, each one tethered to a landing craft. Above the sound of the waves beating the ships' sides, the men could hear an occasional *crump* as German artillery shelled the beach. LCMs and LCVPs pulled alongside the taller LCIs, and the men began to clamber into the assault boats. The crew of Bill's LCI threw a cargo net over the side that reached into the holding space of his LCM. The boat's crew pulled the net taut to give better support for the men to step on the horizontal lines, but the small ships bounced on the waves and the net would slacken then tighten to no particular rhythm. The men had been trained to grasp the vertical lines with both hands when stepping down, and that kept them from falling. With difficulty, thirty-plus men from H Company loaded into Bill's LCM.[7]

The smaller boats marshaled into their assault waves by running in large circles through the swells. When the Wave Commander felt satisfied that all the LCMs and LCVPs had finished loading, he started the run to the beach. Jammed into the boat and tossed about on the open water, the men suffered yet another round of seasickness. By the morning of June 6, they had gone two days without being able to properly digest food. It was an awful way to enter a fight—sick, wet, and weakened by hunger.

Bill double-checked his men to make sure they were ready for action as the LCM surged toward shore. Most had the determined look of soldiers girding themselves for battle, but one man seemed upset and unnerved. Bill went over to the soldier, hoping to calm him. "Are you okay?"

"I'm just a little jumpy."

Each wave or sudden noise made the nervous soldier flinch. Bill tried his best to ease the man's fears. "Look, this whole thing is probably just another training exercise."

A couple seconds later a German artillery shell exploded beside the LCM, sending shrapnel whizzing overhead and showering the troops with a column of seawater. Instinctively, every man hunched over until the effects of the blast subsided. The nervous soldier glared from underneath his helmet at the lieutenant. "Just another training exercise? Hah!"[8]

The LCMs and LCVPs formed on line and raced toward shore. As the water became shallow, the waves grew higher. Each wave jolted the boat and sent spray over the ramp. The coxswain steered the LCM toward a landing spot and ploughed the rising surf at a 90-degree angle. The boat caught a wave inside the breakers and rode it toward the beach, much like a man on a surfboard. A few seconds later, the LCM ran aground. The forward crew removed the safety pawl from the ramp's gears, and the ramp clanked down until it smacked the surface of the water.

The troops pushed forward to disembark. The first soldier to the end of the ramp stepped off and disappeared underwater. The rest of the men stopped short, some teetering on the edge of the ramp. Bill sloshed through the vomit and seawater to the rear of the LCM and shouted to the coxswain, "Raise the ramp. We have to go in farther."[9]

The coxswain shook his head. "No, you get off here."

"It's too deep. Take her in closer to the beach."

"No! I'm in command of this boat, and I say you get off here."

Bill pulled out his .45 cal. pistol and pointed it at the coxswain's head. "Like Hell! Raise the ramp!"

The coxswain quickly changed his mind. The crew cranked the ramp back to vertical and the coxswain gunned the engine. The small boat pushed itself off the bar it had run onto and moved forward to the actual beach. This time, the LCM properly grounded itself in shallow water off the Uncle Red portion of Utah Beach. The ramp dropped a second time and the men charged into the surf. After splashing through the waves, they ran onto the beach at 1130 hours, five hours after the first wave. Although soaked and scared, the troops still felt grateful to be on solid ground.[10]

Just then, more enemy artillery struck the beach. Bill watched the shell bursts lift sand and debris into the air then spray a semi-circular pattern of shrapnel against the surface of the water. He'd seen mortars and artillery shells explode many times in training, but it felt nerve-wracking to be on the receiving end. The reality of combat became clear in that instant—*a guy can get hurt out here*. A soldier could protect himself, somewhat, by moving quickly and taking cover but could do nothing about where the next enemy round struck—no sense worrying about it. Bill understood that cowards fret about getting shot, while real soldiers pay attention to the things they can control. He later said, "The best thing to do is rely on your training and do your job." He rallied his platoon and shepherded them off the beach.[11]

One man, however, dropped to the sand and curled into a fetal position. Bill ran over to him. "Let's go! Get up!" he ordered. The man just shivered. More artillery rounds burst around them sending smoke, sand, and shrapnel into the sky. "Come on. It's not safe to sit here," Bill urged. "We gotta get off the beach." The man refused to budge. Fear had turned him insensible. Bill gave up and left the man cowering on the beach for the medics to round up.

The engineers had blown a gap through the sea berm and linked Utah Beach's exit to Causeway 2. The mortar platoon scurried up the sand incline and emerged into the open area behind the beach. There, General Roosevelt shouted instructions on which direction they needed to march.[12]

Theodore Roosevelt Jr. was the larger-than-life son of an even more renowned icon whose image had already been carved on Mount Rushmore. Known as "Ted" by his friends and "General Teddy" by his troops, he had already accomplished much in an amazing career: graduated from Harvard, earned a fortune in business, became a war hero in World War I, held a series of high government posts, and lost an election for the governorship of New York. In April 1941, he returned to active duty, received a star, and fought in North Africa and Sicily. Brave to the point of recklessness, General Teddy earned the respect and admiration of the troops he led. Unfortunately, his carefree attitude about military formalities and his casual dress, characteristics he shared with the division's unorthodox commander, Major General Terry Allen, irked his senior

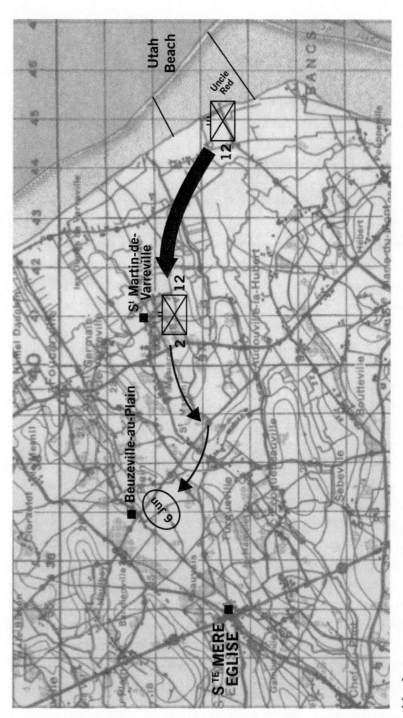

Map I

commanders, Lieutenant Generals George S. Patton and Omar Bradley. Bradley relieved Allen and Roosevelt in an effort to tighten discipline within their battle-weary division.

Not wanting to let a talented combat leader go to waste, Eisenhower scooped up Roosevelt from the Mediterranean Theater and assigned him to the Ivy Division as its assistant division commander. Roosevelt's courage and decisive leadership on Utah Beach would earn the Medal of Honor and confirm the wisdom of Eisenhower's decision.

Bill immediately recognized Roosevelt. He stood out even more that day because of his devil-may-care demeanor, armed only with a cane. Bill noticed something else about Roosevelt's appearance—he had removed his helmet and wore just a soft cap on his head. Worried about the example he was setting for the enlisted men, the young lieutenant approached Roosevelt. "Sir, you're not wearing your helmet. We have strict orders for everyone to keep their helmets on at all times."[13]

Teddy smiled. "Yeah, but I'm a general."

In retrospect, it seems odd that Bill would be the one to admonish a general about wearing a helmet because he had his own peculiar habits about headgear. Most soldiers wore their helmets to shade their eyes and cover their foreheads. Bill hated having anything covering his eyes, so he pushed his helmet back on his head. This habit gave Bill what some might have considered a casual, unprofessional appearance, but he did not care as long his vision was not hindered.

The division's original plan called for the 8th Infantry to hook south to secure the beachhead's left flank and the 22nd to slice northwest to hold its right. The 12th Infantry had intended to use Causeways 3 and 4 to drive up the middle and link up with the 502nd Parachute Infantry Regiment near St. Martin-de-Varreville. Because the division landed at la Madeleine, the initial waves went straight inland on Causeways 2, 3, and 4, jamming them with men and equipment. To get around the traffic, the 12th Infantry advanced northwest from la Madeleine across three miles of the inundated area. The mortar platoon was supposed to have seven jeeps and trailers to move its weapons and ammunition but none of them were available after the landing. The mortarmen shouldered their tubes, base plates, bipods, and rounds, then started slogging along a narrow path away from the beach. Just beyond the dunes they passed a German soldier lying face down by the side of the trail. Bill stared at the corpse as he walked by. He had never seen a dead man before. A short distance past the body, the route of march angled toward St. Martin-de-Varreville and slipped into the swampy ground.[14] (See Map I)

This was the part of the D-Day operation that troubled Bill the most. The low-lying terrain behind the beaches created a shallow moat along the Cotentin's eastern coast. If the Germans dumped gasoline into the water, the fuel could spread for miles over the surface. Twelve square miles might explode into flames at the strike of a match, turning the water obstacle into a fiery death trap. Bill checked for any signs of gasoline. Much to his relief, he saw no evidence that the Germans had poured any into the marshland. Either the German defenders hadn't thought of the tactic or considered it a poor use of precious fuel.[15]

The flooded zone may not have burst into flame but the men still had to wade through waist-deep pools laden with heavy combat loads and life belts. The Germans had dug ditches in the low-lying terrain before flooding it. The unfortunate infantryman who first stepped into one of these submerged trenches would suddenly find himself two feet under water. This threat was especially real for the heavily burdened men of the mortar platoon. Bill's platoon leader commented, "Sometimes we're in shallow water and sometimes we're swimming." Colonel Reeder had warned the men of this danger. He instructed everyone to keep his life belt on and pair with a march buddy who could pull him up if he fell into a water trap. Reeder's sensible precautions and good training paid off. The regiment climbed out of the boggy terrain around 1300 hours near St. Martin-de-Varreville without losing a single man or weapon. The colonel felt elated by that accomplishment. "I knew then that we were going to win the war!" he later said.[16]

After linking up with the paratroopers and reorganizing the regiment, Colonel Reeder ordered the 12th Infantry's first attack to proceed at 1330 hours. The infantrymen pushed west then southwest, using the road running between St. Martin-de-Varreville and Les Mezieres to guide its avenue of advance. Lt. Col. Dominick Montelbano's 2nd Battalion took up position on the south (left) side of the road and surged ahead against remnants of the *919th Infantry Regiment* of the *709th Division*, a static coastal defense unit of questionable quality. Caught between the paratroopers and the 12th Infantry, the German defenders fractured into small elements and managed to put up only a poorly coordinated defense.[17]

Montelbano apportioned the two heavy machine gun platoons out to the two lead companies but kept the mortar platoon in general support of the battalion. Bill's mortar crews mostly followed behind the battalion's riflemen as they cleared the enemy pockets of resistance and the occasional sniper. They did not have to assault the few defenders, but keeping pace with the riflemen while shouldering their heavy loads (the base plate, bipod, and mortar tube each weighed about forty-five pounds) posed a big enough challenge.[18]

The Ivy Division soon encountered the distinctive feature of the Norman *bocage* countryside—hedgerows. For centuries Norman farmers had marked the perimeters of their fields by mounding dirt and planting hawthorn and hazel shrubs on top of the earthen walls. In time, the hedgerows had grown in height and density to become serious impediments to any advance. During their pre-invasion planning, SHAEF's staff had not considered how hedgerows might affect operations, so Allied units had not trained to fight in the *bocage*. Against light resistance, the hedgerows merely slowed their advance. As the men of the Ivy Division and other units soon would learn, hedgerows would pose formidable and deadly obstacles when properly defended.[19]

The rifle platoons swept west, eliminating snipers and overwhelming the occasional German machine gun nest with help from the 81mm mortars. Lieutenant Slaymaker, the mortar platoon leader, recalled a close call during one encounter. "In going across an apple orchard a sniper takes a shot at me. I duck behind a tree and try to locate the source. I see nothing and there is no more firing, so I make a dash to the next tree. I am shot at again and almost at the same time I hear the crack of an M-1 and a German in a camouflage suit comes tumbling out of a tree at our left. My instrument Cpl. has gotten #1 for himself."[20]

The 12th Infantry followed the road for about two miles past Les Mezieres to an intersection short of the hamlet of Reuville. Colonel Reeder directed his two lead battalions to angle northwest from the intersection with Colonel Montelbano's 2nd Battalion again marching on the left side of the formation abreast of the 1st Battalion. At this point, the lead platoons began to contact paratroopers from the 82nd Airborne Division, some of whom were hopelessly lost. The linkup between the two divisions fulfilled one of General Barton's key missions for D-Day.[21]

The regiment advanced another mile to Beuzeville-au-Plain, where the 1st Battalion wiped out an enemy strongpoint and captured a German 75mm anti-tank gun at the crossroads. Colonel Montelbano's men pulled alongside their left flank then halted along the road running southwest from Beuzeville to Ste.-Mere-Eglise. They dug in for the night. The battalion's E and G Companies fronted the road with F Company a couple hundred meters behind them, the classic "two up-one back" defensive formation. For its part, H Company dug in another three hundred meters behind F Company.[22]

H Company spent the rest of the evening preparing a defense. Bill had plenty of tasks to handle after the battalion settled in place. According to Army doctrine, "*The section leader* makes such forward reconnaissances [sic] as are necessary to identify registration points and target areas, and to prepare firing data. He ascertains the location of the main line of resistance and nearby rifle units...Within the firing position areas assigned by the platoon leader, the section leader selects the location for each mortar. Each firing position should be defiladed and concealed, and must be within communicating distance of the observation posts...At least one alternate firing position is selected for each mortar...An observer remains at the observation post. The section leader indicates the sector of fire to the corporal by pointing out definite terrain features." After receiving Bill's instructions, the crews set their mortars up for the planned missions. The section ran telephone wire to the observers to ensure speedy calls for fire if the enemy hit the battalion front in the dark. To help the guns fire swiftly when needed, the squad leaders recorded the descriptions, locations, and firing data for their primary and secondary targets on "range cards." Bill turned these range cards over to Lieutenant Slaymaker, so he could sketch the mortar platoon's target overlay.[23]

That evening, Horsa and Waco gliders flew in to deliver artillery, anti-tank guns, jeeps, and support troops to the interior of the Cotentin Peninsula. The glider pilots used the twilight glow of the setting sun and the illumination from a full moon to search for suitable landing sites near Ste.-Mere-Eglise. German anti-aircraft fire made the task of landing even more perilous. Lieutenant Slaymaker recalled how the mortar platoon jumped into action. "We can see just where their fire is coming from so we open up on them with the mortars; then there is no more fire from that spot." The pilots did their best to maneuver their gliders and avoid the enemy fire, yet several crashed into open fields near the 12th Infantry. "That was a pitiful, bloody thing to see and hear," a member of battalion HQ recalled. The battalion sent out patrols to assist the glider-borne troops. Bill and his men found a few wrecked gliders with dead paratroopers next to them. The sight saddened the young lieutenant. There lay brave, well-trained men who died before even making it into the fight.[24]

After preparing defensive fire missions, the now-exhausted men dug the foxholes in which they'd spend their first night in France and, hopefully, catch some sleep between sporadic episodes of enemy fire and probing. Even with the ever-present danger, the men experienced a general emotion of relief that they had established a foothold in France—and that they had survived D-Day. As one battalion soldier said, "Now we felt we had a chance to live a little longer."[25]

Higher headquarters felt more than relief. The Ivy Division had successfully landed and deployed all three of its regiments with only light casualties. The division's progress, strength, and fighting disposition convinced Maj. Gen. Lawton Collins, commander of VII Corps, and Lt. Gen. Omar Bradley, the First Army commander, that the right flank of the invasion force was secure. The assault on Utah Beach had been considered the most precarious of the five D-Day landings, but it made the deepest advance with the fewest losses. By evening, roughly 21,000 men, 1,700 vehicles, and 1,700 tons of material had poured across the sand of Utah Beach. Strengthened by this surge, the lodgment on the Cotentin Peninsula rapidly solidified.[26]

CHAPTER FOUR

MONTEBOURG

With the initial objective of securing a landing on the Cotentin Peninsula achieved, the VII Corps, of which the 4th Infantry Division was part, turned its attention to the next strategic objective—Cherbourg. The campaign to push the Germans out of Normandy and retake France required vast quantities of fuel, ammunition, equipment, and many more troops. The Mulberry artificial harbors that were set up off the invasion beaches and over-the-beach deliveries by landing craft would suffice for only a few weeks. The Allies needed access to a major seaport to support their titanic logistical effort. The nearest port to the invasion beaches was Cherbourg at the northern tip of the Cotentin Peninsula. The capture of this vital harbor became the focus of the Ivy Division's efforts for the next nineteen days.[1]

During the night of June 6, General Barton conferred with a staff officer from the 82nd Airborne. He decided to shore up the northern flank and begin the drive to Cherbourg in concert with the paratroopers holding Ste.-Mere-Eglise. At midnight, he issued orders to continue the attack toward Montebourg. The orders trickled down to H Company. After Bill finished preparing his mortar section for the night defense, he began planning for the next day's attack.[2]

The 12th Infantry stepped off at 0600 hours on June 7, advancing west-northwest. Without any firm targets, the heavy mortars did not have to fire from their overnight positions and moved with the rest of the battalion. The platoon's jeeps still had not landed, so the men continued to carry their weapons and ammunition as they followed the rifle companies. Bill had targets planned on points of danger along the attack route and pre-designated firing positions for the guns to cover the battalion's advance.

The 2nd Battalion moved forward two and a half kilometers before hitting an enemy position at Neuville-au-Plain, just east of the highway running up to Montebourg. Overnight the Germans had organized a counter-attack against the 82nd Airborne Division in Ste.-Mere-Eglise. They had just arrived in Neuville when the 2nd Battalion's left flank also reached the outskirts of the town. German rifles and machine guns opened fire from nearly every window in the village. Instantly, the rifle companies returned fire.[3]

At the sound of the erupting battle, the mortar squad leaders cried, "Action." The crews executed the drill for putting the guns into operation, something they had practiced often in England. The men carrying the base plates dropped them at the points designated by the squad leaders. Gunners and assistant gunners established the initial direction of fire by driving in aiming stakes on the specified compass heading. The crews aligned the base plates with the aiming stakes. The gunners spread and locked the legs of the bipods then opened the clamping collars. The assistant gunners inserted and locked the bottom of the barrels into the base plate sockets. The crews lowered the barrels into the bipod's cradle then closed the clamping collars. With the guns mounted, the gunners cranked the tubes up to 62 degree elevation and set the deflection scales to zero. The gunners finished by adjusting the tubes for level and alignment. As soon as Bill and his observers called back range and direction to the targets, the section sergeant calculated the correct settings for the

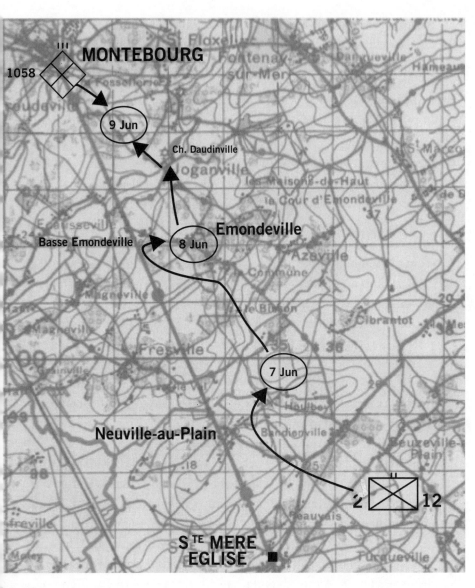

Map II

mortars. The gunners adjusted the deflection and elevation on the tubes. Squad leaders then shouted, "Fire." Within minutes, Bill's crews started dropping 81mm rounds on Neuville to suppress the Germans.[4]

Before the battalion could seize the town, Colonel Reeder called Colonel Montelbano and ordered him to halt the attack. On the right, the 1st Battalion had become entangled with an enemy strongpoint during the morning's action. That caused a gap to form between the regiment's forward battalions. Even more worrisome to Reeder, the 12th Infantry had advanced forward of the rest of the division and now had exposed flanks. At this stage of the war, American tactics demanded an unbroken front when advancing. Later in the war, the Army would learn to exploit any crack in the enemy's defense to reach an objective—and worry less about flank security. Colonel Reeder filled the gap with the 3rd Battalion and pulled Colonel Montelbano's men northeast to high ground between the villages of le Bisson and Bandienville to guard the regiment's rear. The mortar platoon became part of the regiment's reserve but stayed busy the rest of the afternoon clashing with enemy elements that tried to circle behind the regiment.[5] (See Map II)

With no fixed frontlines, both the Americans and Germans had trouble anticipating what direction an enemy probe might come from. The Germans liked to send out a single tank in these situations to scout enemy positions. In one instance, Bill had gathered with part of his section along a hedgerow when a German tank approached. With no weapons capable of knocking out a tank, the men felt defenseless and several panicked, running back to H Company's defensive position. Bill and another man kept their wits about them and crept along a hedgerow to get behind the tank with the idea of disabling it with a grenade. The tank crew saw them but could not target the two infantrymen because of the dense vegetation. Although tanks had advantage in terms of firepower, maneuverability, and armor protection, their crews tended to get very nervous when enemy infantrymen lurked about. The German tank quickly pulled back. The threat having departed, Bill and the other soldier picked up all the loose equipment left behind by the men who had fled and walked back to the company area. When they rejoined their comrades, they dumped all the equipment in a pile in front of them. Point made![6]

The situation remained highly fluid throughout June 7. The regiment had no contact with the other two regiments on its flanks, so Colonel Reeder pulled the Command Post (CP) inside a perimeter and faced the Anti-Tank Platoon to the west. Bill planned targets to protect the regiment's left flank and rear, and his men oriented their guns mostly to the west and south. These precautions paid off. A reinforced company of Germans charged out of Neuville to attack the battalion around 0200 hours. Lieutenant Slaymaker remarked, "There's a lot of scuffling and grenade throwing." The battalion's small arms and mortar fire drove them off without the need to call for artillery.[7]

The action closed with the Germans unable to organize a cohesive defense and the Americans yet to form a solid front. The 12th Infantry had run into some sharp engagements but that had not stopped it from expanding the beachhead. Bill and his men were growing accustomed to incoming fire but, so far, they had not run into any enemy force they could not handle. That situation was about to change. Bill later recalled, "The first two days weren't that bad, but that changed on day three."

During June 7, the Germans brought up two regiments to reinforce the defenders facing the 4th Infantry Division. Drawn from the *91st* and *243rd Divisions*, these units were well-trained and well-equipped combat formations. The German commander had given up hope of driving the Americans back into the English Channel and now sought to establish a solid defense. He designated a main line of resistance (MLR) along the high ground between Emondeville and Crisbecq. The *1058th Infantry Regiment* took up positions directly opposite the 12th Infantry.[8]

Division HQ ordered the 12th Infantry to continue its attack on June 8 with the high ground northeast of Montebourg as its objective. The axis of advance ran first through the town of Emondeville that sat atop a low hill, then continued onto the village of Joganville. From there, the regiment would skirt the eastern edge of Montebourg. Their route meant that they had to cross several farms to reach the objective. Starting this day, the 4th Infantry Division would learn how easily the Germans could defend the peculiar Norman terrain.

The *bocage* frustrated the American advance throughout Normandy. The dense, tangled vegetation and earthen walls of the hedgerows channeled the attackers into narrow roads, running between them, which the Germans covered with mines, machine guns, and anti-tank weapons. The Americans quickly learned to avoid these kill zones and advance through the hedgerows and across the fields.[9]

That did not solve all the problems. The tanks had the power to push through the vegetation but their front ends lifted as they climbed over the barriers, exposing their underbellies to German anti-tank weapons like the *Panzerfaust* or the powerful 88mm *Flak* gun. The Germans tended to entrench on the backside of the open fields, sometimes in the middle. Whenever the Americans broke through a hedgerow and entered the field, the Germans had a clear field of fire. The Germans especially liked to defend the sunken roads that ran parallel to the front. They would dig in along the hedgerow facing the Americans while using the protection of the sunken road behind their position to move troops and vehicles from one sector to the next, as the situation required. The terrain and German defensive techniques obstructed rapid maneuver and concentration of firepower, just the type of offensive tactics the Americans liked to use.[10]

The battle on June 8 kicked off at 0530 hours with naval gunfire pounding Emondeville. The 1st and 3rd Battalions led the attack with the 2nd Battalion in reserve. Despite the Navy's terrific shelling, the attack bogged down against German artillery and machine gun fire only 600 yards beyond the line of departure (LD). The enemy launched a fierce counterattack against the 1st Battalion using the *Seventh Army Sturm Battalion,* supported by a heavy artillery barrage. The 1st Battalion responded with a deluge from its mortars (the 81mm mortar platoon dropped four hundred rounds in ten minutes) and division artillery that beat back the *Sturm Battalion*—barely.[11]

Meanwhile, the 3rd Battalion pushed across the hedgerows toward Emondeville, taking heavy casualties the whole way. Every time the riflemen hopped over a hedgerow, they came under withering enemy fire. By will and sheer determination, L Company forced its way through Emondeville only to have the German defenders emerge from the houses they had bypassed and shoot at them from behind. The company soon found itself isolated on the far (north) side of Emondeville. The rest of 3rd Battalion tried to reach them but German artillery and rocket fire pinned down K Company just short of the village.[12]

Colonel Reeder then committed the 2nd Battalion to envelop the enemy's position and take Emondeville from the west. Colonel Montelbano contacted the 3rd Battalion then directed his attack around their left flank. Tactics dictated that the heavy mortar platoon move forward by echelon (one section at a time) so that at least one section remained in place to deliver immediate suppressive fire on targets of opportunity. The advancing mortar sections picked up their tubes, baseplates, and bipods, then followed the battalion's lead companies as they swung around K Company's left.[13]

The 2nd Battalion had just started its flanking maneuver when the Germans unleashed a barrage of rockets. The Germans had developed a launching system, called the "Nebelwerfer" or "smoke thrower," that fired multiple rocket projectiles a distance of 2,200 meters. Each rocket had a diameter of 280mm and a powerful 110-lb. high explosive warhead. The Nebelwerfers could fire six of these rockets in rapid succession from a towed launcher. When launched, the rockets produced a high-pitched screeching sound. American troops nicknamed them "Screaming Meemies." The rocket projectiles lacked the accuracy of artillery but a launch of six rockets could saturate an area target with deadly effect.[14]

The huge warheads thudded into the fields right in the battalion's path. The ground erupted like a volcano, spitting earth and smoke skyward. Blast waves smacked the riflemen the same moment the deafening roar of the exploding shells boomed in their ears. Colonel Reeder realized how devastating rockets could be to exposed troops. Jumping up and down and waving his arms to the west he shouted, "Everybody go over that way!" Following the orders of their agitated regimental commander, the troops immediately darted to their left. This saved lives but caused confusion. Company commanders, platoon leaders, and squad leaders had no chance to control their formations as the men stampeded out of the impact area. The situation became even more critical when the Germans launched a counterattack out of Emondeville that hit the disorganized 2nd Battalion.[15]

The regiment's executive officer, Lieutenant Colonel James Luckett, marveled at the battalion's reaction. "[T]his counterattack far from routing the 2d Bn seemed to be the thing that straightened them out. The men quickly adjusted themselves into units and went after the Germans." The Americans "opened up with everything they had"—rifles, machine guns, and 81mm mortars—and sent the Germans reeling back to Emondeville.[16]

The revitalized battalion turned its attention back to its objective and advanced. The heavy weapons suppressed the enemy while the riflemen climbed over the hedgerows and maneuvered across the open spaces. Despite the suppressive fire, the Germans held their ground and returned fire with deadly effect. The *crump...crump* of distant American artillery and mortar fire mixed with the *boom...boom* of German shells impacting close by. The rattle of machine guns and rifles melded into a steady, cacophonous din. Losses mounted quickly.

The mortar platoon had its own problems with the Norman terrain. Army doctrine stated that OPs should be "close enough to the mortar position to permit the observer to see both the target and the mortar position." In the *bocage*, the observers could not see past the next hedgerow and could not be seen past the one to their rear. While the platoon had radios, it did not have enough to hand out to the observers. It had telephones and reels of telephone wire but the fast-paced situation made it difficult to lay wire. Enemy artillery and mortars often severed the wires, anyway. Bill's men had to improvise by sending runners back and forth between the guns and observers. They also adapted by displacing mortar sections frequently to keep the guns close to the observers and the front line. The platoon advanced like an inchworm: extend-contract, extend-contract.[17]

When the attack ran into stiff resistance coming from a French farmhouse, the company called up the naval Shore Fire Control Party attached to the regiment, and issued a call for fire against the entrenched Germans. The USS *Nevada* (BB-36) answered the call with its main battery of fourteen-inch guns. Bill had his eyes on the target when he heard the incoming rounds. "The huge shells sounded like a freight train flying overhead." The exploding rounds sent out a massive shock wave. When the smoke cleared, the farmhouse and its German defenders had been obliterated. "Wow! What destruction!" Bill exclaimed.

The attack ground forward. F Company assaulted across an open field against a German position, using "marching fire." The 81mm mortars supported them by dropping rounds in front of the infantrymen until the troops got close to the bursting radius of the shells. Then, the mortar crews added fifty yards to the range and continued to fire. F Company pressed ahead, but lost its commander when he was killed trying to take out a machine gun with only his carbine. One of E Company's riflemen, Technical Sergeant Daniel Stresow, had better luck. He snuck his way along one side of a hedgerow until he was next to a machine gun on the other side of the bushes. He bounded over the shrubs and killed the two-man crew with his bayonet. At one point in the fight, E Company surrounded a German detachment. Six enemy soldiers raised a white flag but appeared to balk at coming out into the open. 2nd Lt. John Everett and a handful of enlisted men went forward to take the Germans prisoner. The two groups were only twenty yards apart when an unseen German machine gun cut down Everett and one of the enlisted men. After that, E Company overwhelmed the German unit with no thought of quarter.[18]

By mid-afternoon the 2nd Battalion had advanced all the way to the Ste.-Mere-Eglise-Montebourg highway and held the adjacent village of Basse Emondeville. Colonel Reeder pulled it back to attack Emondeville from the west. In the confusion, one of the mortar sections got separated going through Basse Emondeville. Lieutenant Slaymaker had to send Bill and three men to guide them back into the attack.[19]

The 2nd Battalion reached the beleaguered L Company late in the afternoon, a few hundred meters northwest of Emondeville. That linkup allowed the regiment to extricate K Company, which had gone to ground under sustained German artillery and mortar fire just south of the village.

While Colonel Montelbano's men fought house to house through Basse Emondeville and Emondeville, the regimental Command Post (CP) came under attack. German artillery observers had noticed a collection of vehicles in nearby Saussetour and correctly guessed that it was an American headquarters. The enemy pounded Saussetour with 88mm and 150mm shells and directed a local counterattack against the soft target. It took part of 3rd Battalion's I Company and a heavy dose of counter-battery fire from the 42nd Artillery Battalion to break up the attack and silence the enemy guns.[20]

The struggle for Emondeville continued into the evening. The German survivors used the cover of darkness to withdraw one kilometer north to Joganville, though nineteen Germans emerged from one house to surrender to the mortars. "We put them to work digging our emplacements." The 2nd Battalion secured the village and H Company set up the 81mm mortars and heavy machine guns around the hamlet. Primary and secondary targets had to be planned to the front and firing positions prepared. Given the fluid situation, Bill had to plan for counterattacks from the left flank and rear, too. Alternate firing positions were designated and potential targets reconnoitered. Bill positioned OPs and had the section lay wire to them. He stayed busy all night working up fire plans and checking the mortar squads' range cards to ensure they recorded data for all planned targets.[21]

The regiment lost nearly three hundred men on June 8; among them was 2nd Lt. Sam Kyle, Bill's best friend. The 12th Infantry had advanced only one third of the way toward Montebourg. After experiencing German rockets, sustained mortar and artillery fire, inter-locking machine gun fire, and stubborn defenders who fought to the death, the Americans had a better idea of how fierce the fighting would become in Normandy. Undaunted by the stiff resistance and the regiment's casualties, Colonel

Reeder ordered an attack on June 9 to seize Joganville but with some modifications. The grinding fight at Emondeville convinced him that the rifle companies could not assault well-defended positions without help. Small arms and mortars were simply not enough to dislodge determined German defenders without absorbing unsustainable losses. The Americans needed more firepower—that meant using tanks.[22]

Tallie Crocker, the H Company commander, summoned Bill to the CP in the predawn hours for a briefing about the upcoming attack. The young lieutenant had not slept for days but he dragged his weary body to the CP to receive the attack order. Bill fell asleep on the way there and collapsed into a hedgerow. Waking up as soon as he landed in the bushes, Bill pulled himself out of the shrubbery, none the worse, except for a small cut on his hand. He would wonder about that cut days later. Coming back after the briefing, Bill felt a strange uneasiness take hold like the time he looked at his parents on the tarmac in San Francisco. This time he knew what the odd sensation meant. He pulled his sergeant aside when he got back with his section. "Stay clear of me today," he said. "I think I'm going to get hit."

The attack by the 2nd Battalion kicked off at 0700 hours, helped by a fog lying atop the *bocage*. The weather was a mixed blessing. The infantrymen could use the extra concealment but the fog also prevented them from getting any air support. The 81mm mortars could hit Joganville from their positions in Emondeville, so the guns remained in place for the initial move as Bill and the observers moved forward with the rifle platoons to locate targets and select forward firing positions.[23]

The observers worked their way through the hedgerows and crawled into spots that gave them observation of Joganville and some cover against enemy fire. With no chance to set up alidades, the observation posts (OPs) could not align with the gun-target (G-T) line. The platoon laid the guns on an initial compass heading toward Joganville (6400 mils). Peeking through brush, the observers estimated their O-T line (5400 mils) and distance from the target (e.g. 400 meters). The observers had to correct their fire orders for the deviation in their line of sight to the target versus the G-T line, using the compass-mil method.

After calculating the correct distance and direction of fire to the targets, the observers called in initial fire orders using telephones wired back to the gun squads. "HE [type of round], 0 [deflection], stake [aiming point], 1200 [range], one round." The observers fixed their binoculars on the targets and spotted the impact of the initial rounds. They called back adjustments for the range and deflection to shift subsequent rounds onto the enemy. Once the rounds landed on target, the observers called "fire for effect." Each gun squad dropped rounds on the enemy every four seconds, saturating the German positions. By comparison, the artillery could only sustain a rate of fire of one round a minute.

Both sides came to appreciate the value of mortars during the close fighting in the hedgerows. The wider dispersion of standard artillery rounds and their greater bursting radius meant that targets any closer than 400–600 meters to friendly troops had to be treated as "danger close" missions. In Normandy hedgerows, an enemy was usually 100 to 300 away. Only mortars could safely fire on an enemy that close. The Germans used mortars extensively, too. Their preferred tactic was to pin down American infantry with small arms and machine-gun fire, then clobber them with mortars. Some estimates showed that German mortars accounted for 75 percent of American infantry losses in Normandy. The Germans also appreciated the threat posed by American mortars and, with increasing frequency, targeted H Company's mortars with their artillery.[24]

E Company riflemen forced their way into Joganville, fighting house-to-house. The Germans fought back with small arms fire and a 75mm howitzer. After a brief, fierce battle, the company seized the town and the howitzer. Over to the right, F Company moved through several fields before they ran into a German combat outpost. The lieutenant commanding the company took a bullet between the eyes while the Battalion S-2 and a platoon leader suffered severe burns from a white phosphorus (WP) round. The enemy held them up until a platoon of tanks from B Company, 746th Tank Battalion joined the fight. The infantry and armor worked together against the enemy. The tanks blasted the dug-in German infantry, forcing their heads down. F Company's riflemen followed with a direct assault. The Americans rooted out the defenders at bayonet point, killing twenty-five of them. The 1st Battalion, on the battalion's right flank, also used tanks from the 746th to advance beyond Joganville. The 12th Infantry had much to learn about combined-arms tactics but its first experience with tanks worked very well.[25]

Just north of the village and across a creek, stood the Chateau Daud-inville, a massive Norman building with four-foot thick stone walls. More a fortress than a residence, the chateau was defended by a company from the *Sturm Battalion*. The enemy made effective use of the chateau's grounds and its wide-open fields of fire to bar the regiment's advance. The motorcycle troops even mined and booby-trapped the outer walls. Colonel Reeder knew an infantry assault would be suicidal but the cha-teau had to be taken. Now that tanks had joined the regiment, Reeder organized a deliberate attack by Combat Team 12 (CT 12), using all the assets he had available. He brought up six tanks from the 746th to bolster the infantry. As soon as the mortar platoon's observers fed firing data to the crews, they started dropping rounds at a furious rate. The short-barreled 105mm howitzers of the regiment's Cannon Company and the regular 105mm howitzers of the 42nd Artillery Battalion joined in. Amer-ican supporting fire plastered the chateau as the tanks and infantry attacked. The tanks hit the chateau with their 75mm main guns and machine guns but the enemy still cut down the infantry as they crossed the creek. It took time, but American firepower turned the tide of battle. Indirect fire whittled down the outlying German positions. Tank fire drove the enemy away from the chateau's windows. Small arms fire picked off more of the defenders who tried to fire back. Under the umbrella of fire, the riflemen worked their way across the creek until they got close enough to launch a final rush to wipe out the defenders. "It was our turn to kill a few," Lieutenant Slaymaker said. "There were no prisoners. They were killed before they could surrender. The men [were] mad...There [was] no mercy in anyone's heart. We [had] seen too many of our buddies killed and wounded this day."[26]

While the 1st and 2nd Battalions reduced Chateau Daudinville, Colo-nel Reeder directed the 3rd Battalion to bypass the action and bound around the eastern flank. The 3rd Battalion succeeded in reaching the regimental objective, the high ground northeast of Montebourg. Reeder wanted to consolidate CT 12 on the objective, so he ordered 1st and 2nd Battalions to resume their attack at 1930 hours from their position northwest of Joganville and come abreast of the 3rd Battalion. Reeder designated a couple of roads that generally ran east-west about one kilometer past the chateau as the LD for the attack by the two battalions.[27]

The 2nd Battalion re-organized after the vicious fight at the chateau. Bill's section had already had a busy day. Lieutenant Slaymaker brought all of H Company's mortars forward to the assembly area northwest of Joganville and prepared to bound the sections to support the attack. Colonel Montelbano started the weary battalion moving around 1915 hours, using the Joganville–Montebourg road as a guide for their right flank. Just as the leading rifle platoons reached the LD, they ran headlong into a German force counterattacking out of Montebourg. Up and down the line, riflemen from both sides hit the dirt and opened fire.

German military doctrine emphasized the necessity of launching an immediate counterattack once an enemy force penetrated a defensive line. "It was a point of honor with them," a G Company soldier once remarked. The fall of Chateau Daudinville and the American push beyond Joganville provoked the Germans into organizing a local assault using their reserves in Montebourg. The two lines of opposing infantry collided along the road that marked the American LD. The mortar platoon had already broken down a section of mortar tubes to carry forward on the evening attack. The sudden counterattack forced them to reset the section. Working quickly, the mortar squads began dropping their remaining rounds just forward of the rifle squads.[28]

The enemy platoons pressed ahead using fire and maneuver but the 12th Infantry held firm. The Germans tried to press their assault but ran into a solid wall of fire. The Germans then sent a small force to envelop the American left. They found a good firing position for their machine guns behind a hedgerow west of the 2nd Battalion. One of the machine gunners spotted a group of Americans across the field and took aim at the officer leading them.

Bill moved forward with some of his observers along a hedgerow, hurrying forward to spot rounds and adjust mortar fire against the enemy. A sudden burst of machine gun fire coming from the left bracketed Bill's head. He felt the heat of the first round as it snapped just in front of his nose, then the warm crackle of the second round as it passed behind his neck. A heartbeat later the Americans heard *tat-tat-tat-tat-tat-tat!* They hit the ground before the machine gunner had a chance to get off a second burst. Bill and his men hugged the ground as more enemy rounds ripped through the shrubs above their heads then low crawled through the growth to get out of the field of fire. By the time they wriggled to the other side, the Germans were pouring fire into the battalion's left flank.[29]

The German machine gun position put the American infantry in a difficult spot. They could not sit still with fire pouring into their flank but they had to cross a thick hedgerow and an open field to get at the Germans.[30]

The commander of the 746th Tank Battalion, Lt. Col. Clarence Hupfer, helped retrieve the situation. He first came forward to make a personal reconnaissance. The hedgerow prevented a direct approach by the tanks against the Germans but Hupfer discovered a gate in the southern extension of the hedgerow. He directed one platoon of his tanks to skirt around the American infantry's left flank and enter the field through the gate. Once the tanks burst into the open field, they fired on the German machine gunners. With tanks bearing down on them, the German machine gunners withdrew, and the enemy counterattack petered out. The tanks' success allowed the 1st and 2nd Battalions to push forward just beyond their designated LD, but that's where they stopped.[31]

The battered American infantry dug in for the night along the front they had just defended. Unfortunately, their positions were within sight of a German OP nestled in the tower of Montebourg's church. Besides spotting artillery fire, the OP could also call for rocket strikes. Later that evening, Bill attended a meeting in the H Company CP. The company leaders had just gathered when they heard a *Nebelwerfer* launch its rockets. The shrill sound of the incoming projectiles alerted them that the rounds were coming their way. Bill and a sergeant dove into a nearby slit trench. The first rocket landed just yards away. *Damn! That was close.* The second round landed even closer. *Uh oh!* The third rocket struck beside Bill's slit trench and everything went black.[32]

The next thing Bill knew he was floating in a mist. For some reason, his arms and legs moved but there was no ground beneath him. He remained suspended in mist, waving his limbs. *Is this what it's like to be dead?* Gradually his senses returned, and he realized that he was neither dead nor suspended in air—he was lying on his back and squirming. The rocket had riddled his torso with shrapnel and cracked his ribs, making it difficult to breathe. The sergeant next to him fared worse—the blast had cut him in two. Bill tried to get to his feet but keeled over. He heard his commander, Tallie Crocker, yelling, "Somebody look after Lieutenant Chapman." Hands came to help. Bill saw his sergeant and noticed that he had tears in his eyes while he helped lift Bill onto a litter. A short time later, he lost consciousness.[33]

The battalion evacuated Bill to a clearing station that stabilized him despite his near-mortal wounds. The medics then transported him to Utah Beach. He came to on the beach but struggled to inhale. The shrapnel embedded in his chest and abdomen made every breath painful. The only way he could cope was to take shallow breaths that did not aggravate the puncture wounds. A medic walked over to check on him. The pained expression on Bill's face and his labored breathing let the medic know that Bill had been badly hurt and suffered severe pain. The medic pulled out a syringe and a vial of morphine. "Here Lieutenant, I've got some morphine that will help ease your pain."

"No doc...Don't...I'm having...enough trouble...breathing as it is."

The medic suddenly realized that he had been on the verge of giving the lieutenant an injection that could have shut down the wounded officer's ability to breathe altogether. His act of kindness might have been fatal. "Oh right!" he said. "Damn! It's a good thing you said something."

The regiment continued losing officers and enlisted men after Bill was evacuated. He was one of the 952 casualties the 12th Infantry suffered during its first week of combat. On June 11 Colonel Reeder was severely wounded by artillery fire, eventually losing a leg. That same day, German artillery killed Lt. Col. Dominick Montelbano, commander of the 2nd Battalion. H Company commander, 1st Lt. Tallie Crocker, went down on June 12. A German 88 knocked the mortar platoon leader, 1st Lt. William Slaymaker, out of the war the next day. The troops in Bill's section had lost all the officers in their chain of command from lieutenant to colonel in seven days. Among the battalion's three rifle companies, only one officer remained.[34]

The Normandy battles chewed up the Germans, too. The *919th Infantry Regiment* had dissolved under the American assault, and the *1058th Regiment* had been reduced to less than half strength. The Americans had killed the commanding general of the *91st Division* on the first day of contact, and an Allied air strike killed the commander of the *LXXXIV Corps*, Lt. Gen. Erich Marcks, on June 12.[35]

Prior to the invasion the German general staff assumed that the American, British, and Canadian armies could be driven back into the sea by a few well-placed and determined counterattacks. German counterattacks, however, failed to produce any significant results. The Americans stood their ground, then punished the attackers with massive firepower, everything from small arms, machine guns, and mortars to artillery, naval gunfire, and aerial bombardment.

The Germans made another huge miscalculation when they underestimated the Allies' ability to reinforce and supply the initial invasion force in the Cotentin Peninsula. They anticipated that the Americans could support two, perhaps three, divisions in the Cotentin in the first week after the landing. The *LXXXIV Corps* had three divisions on hand and could be reinforced with three more in a few days, enough force, they thought, to contain the landing then overwhelm it with strong counterattacks. Instead, the Americans landed with one infantry and two airborne divisions on D-Day then followed up with two more infantry divisions by D+6. The Allies proved that they could surge combat forces onto the battlefield faster than the Germans.[36]

At midnight on June 9, Hitler sent orders to Field Marshal von Rundstedt, commander of *Oberbefehlshaber West* (*OB West*), to hold the *Fifteenth Army* reserves near Calais and assume a strategic defensive posture in Normandy, rather than launch an all-out attack against the Allied beachhead. The Fuhrer had decided to hedge his bets in the West to save Germany's dwindling resources for the looming summer battles in the East. By the time Bill was evacuated to England, the Allies had a permanent foothold on the continent.[37]

CHAPTER FIVE

OPERATION COBRA

Bill arrived at the Royal Army Medical Corps' 83rd General Hospital in Wrexham, Wales. There, the medical staff cleaned his wounds from the rocket blast. He was in bad shape in other ways, too. In the days since D-Day, the vomit and sea salt had been flushed out of his uniform by sweat, rainwater, dirt, and dried blood. Bill had not had his boots off for several days. When nurses removed his socks, the soles of his feet peeled off like paper stuck to adhesive tape.

After cleaning his external wounds, the doctors studied x-rays of Bill's chest to assess the danger posed by the embedded shrapnel. One piece measured three-quarters of an inch in diameter. They saw that his ribs were cracked but failed to notice that his eardrums had been ruptured, too. The punctures in his back worried them most. The doctors decided to leave the chunks of steel in his torso rather than risk further injury trying to dig them out. The hospital staff gave him oxygen, blood transfusions, and fifty-two doses of penicillin over a week. "God, there are holes all over my arms," he complained. Bill responded well to the treatment. Once he got some rest, his breathing became less painful and he gradually regained his strength. In time, he could focus on things besides his soreness.[1]

He first thought about alerting Beth. Like everyone else on the home front, she was thrilled by the news of the Normandy landings but had no way of knowing that Bill had entered combat. Bill knew that the War Department would soon notify her by telegram that he had been wounded. He dreaded the idea of Beth receiving such a telegram unaware. It would certainly put her through a moment of severe anguish until she had a chance to read it. Even after learning that he was not dead, she would still be left to worry about the extent of his wounds. As soon as he was able, he sent an urgent V Mail to tell her that he had been wounded and shipped to a hospital. Bill downplayed his injuries. "There are actually 5 holes in me but you know that I'm too tough to be seriously hurt." He went on to mention that the scars would be on his back. "No, I was not running away." Thankfully, his letter arrived before the War Department telegram. Despite the serious nature of Bill's wounds, Beth felt relieved to know that he was alive and would recover.[2]

While in the hospital, Bill noticed the strange scrape on his hand. It did not fit with his wounds from the German rocket. Thinking back to the battlefield, he remembered falling asleep on his way to a company meeting and cutting his hand on a shrub. Then he recalled the uneasy feeling he had about getting wounded.

Bill, not the sort to believe in premonitions, put his faith in calculations, proofs, and evidence. He openly scoffed at spiritualists, ghost chasers, and followers of the occult. Yet, he could not deny that the strange sensation he felt the morning of June 9 foretold his wounding.

As he pondered this premonition, he remembered experiencing the same uneasy sensation on the day he left home. He had boarded a plane and looked back at his parents when he felt that he would never return. *What did that premonition mean? Am I not going to make it back home?* Bill felt a sudden grip of dread. Even if he did not believe in "extrasensory perception," the premonition about not going home would trouble him until the end of the war.

As his body healed, Bill thought back on his brief experience in France. The short stint in combat seemed disappointing compared to the months of training and preparation for the invasion. "It makes me very angry to be a casualty after 4 days of fighting. I'll be back there soon, though." He did not blame himself for getting wounded but he had hoped to do more. Reflecting on his role in the war, one redeeming thought came to mind. "Remember why I wanted combat?" he wrote to Beth. "I wanted to see how I would react under the pressure of combat and danger. Well, I feel OK about myself now—the question has been answered now and I don't have to admit to anything—thank God."[3]

Bill spent the rest of June recuperating. The time passed slowly. He read, played checkers, and wrote letters to Beth. On June 26, he blew fourteen dollars on a bottle of rum and went out with a couple of other patients to celebrate his anniversary. The party turned out to be more bitter than sweet. He felt terribly lonely and regretted spending the money. When he had been brought to the hospital and stripped for surgery, someone stole his wallet. The government allowed Bill to draw seventy cents per day in casual pay but his mess bill ran ninety cents per day. Without cash or a blank check, he had to run up a debt for his meals in the hospital. Bill had to ask Beth to send money through the Red Cross. That depressed him even more Bill had been short of cash during their entire courtship and he was no ⸱ much better as a husband. "Our marriage has given me a goal, ⸱⸱e in life. It has given me something tangible to fight for. It has a ⸱e a guilty conscience. So far I have given you nothing but an o ⸱"[4]

The surgeons finally stitched his w⸱ ls sh⸱ Bill warned Beth that he would leave the hospital in "a weel ⸱⸱ days." That meant a return to combat. Bill indulged in thinking ⸱⸱ to life after the war. "Well darling, we will live a sensible life af⸱ are together. We know what a precious thing a normal married lif⸱ be." His patriotism mingled with his resentment against the Ger⸱ the disruption wrought on his young life. Philosophically, he ⸱ to destroy the enemy's country to prevent a future war, yet his s⸱ f humanity weighed against retribution. "Who am I to say anot⸱ ⸱ should be killed so that I will not have to fight again in 20 or 30 years? Life is very precious even though it is wasted."[5]

Bill's strength had returned by the first week of July but he still had not fully healed. Meanwhile, the heavy casualties in Normandy put pressure on the medical staff to return wounded men to duty as quickly as possible. Even though his wounds still had to be bandaged, the doctors cleared Bill for frontline duty.

Bill's recovery left his body vulnerable to other health threats. Just as he got orders to return to France, one of his teeth became infected. In his weakened state, the infection developed into an abscess, causing a great deal of pain. The young lieutenant made an appointment with the dental staff to remove the infected tooth before he had to redeploy.

The dentist examined the abscess and agreed the tooth needed to be extracted. However, he saw a problem. "There's so much pus in your abscess I'm afraid the pain killer won't do any good," he said. "We ought to wait for the swelling to go down."

"I don't care," Bill replied. "The abscess is killing me already and I can't come back tomorrow. We have to pull the tooth now."

"I'm sending you back to the hospital for three days then you can come back."

Bill reminded the dentist that as an officer with orders already detaching him from the replacement depot he did not have to comply with his instructions. The dentist relented and did what he could to sedate the lieutenant before prying out the infected tooth. The procedure hurt—a lot—but the abscess had been causing so much aggravation that Bill did not care. "What a relief that was. It had been aching all day and for spells all week." The dentist sent Bill back to the officers' quarters to sleep off the operation.[6]

The hospital staff assigned the recovering lieutenant an enlisted orderly, also known as a batman, as was customary for British officers. When Bill returned to the barracks, the batman had prepared his uniforms and personal gear for transport. The batman asked Bill what else he might need. "Wake me up when the mess hall is serving supper," Bill answered then went to bed. The soldier later roused the sleepy lieutenant for the meal, after which Bill went back to sleep.

The British soldier came back the next morning to get Bill ready for the trip. Still groggy, Bill got up, boarded the train, and immediately fell back asleep. A few hours later the batman woke him again. "Sir, we're about to arrive."

After sleeping for most of the past twenty-four hours, Bill had finally gotten over the effects of the sedative and the tooth extraction. He thanked the batman for his services and boarded the ship. As he boarded, Bill could not help but wonder what kind of impression the British batman had of the American lieutenant who did nothing other than sleep.

The voyage back to France seemed strange and outlandish compared to the last time he had crossed the Channel. Then, he and hundreds of other men had been packed into a sea-tossed LCI smelling of puke. This time, he had a comfortable berth in officers' quarters aboard a merchant vessel. Bill marveled at the "straight grain teak" appointed cabin. Service in the officer's wardroom was equally lavish. "At mess we have a Laskar [sic] boy [servant of Indian extraction] for every table (7 offs.), and he practically breaks his neck waiting on us." As much as Bill enjoyed the accommodations, something about them offended his sensibilities. "You know it is not typical British life here. Those that have wealth have plenty, but they are few."[7]

Bill made his way forward to the front after landing in Normandy for a second time. By July 21, he reached a small village a short distance from the 4th Infantry Division sector. He knocked on the door of a French house to get out of a driving rain. The family readily agreed to let him spend the night. He slept with a roof over his head and out of the rain, a treat he would not enjoy for weeks to come. In his time with the family a few things about their culture and attitudes bothered Bill, particularly the way the farmers treated their women. Every time he requested anything, the French husband would agree then tell his wife to get whatever Bill wanted. "Speaking of the women. You know they do most of the work. You will see the woman pushing a wheelbarrow and her husband walking beside her smoking his pipe!!"

Bill rejoined H Company on July 22 in a soggy assembly area outside the hamlet of le Desert, thirteen kilometers northwest of St. Lo. The sudden reappearance of someone long since written off caused a stir within the unit, especially among the men who had seen the hole next to his heart. He had been one of their past-tense officers.[8]

As happy as he was to be back with his unit, the swarm of new faces and the many missing D-Day veterans dampened his spirits. The 12th Infantry had been through tough times during his convalescence. The VII Corps had driven the Germans back from Montebourg to Cherbourg in the two weeks after Bill had been wounded. The 12th Infantry helped capture the vital port on June 25. After achieving that strategic objective, the 4th Infantry Division moved south of Carentan to expand the Normandy beachhead. In ten days of brutal fighting, the regiment advanced a mere six kilometers, hedgerow-to-hedgerow, against elements of the *2nd SS Panzer "Das Reich" Division* and the *17th SS Panzergrenadier "Gotz von Berlichingen" Division*. The rest of the First Army fared no better. A determined German defense had kept the Allies bottled up in Normandy. General Bradley called off the broad-front push by the V, VII, VIII, and XIX Corps once St. Lo fell on July 18.[9]

The lack of American success can be partially attributed to the Army's tactical doctrine in 1944. The operations manual visualized only two primary forms of attack: an envelopment and a penetration. The manual stated a preference for an envelopment, if an assailable flank was available; if not it called for a penetration. By penetration, the Army meant a rupturing of some point along the enemy's front. "In a penetration the main attack passes through some portion of the area occupied by the enemy's main forces and is directed on an objective in his rear." The manual failed to emphasize a key characteristic of this type of operation—that an attack should strike as slender a slice of the enemy's defenses as possible. It did recommend concentrating forces for the main attack but the guidance left a supposition that the attacking unit would still face the whole breadth of the defender's line. Later, doctrine would draw a distinction between a penetration and a frontal attack, narrowing the definition of a penetration to a concentrated attack against a relatively narrow portion of the enemy's defense.[10]

The early July battles took a savage toll on the Ivy Division. It had lost 2,300 men and radically changed the battalion's officer roster. Tallie Crocker had returned from the hospital but had a new assignment. Captain Earl W. Enroughty, a dependable officer from Virginia, assumed command of H Company on July 20. Major Richard O'Malley took over the 2nd Battalion after Dominick Montelbano was killed outside Montebourg. O'Malley—known as "The Iron Major"—had infused the battalion with his aggressive fighting spirit, but he was killed less than a week before Bill returned. Major Gerden F. Johnson, the 1st Battalion's executive officer (XO), took command in O'Malley's place.[11] (See Fig. 3)

Changes had occurred in the higher echelons, too. Colonel James S. Luckett, an unassuming but capable officer, replaced the dynamic Red Reeder as commander of the 12th Infantry. The division commander, General Barton, remained but the Ivy Division lost its beloved deputy commander, Ted Roosevelt Jr. The hero of Utah Beach died from a heart attack on July 12.

Captain Enroughty assigned Bill to lead one of the two heavy machine gun platoons in H Company. His platoon was organized into two sections, each equipped with two M1917A1 Browning .30 caliber water-cooled machine guns.

The M1917A1 heavy machine gun weighed thirty pounds and came with a six-pound water canister and fifty-three-pound tripod. This considerable weight made them too heavy for rifle companies, which were equipped with the lighter air-cooled M1919 machine gun. The Army placed the M1917A1s into machine gun platoons within the battalion's heavy weapons company. Each of Bill's four gun squads had its own jeep to haul the guns and their ammunition.

The two types of machine guns fired the same M2 cartridge, but each served a separate purpose. The lighter M1919 enabled the rifle companies to carry the firepower of a machine gun forward with its riflemen. The infantry prized the M1917A1 for its incredible reliability and indirect fire capabilities. The War Department purchased the M1917A1 after its inventor, John Browning, conducted a demonstration for senior officers and political leaders. He fired a single "burst" of

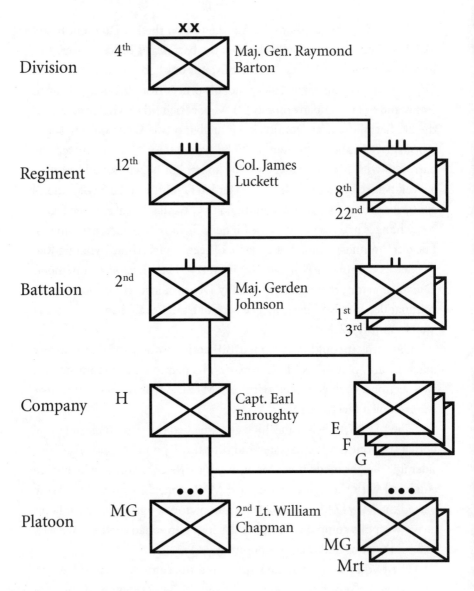

Fig. 3 Organization Jul–Aug 1944

20,000 rounds from an M1917 without a pause or malfunction. The M1917A1 would go on to serve in the U.S. Army and Marine Corps well into the 1950s.[12]

Machine guns were ideal for creating a final protective line (FPL), a defensive tactic meant to stop enemy infantry short of friendly positions by shooting a constant wall of lead across the front line. For them to be effective in the offense, the gunners had to fire either between advancing rifle squads or over their heads using indirect fire techniques, similar to the fire control methods used by the mortars.

Captain Enroughty also told Bill about a big upcoming offensive scheduled to jump off on July 24. General Bradley had abandoned the broad-front attack across the entire American portion of the Normandy line. He now planned to punch through a four-mile stretch of the German frontline with a concentrated attack using the VII Corps, which included the Ivy Division, as the strike force.

A straight length of an old Roman road running between St. Lo and Periers marked the LD for the attack. Beyond that line, bombers from the Eighth and Ninth Air Forces would saturate a target box with bombs to blast away the mixed elements of the *Panzer Lehr*, *5th Parachute*, and *275th Divisions*. Unlike the aerial bombardment that preceded the failed British Operation Goodwood, the Americans would use only bombs of 250 pounds or less to avoid creating massive craters along the planned line of advance. The plan also called for an immediate ground assault after the aerial bombardment to take maximum advantage of its shock effect. As soon as VII Corps penetrated the German front, several armored divisions would pour through the gap. Bradley hoped that this offensive, "Operation Cobra," would achieve a breakthrough that would allow the armored forces to thrust deep into the German rear. General Barton designated the 8th Infantry Regiment as the Ivy Division's spearhead with the 12th Infantry following it into the target box to mop up any pockets of resistance bypassed by the lead regiment.[13]

Rain fell for the next two days, forcing the postponement of the attack and giving Bill more time to get acquainted with his new platoon. On July 24, a few bomber squadrons that had taken off for the scheduled attack did not get the recall message and dropped their bombs, some of them "shorts" that killed a few American troops. The Americans worried that the abortive strike had tipped their hand, but the Germans did not react.[14]

When the men of the 12th Infantry awoke on July 25 and saw clear skies overhead, they knew Operation Cobra would proceed. Some took the opportunity to watch the massive preparation of the target box from the orchards six kilometers back from the St. Lo–Periers Highway. One of the riflemen in Bill's battalion, Private Dick Stodghill, described the unfolding operation.

> The artillery began firing at nine…Every gun within range was taking part…The barrage continued for an hour. Then came the dive bombers. This also seemed never-ending, but it finally stopped and then from behind us came medium bombers…At last it ended…some of us believed that the tank crews and infantrymen of Panzer Lehr had undergone enough pounding…But then…we heard a droning sound approaching from behind. [B]y looking almost directly overhead I saw them, dozen upon dozen of Flying Fortresses and Liberators so high that they looked like toys suspended below a blue ceiling.
>
> [B]ut then the bombs began falling and in stunned surprise we turned again to face the front. For several minutes the thunderous roar of the explosions and the sights of huge clods of dirt flying high in the air drove every thought from mind. Then the idea came over me. No one deserved what the men on the other side of the road were experiencing.
>
> Soon, though, the smoke and dust drifting back over us turned the sky dark. On the far side of the highway it seemed as black as night.
>
> Then came the sickening realization that bombs were beginning to fall on our side of the highway…The explosions drew nearer and nearer until we could see that the bombs

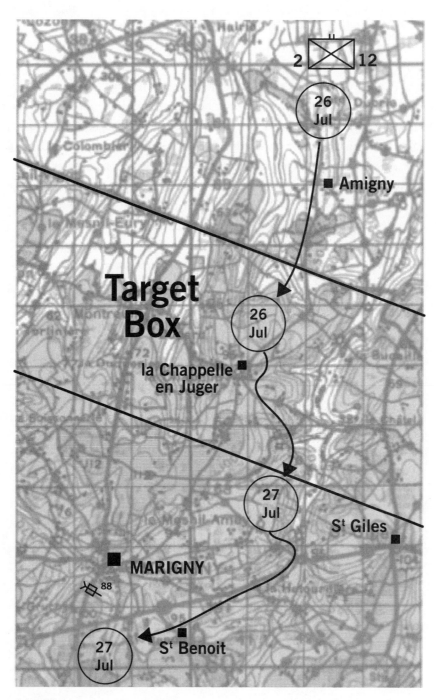

Map III

were falling on the 8th Infantry and in another minute would be falling down on us.[15]

A phenomenon called "creepback" caused the shorts. Bombardiers in the lead formations dropped their bombs a little short of the planned target. The clouds of smoke and debris obscured the targets for those in the following formations, who shifted their aiming points even closer to the American troops. As a result, the bombing crept back from the planned target with each successive bomber formation.

The short bomb loads hit the forward regiments but stopped just short of the 12th Infantry, though the shock waves still vibrated their pantlegs. The end of the bombardment around 1200 hours signaled the time to advance. The regiment pulled out of its assembly area thirty minutes later and marched south. By 1530 hours the 2nd Battalion approached a new assembly area south of le Hommet-d'Arthenay, still short of the St. Lo-Periers highway. There, the men rested, waiting for word on the 8th Infantry's progress.[16]

News from the front did not encourage them. The short bomb loads disrupted the lead elements of the assaulting infantry divisions, especially the 4th and 30th. More than six hundred men were killed and wounded. Although the 8th Infantry's four assault companies had suffered losses and probably needed time to reorganize, the order came down to launch the attack, regardless of the confusion. The only consolation for the still-dazed troops was the thought that the Germans must have suffered far worse, so the attack should face little opposition. The 8th Infantry advanced toward the highway across a devastated landscape. One of the attached tankers described the scene. "The ground was churned up, trees felled, dead birds and livestock everywhere about." Before the 8th Infantry reached the LD, it ran into stubborn German outposts north of the highway. It took the firepower of B Company, 70th Tank Battalion to crush one of the outposts. The 8th Infantry barely made it to the old Roman road by 1600 hours. Up and down the line, the American infantry reported stiff, though sporadic, resistance.[17]

The initial reports coming back to First Army dismayed General Bradley. He had counted on a quick follow-up to the aerial bombardment that would hit the Germans before they could recover. Eisenhower, who had come to the First Army HQ to witness the event, left in a huff, angered by the friendly fire casualties and disheartened that another major Allied offensive failed to punch a hole in the German line.[18]

As the attack proceeded into the evening, evidence began to surface that Cobra had accomplished something. American infantry began picking up groups of German prisoners by 1655 hours. "[T]hese grenadiers from *Panzer Lehr* had been at the center of the air attack and now they stood slack jawed and uncomprehending as a result of concussion...They were bleeding from the mouth, nose, ears and even the eyes." The 12th Infantry still had not moved into the target box but Bill ran into some captured Germans as he trailed behind the 8th Infantry while reconnoitering. "They were dazed and disoriented," Bill recalled. "There was no fight left in them."[19]

More encouraging information trickled back as the lead regiments drove deeper into the target box. At 1804 hours, a battalion of the 8th Infantry had been able to bypass a German pocket of resistance, something the Germans usually stymied. The 8th reached la Chappelle-en-Juger, at the center of the target box, at 2200 hours then consolidated for the night. Back at VII Corps HQ, General Collins noticed that the Germans had not counterattacked anywhere within the target box. The sustained fighting over the previous weeks had severely weakened the Germans and forced them into a defensive scheme that relied on a line of strong outposts supported by units that could conduct vigorous counterattacks when and where needed. The aerial bombardment had smashed most of the Germans' reserves and obliterated their lines of communication, denying them the ability to mount effective counterattacks. Though the initial gains were relatively meager, Collins sensed that the German defense had cracked. He ordered a full exploitation by the infantry divisions and committed the two armored divisions he had in reserve, even though the criteria for launching them had not yet been met.[20]

Orders came down from division just before midnight for the 12th Infantry to advance south of the St. Lo–Periers highway. The 2nd Battalion, in regimental reserve, began its movement shortly after 1000 hours on July 26 to occupy a position previously held by the 1st Battalion near the hamlet of Amigny, still north of the highway. The battalion waited throughout the afternoon for the next order to advance. Finally, Maj. Gerden Johnson led the battalion into the target box around 1845 hours after MPs helped clear a traffic jam on the highway.[21] (See Map III)

The troops crossed over fields dotted with craters, each one surrounded by a splatter pattern of tossed earth and bomb fragments. The stench of rotting flesh hung in the air. German pockets of resistance persisted, so the men had to advance cautiously. The battalion attached Bill's heavy machine gun platoon to one of the lead rifle companies because of the obscure enemy dispositions. Bill moved his platoon with the rifle company and scouted for potential firing positions. The gun crews humped their weapons, tripods, and ammunition while the platoon's vehicles followed, usually one hedgerow back.[22]

It did not take long to run into the enemy. Small detachments of Germans still held their positions and fired on the Americans from behind hedgerows. These isolated enemy detachments lacked cohesion, and the American infantrymen were able to get to their flanks or rear. Bill used the hedgerows to his advantage, concealing his machine guns and flanking the Germans without the advancing riflemen masking his guns' fire. The M1917A1s poured in fire to keep the defenders' heads down until the riflemen wiped them out or the Germans capitulated. Slowly, the 12th Infantry cleaned out enemy stragglers in the target box, opening the way for more tanks and infantry. By nightfall, the battalion made its objective just outside the town of la Chappelle-en-Juger, which one soldier described as "nothing more than dust, scattered stones and roofing tiles."[23]

Bill got little rest. The heavy machine gun platoon had a key role in defending a forward position against potential counterattacks, though that threat had diminished. The 2nd Battalion moved out mid-morning on July 27 toward an assembly area near le Mesnil-Amey. The 1st Battalion had already cleared the route the night before but the troops had to run to ground every German straggler. The battalion closed on its new position by noon. Once in position, the infantrymen began clearing the new area of the enemy in a series of small yet violent skirmishes. "It was an exhausting assignment, one that left us in a state of such debilitating fatigue that when we would slump to the ground for a break of ten or fifteen minutes we rarely spoke to one another."[24]

Around 1645 hours, division warned the 12th Infantry about enemy tanks to the southwest and a possible German force attempting to withdraw south from Marigny. Colonel Luckett issued verbal orders to Major Johnson to join the 1st Battalion in clearing woods south of the St. Lo–Coutances highway. The 2nd Battalion would march south to the highway then west toward a major road junction. Major Johnson quickly rounded up the rifle companies and started the movement from le Mesnil-Amey by 1710 hours. General Barton attached a tank company and platoon of tank destroyers to the regiment to add weight to its attack. It took the 2nd Battalion several hours to get going because clogged roads delayed the arrival of the tanks and the troops had to march six kilometers just to reach the LD near the village of St. Benoit.[25]

The rifle unit and Bill's platoon hurried forward against scattered small arms fire until someone noticed a sign saying, *"Achtung Minen"* posted in the field they were crossing. The infantrymen froze. Buried mines terrified soldiers. One unlucky step could cost a leg or a life. An alert soldier got them out of the jam when he spotted cows grazing nearby. The troops herded the cattle together and drove them across the field. The men followed the path the cows trampled. No mines detonated. Some German had posted the false sign to slow the American advance. They finally reached the St. Lo-Coutances highway at St. Benoit around 2100 hours.[26]

The battalion turned west along the highway and attacked. Without warning, a ground burst sent dirt, branches, and shrapnel flying past the heads of the infantrymen, followed a couple seconds later by a loud boom coming from the direction of Marigny. The men recognized the signature report of the dreaded German 88mm *Flak* gun. The riflemen scurried for cover and the tanks pulled back behind concealing hedgerows.

The Americans learned to respect the "88." Originally developed as an anti-aircraft gun, it could hurl a twenty-two-pound projectile 39,000 feet into the air. In North Africa and Russia, the German Army realized that the high velocity of its projectile—2,690 feet per second—made it a formidable anti-tank weapon. The powerful 88 could shred a Sherman's armor as easily as a .22 cal. bullet hitting a can of beer. One tanker in the 70th Tank Battalion paid reluctant homage to the 88. "It was the finest gun of the war. We had a peashooter 75[mm] with a low charge and were elevating at 200 yards while the Germans were shooting flat trajectory at about 1,000 yards." In Normandy, the Germans employed the 88 in an indirect mode, like artillery, and direct fire role against Allied troops and tanks. One private reported a German gun crew using it as an over-sized sniper rifle.[27]

Upon the impact of the 88mm shell, Bill and his crews ducked for cover. While his machine guns could hardly hope to take on an 88 in a direct-fire shootout, they could put suppressive fire on the gun and its crew using indirect fire. Bill grounded his machine guns behind the concealment of a hedgerow and ordered the crews to establish an initial direction of fire against the enemy gun. A crewmember marked the azimuth by driving an aiming stake into the moist turf forward of the gun. While the crews mounted the machine guns on tripods, an observer tried to get a fix on the German gun. Another jarring explosion along the highway followed by a distant muzzle blast gave the observer the fix he needed. Using hand and arm signals, he gave Bill an estimate of 900 meters to the target. Referring to the firing table, Bill passed the Quadrant Elevation (QE) settings to the section sergeants who bellowed the fire command to the squads. "Prepare for fire order. Lay on base stakes. Boxes [ammunition] per gun: eight. QE: plus nine. Rapid." The gunners elevated the guns by turning a handwheel on the cradle mount while the assistant gunners fed ammunition belts into the receiver. As soon as the gunners signaled they were ready, the sergeants barked, "Commence Fire." The gunners unleashed a long initial burst.[28]

The observer, squinting through his binoculars, spotted the impact of the rounds and signaled adjustments, based on his line of sight (the O-T line). The sections had to correct the adjustments for the guns according to the G-T line. To reconcile the two target lines, they used the newly adopted M10 plotting board. These devices had a pivoting, transparent plastic disk mounted to a base with grid markings. The plastic disk's pivot point represented the location of the guns. The section sergeants marked both the observer's position and initial estimated target on the plastic disk with the help of the grid lines. Once the observer called back adjustments such as "Left 50, Add 100" the sergeants measured the angular correction to the O-T line and the new distance to the target from the OP. After marking the new target point on the disk, the sergeant rotated the disk to the G-T line and measured the corrections from the perspective of the guns. The crews then set new QE and traversing deflections on the gun mount.

The M10 plotting boards allowed the observers simply to report the adjustments from their vantage points. The crews could now correct the observer's spottings for the G-T line, using the plotting boards, then set the guns' QE and deflection. The crews and observers repeated the process until the observer saw tracer rounds kick up the dirt around the 88.[29]

The machine guns could harass and annoy the enemy gun but they could not take it out. Major Johnson called the regiment for help in dealing with the deadly 88, but the S-3, Maj. John W. Gorn, advised him to send out a couple of bazooka teams instead. The German 88 kept the Americans off the highway while daylight lasted.[30]

The German gun may have disrupted tank movement near the St. Lo–Coutances highway, but the American infantry could still maneuver through the brush as daylight waned. The infantry hopped over hedgerows and scurried across fields in the dimming light. They reached the north– south road running out of Marigny and sealed off that line of German retreat. From the south, a German strongpoint poured heavy fire into the battalion's left flank. The rifle platoons, exercising aggressive fire and maneuver, rooted out the enemy as darkness closed in. The battalion then consolidated its position for the night. At midnight, it received orders from Division HQ to continue mopping up any resistance in their current zones on the morning of July 28.[31]

The troops awoke to eerie quiet the next morning. The rifle platoons searched the area south of Marigny but found no Germans. Whatever enemy elements had lingered in the zone of action the day before had slipped away under the concealment of night. The battalion cleared the road coming from Marigny of mines by 1000 hours, allowing the American tanks to rumble south. Troops discovered forty hastily dug German graves west of the highway and a cache of abandoned weapons and ammunition where the German 88 had been the previous day. The evidence left no doubt that the Germans had fled. The tired infantrymen came to a startling realization—they had broken through the Normandy front. The cohesive German defensive line had been torn open like a canvas sail in a hurricane. The frustrating slog through the *bocage* was behind them. The VII Corps could now drive into the depths of the German rear. The war on the Western Front had entered a new phase.[32]

CHAPTER SIX

BREAKOUT

The 2nd Battalion continued scouting for isolated Germans within its zone until the late afternoon of July 28, sometimes shooting it out with pockets of enemy infantry. G Company rousted some youthful enemy soldiers, possibly from a training school. One G Company soldier recalled, "[T]hey fought with a will until caught in a tight spot, then with death staring them in the face they reverted to being boys again." The most excitement came when the *Luftwaffe* made a quick bomb run with four planes. Bill's platoon had an air defense mission but the German planes swooped in from behind the lines, completed their bomb run, and were gone before the crews could engage them. Luckily, they caused little damage.[1]

Colonel Luckett returned from a division meeting at 1720 hours with a fresh set of orders for the 12th Infantry. If anyone had any doubt about the changed nature of the Normandy battle, the movement order erased them. The regiment would march seventeen kilometers into German-held territory with 2nd Battalion serving as the advance guard. That distance exceeded any daily advance since the invasion began.[2]

Given the ground to be covered and the fact that most of it would be hiked in the hours of darkness, the heavy machine gun platoons mounted the guns on their jeeps. Captain Enroughty distributed them throughout the battalion formation to provide security for the entire advance guard. The hedgerows prevented the gun squads from bounding ahead by echelon between firing positions, a technique normally used to keep continuous anti-aircraft coverage along a convoy route. Bill's platoon and the other, commanded by 2nd Lieutenant Jack Gunning, had to move within the same column they had to protect.[3]

The battalion hit the Initial Point (IP) at 1900 hours but quickly stalled because the 3rd Armored Division's vehicles jammed the roads. *Hurry up and wait!* Once the battalion got past the traffic snarl, they marched south, passing west of the Bois de Soulles. Just beyond the woods, the lead vehicles discovered that the intended route over a small bridge dead-ended at the Soulle River. The worn-out infantrymen dropped to the ground to give their sore feet a break while a recon party raced ahead to find an alternate river crossing. The troops barely had a chance to loosen their boot laces before the *Luftwaffe* made another bombing run. The M1917A1 crews, still mounted on the jeeps, swiveled and elevated their guns but Bill ordered them to hold fire. Firing at the planes in the dark would have accomplished nothing except give away their location. Again, the bombs missed. The recon party returned in time to get the advance guard moving before the whole division bogged down. The battalion crossed over an undefended bridge in the town of Soulle.[4]

The long column wound its way through narrow Norman lanes in the pre-dawn hours of July 29. The men finally caught some sleep after digging temporary defensive positions near le Guislain. Bill's platoon had little chance to rest because it had to defend a portion of the perimeter. Bill conferred with the closest rifle company commander to identify possible enemy avenues of approach and select firing positions for his machine guns. He assigned sectors of fire to the crews and designated

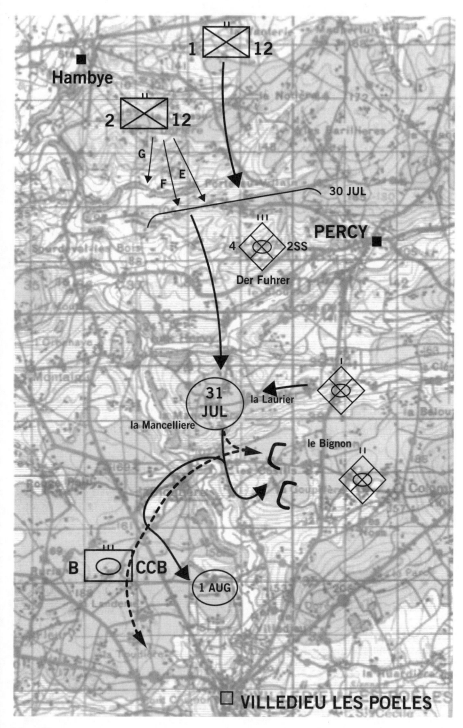

Map IV

FPLs to cover the company front. The squads mounted the guns back on the tripods and filled out range cards. The range cards were hasty sketches, "showing only the probable location of targets and the data as to direction and range or elevations necessary to place fire on them." At best, the crews napped for an hour.[5]

The 12th Infantry resumed its attack to seize the highway between Villebaudon and Hambye four hours after halting. The 2nd Battalion found the highway then turned west toward Hambye. As they approached the town division scouts reported a strange finding—two serviceable enemy tanks, abandoned on the road by their crews. G Company's leading rifle platoon encountered another positive sign—civilians outside their homes. The scene made a lasting impression on Private Stodghill. "By the time the point squad reached the built-up area the street was lined with people dressed in their Sunday best...Soon we were having to push our way through a solid mass of humanity." The Americans shoved their way into the town square. "Then, as the red, white and blue French Tricolor was unfurled in Hambye for the first time in more than four years, the strains of *le Marseillaise* blared forth from [a] record player. Every civilian, the majority with tears streaming down their cheeks, joined in singing what must surely be the most stirring of all anthems."[6]

Reports of a German counterattack cut short the celebration. Scouts spotted four hundred enemy infantrymen coming from the south, using a stream valley for their avenue of approach. The Americans scrambled to set a hasty defense. H Company Commander, Captain Enroughty, organized the battalion's heavy weapons to repel the attack. The 81mm mortar and heavy machine gun crews deployed to deliver long-range fire into the stream valley. When the Germans got within 2,000 meters of Hambye, the eight M1917A1s opened fire, spraying the German column at a rate of 1,000 rounds a minute. At that distance, the trajectory of the rounds followed a high arc before coming down against the enemy (known as "plunging fire"), instead of raking directly over the ground (known as "grazing fire"). Each twenty-round burst sprayed an area 55–65 yards deep and four yards wide, what the Army termed a "beaten zone." (See Figure 4) This plunging fire disrupted the enemy formations

Fig. 4 Machine Gun Fire

and forced their infantrymen to dodge and advance by short rushes instead of charging ahead. The gunners used a traversing handwheel on the mount to shift fire over to cover more of the enemy formation. H Company's mortars joined the fight, dumping 81mm rounds into the valley. The German advance slowed in the face of this fire. The battalion then called in supporting fire from the 42nd Artillery Battalion. That did the trick. The German counterattack dissolved before it got close to the rifle company positions. After the enemy broke off the attack, Major Johnson sent a platoon to check out the small valley. They found nothing. The Germans had completely withdrawn from the area.[7]

The troops, after several armed clashes amid two days and a night of constant marching, were ready to drop in place. Junior officers and sergeants picked out spots to bed the men down. Bill met with one of the rifle company commanders to coordinate the evening fire plan when a call came in from Major Johnson. "Have you cleared all the houses in the town? Over."

"We have the town secured. No reports of any Germans. Over."

"I say again, have you cleared all the houses? Over."

"Negative. Not all of them. We can do that first thing in the morning. Over."

"Negative. Clear all houses, now. Out."

Bill and the company commander looked at each other, bewildered by the insistent directive. But, orders were orders, so the troops spent hours going house-to-house to ensure no Germans skulked around. They finally bedded down late that night.

A heavy rumble of vehicle traffic coming from the north roused Bill before dawn. He scouted the road to see a column of Sherman tanks heading into town. First, one platoon of tanks clanked by then a second. A few half-tracks and jeeps, mixed with more tanks, drove through the village—a whole tank company. But the column did not stop. Tanks, jeeps, half-tracks, and trucks kept coming. Columns of fuel tankers and support vehicles went by, spewing clouds of exhaust into the air. Another column of combat vehicles followed that. Through the pre-dawn hours and into the early morning an entire combat command of an armored division, equivalent in size to an infantry regiment, charged through the French town.

The spectacle amazed Bill and his men. The infantrymen seldom attacked in a column of squads. Yet, right before their eyes it seemed like a whole army of tanks was attacking in single file. They lost count of the vehicles but they could see that the armored march column stretched for miles on the French highway.[8]

The troops in the battalion had little understanding of the greater battle going on around them but the huge flow of men and vehicles surging through the Norman countryside drove home the scale of their success. They began to sense that their advance was more than a breakthrough—it was a breakout.

In the five days since Cobra, the Americans had sheared off the entire western half of the German defensive line. The surviving elements of the German *LXXXIV Corps* had to retreat to avoid being pinned against the Norman west coast. Sweeping west to Coutances, General Collins's VII Corps found nothing to its south other than makeshift fighting formations from miscellaneous enemy units, what the Germans called *Kampfgruppen*. Farther east, the German *II Parachute Corps* struggled to hold their crumbling left flank against the American onslaught.[9]

Collins wasted no time turning his divisions south to exploit the chaotic German defense. The Ivy Division attached tanks to the 12th Infantry on July 30 and ordered Combat Team 12 (CT 12) to seize high ground just north of Villedieu-les-Poêles, a major road hub seventeen kilometers to the south. The 26th Infantry Regiment, temporarily attached to the 4th Infantry Division, was assigned to attack due south from Hambye, alongside CT 12's right (western) flank. The 2nd Battalion had to make room for the 26th Infantry, so it displaced to an assembly area two kilometers farther southeast, near la Chasse-Doriere. The men moved out of Hambye in the early morning to the ominous crunching sounds of a major tank battle near Villebaudon. The 2nd Battalion's avenue of advance ran across three successive east-west streams and ridges. The three ridges pointed like fingers to the Sienne River that flowed along the western edge of the regiment's zone. CT 12 designated the first stream as the LD for the attack and the third hill mass around the village of la Mancellière as its objective.[10] (See Map IV)

At first glance, the regiment's order, and others like it during the summer of 1944, looked sound. The format and task organization met the standards but some details necessary to direct and coordinate the combat action got neglected. The commanders and staff officers in the 12th Infantry had undergone intense training but these young men had gone from lieutenants to field grade officers in two to three years. Their inexperience showed in the order's spotty adherence to doctrine. The Staff Officers' Field Manual stated that a "general location or direction of principal effort" should appear on all orders. The "Plan of Maneuver" in the regiment's field order merely instructed the battalions to "seize objectives shown [on the overlay]", and failed to specify any enveloping maneuvers or directions of attack. Consequently, the battalions and companies used frontal attacks as the standard scheme of maneuver. Doctrine also called for detailed coordination between infantry, armor, and artillery. The regiment's "Plan of Fire," lacked details: no target designations, no instructions for preparation fires, no priority of fire support, and no deception fire missions. Nor did the order task the attached tank platoon with any mission during the attack. In short, the battalions had only broad guidance, not the detailed plans necessary to orchestrate a close-quarter fight against a skilled opponent.[11]

This situation was not limited to the 12th Infantry or the 4th Infantry Division during the summer of 1944. The entire U.S. Army in Northwestern Europe had yet to learn many of the skills necessary to manage combined-arms warfare. The battles in Normandy also revealed many oversights in the Army's tactical doctrine. To their credit, the officers and men would learn these lessons "on the job" and later help the Army update much of its doctrine.

The 2nd Battalion Commander, Major Johnson, attached Bill's heavy machine gun platoon to G Company for the attack. Bill did not welcome the assignment. He had misgivings about the company commander he had to work with.

Since landing on Utah Beach, the regiment had almost completely burned through its officers. A few, like Bill, had returned to duty after convalescing but most had been replaced with green lieutenants. That worked for the platoons but not at the company command level, where experience mattered. Normally, the regimental commander would promote a worthy 1st lieutenant who had some combat under his belt but in July that was not viable. Virtually all the experienced lieutenants had been killed or wounded. Colonel Luckett tried to fix the situation by shifting officers from the battalion and the regiment staffs to command companies, but most of these officers had no time leading troops in the field.[12]

Such was the case of the new commander of G Company. He came from a staff position that required no tactical skills, and he had taken no part in pre-invasion tactical exercises. Bill listened with growing dismay as the commander laid out his plan for the attack. Anyone with firsthand experience fighting the Germans could see obvious shortcomings. The best way to attack a ridge is to flank it then push up the point of the finger. The commander's order directed the platoons to attack down one slope, cross the valley, and charge uphill, taking the German defenders head-on. He neglected to use the natural concealment of woods and hedgerows for his avenue of advance.

The company commander's plan did not include orders for Bill's machine guns, either. Bill interrupted to ask for guidance. "Sir, what do you want my machine guns to do?"

"I don't know. What do you recommend?" the commander asked.

"I think I'll put one section here and the other one over here," Bill said while pointing to the map.

"Okay. Why do you want to put them there?"

"From those positions, we can do a better job of protecting the company when it falls back."

"What do you mean 'falls back?'"

"Well, as I see it, you're going to get stopped the minute the Germans open fire."

"Put your machine guns where they can do the most good and shut up. There'll be no talk of retreat during this attack." The commander ended the meeting and ordered the platoons to prepare for the assault.

The 2nd Battalion launched its attack at 1100 hours. Somehow, neither the division's recon nor the regiment's scouts had located a prepared defensive line along the regiment's LD. At first, the infantry moved forward without taking fire but as the rifle platoons moved down the northern slope into the valley, the Germans opened fire with submachine guns, machine guns, and mortars. To make matters worse, their opponents were no scratch force. The battalion had run into part of the *Der Fuhrer Regiment* of the 2nd SS *"Das Reich" Panzer Division*. These SS troops and other assorted units had collected around the town of Percy after the American breakout. The German high command used them to shore up the western shoulder of the crumbling German defensive line.[13]

Bill hurried his squads forward to positions that could observe the southern slope of the valley. Normally, the machine guns had to elevate their guns and use indirect fire to support a frontal attack because the advancing infantry would mask their positions. In this case, the riflemen had already moved down the northern slope and no longer blocked the line of sight. Bill ordered his men to engage the Germans with direct fire. The gunners pinpointed the enemy MG 42s from their green tracers. Machine gun crews on both sides routinely loaded every fifth round in their ammunition belts with a tracer to help gunners observe where their bullets struck. Using "tracer control" Bill's gunners walked the strike of their own magenta tracer rounds onto the source of the green tracer fire. Streams of colorful, deadly bullets flew in opposite directions over the valley. The Germans had the advantage because they were firing from foxholes with overhead cover. Even with the German guns in their sights, Bill's machine guns could not completely suppress the enemy.[14]

Just as Bill predicted, G Company barely got started before enemy fire stopped it cold. The suppressive fire from Bill's platoon and the company's own machine guns helped the riflemen work their way out of the valley. The company pulled back, with difficulty, after taking some casualties from German indirect fire. The captain lost a finger to shrapnel from a German mortar. Holding his bleeding hand, the commander led his unit's retreat past Bill's position. When Bill saw him, he could not resist the urge to say, "I told you."

The captain said nothing as he passed but his snarl said plenty.

The other two rifle companies in 2nd Battalion had slightly more success. They fought their way up the southern slope but got held up by fire coming from a house. The lead platoon of F Company sent a patrol under Sergeant Everett Worley forward to recon a way to assault the building. As they approached, a group of men in American uniforms waved them forward. The unsuspecting patrol advanced to join them. Too late, they discovered that the men were disguised Germans. Sergeant Worley was taken inside the house where he endured a brutal interrogation from a German officer. Worley refused to talk, so the officer shot him multiple times with his pistol to inflict pain. Luckily, the Americans overran the house and rescued the wounded sergeant.[15]

E and F Companies clung to the slope but could not push to the road running along the summit. Any attempt to move uphill drew severe small arms fire. The rifle companies sorely needed the firepower of the attached tank platoon but the regiment left it back in reserve. The Germans had a Panther tank that cudgeled the Americans, firing at point blank range. A German sergeant shouted to the Americans to surrender, but F Company's infantrymen "told him to go to Hell." The F Company commander, Captain Phineas Henry, and one of his lieutenants grabbed two bazooka gunners and went after the Panther. The rounds they fired at the tank failed to knock it out, but they managed to scare it off. Moments later, the intrepid Captain Henry picked up another bazooka that had already been loaded. The rocket detonated in his hands, killing him instantly.[16]

Late in the day, Major Johnson decided he needed more help from the artillery. His forward observer (FO) from the 42nd Artillery Battalion helped organize a "serenade," the nickname for a time-on-target (TOT) fire mission.[17]

The Army developed the TOT technique to maximize the destructive effect of its artillery. Enemy soldiers scrambled for cover the instant they heard any incoming artillery. The first salvo from an artillery battery might catch some exposed enemy but by the time the second or third salvo landed, nearly every surviving enemy soldier had found shelter. Artillery officers realized that if more rounds landed in the first salvo, more casualties could be inflicted. They created a method that coordinated and timed the fires of multiple batteries to have all their rounds land simultaneously. A TOT required excellent communications and planning by the respective fire direction centers (FDCs). The artillery fire control radio net helped solve these problems. When a FO requested a TOT for a specific time and place, every FDC on the radio net determined whether their guns could reach the target then calculated the time its rounds would take in flight. The FDCs then gave their respective batteries the firing data and the precise moment to fire. The effect of a TOT could be devastating, especially when American artillery crews added the use of timed fuses, or the even deadlier proximity fuses, to cause the shells to burst above ground and kill even more exposed troops.[18]

The FO from the 42nd Artillery Battalion scheduled the "serenade" just before dark. The German defenders on the summit waited for the next American move while the sun set. All at once the heavens filled with a shrieking chorus of incoming artillery rounds. Seconds later a hailstorm of dozens of 105mm and 155mm shells pelted the ridge. The hilltop disappeared as the top layer of sediment lifted into the air.

The sudden strike ended as quickly as it started. E and F Companies' riflemen rose from their hide positions and moved uphill. The enemy, stalwart veterans of the Russian front, recovered from the barrage and pinned down the Americans with small-arms fire. Without tank support, the American infantry could not dislodge the Germans. The Germans counterattacked the two rifle companies holding onto the ridgeline later that night. The attack seemed lackluster compared to most German attacks, and it ended before the enemy made any significant headway. The Americans figured out the next morning that the enemy counterattacked just to distract them while they withdrew from the ridge. Apparently, the artillery serenade convinced them to break contact.[19]

It had not been a good day for the battalion. The Germans held them up with a few well-positioned troops, machine guns, and a couple of tanks. The battalion neglected to reconnoiter its avenue of advance, relied on a simple frontal attack, failed to take advantage of concealed approaches, and did not infiltrate the gaps in the German defense. F Company made some effort to fire and maneuver its way against the Germans but the loss of key men like Worley and Henry denied them success. A more aggressive use of tanks and infantry might have yielded better results without relying so heavily on the artillery.[20]

The operational pace of the American Army revealed another shortcoming in its tactical development. The Americans tended to attack throughout the day, but not into the night. Once the day's fighting subsided, divisional and regimental staffs churned out the next day's orders then went to bed. The 12th Infantry's daily journals showed steady message traffic up to midnight, but little between midnight and 0700 hours, a sure sign of staff inactivity. The quiet in the higher-level CPs did not mean the companies enjoyed long periods of sleep. To the contrary, junior officers and sergeants in the line companies spent hours checking their positions, coordinating fire plans, and resupplying the troops. Often, these junior leaders caught a few paltry hours of sleep before they began preparing for the next attack. This daily pattern of activity soon became apparent to the Germans, who realized that they had little to worry about after the sun went down. For their part, the Germans had no reluctance to conduct night attacks. A senior German officer remarked, "A modern, resourceful and bold commander will happily exploit the dark of night and will move purposefully with his troops under its cover in order to gain operational advantages over a night-shy enemy."[21]

The lack of night operations by the American Army can be traced back to its tactical doctrine that included night operations, but treated them as a separate topic and not as part of standard offensive and defensive operations. Furthermore, the doctrine applied much greater weight to the complications of night attacks than to their advantages. "As a rule," stated a 1944 field manual on battalion-level tactics, "night combat can be conducted successfully only when there is time for the preparation and distribution of a well-conceived plan and for thorough reconnaissance by all leaders during daylight."[22]

Besides doctrine, another reason why American commanders in Northwestern Europe had reservations about night operations can be boiled down to one word—inexperience. The U.S. Army of 1940 consisted of a couple hundred thousand professional soldiers, augmented by another 400,000 reservists and National Guardsmen. By 1944, it measured its strength in the millions, but many of its officers and non-coms, up and down the chain of command, lacked the experience necessary to perform complex military tasks. The leaders in Normandy had to learn on-the-job and would require more combat seasoning before they could sustain twenty-four-hour operational tempo or coordinate night offensive action.

On July 31, the regiment pulled G Company back to serve as its reserve while E and F Companies attacked south. Captain Enroughty attached Bill's platoon to one of the other rifle companies to support the advance. Expecting contact, Bill bounded his gun sections by echelon (one moved while the other overwatched). This ensured that one section was ready to fire the instant the rifle company made contact. The troops moved cautiously over the hill that the Germans had defended the day before. The lead patrols only found a few French civilians who confided that the Germans left the area during the night. Even so, the rifle companies advanced only 1,500 meters by noon. General Barton, impatient with this pace, called the CT 12's CP and directed it to use the roads and bypass small enemy pockets, if need be. Colonel Luckett, in turn, called the 2nd Battalion to help speed its movement. He instructed the executive officer to get the rifle companies out of their line formations and into march column with "just...a little flank protection" to provide security. The battalion moved a bit more quickly after that and consolidated on the objective, the ridge near la Mancellière, by 1540 hours.[23]

Late in the afternoon the 1st Battalion passed through 2nd Battalion's position to continue CT 12's advance toward Villedieu-les-Poêles. Farther back, the 3rd Battalion had endured a counterattack coming out of Percy for most of the afternoon. CT 12 had planned to have the 3rd Battalion follow the 1st but the action near Percy kept it in place. Instead, the regiment ordered the 2nd Battalion to follow the 1st into Villedieu. Just as the battalion organized to resume its march, scouts spotted an enemy force of infantry and tanks to the east.[24]

A German infantry company, reinforced with armor, counterattacked from la Laurier twenty minutes later, following the high ground into la Mancellière. The regimental S-3, Major Gorn, still urged the battalion to follow the 1st Battalion but, with a counterattack bearing down on his left flank, Major Johnson oriented the battalion to fend off the attack. Bill's machine guns had little time to redeploy, so he ordered the squads to swivel the guns to the east and put indirect fire on the enemy column. Luckily, the tank platoon attached to the 1st Battalion had remained at la Mancellière because of a fuel shortage. The Shermans engaged the enemy vehicles while artillery and the battalion's own weapons forced the German infantry to ground. The battalion disposed of the German counterattack by 2100 hours.

The late counterattack meant Bill had another busy night. H Company had to plan primary defensive targets for the mortars and machine guns facing the threat from the east and alternate targets facing south and north. By the time fire plans had been coordinated, guns positioned, and sectors of fire designated, Bill only had an hour or two in which to catch some sleep. The area had several farmhouses and barns available for shelter. After weeks of frequent rain, some overhead cover looked inviting.

Bill and one of his sergeants ducked into a barn already occupied by a few other troops. Bill started to unbuckle his web gear (the belt and suspenders used to carry his pistol, ammunition magazines, canteen, compass, and entrenching tool). Before he dropped his gear on the dirt floor, an uneasy sensation disturbed him. After a previous queasy feeling foretold his wounding near Montebourg, Bill paid more attention to his "sixth sense." Nothing seemed wrong with the barn but the uneasiness kept nagging him. Finally, he turned to the sergeant. "I don't like this. Something doesn't feel right."

"What's wrong with this place?"

"Nothing. Something's bugging me, that's all. We need to get out of here."

Bill convinced the sergeant to leave but the other enlisted men, who were from a different platoon, stayed put. Bill and the sergeant had gone only a hundred meters when they heard the whistle of incoming mortar rounds and dove for cover. *Boom! Boom!* Bill looked back at the barn. Its roof had been blown off and the men inside killed.[25]

CT 12 started the morning of August 1 with its three battalions strung out over a six-kilometer north-south line. The disposition protected the VII Corps' left (east) flank against the German defensive shoulder anchored on Percy. General Barton wanted to do more than just guard the flank. He wanted to thrust south and exploit the American success. The VIII Corps on the far right (western) flank had passed Avranches and roamed free into Brittany. Lt. Gen. George S. Patton had just activated the Third Army and unleashed his armored spearheads into the French interior. Barton felt the time had come to get the 4th Infantry Division rolling, and he exhorted his subordinate commanders to plunge ahead. "I want you, in the next advance, to throw caution to the winds...destroying, capturing or bypassing the enemy and pressing recklessly to the objective." The division still had to take Villedieu but now it made the more distant town of St.-Pois its new objective. To help lead the division's charge, the corps attached Combat Command B (CCB) of the 3rd Armored Division.[26]

General Barton committed CCB on the left (eastern) flank of the regiment and ordered both to move south. CT 12 had the job of seizing Villedieu then advancing toward St.-Pois. Colonel Luckett decided to attack in a column, given that his battalions were already stacked south to north. The 2nd Battalion had to cross a stream immediately south of its position then follow CCB east for 2,500 meters. After passing six hundred meters beyond the crossroad hamlet of le Bignon, it would turn south toward Villedieu.[27]

The battalion moved out at 0800 hours but had only crossed the first stream when the plan derailed. CCB ran into what seemed to be a well-organized roadblock on high ground short of le Bignon. The Germans covered the road and surrounding fields with small arms, mortars, and anti-tank (AT) guns. In this area, the fields were not bound by tall hedgerows, giving the Germans wide fields of fire. CCB's tanks and half-tracks dared not venture into the open against the dreaded 88s, so its armored infantrymen attacked dismounted and without close tank support. This attack quickly stalled in the face of heavy enemy fire. At 0935 hours, CT 12 directed newly promoted Lt. Col. Gerden Johnson to assist CCB.[28]

Colonel Johnson executed a sensible plan of attack. While the armored infantry engaged the Germans, the 2nd Battalion enveloped the enemy position around their southern flank. The riflemen used a draw that sloped up to the German position to make a covered approach.[29]

Bill's platoon had to support the rifle platoons firing uphill. This presented a challenge because the machine guns had to shoot over the heads of their own infantry to hit enemy targets on the crest. The closer the guns followed the advancing riflemen, the higher the angle they had to fire to go over their heads. Too high an angle would send the rounds arcing over the target. To overcome the problem, Bill echeloned the guns. While one section moved forward with the rifle companies to provide direct fire, the other section set up in a defilade position back from the base of the slope to provide indirect fire. Using a compass and map, Bill gave the approximate azimuth and distance to the targets from the guns' defilade positions. The crew members darted forward to place aiming stakes in front of the guns on the compass heading. After sighting the gun on the aiming stake, the gunner clamped the tripod's traverse setting. Next, the crews leveled the gun tube on "zero" horizontal. The gunner raised the tube to sight the top of the hill and called out the setting on the elevation arc (angle of sight). "Plus 57 mils." Bill consulted the firing tables to determine the additional angle of elevation required to hit a target at that range (angle of elevation). "QE, plus 8 mils." The squad leaders adjusted a clinometer to the 8-mil setting and placed it on the gun tube. The gunner clicked the elevation handwheel until the clinometer's bubble leveled on the 8-mil reading.

The combined angle elevated the guns the right amount to hit targets on the hilltop. Bill double-checked the firing table to ensure the QE setting gave a safe margin for riflemen advancing up the slope.[30]

These initial azimuth and elevation settings served only as estimates. To ensure that rounds were on target, someone had to observe their impact and relay any adjustments back to the gun squads. The open terrain around le Bignon and the gentle slope may have allowed observers to communicate via hand-and-arm signals, but the distances involved more than likely forced them to do so with telephones or radios. Bill moved forward with the observers to help adjust fire and control the other gun section.

At 1030 hours, 1st Lt. Martin MacDiarmid led E Company up the draw. Colonel Johnson brought up an attached platoon of tanks from C Company of the 70th Tank Battalion to give the company more firepower. The convex shape of the slope concealed their approach from the German roadblock at le Bignon. MacDiarmid planned to pounce on the Germans' left flank once his platoons crossed the "military crest," the point where the bulge on a slope permits observation to the bottom of the slope. However, the moment the lead elements moved over the military crest they started taking fire from the high ground to their right (south). The Americans discovered, to their dismay, that enemy infantry had dug in all over the high ground. E Company's riflemen went to ground and returned fire but the extended enemy position had them trapped in the defile. German anti-tank fire kept the Shermans at bay while the enemy infantry moved to better firing positions to pick off the American riflemen caught in the low ground. Despite his good intentions, Colonel Johnson found his battalion stuck in a prolonged firefight.[31]

Bill's platoon concentrated on the highest priority targets, the German AT guns and machine guns. The forward machine gun section mounted their M1917A1s and put direct fire on the enemy. Bill and the observers called the rear section and adjusted their indirect fire. The two sides blasted each other through the middle part of the day but the Germans held the better position.[32]

The reports coming from CCB and CT 12 rankled General Barton. He had instructed his subordinate commands to attack "recklessly" and bypass pockets of resistance. Now, his primary armored force and an infantry battalion had gotten tied down on the eastern flank. He decided to extricate his forces from le Bignon. Barton coordinated with the 1st Infantry Division on his western flank for permission to use some of their zone to maneuver CCB. At 1520 hours, Division HQ advised Colonel Luckett that CCB would turn around and switch their avenue of advance along the division's western (right) flank.

"Do you still need my Second Battalion?" Luckett asked.

"No."

"Then I'll disengage them."[33]

About the time that the Americans decided to break off the engagement, the German commander, who realized that his outpost at le Bignon had fixed a large American formation, took the opportunity to hit back at the American infantry pinned in the low ground.

The 2nd Battalion's scouts spotted several hundred German infantrymen moving west from the hamlet of la Goupiliere and advancing up the eastern slope of the high ground separating them from E Company. If the Germans were masters of the art of maneuver, the Americans were masters in the application of firepower. Colonel Johnson drew E Company back a couple hundred meters to establish a safety buffer then requested a 'serenade.' The artillery FO timed the strike to coincide with the moment the enemy counterattack reached a patch of woods along the crest of the high ground.[34]

Around 1745 hours, the hilltop erupted with the impact of seventy-two artillery shells. Smoke, dust, and debris shrouded the German position. Johnson began withdrawing E Company from the battle as soon as the rounds landed. Bill shouted to his forward gun squads to displace. The men broke down their weapons, hoisted them on their backs, and hurried down the slope. E Company moved back only a short distance before the smoke cleared enough for the Germans to resume firing. Bill's crews could not move away without first suppressing the enemy's guns but they could not do that without putting the guns back into action. Colonel Johnson solved the dilemma by ordering another "serenade." After the dust cleared a second time, only a single, foolish AT gun crew harassed the Americans. A third serenade put a stop to that.[35]

The battle near le Bignon had one footnote. The Americans caught three German soldiers dressed in American uniforms. With the memory of Sergeant Worley's patrol still fresh, the captors shot the Germans on the spot.[36]

The battalion marched unmolested across the Sienne River then turned south-southeast along the Hambye-Villedieu highway. By 2110 hours, the men settled into an assembly area on ground overlooking the northern edge of Villedieu. They spent the night preparing for the attack to seize the strategic town.[37]

In the three days since Hambye, adjacent units on the west (right) flank enjoyed clear sailing with few enemy to impede their advance. Meanwhile, CT 12 had advanced south while fighting off heavy German pressure coming from the east (left) flank. Colonel Luckett's men found themselves rubbing against the line of friction between the German defensive shoulder and the American breakout. Unlike Patton's Third Army, CT 12 had to fend off the enemy with every forward step. This campaign of long marches, punctuated by fierce clashes, kept chipping away at the fighting spirit and power of the already depleted unit. The days ahead would present an even graver threat to the 12th Infantry.

CHAPTER SEVEN

VILLEDIEU TO ST.-POIS

Villedieu-les-Poêles lay at a bend in the Sienne River Valley where the flow changed from a westward to a northward course. The town sat in low ground overlooked by hills to the north, west, and south. Field Marshal von Rundstedt and his successor, Field Marshal von Kluge, considered Villedieu essential to the German defensive scheme in Normandy because it served as a crucial transportation hub. Highways radiated from Villedieu in six directions and a major rail link passed through on an east-west axis. Yet, the Germans still abandoned it on August 1 when the 4th Infantry Division's cavalry moved in, supported by CT 12's 3rd Battalion.[1]

At 1000 hours on August 2, the 2nd Battalion received orders to march through Villedieu and seize Hill 213, a finger ridge southeast of town overlooking the river valley. The battalion entered the undefended town around midday with rifles slung. Bill's platoon mounted its jeeps to move more quickly. Civilians greeted the column of American troops, cheering as the soldiers advanced past the cathedral.[2]

A short time later, a motorcycle with a sidecar roared into Villedieu and pulled up in the square. A large mustachioed man, riding in the sidecar and clad in a war correspondent's uniform, removed his goggles and smiled expansively at the crowd—Ernest Hemingway. Officially, Hemingway worked as a correspondent for a major magazine, *Collier's*. Unofficially, he organized his own band of adventurers, who shared his determination to get close to the action and celebrate France's liberation all the way across the country. His armed retinue violated several, if not all, regulations for the conduct of war correspondents but Hemingway cared little for convention. The famous author had adopted the 4th Infantry Division as his own, and formed a close bond with the commander of the 22nd Infantry, Colonel Charles "Buck" Lanham. He would follow the division into Germany.

Reveling in the cheers of the citizens and the excited atmosphere of liberation, Hemingway waved to the troops from the sidecar that he had littered with champagne bottles and hand grenades. He bragged to passing infantrymen that he had captured a few German stragglers that morning. After soaking up some of the communal adulation and pressing the flesh with the regiment's riflemen, he and his driver pulled the motorcycle around the corner to a nearby *taverne*. He forced the owner to open his doors then broke into the cellar. After popping a few corks, the famed author toasted the passing infantry.[3]

F Company and a platoon of tanks from B Company, 70th Tank Battalion led the movement out the other side of Villedieu to the highway heading southeast. Just as the column crossed to the south bank of the Sienne River, four German soldiers took a shot at the lead Sherman with a *Panzerfaust* but missed. The tanks immediately turned and fired at the German infantrymen who scrambled for refuge in the nearby rail station. It did little good. The tanks fired on the station with their 75mm main guns and brought the building down on their heads.[4]

After that distraction, Colonel Johnson put the rifle companies into formation for the advance toward Hill 213. The Intelligence and Reconnaissance (I&R) Platoon reported that the Germans had withdrawn from Hill 213, so he hoped for an easy afternoon.[5] (See Map V)

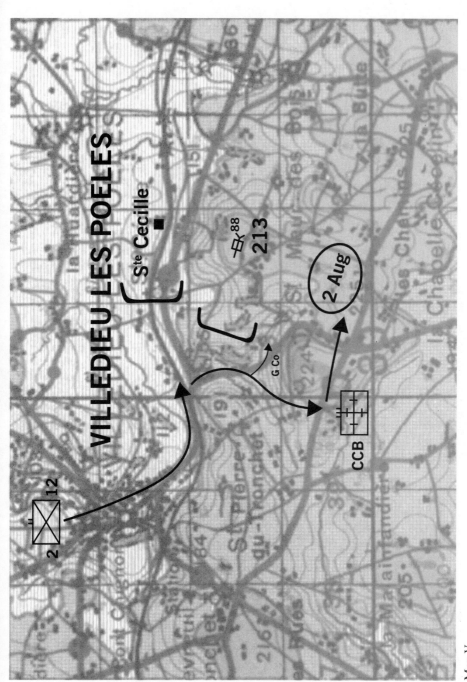

Map V

Given the open terrain of the river valley, H Company's machine gun platoons worked under battalion control rather than being attached to the rifle companies. Picking out positions from which his platoon could support the whole battalion, Bill bounded the sections forward by echelon. One section stayed ready to fire while the other section drove forward to the next overwatch position.[6]

F Company approached a road junction with one fork heading southeast up the slope to the top of Hill 213. Up to this point, it had faced some small arms fire but not enough to stall the advance. A patrol at the front of F Company began moving up the slope around 1330 hours. Suddenly, two dug-in machine guns started shooting, raking the ground with grazing fire. At the same time, German machine guns in Ste. Cecile, eight hundred meters to the east, engaged the Americans. The patrol threw themselves to the ground while the rest of the company scrambled for the cover of a road embankment at the bottom of Hill 213. A few riflemen tried to advance to deal with the guns but every time someone lifted his head a stream of bullets flew by. The company commander called the attached tank platoon forward to rescue the patrol and blast the enemy machine guns.[7]

Five M4 Shermans charged to the road junction and jockeyed into firing positions. Before they got off a shot, a round from an 88 smashed into one of the tanks, knocking it out. The other four tanks slammed into reverse and started pulling back as more 88 shells burst around them, fired from a battery of self-propelled guns on the top of Hill 213. One of the Shermans had a dozer blade attached to its front end. Extremely useful in hedgerow country, the blade became a hindrance and stuck in the dirt as the tank's driver tried to maneuver out of the kill zone. A few seconds later, the dozer tank took a direct hit. The crew bailed out with one man injured.[8]

The defending Germans had the upper hand. Their MG 42s had the American infantry pinned down, and the 88s had driven off the battalion's tank support. The 88 gunners turned their attention to the American infantry. Their first salvo fell just short of the American troops huddled in the ditch. The next volley landed just beyond their position.

The veterans knew what that meant—the Germans had them bracketed. As soon as the 88 gunners split the difference between the first two elevation settings, the next rounds would land on top of them. The infantrymen gritted their teeth and burrowed deeper into the dirt. The next salvo blasted the embankment but the rounds landed short, again. Another minute went by before the next salvo, this time long. Back and forth the 88 rounds dropped but never on the Americans hunkered under the embankment. An artillery FO figured out the reason for the Germans' inaccuracy. Even at 1,500 meters, the trajectory of the 88mm shells did not have enough arc to split the distance. F Company sat in a "dead zone" within their range fan. Had the Germans used mortars, the Americans would have been in a much tougher spot.[9]

Sitting at the bottom of the hill, Bill couldn't do much. His M1917A1s had the range to hit the 88s but, without observation of the target, they had little chance of suppressing them. Ever the engineer, Bill took a morbid fascination with the 88's strange acoustics. When an 88mm shell detonated nearby, Bill detected what sounded like a second burst, just after he heard the round explode. He heard the report from the gun's muzzle blast a second or two later. The 88mm projectile traveled over two times the speed of sound, so he should have only heard the impact of the round then the report from the gun. He theorized the 88mm shell was so large it pushed a sonic wave that produced the mysterious secondary boom.

Colonel Johnson crawled forward to consult with F Company's commander and assess the situation. Ruling out a frontal attack in the teeth of intense machine gun fire, he decided to pull back and make a wide detour through a draw that put a hill mass between the battalion and the dreaded 88s. The battalion used the cover of the draw to move south around the west side of Hill 224. The maneuver proceeded nicely until G Company turned onto a side trail, taking them east into Hill 213. Within minutes, the disoriented company found itself tied up in a firefight.

Back at the regimental CP, the fire support officer for 42nd Artillery Battalion itched to get into the fight. After receiving a fire request from the 3rd Battalion, he asked for clearance to fire at the western slope of Hill 213. The CP checked the latest coordinate for the 2nd Battalion and, believing that it was on the opposite side of Hill 224, approved the fire mission.[10]

One of the G Company soldiers fighting on Hill 213 described the result. "[T]here came from our rear a strange and deadly sound unlike any I had heard before. It was a low pitched...unearthly moaning that continued far longer than normal shellfire. I listened for what could have been a fatal second, then dived into the space between the cordwood and out building. Leaves, and dirt came down on me as shells hit close by and another landed in the draw."[11]

G Company would manage to pull back from Hill 213 and rejoin the battalion after dark but the misdirected fight and friendly fire incident cost it six casualties.[12]

Colonel Johnson moved at the head of E and F Companies as they climbed out of the protective draw. The wide enveloping move kept Hill 224 between them and the Germans. Moving cautiously onto level ground, Johnson searched for the highway he planned to follow to get due south of Hill 213 and the Germans. He found the highway but stumbled onto something he never expected—a traffic jam. American trucks, jeeps, tanks, and ambulances clogged the road. The confused battalion commander crossed the highway where he found a medical station in full operation. Johnson asked what type of medical outfit it was.

"This is a clearing station," said a medical officer.

"You mean a collecting station."

"No," he said. "A clearing station."[13]

Medics used collecting stations close to the front lines to gather wounded soldiers and decide which ones needed immediate evacuation to the clearing stations, where doctors and nurses would perform triage and stabilize seriously wounded soldiers. Out of necessity, units located clearing stations farther to the rear. Astonished, Johnson learned that his enveloping attack against Hill 213 had bumped into the tail end of CCB's rear echelon, the same armor unit they fought alongside the day before. While CT 12 had been butting against the stubborn western shoulder of the German defense, CCB had swept around Villedieu then raced southeast along highways to Coulouvray-Boisbenatre, an impressive fourteen-kilometer advance.[14]

Johnson secured help in evacuating G Company's wounded then moved the battalion north to strike the southern flank of Hill 213. He had hoped to hit the Germans from an unexpected direction but they had already been alerted to the flanking maneuver once G Company mistakenly walked into their defense. With dark descending and German resistance ahead, Johnson became "night-shy" and decided to attack the following morning.

Throughout the night, Captain Enroughty and H Company's lieutenants planned machine gun and mortar fires against Hill 213. The high ground south of Hill 213 and Hill 224 overlooked the German position. The machine gun platoons could set up in separate elevated positions and pour fire into the enemy from two different directions. As they made their calculations, the officers could see that their guns would have less masking from the forward riflemen, meaning the rounds would have less arc in their trajectories. The lower trajectories would disperse the rounds into longer, narrower beaten zones. No matter along what axis the Germans dug in their defensive positions, they would be aligned with the long axis of some of the guns' beaten zones.

The 2nd Battalion attacked Hill 213 promptly at 0800 hours on August 3. Bill advanced alongside the rifle companies with one of his heavy machine gun sections while the other sat back on high ground ready to lay down fire on any enemy encountered. Expecting contact at any moment, the lead troops advanced by bounds, carefully searching for the enemy. Colonel Luckett had to prod the battalion "to keep rolling" after getting the first situation report. By 1000 hours the battalion gained the summit of Hill 213 without a fight. Local farmers told them the Germans pulled out the night before.[15]

For the third time in four days the battalion had endured a cycle of events in which an attack had been stopped by well-positioned German machine guns and/or the damnable 88s. By the time they were ready to deliver a crushing blow, the Germans slipped away under cover of night. "The Germans were masters of escape," Bill often noted.

Bill, along with most of the experienced men, noted something else—the regiment lacked the punch it had on D-Day. The infantrymen in the ranks at Villedieu barely resembled the troops that fought their way into Emondeville or assaulted the Chateau Daudinville. "More than half were fresh replacements…the rest of us were spent in both mind and body."[16]

In this, the 12th Infantry was hardly alone. The ponderous casualties in Normandy had over-taxed the Army's replacement system. One in seven soldiers sent to Europe were infantrymen but they made up 85 percent of those sent to aid stations or cemeteries. The vicious rate of infantry casualties drained the Army's replacement pool by early August down to a single rifleman for the entire European Theater. To keep frontline divisions up to strength, the Army curtailed recruit training and combed out men from over-strength rear-echelon units. The new men had no basic fighting skills. The Army callously assumed that the veterans in their new units would train them on the job. Given the relentless nature of the summer's fighting, that proved to be wishful thinking. A platoon sergeant in F Company pointed out, "We have had no time to train them; the only training they get is in actual fighting with the enemy."[17]

These ill-prepared soldiers often failed once the bullets started flying. The military historian S. L. A. Marshall accurately portrayed the terrifying experience of raw troops in their first fight in his 1947 book, *Men Against Fire*. "The unit enters upon the battlefield and moves across ground within range of the enemy's small arms weapons. The enemy fires. The transition of that moment is wholly abnormal. He had expected to see action. He sees nothing. There is nothing to be seen. The fire comes from nowhere. He knows that it is fire because the sounds are unmistakable. But that is all he knows for certain…The men scatter as the fire breaks around. When they go to ground, most are lost to sight of each other. Those who can still be seen are for the most part strangely silent."[18]

The sergeants in 2nd Battalion confirmed Marshall's description. "[O]ur biggest trouble with new men is getting them to move forward under fire and to fire while moving. They get pinned down too easily; then when they do get a chance to move they just get up and walk and make no effort to keep firing on the enemy." Even H Company, with its crew-served weapons, had trouble getting replacements to fight under fire. Bill recalled "grabbing a man by the nape of the neck and jerking him out of a hole and pushing him to a firing position." CT 12 remained a large, impressive force but its most basic combat element, the individual infantryman, had depreciated in value.[19]

The 2nd Battalion moved on after clearing Hill 213. Colonel Johnson dispatched one company to Ste. Cecile and another to the battalion's intermediate objective, a hilltop near the hamlet of la Butte. The troops moved overland without opposition and by midday passed la Butte on their way to another intermediate objective, the town of Bois-Yvon. After anticipating a severe fight for Hill 213, the troops now looked forward to a restful day of marching.[20]

Bill and his platoon resumed their customary duties for an approach march as the battalion neared Bois-Yvon. Bill wrote to his mother about an incident when his unit came to one small French town. As they got to the outskirts of the dwellings, a church bell started ringing. The Germans often used church bells or flags in tall buildings to signal a distant artillery battery. At the sound of the bell, Bill and his men dove for cover and waited for incoming shells. The bell continued ringing for a couple of minutes without any shellfire. The Americans figured something was amiss. Bill and a few troops went into town to investigate. They made their way to the church where they discovered a woman vigorously pulling the bell ropes. When asked, she explained that she was ringing the church bells to celebrate the town's liberation.[21]

The fact that the Germans had to rely on unconventional means, such as church bells, to communicate, illustrated what Bill considered one of the key advantages of the American Army. The Americans could operate radio nets down to the company level. In addition, the attached artillery observers had their own dedicated radio net. If the command radio net failed, company commanders could still communicate with battalion by relaying messages through the artillery radio net. This flexibility in communications enabled the Americans to react faster and place fire more quickly in fluid combat situations. The Germans depended on pre-planned targets and one-way signaling tricks to put fire on targets of opportunity.

The battalion continued its advance, but enemy activity picked up. The Germans had pulled their artillery back to the Forêt de St. Sever, seeking the concealment of the trees from Allied air attack. Now, as the battalion got closer to the forest, enemy artillery strikes became more frequent.

During the advance, Bill walked with his platoon across a field bounded by tall hedgerows. Everything looked peaceful, yet Bill started to get an eerie feeling that someone was staring at him. He paid more attention to these subtle sensations since getting wounded. The platoon continued moving past a line of trees. Bill turned his head and saw a ridge come into view three kilometers to the east. The instant he spotted the distant high ground he knew a German artillery observer had them in his sights.

Bill called out to his men. "Move out! On the double! Get out of here!"

The platoon raced to the protective cover of the next field. Jumping the hedgerow, they shifted to a hidden spot. Seconds later enemy shells pounded the field where they had just been walking.[22]

Other than instances of incoming artillery, the battalion avoided contact until its lead element crossed a small bridge two kilometers east of Bois-Yvon. The lead platoon and two attached tanks turned south to Coulouvray-Boisbenatre without incident but the moment the main body got to the bridge German machine guns opened fire from hidden positions. Rather than fight through the enemy outpost, Colonel Johnson turned the battalion away from the crossing and on to a different route to Coulouvray-Boisbenatre.[23]

The matter would have ended there until someone reported that two casualties had been left at the crossing site. The Battalion Surgeon, Capt. Francis Ware, did not want to risk any more casualties but the medics persuaded him to let four men in a jeep attempt the recovery under a

Geneva flag. The medics found the body of one man and were searching for the second casualty when a German machine gun opened fire and wounded one of them. The medics crawled back to the surgeon and his party. A German medic walked up to the Americans a short time later, under a flag of truce. He handed over a letter expressing regret for mistakenly firing on the medics and offering them the opportunity to evacuate their vehicle and dead, unmolested. Captain Ware, with much trepidation, agreed to send a second team to pick up the bodies, escorted by the German medic. True to their word, the Germans allowed the Americans to recover their jeep and the dead. Once the jeep returned, the German medic waved and departed.

Four days earlier Germans, disguised in American uniforms, had captured, tortured, and shot F Company soldiers. This time Germans acted as repentant gentlemen to rectify their inadvertent violation of the Geneva Convention. Sometimes the contradictions in war defy understanding.

The battalion moved onto Coulouvray-Boisbenatre while General Barton worked to protect the eastern flank of the American breakout and shove back the German defensive shoulder. He attached the 2nd Battalion of the 8th Infantry to CT 12. The battalion from the sister regiment had already taken Hill 232 just north of St.-Pois. Colonel Luckett bounded his battalions southeast to establish a wall facing the Germans who lay in wait inside the Forêt de St. Sever. As soon as Bill's battalion reached their fourth objective of the day, they received orders to push another 1,500 meters southeast to Hill 290.[24]

Bill's squads moved within the battalion formation rather than bound by sections. The long march, thirteen kilometers to this point, forced the squads to use their jeeps to keep up with the rifle companies and reduce fatigue. They stopped just short of Hill 290 and the crews hoisted their guns off the jeeps, in case they had to fight their way uphill. The lead rifle squads moved forward in the waning daylight with no difficulty until the men heard the rising shriek of enemy artillery followed a second later by the blast of impact. They had crossed a German pre-planned target still under observation from high ground to the east. Bill and the rest of the troops hurried uphill to escape the impact zone. Shock waves and debris buffeted them as they struggled under their loads. Once they got beyond the reach of shrapnel, the men hit the dirt and crawled for cover. The growing darkness soon provided enough concealment to allow the battalion to lay out its defense on Hill 290 and dig in.[25]

Their day was not over. Division HQ sent down word that a company from the 22nd Infantry would take their place on Hill 290 so they could relieve the 2nd Battalion of the 8th Infantry on Hill 232. The men had to march another three kilometers and move into someone else's positions in the middle of the night. Sergeants booted everybody out of their freshly dug foxholes. One rifleman complained, "This was too much. The veterans arrived by rote, stumbling along in the dark like cattle just keeping up with the herd. And now we were off again, mindless animals trailing behind an unseen leader somewhere up ahead."[26]

Bone-tired, the men crawled up the northern slope of Hill 232, making contact with the 2nd Battalion 8th Infantry at 0200 hours on August 4. While the other battalion gathered itself to leave, Bill's battalion deployed and posted security. Many of the men collapsed in place; few had the energy to dig a foxhole.

A private in G Company, Dick Stodghill, stood the first shift of guard duty for his squad. He had to perch his chin on the point of his bayonet to keep himself awake. "When the moon made another abrupt appearance I turned my head and looked out over the field, started to turn again and then did a double-take, blinking several times to make certain I wasn't seeing things that were not there. But they were there, dozens of men coming up the incline in a semi crouch, weapons trailing in their right hands the way Germans carried them on the attack. This was not a patrol or even a large raiding party, it was a full company of men… Suddenly there was bedlam out front. Rifles, burp guns, BARs and machine guns were firing, grenades were exploding, Germans were shouting above the din." The enemy dumped artillery and mortars on the north end of the hill to support their attack. The German infantry got close enough to start a hand-to-hand brawl but they lacked the strength to drive off two American battalions. Had they timed their attack two hours earlier or two hours later they would have faced only one battalion and might have stood a better chance of success.[27]

Bill's men finally closed their eyes an hour before dawn broke on August 4. As soon as daylight permitted, they tried to reorganize their defense. Three things became immediately apparent. First, the battalion from the sister regiment had not occupied the summit of Hill 232, only its northern slope. Second, the two battalions had become mixed during the night and had to be separated before defensive positions could be dug. Third, the Germans had them zeroed in. Machine gun, mortar, and artillery fire fell on the Americans from the tops of Hills 232, 321, and 329 to the south, east, and north. The Germans had committed the *116th Panzer Division* to hold St.-Pois and it brought its considerable indirect fire assets to bear against the Americans on Hill 232. Enemy fire harassed Bill and his men throughout the morning as they tried to orient their machine guns against multiple threats.[28]

The regimental HQ did not fully appreciate the 2nd Battalion's tenuous situation and ordered the battalion to attack farther east against the Germans defending Hill 321. Colonel Johnson called back to the regimental staff to make them understand that another attack was out of the question. They had to gain complete control of Hill 232 first. He tried to convey the troubles facing the battalion to Major Gorn, the S-3. "Men [are] very tired, could barely stay awake during last night's counterattack." Johnson went on to explain that the Germans had a couple of tanks on Hill 232 and had the bridge on the battalion's only supply route under observation and artillery interdiction. On top of that, the Germans stole most of the rations during the night. Gorn relented. He told the battalion to concentrate on Hill 232 "then move to your objective."[29]

The higher-level staffs missed signs of the regiment's wilting morale. Many of the men were close to or had passed the limits of their endurance. Physically exhausted by eleven days of marching, emotionally drained by the mounting loss of comrades, and stressed by almost continuous enemy small arms and artillery fire, some men succumbed to combat fatigue. A few exhibited classic symptoms of "shell shock" while others simply fell out of the fight. Bill reacted to the relentless strain by detaching his compassion and empathy. His use of gallows humor during this part of the campaign revealed this emotional void.

The battalion attacked up the incline of Hill 232. Bill moved forward with the assaulting rifle companies to spot forward firing positions for his gun squads. Under fire, the Americans scurried from cover to cover, a rock ledge, a tree, a stump, anything that offered protection from a bullet. Bill and a sergeant ducked behind a mound of dirt as enemy rounds cracked overhead. The moment Bill peeked around the pile, bullets splattered into the dirt. He pulled his head back. The sergeant drew rifle fire when he peered over the top of the mound.

"We better keep our heads down," Bill told the sergeant.

A few seconds later the sergeant raised his head, looking for another place to find cover. Again, rifle fire snapped above them. "Don't do that," Bill said. "They have us pinned down."

"I'm just trying to find a way to get out of here," the sergeant replied.

"Stay down. We have to wait for someone to get us out."

The impatient sergeant lifted his head above the dirt, again. This time a German rifleman hit him square in the forehead. Bill hunkered down beside the dead sergeant until a rifle platoon pushed the Germans back. The platoon's lieutenant came over to check on Bill. As the two officers stared at the sergeant's shattered skull, Bill indulged in tasteless mockery. He pointed to the open wound. "Typical non-com, no brains."

The scornful joke did not go over. The other lieutenant glared at Bill as if he were some heartless bastard. By this point, perhaps he was, or maybe he had become too inured to the mayhem around him.[30]

The battalion's attack on Hill 232 soon ran out of steam. German artillery plastered the mortars, forcing them to displace. The rifle platoons simply did not have the energy to carry the assault all the way to the top of the hill. The battalion drew back to a defensive posture while the Germans continued to rain fire down on them.[31]

Alarmed by the condition of the 2nd Battalion's troops, Captain Ware, the regimental surgeon, barged into the regimental CP and argued with Colonel Luckett that the men could not go any further. Luckett called the division chief of staff and told him that his whole regiment was in no condition to resume any offensive operations. Word reached General Barton, who drove to the 12th Infantry's CP. After seeing the situation first hand, he instructed Colonel Luckett to hold in place. He then called in air strikes on the German held hilltops and directed the 22nd Infantry to drive on St.-Pois. The 12th would secure the division's left flank while the other two regiments attacked.[32]

Bill reset his guns to establish defensive sectors of fire and final protective lines along the company fronts. With the possibility of an enemy attack from three different directions, he assigned alternate firing positions to each gun squad to give the battalion all-around coverage.

Grimly, the battalion clung to its precarious position on Hill 232. The Germans kept up machine gun and artillery fire throughout the day. Ever since the 2nd Battalion left Villedieu, the Germans had taken potshots at them with a large caliber siege gun mounted on a railcar, most likely a 240mm *Theodor Bruno Kanone*, which lobbed giant 330-pound projectiles from a siding hidden in the Forêt de St. Sever. The unwieldy gun had trouble hitting a target on the move, but, with a stationary target, the monstrous gun could be brought to bear with effect. One rifleman observed, "When a shell hit it would blast a huge crater in the ground and hurl clods of dirt as big as a jeep sixty or more feet into the air."[33]

In the middle of the day, Ernest Hemingway watched the German artillery work over Hill 232. "The side of the hill was jumping into the air in spurting dark fountains from the multiple bursts." A sudden increase in enemy artillery and mortar fire alerted the Americans to another counterattack. "The Germans were yelling again as they came at us, but yelling does not scare men who are already keyed up, it just keeps the men doing it from thinking as clearly as they should. Anyway, their shouts were soon lost in the clatter of rifle and machine gun fire... We had all the advantage, being in prepared positions while they were in the open. How often that situation had been reversed." Heavy small arms and machine gun fire stopped the enemy charge.[34]

The riflemen slumped back into their foxholes while medics tended the wounded. Bill watched as a litter team picked up a soldier whose foot had been blown off. He noticed that they left the man's foot behind. He picked it up and tossed it onto the litter. One of the bearers scowled at him, apparently irritated about the extra weight. Private Stodghill described his reaction to the scene. "I felt empty inside, drained of all emotion. Only a sick sense of hopelessness was left. Not just for G Company and myself, but for all of mankind."[35]

For the remainder of August 4, the men stayed in position. With observers on three surrounding hills, the enemy had nearly complete visibility into the 2nd Battalion position. Any movement drew artillery or mortar fire. The artillery also shelled the small bridge that served as the battalion's lifeline for communications and resupply. The arrival of darkness offered concealment, but throughout the night, the Germans fired artillery at the battalion, and the *Luftwaffe* made occasional bomb runs.[36]

That night Hemingway paid a visit to General Barton. "I found him in the trailer, stretched out in an old gray woolen union suit. His face that was still handsome when he was rested was gray and drawn and endlessly tired.

"The people are very tired, Ernie," he said. "They ought to have a rest. Even one good night's rest would help. If they could have four days… just four days. But it's the same old story." Hemingway wrote pointedly and poignantly about the mental state of the exhausted men. "No one remembered separate days any more, and history, being made each day, was never noticed but only merged into a great blur of tiredness and dust, of the smell of dead cattle, the smell of earth new-broken by TNT, the grinding sound of tanks and bulldozers, the sound of automatic-rifle and machine-gun fire, the interceptive, dry rattle of German machine-pistol fire, dry as a rattler rattling; and the quick, spurting tap of the German light machine-guns—and always waiting for others to come up."[37]

General Barton organized a concerted effort to take St.-Pois on August 5. With the 12th Infantry still securing the left flank, he directed the 22nd Infantry to attack the town. Barton ordered the Twenty-Second's 3rd Battalion to seize Hill 232 from the west while Bill's battalion supported the attack with fire. Help was on the way from the north, too, in the form of the 9th Infantry Division driving against the Germans on the high ground east of Hill 232.[38]

Sensing that this was their last chance to hold onto Hill 232 and St.-Pois, the Germans launched one more counterattack at the 2nd Battalion. German artillery and mortars pounded the Americans to pave the way for their infantry. One mortar shell dropped through the front door of the battalion CP, wounding the F Company commander. Despite the accuracy of their indirect fire, they had too few infantrymen to dislodge the battalion. The Germans pulled back and prepared to evacuate St.-Pois.[39]

After helping to repulse the counterattack, Bill and his sections prepared to support the 3rd Battalion 22nd Infantry's attack on Hill 232. They selected firing positions with adequate standoff distance to place plunging fire on the summit. The rest of H Company's heavy weapons and the rifle companies passed down firing instructions to their crews and riflemen. Back from the front line, two battalions of 105mm and 155mm artillery also plotted supporting fires. The 3-22nd attacked in the late afternoon while the supporting fires plastered the objective. The Germans quickly withdrew. The 22nd Infantry reached the top of Hill 232 with little trouble.[40]

The 2nd Battalion finally made its way to the top of Hill 232 and relieved the 3-22nd at 0100 hours on August 6, forty-seven hours after it first arrived. This time, the relief went peacefully. The 9th Infantry Division, pushing down from the north, soon pinched out the Ivy Division's zone on the flank of the American breakout. That allowed the division to pull out of contact.[41]

Many portray the Normandy Breakout in terms of sweeping armored movements and rapid gains of territory. They forget that while Patton's army ran amok in Brittany and raced on to distant cities like Le Mans, the Ivy Division held the breakout's flank. For nearly two weeks, it marched and fought every day against a desperate and determined enemy. The Ivy Division did its share of advancing, but each day's progress was punctuated by grueling battles that drained the men physically, spiritually, and emotionally. By the time the worn-out troops left St.-Pois, the

12th Infantry required a sustained period of rest and reorganization to restore itself to combat effective status.

The Ivy Division finally scheduled them for "downtime." The regiment issued an order to move by truck to an assembly area near Brecey. "For the first time since D-Day the hollow eyed, gaunt cheeked men of the 12th [Regimental] Combat Team could relax."[42]

The trucks pulled into a lovely, quaint bivouac site around 1530 hours. As an officer, Bill was entitled to a daily liquor ration. The supply section handed him a bottle of vodka to make up for all the days he had missed. After peeling off his filthy unionalls and showering, he donned a fresh uniform. Feeling somewhat human for the first time in many days, Bill, Dave McElroy, Jack Gunning, and a couple other officers spent the rest of the evening guzzling their accumulated liquor rations. No one cared what the liquor tasted like so long as it helped erase the memory of the last two weeks. Once finished with his bottle, Bill passed out on his bedroll.

CHAPTER EIGHT

MORTAIN

"**W**ake up! Everybody up! Outta bed!" Orderlies poked their heads into the officers' pup tents, shaking the lieutenants awake.

With his head still spinning from the previous night's drunk, Bill looked at his watch—0430 hours. "What?"[1]

"Orders. Every officer has to report immediately," the orderlies said.

The other lieutenants struggled out of their bedrolls and got dressed. Not an easy task, hung over as they were. They hurried over to the battalion CP while the sergeants rousted the enlisted men.

Overnight, the Germans had launched a surprise counterattack against the 30th Infantry Division and overran the key town of Mortain. Unlike past, localized counterattacks, the Germans struck the eastern flank of the American breakout with four panzer divisions.

General Collins ordered the 4th Infantry Division to shore up that flank to keep the Germans from driving to Avranches on the Normandy coast, a move that could cut off the entire American breakout. So much for the rest period. To secure the regiment's assembly area, Colonel Luckett sent the 2ⁿᵈ Battalion to guard a bridge over the See River southeast of Brecey. Bill's head still swirled from the vodka consumed the night before as his platoon hustled to load their vehicles. The battalion secured the See River bridgehead by 0847 hours.[2]

The men of the 12ᵗʰ Infantry knew that the German counterattack signaled something big but they had no concept of the strategic significance of the Germans' *Operation Luttich*. Since mid-June, Hitler had ordered a strategic defensive in Normandy, partly due to his low opinion of the fighting qualities of Allied armies. During June and July, the German high command fed available units piecemeal into Normandy to contain the Allies. Hitler and his general staff (*Oberkommando der Wehrmacht—OKW*) turned a deaf ear to the complaints of Rommel, von Rundstedt, and, later, von Kluge about the grinding attrition suffered by the *Seventh Army* and *Panzer Group West* as long as the Allies seemed to be bottled up in the hedgerows. The sudden breakout and rapid exploitation by the Americans startled Hitler and *OKW* who now perceived the potential collapse of the Western Front. Hitler decided to gamble by adopting a strategic offensive to pinch off the American penetration and throw them back into the Cotentin Peninsula. On August 2, he issued orders to von Kluge, commander of *Oberbefehlshaber West* (*OB West*), to launch a massive armored attack that would split the American forces along the Mortain–Avranches axis. *OKW* named the ambitious offensive *Operation Luttich*.

Field Marshal von Kluge had already begun planning a tactical counterattack against the waist of the American breakout in hopes of blunting the onslaught and buying time for a strategic withdrawal to the Seine River.

Von Kluge decided to attack on the night of August 6-7 with the *1ˢᵗ SS Panzer, 2ⁿᵈ Panzer, 2ⁿᵈ SS Panzer,* and *116ᵗʰ Panzer Divisions*, all the panzer divisions he dared pull from the line without risking disaster. The strike force looked impressive on paper but these units, depleted by the hard fighting in Normandy, mustered only 100–130 tanks among them. At the last minute, Hitler offered von Kluge more tanks but the field marshal did not want to delay the offensive and refused.[3]

At 0200 hours on August 7, the *2ⁿᵈ SS "Das Reich" Panzer Division* slammed into the 120ᵗʰ Infantry Regiment of the 30ᵗʰ Infantry Division at Mortain, achieving complete surprise. The division's *Deutschland Regiment* swept into Mortain around the southern side of Hill 314 and trapped the 120ᵗʰ Infantry's 2ⁿᵈ Battalion on the hilltop. Its *Der Fuhrer Regiment* tried to enter the town around the northern side of Hill 314 but ran into well-positioned 3" towed anti-tank guns near l'Abbaye Blanche that stopped the assault and forced the *Panzergrenadieren* to dismount. One kilometer north of l'Abbaye Blanche, the *1ˢᵗ SS "Leibstandarte Adolf Hitler" Panzer Division*, driving up the highway from Sourdeval, reached the vital intersection with the main highway running from Mortain to St. Barthelemy, Juvigny, and Avranches. The panzers turned north at the road junction (called RJ 278 by the Americans) and attacked the 117ᵗʰ Infantry Regiment at St. Barthelemy. At the same time, the *2ⁿᵈ Panzer Division* struck St. Barthelemy from the opposite direction. The panzers took the small town but their advance stalled under increasing resistance from the American infantrymen. Another column from the *2ⁿᵈ Panzer Division* found a gap in the American defense and pushed west along the See River valley to le Mesnil-Adelée. That attack ended when they ran into a force of tanks from the U.S. 2ⁿᵈ Armored Division. Farther north, the *116th Panzer Division's* commander, discouraged by what he considered to be poor prospects of success, elected not to participate in the initial attack.

The Germans held Mortain and St. Barthelemy, RJ 278, and the highway leading back to Sourdeval. They also had an American battalion trapped on Hill 314. Even with these local successes, the all-important, last-ditch effort to cut off the American breakout had ground to a halt by noon of its first day. The Germans reverted to a tactical defense, at least until darkness fell. The German tank commanders knew better than to move around in clear weather. When the morning fog burned off, British Typhoon fighter-bombers swarmed the German columns like a flock of seabirds diving on a bait-ball. The British 'Jabos' strafed and bombed any German vehicles left on the roads or lacking adequate camouflage.⁴

By the afternoon of August 7, *OB West* and von Kluge realized *Operation Luttich* had failed and prepared to withdraw. Hitler, who had an uncanny habit of turning defeat into disaster, ordered von Kluge to double-down on the attack with three more panzer divisions. He directed von Kluge to pull the additional panzer units from the British front and organize a combined strike force under Lt. Gen. Heinrich Eberbach. Because of the time needed to collect the additional forces, Eberbach planned to launch the second phase of *Operation Luttich* on August 11. This attack failed to materialize because all three panzer divisions got siphoned off to shore up crumbling German defenses elsewhere. The four panzer divisions already committed at Mortain could only defend in place, waiting for a second attack that would never come.[5]

General Collins may have been relieved that the German counterattack had been stopped but the 30th Infantry Division's situation still worried him. He decided to attach the 12th Infantry to the 30th Infantry Division as a reserve force. Back in Brecey, the Ivy Division alerted Colonel Luckett to get a battalion on the road that afternoon. All of Combat Team 12's trucks, tanks, and tank destroyers rolled out at 1930 hours on August 7 with the 3rd Battalion in the lead, followed by 2nd Battalion.[6]

The convoy passed through Montigny on its way south, fighting traffic the whole time. Tanks, supply vehicles, and other unit convoys crammed the road and broke into the regiment's march serials. The miserable motor convoy turned into a nightmare when the *Luftwaffe* showed up at 0150 hours.[7]

Bill heard the German fighter-bombers bearing down on the stalled column. He dove out of his jeep into a ditch then wedged himself into the available cover with twenty other men. "There was enough room for three," he recalled. The planes roared by with their cannons blazing. Seconds later the bombs hit. One of the Cannon Company's halftracks, farther back in the column, blew up. It carried a basic load of 105mm artillery rounds. Some of these detonated, tossing more rounds into the air. The exploding ammunition caused an inferno and lit up the countryside. As soon as the German fighter-bombers left, Bill's march serial continued moving. The Cannon Company and the 1ˢᵗ Battalion had to back up and take an alternate route to get around the demolished halftrack.

Bill's convoy reached its destination near the hamlet of Fontenay, eight kilometers west of Mortain, around 0400 hours on August 8. Their new masters in the 30ᵗʰ Infantry Division hardly gave them time to pee before they started issuing orders. They had already detached the 3ʳᵈ Battalion from the regiment and sent it to reinforce the 117ᵗʰ Infantry's attack against St. Barthelemy. Now, they told Colonel Luckett to seize the crucial Road Junction (RJ) 278 (278 represented the intersection's elevation in meters) that lay between St. Barthelemy and l'Abbaye Blanche with his two remaining battalions. The division scheduled the attack for 1000 hours. So much for being held in reserve.[8]

The 2ⁿᵈ Battalion led CT 12's movement from Fontenay to la Chevalaye. The battalion turned east and shifted into its attack formation. Lt. Col. Gerden Johnson used a standard attack formation of two companies (F and G) up and one (E) back. Bill's platoon supported F Company. With five kilometers to cross before the objective, Bill would have had his sections in echelon, two machine guns dismounted up front, the other two riding in jeeps. By 1250 hours the battalion crossed a stream 1600 meters east of la Chevalaye that marked their LD.[9]

The advance proceeded smoothly for the first three kilometers with the lead companies following a compass azimuth in the general direction of St. Barthelemy. At 1430 hours the battalion reached a trail crossing atop a ridgeline that the regiment designated "Point B." It lay 1900 meters due west of RJ 278. Looking ahead, Bill could see low ground with a small stream dribbling southward across the avenue of advance. Once past the stream, the battalion would have to climb a gentle grade to the vital Mortain-St. Barthelemy highway running along a ridge. Colonel Johnson halted the advance while he sent scouts ahead to check out the nearest stream crossing. The temporary halt gave Bill's platoon a chance to set up its guns to overwatch the open ground ahead. The stream, la Rivière Dorée, did not look like much on the map but only one small bridge—marked on American maps as "Point D"—crossed it along its four-kilometer course. The infantry would have no trouble crossing the stream but Johnson worried about the jeeps and trucks that had to bring forward the battalion's supplies, as well as the Sherman tanks of B Company, 70th Tank Battalion.

The scouts returned an hour later with discouraging news. The Germans defended the small bridge at Point D one kilometer to the southeast with twenty-three armored vehicles and dug-in infantry. The trail over the bridge ran between two positions defended by the *Der Fuhrer Regiment* of the *Das Reich Division*. The scouts discovered another German defensive position 1,600 meters south-southeast from Point B on a wooded hilltop called Roche Grise.[10] (See Maps VI and VII)

Colonel Luckett modified his attack plan. He ordered Johnson's 2nd Battalion to attack east across la Rivière Dorée to the original objective, RJ 278. Luckett then detoured the 1st Battalion south to hook up with a battalion from the 120th Infantry. Together, those two battalions would drive toward Mortain, overrunning the German outpost on Roche Grise in the process. Luckett's decision effectively split the regiment's two remaining battalions into two separate and non-supporting avenues of advance.[11]

Bill's battalion resumed the attack at 1830 hours, without its attached tanks, staying well north of the *Panzergrenadieren* at Point D. Bill moved forward with two of his machine guns while the other two provided overwatch. As they moved into the low ground, the troops found their boots sinking into the soggy terrain. The men splashed across la Rivière Dorée and continued east through more water-soaked ground. The officers in H Company immediately realized the soft ground could not support vehicles. Bill's jeeps brought the other machine gun section as far forward as they could. From there the crews carried everything forward.[12]

After the Americans climbed out of the wetlands, they advanced up the long slope through several fields filled with ripening wheat. Scouts crept along rows of tangled hawthorn shrubs and oak trees. Behind them the lead rifle squads stepped across the open spaces, rifles at the ready. Other squads overwatched their buddies until they shuttled forward to

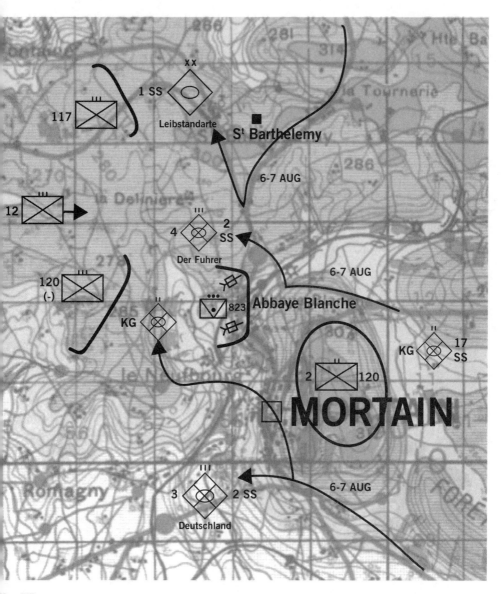

Map VI

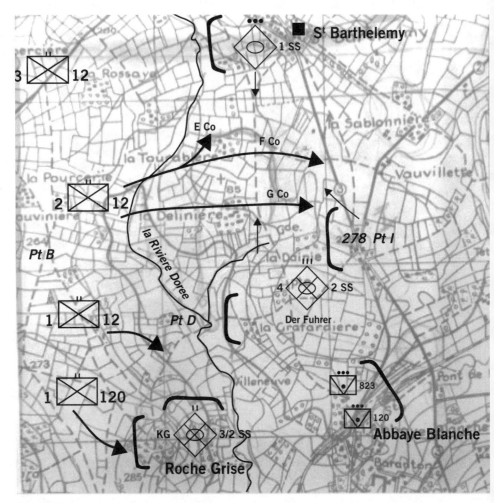

Map VII

take over the lead. Bill's platoon stayed with F Company on the left (north) flank of the battalion, blending into the cover of la Tourablere's orchard. G Company hugged the orchard at la Deliniere three hundred meters to the south. Just beyond the two orchards, the infantrymen crossed a north-south trail. While they inched ahead, the men could hear the rattling of small arms and the *crump...crump* of artillery to the north near St. Barthelemy and to the south by Roche Grise. Both sister battalions had run into fierce fights. The men in F and G Companies wondered how long before they caught hell from the Germans.[13]

The 2nd Battalion advanced against only minor resistance because it hit a seam separating the *Das Reich Division* defending Mortain and the *Leibstandarte Division* holding St. Barthelemy. The Germans had used the north-south trail as a line of communication between the two panzer divisions. When they spotted the Americans crossing it, they reacted with vigor. The battalion's lead elements ran into *Panzergrenadieren* defending the highway, just as they picked up the squeal of incoming shells and dove for cover. Artillery, mortars, and rockets rained down on the exposed infantry. Private Dick Stodghill described the terrifying attack. "The ear-splitting explosions all around and the howling of the Screaming Meemies made a preacher's threat of Hell seem laughable." To get out from under the intense barrage, the riflemen had to keep moving forward. The threat from enemy rifle fire and machine guns paled next to the horrific shelling. It seemed better to take chances against an enemy you can shoot. "We had the advantage of fear driven desire to get close to them and stay close to them...The result was a brutal firefight, but now we could return shot for shot...Fire and movement—fire at the enemy, and if you can't see him then empty a clip at the place where you think he is. Move ahead, fire and then move again." The two companies crawled within sight of RJ 278, so close to the German positions that the enemy dared not bring artillery on them. "By nightfall each side held grimly onto a section of roadway, but neither could claim it as their own."[14]

The Germans launched a hasty counterattack near sunset, spearheaded by two tanks, three armored cars, and six motorcycles. The armored vehicles sprayed the hedgerows with their machine guns and the tanks fired high explosive (HE) main gun rounds anywhere their crews thought the American infantry might be hiding. Without heavy anti-tank weapons, the hapless American riflemen had nothing to fire back at the German armor, yet they held on. Colonel Luckett ordered Johnson to pull back a couple hundred meters from RJ 278, enough so he could bombard the intersection with artillery, hoping to drive off the enemy counterattack. F and G Companies stayed within "danger close" range of the incoming friendly artillery shells that hammered the intersection. The shelling forced the German armor to withdraw, but the enemy infantry clung to RJ 278. Although the Americans did not occupy the road junction, their machine guns still covered the roadway with fire. Stalemate.[15]

The enemy devised a new plan to sever F and G Companies from the rest of the battalion. An enemy tank pulled into the north-south lane at its north end, just outside of St. Barthelemy. From there, the trail ran straight south for a distance of nine hundred meters. At the south end of the straight section, a second tank pulled into the lane facing north. Both tanks opened fire with their machine guns, bookending the north-south trail. A machine gun bullet has a flat trajectory for 500-600 meters before it begins a downward arc. The fire from the two German tanks covered the straight length of the trail with an overlapping wall of fire, yet the rounds fell to the ground before reaching the opposite tank.[16]

The battalion had a platoon of tanks and a platoon of towed 57mm anti-tank guns but they were stuck on the other side of the stream. That left the rifle companies with only bazookas to use against the tanks. The German tank crews had little to fear from the American riflemen.

The battalion's inability to knock out German tanks illustrated the relative weakness of American anti-tank weapons in 1944. The Germans had the fabulous 88 that could take out any Allied tank at long range. The Americans' 57mm anti-tank gun was barely effective against the German Mark IV but virtually useless against a Panther or Tiger. The German *Panzerfaust* could punch through 200mm of armor whereas the American bazooka could only penetrate 100mm, less than the frontal armor of late model German tanks. Even Sherman tanks and M10 tank destroyers could not stop Panthers or Tigers head-on.[17]

Colonel Johnson moved his CP forward into the farmhouse at la Tourablere. With his rifle companies so close to the vital objective, he decided to hold the battalion's position overnight, tenuous as it was. The 2nd Battalion suffered the consequences of the 12th Infantry's three disjointed attacks. The battalion made it to the objective but the regiment had no reserve force to help them finish the job. The other two battalions were stuck at St. Barthelemy and Roche Grise. None of the three attacks had sufficient strength to succeed, although 2nd Battalion came closest. Johnson determined that the enemy tanks sitting on the battalion's flanks posed the biggest threat. He told the companies to shore up both flanks along the north-south trail with bazookas. Bill positioned his machine guns to stop any infantry attack against the left flank coming from St. Barthelemy. He also established sectors of fire and FPLs covering the approaches over the adjacent fields.[18]

The Germans shelled the battalion incessantly. The Americans burrowed into their hasty foxholes as enemy 105mm and 150mm shells burst around them and overhead. Shock waves and shrapnel tore through the vegetation and gashed the soil. The air filled with smoke, dust, and falling debris. Bill covered his ears and held his mouth open to relieve the over-pressure from the blasts. Each near miss felt like a punch from Joe Louis. The infantrymen could do nothing but pray that the next incoming round missed their position.

The 30th Infantry Division's deputy commander, Brigadier General William Harrison, contacted Colonel Johnson directly to gauge the 2nd Battalion's status. Johnson told the general that the rifle companies were isolated and in serious jeopardy. Casualty evacuation and re-supply had to be done by foot over a swamp. Worse, they could not get any tanks or tank destroyers forward to drive off the enemy armored vehicles. General Harrison promised Johnson that the engineers would give top priority to bridging the stream and bog. He confirmed that the attack on the original objective would continue the next morning, presumably after the tanks and tank destroyers joined the rifle companies.

That night Colonel Johnson learned, firsthand, the degree of fanaticism the battalion faced. A prisoner, an arrogant and sullen nineteen-year-old SS *Panzergrenadier,* was brought in for interrogation. When the colonel asked where he was from, the prisoner said that he had enlisted from Hamburg. "Then, doesn't it worry you to be up here in Western France fighting us and wondering what is happening back home?" Johnson asked.

"No, why should it?"

The colonel inquired about any family members who might be in Hamburg and subjected to Allied bombing. The prisoner confirmed that his parents and sister still lived in Hamburg. Johnson asked, "Don't you worry about their safety?"

"No. It's up to them to look out for themselves. It makes no difference to me."

"Don't you feel that you owe anything to your family?"

"No, of course not."

"Then just who do you think you owe anything to in this world?"

"Hitler. Heil Hitler!"[19]

That night, the 4th Engineers, augmented by the regiment's pioneer and wire sections, threw themselves into the work but they had more to do than put up a small bridge; they also had to build a path that could support thirty-ton Shermans over several hundred meters of soggy ground. Until this work was completed, the tanks attached to CT 12 could do nothing but wait. One of the tankers observed, "When we pulled up, the fire was everywhere in an arc in front of us. There was a lot of infantry around, and they were really getting shot up. We pulled into a field, put our tanks in a ring, and got them camouflaged. All we could do was sit there and let them shell us for several days."[20]

The Battle of Mortain appeared to be the one time in the Normandy campaign in which the Germans matched the Allies, round for round, in artillery. Besides hitting the frontline companies, the enemy pounded American artillery, mortar, and support positions. Even back at the regiment's CP, the enemy artillery had effect. One of the men in the counterintelligence section, J. D. Salinger, confessed in a letter, "I dig my fox-holes down to a cowardly depth." The Americans had abundant artillery on hand to suppress the German guns with counter-battery fire, but the enemy guns stayed mostly hidden from the American observers because of the terrain and their effective camouflage. The division devoted much of its artillery fire to protecting the isolated battalion on Hill 314.[21]

As soon as dawn shed enough light, the German observers spotted the American engineers at work in the streambed and called fire on the crossing site. Everyone watched with dismay as the enemy artillery demolished much of what had been done overnight. Without tanks, tank destroyers, or a line of resupply, the battalion now had little chance to take the road junction.[22]

At 0750 hours, German tanks and infantry joined the artillery in firing on Bill's battalion. The situation at the battalion forward CP inside the farmhouse became tense. A tank round knocked down the adjacent building. A few seconds later another tank shell hit the farmhouse, wounding one of the company commanders. The aid station had already accumulated a large number of casualties, including several with combat fatigue. Under this intense fire and faced with the knowledge that he would receive no armor support, Colonel Johnson ordered the rifle companies to pull back behind la Rivière Dorée. At least from there they could evacuate the wounded, reorganize, and rearm before resuming the attack.[23]

Bill saw a big problem in moving his platoon back to the streambed. With all his guns on the east side of the north-south trail covered by the German tanks, he had to find a way to cross the dangerous lane. Scouting along hedgerows, he found a spot on the road with a slight crest. The minor hump in elevation offered only a foot or two of masking from the southern end of the trail. If the troops hunched over, they could slip across with minimal exposure to the direct fire coming from that direction. The dust kicked up by the incoming artillery added a veil of concealment from the north end. He scurried to the west side of the trail to test the crossing site. Safely across, he reconnoitered a path back to la Tourablere's orchard. Bill re-crossed the road, returned to his platoon, and gathered the men. Bill's crews moved along hedgerows, hidden from the Germans, as he led them to the trail crossing. After getting careful instructions from their lieutenant, the men scampered to the west side. Bill then led them back to the battalion rally point. F Company followed Bill's platoon along the same path to safety.[24]

Colonel Johnson pleaded for airstrikes against the Germans to cover the withdrawal but the regiment could not get the mission approved. Major Gorn told Johnson to "use all the artillery you need." The 42nd Artillery Battalion, in direct support to the regiment, responded to Johnson's requests. They took out a tank and self-propelled gun but it only helped a little. German direct and indirect fire continued to pelt the area. Meanwhile, Captain Ware, the battalion surgeon, and his medics mounted a frantic effort to carry out the wounded from la Tourablere. A couple of men, too badly wounded to be moved, had to be left. One of the medics agreed to stay with them and find a place to hide, if the Germans retook the position.[25]

The withdrawal became a dicey affair. G Company pulled back from its forward position but remained stuck on the east side of the trail. The isolated rifle company told the colonel that they did not know how to get across without taking casualties from the enemy fire covering the trail. At this point, Bill reported to the forward CP that he had succeeded in pulling his platoon back to the rally point. Hearing that G Company was still caught on the other side of the trail, he volunteered to guide them out. Johnson gave his okay then requested an artillery strike with a mix of smoke and HE rounds between the German tanks at the north end of the trail and the designated crossing site.[26]

Bill dashed across the trail a fourth time then worked his way along the hedgerows until he located G Company. He conferred with its commander, Capt. Fred Sullivan, to plan the extraction. Once again, Bill took the lead. The G Company troops fell in behind him and snuck to the point Bill had found earlier. The friendly HE and smoke rounds were already impacting barely three hundred meters north of their position, well inside "danger close" range. The riflemen slipped across the road using the slight elevation to cover their southern flank and the artillery fire to conceal the other. Bill took them back to the rally point and notified the battalion CP that everyone had withdrawn.

Once he got the word, Colonel Johnson looked at the few men remaining in the forward CP. "We are the only troops left in the area," he said. Then he laughed, "So, let's go."[27]

The Germans continued to pour artillery and tank fire from a sunken road near Fantay into the 2nd Battalion as it withdrew. In response, the battalion called for more smoke rounds to help conceal its movement. Not until 1145 hours did Colonel Johnson collect his entire unit on the west side of la Rivière Dorée.[28]

The regiment and the 30th Infantry Division squandered the advantage gained by the battalion's penetration and interdiction of the St. Barthelemy-Abbaye Blanche highway. The disappointing results of this initial attack can be traced back to the inexperience of American officers with combined arms operations. The Americans planned the attack from an infantryman's perspective. The 30th Infantry Division had committed the CT 12 in a sector constrained to one small bridge across a boggy lowland, impassable to vehicles. In contrast, the Germans thought in terms of armored warfare. They realized the Juvigny-St. Barthelemy ridgeline and the high ground to the south around Roche Grise and le Neufbourg were the only viable avenues of approach available for American armor. That's where they concentrated their armor and infantry. The Germans covered the three-kilometer gap between the two avenues with just the outpost at Point D, the small bridge over the little stream. The penetration by the 2nd Battalion vexed the Germans and forced them to allocate resources to contain it. Yet, they correctly surmised that the Americans could not exploit any success without tanks and support vehicles.

General Harrison arrived at Colonel Johnson's new CP a short time later. Harrison saw the battlefield the same way the Germans did. He figured nothing could be accomplished by attacking over the swamp, and decided to put 2nd Battalion to what he considered better use—reinforcing the attack against St. Barthelemy. Although he was only the deputy division commander, General Harrison took a more hands-on approach to managing a battle than the division commander, Major General Leland "Hollywood" Hobbs. Harrison ordered Colonel Johnson to renew the attack but in a new direction, northeast in conjunction with 3rd Battalion and the 1st Battalion of the 117th Infantry. Colonel Johnson called Colonel Luckett to inform him that General Harrison had over-ridden his orders. Luckett immediately called General Hobbs to ask him if the 12th Infantry still commanded its 2nd Battalion. Hobbs convened a conference between senior officers at 1300 hours. He reassured Colonel Luckett that he retained control of his 1st and 2nd Battalions. He then changed the 2nd Battalion's mission to conform to General Harrison's plan to attack St. Barthelemy. This attack arrayed three battalions abreast (north to south: the 1-117, 3-12 and 2-12). Hobbs did not return the 3rd Battalion to Colonel Luckett's control, nor did he give Luckett control of the attack even though the 12th Infantry now supplied two-thirds of the force against St. Barthelemy. Worse, the revised order, again, split the two battalions the regiment did control (1st and 2nd) into two separate missions.[29]

News of the squabble reached the ears of General Barton. He already had heard reports about his regiment's heavy losses. In frustration, he pleaded with General Collins to return all of the units detached from his division and let him take responsibility for driving the Germans out of Mortain. The corps commander did not oblige.[30]

After diverting the 2nd Battalion toward St. Barthelemy instead of RJ 278, General Hobbs combined a tank battalion from CCB of the 3rd Armored Division with the 2nd Battalion 119th Infantry into Task Force 3 (TF 3) and ordered it to seize RJ 278 from the south. TF 3 swung well to the south to bypass the Germans around Hill 285 and Roche Grise. They passed through le Neufbourg and reached l'Abbaye Blanche without encountering any opposition. As soon as TF 3 reached l'Abbaye Blanche, however, the Germans responded with heavy artillery fire that forced the American infantry off the tanks they were riding. TF 3's tanks pressed ahead without its riflemen but ran into the same Germans who had defended RJ 278 against Bill's battalion the night before. After losing nine tanks, TF 3 pulled back from the intersection. The failure of TF 3 to take RJ 278 mirrored the 2nd Battalion's misfortune. The Germans repulsed, in sequence, an infantry attack without armor then an armored attack without infantry.[31]

While TF 3 languished near RJ 278, the three-battalion attack, overseen by General Harrison, launched at 1600 hours. The 2nd Battalion immediately ran into German tank, small arms, and indirect fire coming from St. Barthelemy and *Leibstandarte's* tanks on the ridgeline near Fantay. F and G Companies advanced only one hedgerow before calling for help from the artillery. The rifle companies got some relief from an air strike that knocked out one of the tanks that had held them up—although it also took out two American tanks. The battalion eked out another two hundred meters and linked up with the 3rd Battalion at 2025 hours. The exhausted troops, pounded by enemy artillery, could do no more than push to the northern end of la Rivière Dorée. Orders came down at 2121 hours to halt the advance and dig in. The poorly coordinated attacks by the 12th Infantry, 117th Infantry, and TF 3 had failed to take either St. Barthelemy or RJ 278. Generals Hobbs and Harrison appeared to have worked at cross purposes. Had they concentrated CT 12 and TF 3 on either St. Barthelemy or RJ 278 the results would likely have been much better.[32]

In the twilight Bill positioned his squads for night defense. He directed the crews to sight primary targets against the high ground east of the stream, cover the exposed southern flank, and sight FPLs along the rifle companies' front lines. When he felt satisfied with the platoon's disposition, Bill headed to his own foxhole. He had been on his feet for forty-four hours straight, most of that time under direct and indirect enemy fire. He collapsed just short of his foxhole.

Bill's eyelids had barely closed when the *Luftwaffe* paid the battalion a visit. Five fighter-bombers rolled in to make strafing runs over the American position. Bill craned his neck to the sound of a German plane diving toward him. He was within arm's reach of his foxhole but could not muster the energy to crawl the remaining two feet to safety. He rolled over and fell back to sleep.[33]

New attack orders came down in the pre-dawn hours. The 30th Infantry Division planned a concentrated attack to seize RJ 278. They returned Bill's battalion to Colonel Luckett's control then instructed him to attack from the battalion's overnight positions to the critical intersection. Once on the objective, it would link up with TF 3. Luckett directed the 1st Battalion to attack due east from the vicinity of Point B (RJ 264) to seize RJ 278. The 2nd Battalion's mission barely changed from August 8. Bill and his men would attack across the same ground and the same stream that had frustrated them earlier to seize part of the highway immediately north of RJ 278. This would be one of the few times during the entire war they had to attack over ground previously covered.[34]

The attack, scheduled for 0600 hours, kicked off at 0700. Colonel Johnson led with F Company on the right flank, G Company on the left, and E Company trailing. Bit by bit, the rifle companies shoved their way to the orchard that they occupied two days earlier. To everyone's amazement they found the medic with one surviving wounded man they had left on the scene when the battalion withdrew the day before.[35]

Just like the attack two days earlier, F and G Companies crossed the deadly north–south trail and E Company covered the rear. Bill's platoon moved with one of the forward companies. At 0755 hours the Germans counterattacked. Again, tanks on the Fantay-St. Barthelemy ridgeline opened fire on the battalion's advance. Again, the enemy dumped massive amounts of artillery and mortar fire on the battalion. Again, a German tank appeared at the north end of the lane to sever the forward rifle companies from the rest of the battalion. Three more tanks counterattacked from the east. Again, the American infantrymen hunkered down, absorbing the fire from the tanks and artillery. Again, enemy armor could not drive back the Americans, and the few *Panzergrenadieren* got nowhere against the battalion's riflemen. Again, stalemate.

Meanwhile, the work on the critical stream crossing stalled—in part, because the 30th Division engineer company had wandered from the scene during the night and failed to return. Colonel Luckett complained to the division staff, and General Hobbs intervened to chase down the errant engineers. They finally arrived at the work site at 0930 hours. The engineers from the 4th and 30th Infantry Divisions piled gravel over the swampy streambed, straining to complete the vital crossing while the

Germans pummeled them with artillery fire. The delay forced the rifle companies to fight without armor support. The situation seemed to play out for the 2ⁿᵈ Battalion as it had two days before, but this time, it was not fighting on its own.[36]

The 1ˢᵗ Battalion crossed the streambed and advanced toward la Delinière, where it ran into stiff opposition and took heavy casualties. By 0935 hours TF 3's Sherman tanks had driven to within two hundred yards of RJ 278 and drew off the three German tanks confronting F and G Companies.[37]

The attack ran into more problems. The 1ˢᵗ Battalion fouled the 2ⁿᵈ Battalion's attack when it pushed north of its designated avenue of advance and crossed in front of F Company. Colonel Johnson halted the battalion's movement to avoid fratricides. He joined the 1ˢᵗ Battalion Commander, Lt. Col. Charles Jackson, in a hasty conference to sort out the confusion on the ground. The two commanders decided to hold 1ˢᵗ Battalion in place while the 2ⁿᵈ Battalion swung around them to the north. The Second would then turn to attack the objective, RJ 278, from the north flank.[38]

Despite the pressure, the Germans held firm and fought back. TF 3 reached RJ 278 at 1016 hours but Mark V Panther and Mark VI Tiger tanks began picking off its Shermans. The *Der Fuhrer Regiment* recorded the action. "Individual enemy [American] tanks that broke through were taken out in close combat." A German outpost in la Dairie orchard continued firing into the 1ˢᵗ and 2ⁿᵈ Battalions even though TF 3 had taken the ground behind them. The task force sent an infantry force to link up with 1ˢᵗ Battalion, only a few hundred meters away, but German fire pinned them down. The Germans could no longer launch large-scale counterattacks but they could still punch back with their remaining Panthers and Tigers in local assaults. By 1100 hours F Company had pushed to within four hundred meters of RJ 278 but still could not link up with TF 3.[39]

The 12ᵗʰ Infantry and TF 3 had completely ruptured *Das Reich's* defensive front but the tenacious *SS* troops refused to withdraw. American units, including the 12ᵗʰ Infantry, felt very uncomfortable whenever they lost contact with friendly units on their flanks. The Germans worked differently. They sought opportunities to insinuate themselves between American units, even if it meant they got isolated themselves.[40]

Three American and two German battalions thrashed each other over terrain no larger than a square kilometer, about the size of a municipal golf course. The two sides saturated the area with one hundred plus heavy guns and mortars while small arms fire pinned the other side's infantrymen in place. The steady percussion of exploding artillery forced sergeants to shout instructions to men huddled next to them. American artillery observers had to duck from incoming rounds, too, and could not get eyes on the enemy guns to suppress them with counter-battery fire. Around 1445 hours the Germans launched rockets at the crossing site. Fortunately, an aerial spotter plane located the *Nebelwerfers* and brought in fighter-bombers to take out the battery. H Company's mortar platoon had dug firing emplacements behind la Tourablere. Even then, they had to displace to different positions once the enemy observers called in artillery on top of them. "One artillery shell dropped down a mortar tube, exploding inside and destroying the mortar. The gunner climbed out of his dug-in position, lit a cigarette, and walked away. About twenty seconds after he left the hole a second shell hit in the hole and blew a large crater where it had been."[41]

Not everyone handled the enemy shelling as calmly as the mortar gunner. "Several of the men started cracking up." As early as August 8, the commander of the 117th Infantry had complained to the 30th Infantry Division HQ about the battle worthiness of the sister battalion attached to them. "I think they all have battle fatigue." By August 10 the regiment's aid stations had collected a sizable number of combat stress cases.[42]

Bill watched one of his men "crack up." Some of his men were crossing a field when an enemy machine gun opened fire. One soldier took cover behind a dead cow, the most common bovine variety in Normandy that summer. The cow had been dead for a couple of days. Its hooves pointed skyward from the buildup of gas inside the carcass. A few seconds later a shell landed nearby. The shrapnel punctured the dead animal's skin, and the carcass exploded. Cow guts spewed in every direction, drenching the soldier in decomposing entrails. The sight, the smell, and the slime overpowered him. He went nuts. The man began screaming in horror. Other troops hurried over to the crazed soldier before he exposed himself and started running around in his frenzied state. The platoon managed to evacuate him until he could come to his senses.[43]

The 12th Infantry desperately needed tanks to reinforce its drive but the attached armor remained on the other side of la Rivière Dorée. The regiment queried the 2nd Battalion throughout the day for updates on the engineers' progress: 0947 hours—"should be finished in 15 min," 1013 hours—"tanks should go across shortly," 1139 hours—"using more gravel to enable tanks to cross," 1246 hours—"tank bogged down trying to cross," 1254 hours—"now 2 tanks bogged." By early afternoon the regiment realized that more work had to be done before the tanks and tank destroyers could make it over the streambed. Colonel Luckett ordered the 1st and 2nd Battalions and TF 3 to continue the attack without the additional armor. Bill's battalion struggled north at 1610 hours while the other two units supported by fire.[44]

F Company now led the attack, followed by G Company and E Company. The troops crept along hedgerows to a small trail that cut east-west. The sunken lane gave the riflemen a little cover as they approached the main St. Barthelemy-Mortain highway from the west. The advance ended when a German machine gun opened fire from a hedgerow, two hundred meters to their west, pinning them down.[45]

TF 3 sent a platoon of tanks north along the highway to augment the 12th Infantry, but German defenders managed to keep the tanks separated from the 1st and 2nd Battalions.[46]

By 1900 hours the American attack reached its culminating point. The steady *crump...crump* of artillery shells sounded across the battlefield. Casualties mounted to an alarming level. Ammo bearers carried cans of .30 cal. rounds forward and stretchers of wounded back. TF 3 reported the loss of twelve tanks. Bill's battalion had lost 160 men, the rough equivalent of an entire rifle company, over the previous thirty-six hours. With diminished strength in its rifle companies, the 2nd Battalion's attack ground to a halt and reverted to a hasty defense. Colonel Johnson re-deployed E Company on a line extending behind F and G, facing north to cover an exposed flank. TF 3, 1st Battalion, and 2nd Battalion had seized portions of the St. Barthelemy-Mortain highway but failed to link up with each other or clear the objective.[47]

True to form, the Germans launched a counterattack from the north aimed at forcing the 2nd Battalion to withdraw. E Company spotted troops in American uniforms slipping south along the lowland. Suspecting they were SS troops up to their old tricks, E Company opened fire and drove them back.[48]

At 2105 hours on August 10, the regiment instructed its two battalions to dig-in for the night. The heavy casualties of the past three days forced the rifle companies and H Company's machine gun platoons to stretch out just to cover their frontage. TF 3 pulled its tanks back five hundred meters where, in accordance with American armored tactical doctrine, they formed a defensive "lager" to refuel, rearm, and perform maintenance. These nightly withdrawals made sense for the tank crews, but they also ceded any ground won during the day.[49]

As to the Germans, the commander of the *Der Fuhrer Regiment* admitted, "Our own casualties were considerable." While they had lost much of their combat power, they stubbornly hung on to their outposts at Roche Grise, St. Barthelemy, la Dairie, and RJ 278. Individual German tanks stayed forward with their infantry. The enemy kept the pressure on the 2nd Battalion throughout the night of August 10 with incessant artillery fire and probes.[50]

One German Tiger tank came barreling down the north-south trail into E Company's position. Private Michael Burik grabbed a bazooka, loaded a round, then bravely walked into the lane, challenging the German tank to a duel. Burik pulled the bazooka's trigger but nothing happened. He had forgotten to release the safety. By the time he armed the bazooka, the tank was nearly on him. He quickly fired at point blank range. The 2.36-inch rocket bounced harmlessly off the Tiger's 120mm armor plating. The tank crew replied by firing its massive 88mm main gun at the lone American rifleman. The shell missed, but the blast sent

Burik toppling backwards head over heels. Undismayed, the private reloaded, kneeled, and fired a second time. Again, the round pinged off the Tiger with no effect. The Germans again fired the main gun at Burik, turning him into a human tumbleweed. Wobbling from the blast, the infantryman refused to back away. He loaded and fired a third rocket into the Tiger. The round did nothing to the tank, but the crew had enough of the crazy American bazooka gunner and retreated. After helping another soldier take cover, Burik called for more bazooka ammunition. Before he could fire a fourth time, he succumbed to shock. Sadly, he later died from his wounds.[51]

Under intermittent artillery fire throughout the night, the engineers graded a path atop the swampy ground and reinforced the bridge over the stream. This allowed wheeled vehicles, ambulances, and jeeps to bring in supplies and carry out casualties. That helped, but what the battalion really needed was armor. As dawn broke the engineers' work had progressed to the point that the regiment planned on getting the tanks and tank destroyers into the fight. Luckett ordered a new attack at midday. First Battalion would launch the main attack to RJ 278, supported by 2nd Battalion and TF 3. Colonel Johnson could only muster 270 men—36 percent of the battalion's authorized strength—for the attack.[52]

The battalion's executive officer had been wounded a couple days earlier and Johnson neared exhaustion trying to run the battalion on his own. Luckett sent Major Ken Lay from the regimental staff to assist him.[53]

At 0934 hours on August 11, four tanks and two tank destroyers finally made it across the streambed. More were on the way. Eventually, the rest of B Company, 70th Tank Battalion along with tank destroyers and the regiment's towed 57mm AT guns, crossed la Rivière Dorée. Getting the armor through the hedgerows proved troublesome. The tanks had a "Hell of time getting into position." The two battalions coordinated their attacks for 1330 hours, beginning with a fifteen-minute preparation by the 42nd Field Artillery Battalion.[54]

Finally configured as a combined arms force, CT 12 attacked the minute the artillery finished firing. Each battalion jumped off and advanced one hedgerow before running into stiff German resistance. Bill and his machine gun crews returned fire as the infantry platoons tangled with the enemy from one hedgerow to the next. Colonel Johnson and Major Lay stayed with the lead platoons to help coordinate the efforts of the tanks and infantry. One of the first things Major Lay noticed as they advanced were the bodies of dead 2nd Battalion infantrymen that had been left on the field over the course of the past three days. The stench of moldering flesh added to the din of exploding shells to further torment the soldiers' senses.[55]

During the exchange of fire, an F Company rifleman spotted troops in American uniforms acting like they were trying to infiltrate the friendly position. He opened fire and wounded a few of the suspicious troops who turned out to be SS Panzergrenadieren. At this point in the melee, a German medic waved a Red Cross flag and asked for a truce to allow some of the wounded to be evacuated. The Americans consented and the slaughter paused in this part of the battlefield. The killing promptly resumed the moment the two sides cleared their casualties.[56]

F Company pressed toward the highway with G Company following. Men ducked as enemy machine gun bullets snapped overhead and flinched each time a howitzer shell exploded nearby. Moving in short spurts, they worked their way along the hedgerows with the help of the attached tanks. Colonel Johnson reported the action. "Of [the] two remaining tanks, one concentrated on knocking out machine-gun nests in a stone house on the left flank while the other placed its fire on the dug-in positions holding up the advance of the 1st Battalion." Johnson and Lay were not the only senior officers leading from the front. One rifleman staggered back through a gap in a hedgerow after getting hit by machine gun fire. When he looked up he saw Colonel Luckett moving forward with another rifle platoon. Luckett ordered the lieutenant with him to watch the wounded rifleman then led the platoon forward. F Company's platoons used the sunken east-west trail to reach the St. Barthelemy-Mortain highway. Two intrepid sergeants succeeded in taking out a couple of machine gun positions with hand grenades to clear the way. The battalion had finally severed the highway five hundred meters north of RJ 278. Now it had to hold while the 1st Battalion and TF 3 attempted to seize the road junction.[57]

Sensing enemy pressure building along his left (northern) flank, Colonel Johnson requested assistance from the 3rd Battalion. The regiment replied that the 117th had already committed the sister battalion to a fight near St. Barthelemy. As Johnson feared, the *Leibstandarte Division* in St. Barthelemy responded, just as it had on August 9 and 10.[58]

The 2nd Battalion brought up a couple of anti-tank guns towed by halftracks to shore up the north flank. At 1552 hours a German tank coming out of St. Barthelemy hit the two halftracks while they crossed the north-south trail. One halftrack driver, Private First Class Vierse McWilliams, refused to abandon his vehicle. The German tank hit the halftrack two more times before he finally bailed out. Fortunately, the 57mm guns were still serviceable and the crews positioned them to fire back at the Germans. Right after taking out the halftracks, the tanks supported a *Panzergrenadier* counterattack out of St. Barthelemy. Bill's squads unleashed a torrent of bullets, adding to the intense fire from mortars and rifles that stopped the enemy cold. That did not stop the German tanks from firing at will into the Americans.[59]

Throughout the afternoon, Bill's guns suppressed enemy machine guns and helped drive back German infantry. The short distances in hedgerow country forced the heavy machine guns to rely more on direct fire to drive back the enemy. With enemy activity ranging from the southeast to the northwest, Bill had to continually re-position the squads.

Colonel Johnson observed an enemy tank firing at his command group from behind a hedgerow. He turned to the Anti-Tank Platoon Leader, Lieutenant Morgan Welch. "Welch, there's a tank aiming at us. Take a bazooka team and knock him out." Welch and his team began stalking the German tank. They crept up close to the tank, hidden by a hedgerow. His team loaded the bazooka round and the lieutenant rose above the shrubs to aim at the tank, a Mark VI Tiger. Welch fired at point blank range but the round bounced off the turret. To their horror, the team of Americans watched the 88mm gun turn in their direction and fire. The shock wave knocked them senseless. Lieutenant Welch came to flat on his back. The next thing he heard was *plop...plop-plop...plop.* It took him and his team a few seconds to realize the strange sound was caused by their helmets falling from the sky to the ground. As the team cleared their heads, the Tiger drove away. Apparently, they convinced the tank to withdraw even though they could not take it out.[60]

Others besides Lieutenant Welch had difficulty knocking out German tanks. One of the attached tanks from B Company, 70th Tank Battalion moved forward a couple hedgerows during the action. Its commander, Sergeant Carl Rambo, spotted a German tank facing south against the 2nd Battalion flank. "I picked up a German tank sitting sideways to me. I told my gunner to 'hit him low.' We threw three rounds into the belly, and smoke rolled out of that tank." Excited by the kill, Rambo shouted, "We got him." The tank commander then turned to engage other targets until his main gun jammed from over-heating. Later, another tank commander burst his bubble when he told him that he had not taken out the German tank. "Man, that thing just drove off!"[61]

While Welch and Rambo sparred with German tanks, Colonel Johnson and Major Lay moved over to one of E Company's platoons as it crossed another shell-pocked wheat field. A German machine gun opened fire at the exposed Americans, sending everyone scurrying behind a hedgerow. The platoon sergeant had to yank some of his soldiers over the top of the bushes to safety. While the infantrymen hunkered down, a Sherman tank approached. Johnson organized a local combined arms attack, ordering the tank to suppress the enemy machine gun while the infantry charged across the field. The colonel stood up to direct the tank's fire but spotted a German vehicle next to a building. He gave the tank commander the new target information then got the rifle platoon ready for its assault.[62]

The Sherman pushed forward on Colonel Johnson's signal and opened fire on the German vehicle that quickly pulled behind the building for cover. Just as the American assault got underway, three German Panthers appeared and opened fire. Their opening salvo landed in the middle of the command group. The blast killed two radio operators and wounded both Johnson and Lay. The colonel suffered severe wounds to his face, arm, and legs. He required immediate evacuation. For the third time in nine weeks, the 2nd Battalion had to cart off its commander. At least this one was headed for a hospital instead of a grave. Major Lay stayed forward, despite his wounds, until Lt. Col. Franklin Sibert arrived from the 1st Battalion to take command.[63]

The loss of Johnson and Lay took the steam out of the battalion's attack. Most of E and G Companies' officers had become casualties. F Company had no officers left. The unit did not have enough leaders on hand to direct an attack, but, it could—and did—stand its ground and repelled the German counterattack. The troops even managed to knock out one of the three Panthers with a lucky shot from a bazooka. Colonel Luckett called a halt to the attack at 2025 hours. Both 1st and 2nd Battalions pulled back to their positions of the previous night while the 42nd Field Artillery blasted RJ 278, yet again. The regiment had little to show for the day's attack other than plenty of casualties. Once again, CT 12 failed to clear and hold the vital intersection, though it finally had armor assets forward of the streambed.[64]

The attack did serve its purpose—the Germans threw in the towel. The *Der Fuhrer Regiment's* commander later wrote, "The enemy drove into the regiment's flank with tank support. Under artillery fire and continuous strafing attacks, our positions west of the Mortain–St. Barthelemy road had to be pulled back." It was time to leave. The *Das Reich Division* covered the withdrawal of the other panzer divisions from north of Mortain as the Germans tried to escape the jaws of Patton's Third Army closing in behind them.[65]

Lieutenant James Piper led a patrol across the main highway after dark to explore high ground west of the la Sablonniere orchard. The patrol moved to their objective without running into any Germans. Piper continued patrolling down to RJ 278 then northeast for a short distance up the highway leading to Sourdeval. He discovered that the Germans had vacated their forward defensive positions and regrouped. The battalion took advantage of the situation to send forces across the highway onto the ridgeline. This minor advance marked one of the few times the American infantry followed up a nighttime patrol by seizing ground during the hours of darkness.[66]

A little before midnight, the regiment issued orders to resume the attack on August 12. The regiment tasked the 1st Battalion to seize the now-familiar objective, RJ 278. With only fourteen officers and 196 enlisted men left, the 2nd Battalion would hold the north flank while the 1st Battalion took the road junction.[67]

Shortly after the regiment's attack order came down, the eastern sky lit up. German artillery deluged the 12th Infantry's area like a Kansas thunderstorm. To the American infantry hunkering down in their foxholes, it seemed that every enemy gun within range was firing at them. The regiment described the strike as "the heaviest arty fire yet felt in this sector." Fortunately, most of the enemy shells fell between the rifle companies and the support elements.[68]

A spot report from E Company provided a clue why the Germans had fired the massive artillery barrage. From their position on the high ground east of the St. Barthelemy-Mortain highway, E Company could see a long line of German vehicles, bumper to tail, heading northeast on the highway to Sourdeval. The German used the artillery to cover their withdrawal from Mortain. The 42nd Artillery Battalion responded with interdictory fires along the Sourdeval highway.[69]

The attack kicked off at 0800 hours on August 12. The Germans left a screening detachment in the area to slow the American advance but it lacked the firepower and zeal of previous days. The 1st Battalion pushed through enemy small arms fire on its way to the objective. The 2nd Battalion's troops knocked out a Mark IV tank near St. Barthelemy with a bazooka. With better observation on the higher ground, the American forward observers could finally target the enemy with some degree of accuracy. A 1st Battalion 81mm mortar destroyed a Tiger when it dropped a round right through the tank's hatch. The 42nd Artillery Battalion killed four more tanks. The 1st Battalion occupied RJ 278 by 1023 hours. The 2nd Battalion dispatched more patrols to locate the German defensive line but they found nothing nearby. The 117th Infantry, with the 3rd Battalion, entered St. Barthelemy at 1230 hours. An hour later the regiment received word from the 30th Infantry Division to consolidate around RJ 278. The isolated battalion on Hill 314 had been relieved and the mission accomplished.[70]

At long last the 117th Infantry returned the 3rd Battalion to Colonel Luckett. That evening the entire regiment clustered around the vital intersection it had fought so hard to control for five days. The Germans continued to lob artillery and 88mm rounds at them, reminding everyone that more hard fighting lay ahead.[71]

At 1000 hours on August 13, the 117th Infantry relieved the 2nd Battalion at la Sablonniere. The battalion's survivors marched six kilometers by foot to an assembly area a little south of Juvigny. Two things greeted them when they arrived. First, they got official word that the 12th Infantry had been placed back under General Barton's control. Second, trucks stood by to carry them from Mortain to a bivouac site. The trucks hauled off only 28 percent of the men they had dropped off August 8.[72]

When asked, Bill always said that the most savage fighting he ever saw was at Mortain. He and the other exhausted survivors may not have realized it but Mortain marked a major milestone. The failed *Operation Luttich*, followed by the slaughter of the Falaise Pocket, effectively destroyed the fighting prowess of the *SS Panzer* divisions. Though the 12th Infantry had many months of tough fighting ahead, from this point on, they would fight with greater skill and grit than their opponents.

CHAPTER NINE

PARIS

The remnants of the regiment pulled into an assembly area five kilometers southwest of le Teilleul the evening of August 13. Their location, safely tucked away from any action and beyond the reach of German artillery, finally gave the men a respite from danger and a chance to relax.[1]

The 2nd Battalion responded to the down time with enthusiasm. "We got the works. There were movies, Red Cross doughnut wagons, Red Cross clubmobiles, USO shows, showers and a close by mill pond which provided a swimmer's paradise." Bill took full advantage of the opportunities to clean up, sleep, and take things easy—and put the memory of Mortain behind him.[2]

Mortain had wrecked the 12th Infantry. The brutal combat had steadily eroded the regiment's fighting strength and morale until little remained of either. Suffering so much while attached to a different division made the men feel they had been treated like a rented mule. General Barton knew the critical condition of his returned regiment and its urgent need for rest. He heard about the command squabbles between Hobbs, Harrison, and Luckett. He understood the disgruntled feelings about the hard luck mission they drew. He saw the casualty list with 1,150 names. Most alarming of all, he learned about the three hundred cases of combat fatigue.[3]

Barton welcomed the 12th back to the fold of the Ivy Division, showing as much compassion as the father of the Prodigal Son. He issued strict orders for the regiment not to be disturbed "for anything." True to his word, the regiment's journal only had two innocuous entries in each of the next three days.[4]

The wise general also applied some "tough love." That evening, he issued a message to the division, alerting its leaders to a dangerous attitude he labeled "silent mutiny." He faulted some individuals for feeling sorry for themselves because of what they'd been through and assuming that no one in command cared about their welfare. Barton reminded his subordinates that no matter how rough things got they must persevere like soldiers and do their duty. He lectured the officer corps to counter any discouraging thoughts among their men. "[T]hey must be Pollyannas" to keep the soldiers' fighting spirits up. The general carefully avoided pointing any fingers but he clearly intended the message to counsel the 12th Infantry against falling into despondency.[5]

This struck close to home for Bill. One of his friends, a lieutenant who had been with the battalion since Montebourg, announced to his company commander that he would no longer lead men into battle. He had reached his capacity for carnage. The lieutenant openly declared that he did not care what the command did to punish him.

This put the chain of command in a tough spot. Under Army regulations, refusal to follow orders in combat could bring a charge of disobedience and cowardice. A charge of cowardice seemed inapt. The lieutenant had fought courageously and effectively for weeks. He was no coward, and he was not trying to avoid danger, either. He just could not accept responsibility for more deaths.

Rather than lose a valuable officer, the senior officers agreed to reassign the lieutenant to support duty within the battalion. The young officer would serve in that capacity and perform very well throughout the rest of the war.

This was not the last time "frontline justice" would prevail over regulations. The dangers and horrors of combat could turn jurisprudence on its head. In the months ahead, Bill too would wrestle with difficult issues of law and justice.

The regiment spent the next three days resting and taking care of routine maintenance. The supply sergeants issued new gear to the platoons to replace the equipment and clothing lost or ruined by the recent fighting. Combat fatigue cases returned to the ranks. Most of them only required a hot meal and a quiet night to recover. Replacements arrived to fill the vast number of vacancies within the regiment. The mood in camp rallied with the extra sleep and influx of fresh blood.[6]

Outside the bivouac, the strategic situation shifted rapidly. Patton's Third Army and Hodges's First Army raced east to Orleans and Chartres. The Canadians and Americans crushed the flanks of the German *Seventh Army* and *Panzer Group West* inside the Falaise-Argentan pocket. Hitler relented and allowed *OB West* to conduct a withdrawal from the pocket on August 16. The withdrawal turned into a stampede. The German defense in the West verged on collapse.[7]

One morning Bill indulged himself with a hot shower. As he soaped the grime off his body a replacement walked into the shower tent. The recent arrival started talking about the rapid advance of the Allies and the rout of the German army. "Did you hear the news?" he asked. "The Germans are falling back all across the front. Patton's army is chasing them back to Germany. The war should be over in a month."

"I doubt that," Bill replied. After surviving the desperate struggle at Mortain, Bill knew the Germans had no intention of giving up.

"Why do you say that? They know they're beat."

"The Germans won't give up that easily. To them this is a setback. They still have fight left in them."

"No way! They quit in 1918 as soon as we got to their border."

"I don't see them quitting now. They'll fight to protect their land. Besides, Hitler will never give up."

"Hell, they already tried to kill Hitler. I say they're finished."

The two men finished rinsing and moved to the changing area to dry off. They continued arguing until Bill pulled on his shirt. Once the enlisted man saw Bill's gold bar he bit his lip. A few weeks later the replacement found out for himself that the Germans had plenty of fight left.

As the Allies crushed the Falaise-Argentan pocket, VII Corps became concerned about potential German armored attacks to break out of the trap. The 4th Infantry Division received orders to reinforce the southern jaw of the Allied pincers. Late on August 17, the 2nd Battalion climbed aboard two-and-a-half-ton trucks—the Army's famous "deuce-and-a-half"—to move to a new assembly area three kilometers south of Carrouges. By the time they arrived in position the threat had passed. The Germans were already fleeing in large numbers through the narrow mouth of the pocket. The German *Seventh Army* escaped complete encirclement but Allied aircraft and artillery slaughtered tens of thousands of Germans caught in the vice. Other American units pinched out the Ivy Division's front then sucked up the available transport to chase the Germans east. The First Army put the division back in reserve and gave the whole unit a rest period.[8]

With a roster filled with replacements, General Barton directed the division to use the extra time to conduct training. For its part, H Company brushed up on employing the machine guns and mortars. The company commander tasked Bill to organize training for the mortar platoon. Bill walked into the mortar platoon bivouac area and announced that they would spend the day practicing drills instead of lounging in their tents.[9]

The troops groaned in protest. "Why do we need training? We've been in combat for two months." The men had a point. They had fired thousands of rounds since D-Day. The lieutenant persisted and laid out crew drills similar to the ones he had conducted back in England. He even set up a live-fire range. The men grumbled while they set up the tubes and prepared the munitions for firing. With all their combat experience the men failed to see any purpose in the training but Bill knew better.

The squads and sections ran through their drills but their performance fell below the standards they had achieved prior to D-Day. The crews had trouble aligning the tubes. It took them too long to get rounds down range. They had to fire extra spotting rounds before firing for effect. As Bill figured, casualties, bad habits, and loss of key leaders had eroded crew proficiency. He met with the sections and shared the results. The men got the message and put more effort into performing their tasks correctly. By the end of the day, the grousing about the lost rest time ceased, and the platoon's morale lifted because of their increased confidence in themselves.

The mortar platoon's training did have one, unintended consequence—the sound of impacting rounds in the otherwise quiet sector startled the division's HQ. The division intelligence officer (G-2) called the regiment. "Did you receive some arty fire in your area this A.M.?" The regiment reassured the G-2 that the explosions came from practice rounds.[10]

Bill believed in the Army's training and doctrine. As an engineer, he gravitated to the idea that tasks should be done properly to ensure a safe and reliable outcome. He approached tactical operations the way he solved math problems—in an orderly and thorough manner, not skipping any steps.

In this, Bill differed from the typical GI who had spent less than a year in the Army. Many of the young troops, like Bill Mauldin's cartoon characters, Willie and Joe, disdained the Army's formal courtesies and procedures. They constantly looked for shortcuts around standard operating procedures. Skipping steps sometimes worked but often caused mistakes and errors in performance—and deaths on the battlefield. Bill understood that soldiers should avoid taking shortcuts without first knowing the purpose of each step in the process. He closely supervised his men to maintain discipline and correct oversights.

For a brief period, the troops' lives reverted to the routine of an army field encampment rather than duty in a combat zone. Officers and enlisted men attended training sessions, put on demonstrations, and familiarized themselves with their individual weapons. Senior officers inspected unit bivouacs and issued orders to correct shortcomings in sanitation and orderliness. Once, the battalion even stood formation for evening retreat, conducted to the sound of a bugle. The respite did not last. Movement orders came down on August 22. The regiment prepared to depart but traffic jams and a rapidly changing situation forced the 12th Infantry to stay put. Just as well. The next morning General Barton called in all the subordinate commanders to brief them on a new mission.[11]

Paris suddenly became the strategic focus of Eisenhower, Bradley, and, consequently, the Ivy Division. As the Allies thrust across northern France and a Franco-American force landed in southern France on August 15, the people in France's capital could no longer restrain themselves and took a hand in their own liberation. Following a strike by Metro workers, postal workers, and police on August 15, a general strike began on August 18. The next day, resistance fighters, loosely formed within the French Forces of the Interior (FFI) started fighting German troops and seized many buildings, including the Prefecture de Police on the Ile de la Cité and the Hôtel de Ville. On August 20, ordinary Parisians joined in, throwing up barricades.

The German garrison defended itself effectively but lacked the troops to restore order throughout the city. The German commandant of Paris, Lt. Gen. Dietrich von Choltitz, negotiated a shaky cease-fire with the FFI that spared the city and its German occupiers from full scale fighting. Both sides found the cease-fire expedient, but the city ceased to function in the meantime. Utilities failed, critical services stopped, and the influx of food halted.

Gen. Charles de Gaulle, the leader of the Free French, and his military subordinates chafed at the delays in taking Paris. De Gaulle wanted forces loyal to him to enter the capital at once to help him establish his government. Maj. Gen. Phillipe Leclerc, commander of the *2e Division Blindee (2e DB)*, a French armored division, petitioned the Allied high command to send his unit to liberate Paris. Eisenhower initially wanted to avoid the military burden of seizing and sustaining Paris but, with the cease-fire expiring on August 23, he could no longer delay matters. He ordered Maj. Gen. Leonard "Gee" Gerow, commander of V Corps, to take responsibility for securing Paris—and gave him the *2e DB* and the 4th Infantry Division to do the job.[12]

Colonel Luckett returned to the regimental CP at 1106 hours on August 23 and told the battalion and attached unit commanders that CT 12 would support the *2e DB's* advance into Paris by securing important bridges south of the capital at Juvisy-sur-Orge. The units scrambled to prepare for a 145-mile road march. Before noon word went out that movement would begin at 1700 hours. An hour later the men got an appreciation for how fluid the strategic situation had become—all the routes had changed. The regiment ordered the 2nd Battalion to provide road guides for the revised convoy route. The column finally got under-way at 1900 hours.[13]

The weather turned raw and made the road march hell. Storms and heavy rain lashed the convoy. The men got soaked and chilled riding in the backs of deuce-and-a-half trucks. As much as they struggled to hold the canvas tops in place, the rain still dripped and splashed on them. Because he was an officer, Bill rode in the cab of a truck but he still got wet. The drivers had a difficult time, too. Besides dealing with poor vis-ibility, they had trouble keeping the trucks on the road. The route fol-lowed many secondary roads that were winding, slick, and poorly drained. Numerous vehicles slid off the roads. Maintenance teams spent the whole night towing and winching trucks out of the ditches. No one thought about sleep.[14]

One of the battalion's riflemen described the routine inside the trucks. "Every few hours we stopped to let the men stretch their legs and make the necessary nature calls. I remember one guy in the front part of the cargo space who had very little control and had to relieve himself several times during the night. Naturally, he used his helmet, the all-purpose accessory of the infantryman. As we were moving forward, he had to pass it back to have someone in the rear to empty it so as not to blow into the side of the truck body. By morning, all of us were losing patience with the guy and about the only thing to relieve the tension was to curse at him."[15]

Sometime after dawn on August 24, the rain let up. The convoy pulled into a temporary assembly area near Orphin at 1049 hours, minus thirty-one vehicles that fell out of the column. The troops got out to wring the water from their uniforms and shake out the cramps. The mess units set up chow while the fuel tankers gassed up the vehicles for the second stage of the road march. Word of another change came shortly after arrival. General Leclerc's *2e DB* had shifted its avenue of advance south of the zone V Corps had given it and crossed part of the regiment's route, jamming the roads. CT 12 altered course to a new designated assembly area near Nozay.[16]

Movement resumed at 1500 hours. News of their mission traveled faster than the convoy. All along the route, French citizens poured from their homes and lined the roads. The division staff noted, "Most of the people were well dressed, seemed well-to-do and a great many shouted greetings in English. Hundreds had brought flowers, fruit and vegetables." The tankers attached to the regiment experienced the thoughtful gratitude of the crowd during one halt. "As vehicles stayed in place, people emerged from a pharmacy with eyewash and cotton, and went from tank to tank tenderly washing dirt from the eyes of tankers," one of them remembered. "What a magnificent gesture!"[17]

At one point, Bill's march unit stopped, and bystanders swarmed forward to shake the soldiers' hands. Some of the Frenchmen shoved open bottles of champagne at the Americans while French women jumped in to kiss the liberators.

One old woman stood next to Bill's truck. She looked at the veteran infantrymen in the vehicles with a somber expression. Bill could hear her say, "*Si fatigue. Si fatigue,*" as she looked at the lined faces and slumped postures of the battle-weary men. The old woman started fumbling with her belongings. Bill could tell that she wanted to give something to the soldiers but the only thing she had with her was a tomato she had just purchased at the local market. She gladly handed it to Bill.

He thanked the woman as the convoy got moving again. He looked at the old woman's gift and marveled. The tomato, huge with a bright red skin, looked ripe and tempting. When he bit into the vine-ripened fruit, it flooded his mouth with wonderful flavor. He devoured the tomato, savoring its freshness. After weeks of nothing but bland Army food and K rations, the tomato gave him a pleasant reminder of life back in the States. The old woman had no idea how much Bill appreciated her small token of thanks.

The convoy coiled into the Nozay assembly area shortly after sunset. The troops dug in a defensive position, though the threat of enemy action seemed remote.[18]

Close to midnight Colonel Luckett returned from the division CP with new instructions based on yet another shift in the strategic situation. Stiff resistance on the *2e DB's* southerly approach into Paris and roads clogged with their cheering fellow countrymen had slowed the French column, considerably. Bradley, Hodges, and Gerow had expected the French armored division to relieve the city on August 24. An irritated Bradley gave General Gerow the green light to commit the Ivy Division. "To Hell with prestige, tell the Fourth to slam on in and take the liberation." General Barton chose the 12th Infantry to seize the Palais de Justice in the center of the city, a gesture he hoped would partially compensate for the ordeal of Mortain.[19]

The attached 38th Cavalry Reconnaissance Squadron and the 3rd Battalion moved out at 0600 hours on August 25 to lead the regiment into Paris. The 2nd Battalion pulled out by 0910 hours. Their route went through Longjumeau and Athis-Mons then skirted Orly Airport through Villeneuve-le-Roi. The move turned into a triumphal march as the entire capital turned abuzz with word of "liberation." A G Company rifleman thrilled at the joyous reception. "As we entered the Rue d'Itale [sic], our tactical motor march became a huge victory parade, and our vehicles became covered with flowers." Bill and his men entered what was perhaps the most jubilant fête of the twentieth century. "The pent-up emotions of four bitter years under the Nazi yoke suddenly burst into wild celebration, and the French citizens made us feel that each of us was personally responsible for the liberation of these grateful people. We felt wonderful!"[20]

The American vehicles nudged up the clogged avenues toward the Ile de la Cité. Official histories of the regiment and battalion waxed poetic in their descriptions of the rapturous greeting they received. "The men, women and children surged against the mounted troops on all sides in a riot of frantic acclaim...Repeatedly above the din of exuberant throats were the cries: 'Merci! Merci! S'ank you, s'ank you-Viva la Ameriques [sic]!'" "Some were crying, some were laughing and shouting, others...a minority...stood silently and admired us but the reactions of the mademoiselles were unanimous. If a man wasn't kissed a hundred times, he had a bad seat." Bill had a good seat. He rode in the cab of a deuce-and-a-half shaking hands and kissing the women, girls, and babies lining the avenue. [21]

While the regiment's column plowed through the crowds swarming the Rue d'Italie, the Allies communicated with General von Choltitz to secure the surrender of the remaining Germans. One of General Leclerc's subordinate commanders, Colonel Pierre Billotte, issued an ultimatum at 1000 hours to von Choltitz, holed up in the Hôtel Meurice. By then Leclerc's tanks and the FFI had the German defenders cornered in a handful of strongholds such as the Palais Bourbon, the Prince Eugene Barracks, and the Place de la République. Von Choltitz was ready to surrender but worried that once he accepted Billotte's terms, the FFI would string him up along with most of his officers. He also had to think about the future of his family in Germany should the Fuhrer condemn him for surrendering without a fight. The German commander turned down the demand, at least until a greater show of force could justify it. [22]

Colonel Luckett arrived at the Prefecture de Police at 1230 hours. He conferred with Colonel Billotte and the Prefect, Captain Edgard Pisani. The Frenchmen explained the Germans' reluctance to surrender. The colonel and his party drove in their jeep to the Place de la République, armed with tommy guns, to add to the show of force. Meanwhile, Billotte's troops and tanks cleared the Rue de Rivoli and Tuileries Garden. Von Choltitz and the Germans offered no resistance as uniformed French troops entered the Hôtel Meurice and took them prisoner. Billotte's men brought von Choltitz to the Prefecture where Generals Leclerc and Barton had assembled, along with members of the FFI: Jacques Chaban-Delmas, Charles Luizet, Henri Rol-Tanguy, and Maurice Kriegel-Valrimont.[23]

Satisfied by the show of force and reassured by the presence of the Americans, von Choltitz agreed to surrender the entire German garrison. He and Leclerc signed one surrender document at the Prefecture then moved to Leclerc's CP at the Gare Montparnasse where von Choltitz signed a second surrender document. Leclerc and Rol-Tanguy, as commander of the FFI in Paris, jointly signed this surrender document in the name of the French Provisional Government. American and British representatives were not asked to sign.[24]

The 12th Infantry's column reached the Ile de la Cité by mid-afternoon. Bill and his men pulled into the courtyard of Notre Dame while the cathedral's bells pealed in celebration. The regiment had responsibility for patrolling and clearing the southeast portion of the city, roughly the 11th, 12th, 13th, and 20th Arrondissements. Colonel Luckett set up the regimental CP in the Hotel du Levant on the Left Bank. The 2nd Battalion occupied a slice of the Rive Gauche by the Jardin des Plantes. Lt. Col. Franklin Sibert, the battalion commander, tasked Bill's platoon with controlling the movement of vehicles and people between the Left Bank and the Ile de la Cité. Bill positioned one section of machine guns on the Petit Pont and the other section on Pont St.-Michel. From these positions, they could guard the southern approach to the Prefecture de Police and Palais de Justice. The platoon enjoyed the easy mission. They only fired their weapons one time and that was done to separate opposing factions of the FFI.[25]

The Allied advance into Paris swelled the ranks of the FFI tenfold, a hundredfold from the week before. The orderliness of these combatants seemed to coincide with the length of time they had been active in the resistance. To the American soldiers, what this amateur force lacked in military appearance it more than made up in earnestness and deadly intent as they helped French and American troops clear out isolated pockets of Germans. "The majority of the FFI were clad in mufti or partial uniforms. Their weapons were of German or American make. They were everywhere, rounding up the stunned Hun with a fierce intensity of purpose...In typical Latin fashion these armed civilians raced madly about in nondescript vehicles. Men were lying on front fenders in firing positions; rifles were sticking out of car windows like the quills of a porcupine. Some vehicles even had men in the rear trunk with rifles ready for action."[26]

The Americans also witnessed the darker side of liberation—retribution. Hostile Parisians rounded up women who had fraternized with German soldiers and shaved their heads. Two sergeants from the regiment's counter-intelligence section, J. D. Salinger and John Keenan, arrested a suspected collaborator only to watch helplessly as a vengeful crowd beat him to death.[27]

The undercurrent of political competition and revenge could not dampen the overall euphoria that leavened the City of Light. Parisians filled the streets, most of them shouting, drinking, and singing. The revelry went on all day and night. Hemingway and his merry men seized the Ritz and drained bottle after bottle of rare vintages of *Premiers Grands Crus Classes A* clarets. Sergeant Salinger claimed, "you could stand on the hood of your jeep and take a leak on it and it wouldn't matter...anything you did would be fine."

Courteous Parisians invited soldiers into their homes for meals, showers, and cognac. The homesick Americans lapped up the fawning attention, especially from the ladies. One by one, soldiers disappeared into neighborhood homes, returning an hour later with grins on their faces. "I think I was the only guy in the platoon that didn't get laid that night," Bill later grumbled.[28]

Perhaps the most touching incident of the liberation for Bill occurred when an elderly Frenchman approached the machine gun position on Pont St.-Michel. He looked over the American soldiers and recognized Bill as the officer in charge. With tears in his eyes he walked up to Bill and spoke in halting English. "Thank you, Americans, for liberating us."

"You're welcome," Bill replied. "I'm glad we could help free your city."

"It is important to me to speak with you in English."

"Why is that?"

The old man could barely contain his emotions as he explained. "When the Germans came I knew only the Americans could drive them out. I did not speak English then but I taught myself. I did that because I hoped that one day I could speak English to our liberators. That day has come and now I can speak English with you."

Bill smiled and shook the old Frenchman's hand. "You speak English very well."

"Thank you. That is good to hear from you." The man looked very relieved by Bill's compliment. "I tried to speak with another American but I could not understand anything he said. I can understand you."

"That's okay. The other guy was probably from Alabama."

The troops settled in for the night, most near their designated positions, a few in warm beds. Each knew that he had been part of a history-making event, made all the sweeter by the adulation of the grateful Parisians. A Signal Corps private attached to the regiment, Irwin Shaw, summed up August 25 the best. "This was the day the war should have ended."[29]

The next morning, the regiment received orders to move from the city center to the 12th Arrondissement in the southeastern part of the city. The new assembly area lay within the Bois de Vincennes, the former hunting grounds of French monarchs.[30]

The regiment's move may have served a political purpose. The American participation in Paris' liberation did not fit the narrative de Gaulle asserted. In a rousing speech in front of the Hotel de Ville he proudly proclaimed, "Paris! Paris outraged! Paris broken! Paris martyred! But Paris liberated! Released by itself, liberated by its people with the help of the armies of France, with the support and assistance of all France, France who fights, the only France, the real France, eternal France." Ironically, Bill's platoon stood guard only five hundred meters away when he delivered his address.[31]

Before departing the Ile de la Cité, the regiment's Catholic soldiers received a rare treat. The 12th Infantry's Catholic chaplain, Father Leonard Fries, was granted the honor of being the first priest, following the liberation, to celebrate Mass in Notre Dame, France's most sacred cathedral.

The French worshippers welcomed the troops who, nonetheless, felt awkward about their presence. "It was a strange sight for Notre Dame to see us doughboys sitting at Mass with our rifles and battle gear."[32]

The move and occupation of the assembly area in the Paris park went without a hitch. The main body pulled into the woods shortly after midday and began setting up a defensive perimeter. Their appearance drew an immediate crowd. Eager to contact Americans, the Parisians clustered around every soldier. After a while the command became annoyed. The well-meaning but plentiful citizens kept the soldiers from their duties. One of the attached tankers recalled, "We could hardly eat, shave, change clothes, or do anything of a personal nature." The company commanders finally explained to the well-wishers that the soldiers needed to be left alone. "Immediately, with profuse apologies, the civilians left." The tank company first sergeant decided the time had come to reassert discipline. "Alright, goddammit, tear off the goddamn crepe paper. The goddamn circus is over."[33]

The FFI continued its rampage around Paris. The generals figured they could prove useful in rounding up German stragglers and locating points of resistance. Throughout the day intelligence reports from the French irregulars poured into the regiment's S-2. Some French spot reports had dubious value—e.g., "100 enemy tanks reported...vicinity of Boissey St. Leger" and "800 Germans digging in." American intelligence did confirm some FFI reports, including "German group [in the vicinity of] Champigny sur Marne holding hostages."[34]

Colonel Sibert dispatched a force under Capt. Tallie Crocker, now the G Company Commander, to deal with the situation. A heavy machine gun platoon and an 81mm mortar section from H Company reinforced G Company's riflemen. A platoon of tanks from B Company 70th Tank Battalion and a couple of M10 tank destroyers rounded out the force. This combined-arms team arrived on the scene around 2100 hours and conferred with the FFI's Captain Perrette. The Germans were holed up in Fort de Champigny, a concrete fortress dating back to just after the Franco-Prussian War. The two captains figured the Germans were holding out to avoid surrendering to the FFI. An American party advanced to the fort under a flag of truce, only to duck for cover when the enemy opened fire. Battalion ordered Captain Crocker to pull back to a cross-roads and try again in the morning.[35]

Near midnight the *Luftwaffe* raided the Bois de Vincennes and the Seine River bridges, as if to remind the regiment's troops that the war was not over. The bombing failed to injure anyone but narrowly missed a large ammunition dump. It did have one effect—the 2nd Battalion relocated its CP the next day to a nearby fort that had "a very secure bomb shelter."[36]

Captain Crocker's team and the FFI scouted Fort de Champigny again the next morning. It was empty. As so often happened, the Germans used the cover of night to slip away.[37]

The 12th Infantry remained in Paris on August 27 to guard the Seine River bridges while the rest of the Ivy Division moved out to the northern suburbs.[38]

As Bill and his men dug in that evening, a torrential storm blew over the Bois de Vincennes and drenched them. It was August but the rain still chilled them to the bone. What a let down from the warm hotel rooms, free drinks, and kisses from two nights before!

Bill and an enlisted man shared time with an entrenching tool, lifting spade loads of mud out of their miserable foxhole. After the young officer dug down a couple of feet, the soldier jumped into the hole to take his place. The soldier tossed a few more spades of mud then looked up at Bill, rain drops splattering his face. "You know, lieutenant, I wouldn't put a dog out in weather like this...but that son of a bitch Eisenhower has four million of us out here!"

A warning order arrived early the next morning, August 28, advising the regiment to prepare to move out. Bill's battalion would march from the Paris park on foot at 1100 hours. "Everyone hated to leave, but as far as we were concerned, the war was still a long way from being over."[39]

CHAPTER TEN

PURSUIT

Tramping eastward through the streets of Paris on a warm August day put an unexpected strain on CT 12's infantrymen. For the past two weeks, they had moved by truck. Now the veterans had to reacquaint themselves with the ground-pounding routine of Normandy days while the replacements got their first taste of a foot march. One of the regiment's lieutenants watched the troops adjust. "[The] men had stashed bottles of wine, loaves of bread, jars of jam under their shirts. It was a very hot and humid day. The farther we walked, the hotter it got, and more bread, jam, and wine ended up on the road."[1]

The machine gun platoons had their own jeeps. With little threat of running into the enemy, Bill had the gun squads mounted to serve as air guards. He walked, something he dreaded because he had developed a severe case of hemorrhoids. He wondered if he could handle the pain while marching for miles but he toughed it out.

The 2nd Battalion crossed to the north side of the Marne River near the huge railroad marshaling yard at Chelles. They spent the remainder of the day marching east-northeast to a position just beyond Villevaude. The Germans left a rear guard in a fortified house in the town but the artillery drove them off before the infantry arrived.[2]

CT 12 issued a verbal attack order and overlay the next morning, August 29. The 2nd and 3rd Battalions advanced abreast at 1000 hours in a northeasterly direction. Apart from a scrape with an enemy outpost, the attack proved to be no more than a simple foot march on paved roads. The battalion turned north at the village of Charny. By this time, sixty men had fallen out for blisters and sore feet. Happily for Bill, the seventeen-kilometer march cured his hemorrhoids. He theorized that the constant friction rubbed away the inflammation and cauterized the sores. The rest of the battalion limped along and rounded up twenty to thirty German stragglers on the way through le Plessis-l'-Évêque. They ended their day on a wooded ridge about a mile short of St. Soupplets.[3]

The Ivy Division's zone of action followed the double-track rail line running between Paris and Saint-Quentin. That pointed the division toward Belgium, not Germany. Bill and his buddies had no way of knowing that a power struggle within the highest echelons of the Allied command had dictated the division's direction.

Even as the Allies clamped down on the Germans in the Falaise-Argentan Pocket, British General Montgomery opened the battle over grand strategy for operations beyond the Seine River. Montgomery outlined his plan to Lt. Gen. Omar Bradley on August 17. He proposed a single forty-division thrust, "so strong that it need fear nothing," that would go through the lowlands north of the Ardennes, into Germany's Ruhr Valley, and, eventually, onto Berlin. Given that Montgomery's 21st Army Group lacked the strength for this ambitious mission, he would take half of Bradley's 12th Army Group. To ensure adequate fuel and supplies for this thrust, Monty envisioned that the rest of Bradley's army group and Lt. Gen. Jacob Devers's newly arrived 6th Army Group would halt their advances. He also insisted that, for his plan to succeed, it required a single ground-forces commander—himself.[4]

Bradley met Monty's proposal with a grim silence that Monty took as concurrence. Quite the contrary, Bradley was aghast. The "narrow thrust" looked more fitting for a penetration than a pursuit. Further-more, a five hundred-mile drive across numerous rivers, canals, and flood plains would have left a huge exposed flank, ripe for a major German counterattack. Worst of all, Montgomery's plan idled half of the Allied force—the American half. Bradley favored the original "broad front" plan of two major assaults into Germany, one north of the Ardennes by Montgomery and one south of the Ardennes by his army group. For the next week, debate raged within the Allied high command over the "single thrust" versus the "broad front" strategy and Monty's attempts to retain overall command of Allied ground forces.[5]

The issue came to a head during Eisenhower's visit to Montgomery's "Tac HQ": in Condé-sur-Noireau on August 23. Eisenhower held firm to the broad front approach. Patton's Third Army would continue its advance toward Metz and link up with Lt. Gen. Alexander Patch's Seventh Army, part of Devers's army group, that was driving from the south of France. Eisenhower granted two major concessions. First, he designated the 21st Army Group's push into Belgium and the Netherlands as the Allied main effort. Second, he agreed to redirect Lt. Gen. Courtney Hodges's First Army on a northerly course to protect Montgomery's flank. On one key point, Eisenhower did not give an inch. He, not Montgomery, would serve as the overall ground forces commander.[6]

Montgomery vented his frustrations at Eisenhower's decision to Field Marshal Alan Brooke, Chief of the Imperial General Staff. "We are throwing overboard the principle of concentration of effort." Such petulance was unwarranted. Montgomery still controlled a twenty-eight-division force and Ike gave it top priority for fuel and ammunition. He had the resources for a full-blown thrust into Germany. As General Bradley stated, "Everything now depended on how aggressively Monty conducted the pursuit."[7]

The 12th Infantry resumed its march on August 30, oblivious to the generals' quarrel. With fuel at a premium and many of the Army's trucks diverted to the urgent resupply problem, the battalion stayed on foot. The machine gun crews rode on jeeps but Bill walked up front with the leading rifle platoons, the best place to decide how the machine guns should react to a meeting engagement with the enemy. The men trudged through two uneventful days, heading northeast.[8]

The division and regiment had cavalry and motorized scout patrols ahead of the main force to spot any delay positions or roadblocks. That allowed the companies to march at a steady pace. The rifle companies set a daily goal that became a motto for the campaign. "March fifteen miles—kill three Germans." In reality, blisters and tedium were the main opponents. Bill discovered something during these tiresome days on foot—he learned how to sleep while marching. At least his brain got a little rest even if his feet did not.

Other leaders, besides Bill, suffered from sleep deprivation. The officers and non-coms marched all day with the troops but spent hours every evening laying out defensive positions, securing resupply for the men, and receiving orders for the next day. They had to rise before dawn to organize their units for movement and possible action. Getting only two hours of sleep tended to make some of them grumpy. Captain Crocker earned a reputation for being particularly difficult to wake up. Bill, who was frequently attached to G Company, had to shake the captain to awaken him on several mornings. Most mornings Crocker just complained or swore but one time he pulled a knife and swung it at Bill. After that, Bill and the other lieutenants resorted to poking the drowsy captain with a chair.

The 2nd Battalion entered the Forêt de Retz by mid-afternoon on August 31 and climbed its steep ridgeline. While passing the rail line, troops discovered caches of German ammunition. Probing deeper, they found a vast quantity of small arms, tank and artillery rounds stockpiled in huts. The S-2 figured it was sufficient to supply an entire German army. Veterans, like Bill, marveled at the change in the campaign. In Normandy, German infantrymen refused to budge from defensive positions unless the Americans blasted them out. In northern France, the enemy fled so fast they failed to carry off mountains of precious supplies.[9]

The footsore infantrymen got a break the next day, September 1. General Barton gave orders to increase the tempo of the chase by moving the men on trucks. The new orders gave the regiment a deep objective,

Valenciennes, over one hundred kilometers to the north. Bill and his platoon mounted on jeeps and trucks at 1500 hours for the advance. The column jumped the Aisne River unopposed at Vic-sur-Aisne and pressed forward to Nampcel by evening. The German Army had planned to establish a defensive line along the Somme and Aisne Rivers, called the Kitzinger Line, but they abandoned the idea when they ran out of time to prepare positions.[10]

Riding on trucks, jeeps, tanks, and tank destroyers, the men of CT 12 bounded over Mont de Choisy on September 2. They passed through Cuts then came to a stop at Bretigny where the Germans had blown the bridge over the Oise River. A platoon from the 4th Engineers immediately went to work on the bridge. A few hours later the regiment headed north on the road from Appilly and wound around Mont de Grandru. CT 12 drove to Berlancourt then angled northeast all the way to Saint-Quentin, following the east bank of a canal. The battalion staff aptly summarized the pursuit, "No fighting—just riding through one cheering town after another."[11]

Near the village of Contescourt, the tankers of B Company, 70th Tank Battalion scanned a parallel road to the east and spotted a German column of "vehicles, troops and horse-drawn carts and wagons" retreating toward Saint-Quentin. The German army still relied on horse carts for logistical support. The Shermans lobbed HE rounds on the enemy, out to a range of 3,000 to 4,000 meters. The 75mm shells exploded within the file of wagons and trucks. Vehicles burst into flames and wounded horses screamed. Panicked soldiers ran for cover. Drivers hit the gas or whipped the draft animals to get out from under this storm of fire. The tankers lit up the retreating Germans until they hustled out of range.[12]

Later that afternoon the 2nd Battalion entered Saint-Quentin and set off another celebration. The townspeople responded joyously to liberation. "The usual welcome of flowers, bread, apples and any foodstuffs available, prevailed." One of the attached tankers observed, "The whole city was rocking with liberation parties."[13]

The soldiers also saw proof of the deprivation the French suffered under German occupation. The retreating German supply column left several dead horses behind. The minute the Americans entered the city, the townspeople rushed from their homes and slaughtered the carcasses. By the next morning only the head of one horse remained, and someone was rinsing that in a fountain.[14]

The celebrations in Paris and Saint-Quentin bookended an amazing advance beyond the Seine River. The 12th Infantry had travelled 150 kilometers in six days with little enemy contact. The march left the men exhausted but exhilarated. In Normandy, they had left a body every ten meters. After Paris, the regiment covered twenty-five kilometers a day with barely a scratch.

The electrifying advance could not continue. The First Army's northward axis threatened to pinch off the 21st Army Group's zone of action against the English Channel. Of greater concern, elements of the First Army had begun running out of gas—literally. Early on September 3, General Barton ordered the 12th Infantry to halt and await instructions. Bill's battalion spent that day and the next establishing a defensive position west of the city at Francilly-Selency. A change in the strategic situation gave the men a two-day reprieve from marching.[15]

On the day CT 12 captured Saint-Quentin, Eisenhower approved a plan to reorient the First Army's attack to the northeast, though it still had to protect Field Marshal Montgomery's right flank. Patton's Third Army would continue its attack south of the Ardennes. To cover the widening gap between the two armies General Hodges committed General Gerow's V Corps to attack through the Ardennes. The plan forced Gerow to stop his northward movement and redirect his three divisions (4th and 28th Infantry and 5th Armored) east toward the German frontier via Belgium and Luxembourg.[16]

The enemy strategy also shifted while the 12th Infantry drove on Saint-Quentin. On August 31 General Jodl, *OKW* chief of staff, finally focused Hitler's attention to the dire situation on the Western Front. Jodl convinced the Fuhrer of the necessity to prepare a defensive line along Germany's western border. Hitler reappointed Field Marshal von Rundstedt to command *OB West* and ordered him to coordinate the defense of the "West Wall," a series of fortifications that the Allies dubbed the

"Siegfried Line." The Germans now allocated manpower and material to rehabilitate these fortifications, which they had abandoned after their 1940 victories in France and the Low Countries. Von Rundstedt pulled together what forces he could to delay the Allied surge while the repairs took place. He noted that many formations lacked vehicles, weapons, and men but still had functioning headquarters. Using them, *OB West* started rebuilding its depleted units. Von Rundstedt anticipated that the Allied advance would eventually lose steam due to logistical shortages, long enough, he hoped, for the Germans to complete their defensive preparations. He advised Hitler that the West Wall's defense would be ready by late October. The Allies would hit the Siegfried Line much sooner than that.[17]

The trucks showed up in Saint-Quentin in the early morning of September 5. Bill and his men climbed aboard the deuce-and-a-halves and their own jeeps for a long road march to the Meuse River. The convoy motored east across northern France, taking the regiment to its new zone of action. Screened by the 38th Cavalry Squadron, CT 12 rumbled through Guise, la Cappelle, and Hirson without incident. The route continued east past the fortress city of Rocroi where 301 years earlier the great French commander, le Duc d'Enghien (then all of twenty-one years old), defeated Spain's vaunted Army of Flanders, a victory that heralded the coming supremacy of France and set him on his way to earning the moniker—*le Grand Conde*. The 2nd Battalion's 130-kilometer road march ended at the town of Fumay, a small town sitting inside a loop of the Meuse River.[18]

The men hopped off the trucks at 1745 hours, glad to finally stretch their legs. The cavalry secured Fumay the day before and the engineers had already replaced the bridge over the river. The rifle companies and H Company's machine gun platoons hurried over the pontoon bridge then started setting up outposts on the far side of the Meuse.[19]

An urgent call from the 38th Cavalry interrupted their preparations. The cavalrymen had pushed east from the river into the Ardennes foothills. They caught up with the retreating Germans in the town of Hargnies adjacent to the Belgian border. The Americans had chased German infantry from the town but an *SS* unit with four tanks counterattacked. At 1821 hours the regiment ordered the 2nd Battalion to help the cavalry retake Hargnies.[20]

The battalion hustled on foot from the east bank of the Meuse up the slopes of the wooded bluffs. Bill and his men got their first taste of the Ardennes when they had to climb five hundred feet in elevation through the thick Bois de la Houssiere. By the time the infantrymen reached the scene, the cavalrymen had already driven the Germans from the town with help from the 42nd Artillery Battalion.[21]

As battle hardened as the men were, what they saw in Hargnies tore at their hearts and filled them with rage. Smoke filled the town and dazed civilians wandered about, some sobbing in anguish. Bodies littered the streets. Before retreating, the *SS* troops had fired the town. Entire families perished after the Germans herded the townspeople into their homes then set the houses ablaze. The *SS* gunned down or slit the throats of anyone who tried to escape. Bill and his men had seen plenty of brutality in the preceding months but they had not witnessed wholesale atrocity before. The troops now saw for themselves the depraved nature of the enemy they fought.[22]

CT 12 had to adapt to different terrain in the Ardennes. Gone were the expansive plains and gentle rivers of Picardy, replaced by steeply carved stream valleys covered with oak and pine. Narrow roads ran under an almost solid canopy of leaves and conifer needles. Small, quaint towns, situated within pockets of cleared land, dotted the Ardennes creating an overall feel of "country like the illustrations for Grimm's Fairy Tales only a lot grimmer." The dense forests also confined vehicles to soggy roads and provided the Germans with plenty of natural material for hasty obstacles.[23]

Colonel Luckett configured CT 12 for pursuit operations into this terrain on September 6. He formed two columns to attack along separate routes deep into enemy territory. Luckett assigned 2nd Battalion the southern avenue and attached cavalry, tanks, tank destroyers, and an artillery battery to give Colonel Sibert what he needed to attack independently. CT 12 launched into Belgium at 0900 hours. Luckett planned an aggressive thrust to the east but the promised trucks and tanks stayed back in the division motor pool—lack of fuel. The infantry advanced on foot behind Troop A of the 38ᵗʰ Cavalry.

The Germans only fought delaying actions, as they would for most of the next week. The *SS* commander had five tanks, eleven halftracks, and a couple hundred infantrymen, enough to put up a considerable fight. However, with no replacements on the way, he had to preserve this small force. The retreating Germans blew up several bridges across the Huille River on the 2ⁿᵈ Battalion's route, slowing the American advance. The combat vehicles had to wait until the engineers replaced the missing span at Willerzie, Belgium before continuing their push. As they did, German tanks took potshots at them from the neighboring town of Rienne.[24]

G Company reinforced Troop A as it maneuvered against the enemy tanks and infantry in Rienne. The Battalion Assistant S-3, moving with G Company, reported, "We entered from the west just as the cavalry patrol entered from the south and both of us watched an enemy tank disappear in the distance." The *SS* force pulled back to Gedinne three kilometers farther east. Late in the day Colonel Sibert developed a plan to bag the *SS* rear guard. He posted all the battalion's anti-tank weapons and attached tank destroyers on the east side of Rienne while sending the cavalry in a wide flanking maneuver to the south. He planned to create "a shooting gallery" once the cavalry flushed the enemy tanks and halftracks from Gedinne, but the onset of darkness delayed the operation until morning. By then the "masters of escape" had pulled out of Gedinne, confounding Sibert's plan.[25]

This scenario played out repeatedly, as noted by an *SS* commander. "Only the arrival of darkness, in which the enemy almost never fought, enabled all of the elements of the regiment to escape encirclement." The Germans felt bewildered by the American habit of halting at sundown but grateful. "[W]e often wondered why their strong motorized forces never attempted to drive east and northeast during darkness just as unconcernedly as our forces had done in the opposite direction in 1939 and 1940."[26]

High-level American doctrine concerning the pursuit encouraged "relentless pressure" to accomplish "the annihilation of hostile forces." It also urged pursuit during hours of darkness. "The enemy's attempts to organize his retreat under the cover of darkness must be frustrated. Under no circumstances must he be allowed to break contact. Units which have advanced without serious opposition continue their march during the night." However, battalion-level doctrine on pursuit operations only recommended "limited objective night attacks" for "disrupting" an enemy's withdrawal. The resulting failure of the Americans to mount even limited night attacks gave the Germans time to withdraw and reorganize.[27]

The 12th Infantry got a temporary commander on September 6 to allow the colonel ten days of leave. The division brought in Colonel Robert H. Chance to run the regiment during Jim Luckett's absence.[28]

As they drove deeper into the Ardennes, the Americans relied increasingly on local citizens to navigate the trails and track enemy movements. The Belgian Resistance provided a steady stream of intelligence on the Germans' whereabouts. Nearly every cavalry unit had Belgians, many of them army veterans, riding in their combat vehicles. As soon as the 12th Infantry seized a town, local Belgians secured the area, including the wide gaps between the advancing columns. They did not restrict themselves to aiding the Americans. The *Der Fuhrer Regiment's* commander reported "growing terrorist activities" behind German lines. "Runners were shot at, and large quantities of iron hooks were strewn on the roads in order to puncture tires."[29]

The Germans retaliated against the Belgians. During a reconnaissance mission to a Belgian village, Bill noticed a woman sitting on her porch with her children. When the battalion later drove the Germans out of the village his platoon passed the same house. He saw the woman still sitting on her porch but noticed that she was not cheering like the rest of the townspeople. She remained motionless. Bill discovered that the Germans had slit her throat.[30]

With the Germans gone from Gedinne, the 2nd Battalion resumed its foot march to the east through a steady, chilling rain on September 7.

The 38th Cavalry stayed a step ahead reporting roadblocks and chasing off the enemy rear guard. The attached engineers made quick work of the abatis thrown up by the enemy, although some were booby-trapped. The battalion managed steady progress throughout the day. For Bill and his men, moving through the Ardennes took on the character of the march across northern France. *March fifteen miles—kill three Germans.* It still put a strain on the troops. Bill's crews had to hoist the M1917A1s and tripods as they trudged mile after mile in rain-soaked uniforms. Their mud-caked boots felt as heavy as anvils. At every halt, they scraped off the muck with sticks or bayonets. The advance stopped at twilight in Transinne. While Bill set up his firing points for the evening, the regiment's S-2 distributed some interesting intelligence. One of the German stragglers picked up during the day told his interrogators that the *Der Fuhrer Regiment* was down to a mere five hundred men who had to forage for supplies as they retreated.[31]

The action on September 8 followed the same pattern. The Germans fell back toward the Ourthe River and the rain fell steadily. The cavalry did most of the work to keep the Germans back-pedaling, often bypassing the hasty obstacles. The rifle companies and engineers pushed through the numerous abatis and roadblocks that barely slowed the advance because of their poor construction. The main body marched through Smuid and by late afternoon approached the town of St. Hubert, their objective for the day. Intelligence alerted the battalion that the Germans still held St. Hubert, so Colonel Sibert prepared a deliberate attack. He sent G Company straight up the road toward the town center while E Company looped around to the north onto high ground overlooking the objective. Bill's platoon moved forward with one of the two attacking companies, but its firepower was not needed. The Germans fled before the battalion assaulted. The infantrymen entered St. Hubert "to receive the usual quota of champagne, cognac, bread, and fruits, which led to the usual celebrations."[32]

CT 12 planned an easy day for the 2nd Battalion on September 9. The men only had to march twelve kilometers to the six-forks crossroad village of Champlon. The cavalry screened the route for the infantry and reduced several roadblocks. The battalion started its movement at 0905 hours, heading northeast on the highway to La Roche-en-Ardenne. They had to cross heavily wooded and swampy terrain through the Foret de Freyr but the march went well. By 1100 hours the main body had passed the halfway checkpoint despite the chilling rain. Pleased by the progress, the regiment told Colonel Sibert to extend the movement another eleven kilometers to La Roche-en-Ardenne where the highway crossed the Ourthe River.[33]

Things got more interesting that afternoon when the 38th Cavalry discovered "a strong enemy force" in La Roche. Colonel Sibert sent scouts and artillery observers forward to get a sense of the battlefield. The reports from the front provided encouraging news. The Ourthe River carved a steep gorge in this part of the Ardennes. The main part of La Roche nestled within a loop of the river on the far (eastern) bank. The cavalry identified four enemy tanks and about 150 infantrymen holding La Roche. The German infantry occupied a medieval castle sitting across the river just above the town. The highway bridge crossed the river from the south side within view of the castle's ramparts. The German force appeared to hold a formidable position for disputing a river crossing, except for the dominating high ground on the near (western) bank where tall bluffs stood three hundred feet above La Roche. H Company and the battalion Anti-Tank (AT) Platoon rushed onto the escarpment. Bill positioned his four guns with near perfect fields of fire and issued instructions to the section leaders. "Range 700. First Section, castle wall. Second Section, houses far side of river. Suppress enemy weapons." At that range, they could lay direct fire on the heads of the Germans, even the ones inside the castle.[34]

The assault kicked off at 1800 hours under the "withering fire of machine guns and mortar shells." The heavy weapons on the bluff plastered the Germans. The rifle companies put their own machine guns in the windows of hotels and houses across the river and rained more fire on the defenders. G Company, reinforced with platoons of tanks and tank destroyers, led the drive into La Roche from the south. The instant the Germans started firing, Bill's squads showered them with suppressive fire. Watching their magenta tracers, the gunners walked their rounds right into enemy firing positions or individual windows. The Assistant S-3 admired the action from an OP on the bluff. "Every time a German opened up, he got everything from rifle to three-inch shells right back." With Bill's machine guns clearing the defenders off the castle's battlements and the mortars pouring rounds behind its walls, the Germans gave up. "Lots of Germans ran, and lots are still there." The Germans blew up the highway bridge but failed to collapse it into the river. The rifle companies stormed across the broken spans, with help from the engineers, and captured the castle. The heavy machine guns and 57mm AT guns raked the Germans as they pulled out of the river town. From their vantage point, the American gunners fired on the retreating Germans until they climbed over the eastern bluffs 1,500 meters away.[35]

The battle provided a welcome moment of excitement after so many days of dogging the enemy. When the battalion finally caught up with the fleeing Germans, they routed them and captured La Roche without suffering a single casualty. Bill described it as a "sharp decisive battle."[36]

As soon as the firing stopped, "the people came out with the customary methods of thanks." Bill moved his platoon across the river to occupy positions in La Roche. While he bedded down his men, an old lady approached the young lieutenant and asked him to stay at her house for the evening. He accepted, welcoming the chance to spend a night out of the rain.[37]

Bill would remember his time in the Belgian home, not for its comfort, but for the lesson he learned about the Aryan race's cruel mindset. The old lady shared the house with her daughter and five-year-old granddaughter. The local SS commandant had forced the younger woman, a widow, to serve as his concubine while the Germans occupied La Roche.[38]

Inside the house Bill noticed that the young woman and child fidgeted and hung back in the shadows. At first, he thought his dirty, unshaven appearance might be frightening them but then the little girl asked him a question. "Are the Nazis coming back?"

Bill picked up the girl and sat her on his lap. "No, the Germans are gone forever." Despite his reassurance the girl and her mother still trembled. "Why are you still afraid?"

The young woman explained that the SS commandant told her not to talk with the Americans.

"Look, we've taken Belgium and we're sure not going to give it back. You don't need to be worried about the Germans anymore."

The young woman still shook with fear then related what the SS officer said before he left town. "We're going now but when we come back—and we will be back in three months—if I find out that you've spoken to the Americans, I'll shoot your daughter." The SS officer then left the terrorized woman and fled toward Germany.

Three months later, during the Ardennes counteroffensive, the Germans retook La Roche-en-Ardenne. When news of the German counteroffensive reached Bill, he could not help but note that the SS officer's promise had been better than his. "Damn those krauts!"[39]

The tiresome pursuit resumed September 10, but the regiment changed its plan of attack. Instead of using two avenues of advance, the regiment put all three battalions in column. The 2nd Battalion was supposed to lead the attack, but once the engineers completed bridge repairs the regiment switched the order of march. The 1st Battalion passed through Colonel Sibert's battalion and led the advance from La Roche northeast along the highway. The 2nd Battalion followed them through Samree to Fraiture, again on foot. They reached their objective at 2100 hours and settled in without any enemy contact.[40]

Expecting resistance along the Salm River, the regiment split the attack back into two avenues of advance the following day. The 1st Battalion took the direct route east toward Salmchateau while the 2nd Battalion moved on a more southerly course through Bihain and Petite Langlir. Bill's platoon, along with the rifle companies, slogged all day on secondary roads and trails that had turned to slush. September 11 was looking like one of those "March fifteen miles—kill three Germans" type of days. The battalion's route aimed for a crossing of the Salm River by the rail station at Cierreux. The lead elements drove off a German security outpost on the high ground west of the river around 1700 hours. Colonel Sibert sent F Company across the river while the heavy weapons occupied the bluff overlooking the valley. The Germans contested the crossing and briefly pinned down F Company. The Americans did not have any attached tanks or tank destroyers but they still outgunned the Germans with their machine guns and 57mm guns posted on the high bluff and the mortars in defilade. With superior fields of fire, the Americans rained fire on the enemy. By 1945 hours the Germans abandoned the field. The battalion crossed the river and continued its advance. The weary troops set up their nightly defense in Rogery while the 1st Battalion consolidated its crossing site at Salmchateau.[41]

The *Das Reich Division* continued back-pedaling before the Americans but set a defensive line just west of the Our River along the last ridgeline inside Belgium. The 1st and 2nd Battalions moved out by 0800 hours on September 12. The 2nd Battalion attacked east three kilometers to its intermediate objective, the village of Commanster. Meeting no meaningful resistance, the rest of the regiment consolidated with them. At 1345 hours Colonel Chance ordered the attack to continue for another fourteen kilometers. The Germans had an outpost in St. Vith on the 1st Battalion's line of march but, with the help of the cavalry and fighter-bombers, the Americans drove them out. Bill's battalion, advancing south of St. Vith, had smooth sailing all the way to Schlierbach. They helped 1st Battalion occupy Schlierbach, then set up their defense for the night.[42]

The battalion history sounded almost regretful about the lack of action. "The fun was taking place on our left, where the [1st] Battalion was liberating St. Vith." That night the *Das Reich Division* retreated to the Siegfried Line.[43]

The 12th Infantry had pushed to within a few kilometers of the German border and a mere eleven kilometers from the Siegfried Line. The men noticed fewer cheers and waves from the civilians than in previous days. This part of Belgium had been claimed by Germany after 1940 and many native Germans had settled in the area. In St. Vith, the *Burgermeister* and town officials, all of whom were ethnic Germans, fled along with the retreating *SS* troops. An Ivy Division officer observed "that people were very sullen and hostile; many of the women crying; there was also a look of dazed incredulity."[44]

The order for September 13 called for a modest advance of ten kilometers, intentionally stopping short of the German fortifications. The short movement stemmed from the concerns of First Army Commander General Hodges about the acute shortage of fuel and ammunition. If the Germans defended the Siegfried Line, he worried that his troops lacked the necessary ammunition, especially artillery shells, to prosecute a successful attack. Hodges enjoined the V Corps from launching a deliberate attack against the Siegfried Line before September 14. The regiment's attack order for September 13 reflected the over-arching logistical constraints. "It is desired that a heavy engagement involving a major expenditure of artillery ammunition be avoided...Forward advance will be so limited so that combat vehicles will always have sufficient gasoline on hand to fight and replenish."[45]

The 2nd Battalion got off to a leisurely start at 1015 hours. They trailed the 1st Battalion in column to a crossing site on the Our River near Roagen, Belgium. The troops continued hiking a forest trail to the east. At 1330 hours the battalion discovered a stone marker that denoted the German border. A lot of the men paid their respects by spitting or pissing on the boundary stone as they entered Germany for the first time. They passed through Mutzenich on the way to Radscheid, their objective for the day. Before reaching Radscheid, the Germans fired artillery at the column. The incoming rounds failed to hit anyone but it made the men wonder. *How long had it been since the Germans employed any artillery?*[46]

One month had passed since the 12th Infantry pulled out of Mortain. In the intervening weeks, Bill and his compatriots had covered vast distances and shared the euphoria of liberation. The nightmare of Normandy had receded. Strength and fighting spirit had returned. Having reached German territory, the men felt a sense of accomplishment and optimism about the approaching battle for the enemy's homeland. After weeks of facing feeble and disorganized enemy resistance, the 4th Infantry Division's staff anticipated a quick campaign to finish the war.

"Everyone now believes the war is practically over. The longest current estimate of the time it will take us to go through the Siegfried Line is three days after which we will do no more serious fighting. Some say we will do it in 24 hours."[47]

The battalion's position near Radscheid put them on the hillside opposite the Siegfried Line. That night Colonel Sibert sent out a strong patrol to test its defenses in preparation for a full scale attack the next morning. The V Corps intended to hit the Germans with all three of its divisions spread across a broad front, the same configuration used during the pursuit. The plan indicated that the corps believed it could smash through the German line without planning a penetration. General Barton also expected to find only a thin crust defending the Siegfried Line and pinned his hopes on breaking through using the division's momentum.[48]

To everyone's dismay, the next several days upended these rosy predictions. If Mortain had become known as the 12th Infantry's most savage battle, the upcoming battle would certainly go down as its most disheartening.

CHAPTER ELEVEN

SCHNEE EIFEL

N ot nearly as elaborate as the French Maginot line, Nazi Germany's Siegfried Line consisted mostly of bunkers with interlocking fields of fire, stretching from the Dutch border to the Swiss frontier. The fortifications may not have been intricate, but the individual structures offered amazing protection. The Germans used steel reinforced concrete to construct pillboxes that could house up to twelve men. The walls varied from four to seven feet in thickness. Twelve-inch steel I-beams supported seven-foot-thick concrete roofs. Infantrymen could fire their weapons through embrasures in the concrete walls. If threatened, they could lock themselves inside the bunkers by closing the steel doors guarding the entrance. The heavy construction made the bunkers almost impervious to artillery fire.[1]

The individual bunkers were solid but the Siegfried Line itself was anything but. Had the Allies known its true state they would have been even more confident of a quick breakthrough. Since their victories in 1940, the Germans had neglected the fortifications and the bunkers had fallen into disrepair. Telephone communications to the pillboxes had degraded. Water, food, and medical supplies had disappeared. No protective minefields had been laid. Local civilians had turned some of the bunkers into shelters and potato cellars. Worse yet, the embrasures could not accommodate the MG 42 machine gun and larger caliber anti-tank guns. The *Das Reich Division* had trouble finding some bunkers in its sector because they had become overgrown with vegetation. Many pillbox doors were locked and the division had to send someone to Bitburg, Germany for the keys.[2]

Even the best fortifications are worthless without troops to man them. Everyone assumed the Germans would try to hold the Allies along the last defensible line short of the Rhine River, but one Allied intelligence report estimated they could muster only nineteen divisions, a force far from adequate. Estimates like that convinced Generals Eisenhower, Bradley, and Hodges to continue the offensive and blast through the Siegfried Line before the Germans had a chance to resurrect their shattered army.[3]

The Germans were busy doing exactly that, but it was a haphazard affair. The commander of the *1st SS Panzer Corps* rebuilt his depleted units "by assigning local defense detachments, superfluous personnel from the *Luftwaffe*, and candidates for commissioned and non-commissioned ranks."[4]

The approaching American forces had their own problems. The dash from the Seine River through Belgium stretched the supply line to its limits. The Ivy Division's trucks had to drive sixty miles to the ammunition supply point and 250 miles to the nearest fuel depot. Gasoline had to be rationed. The 12th Infantry's operations orders inserted instructions to maintain enough fuel in all vehicles to be able to displace in case they made contact with the enemy. The most critical shortfall was ammunition. The First Army did not have enough artillery rounds on hand to sustain a battle lasting more than a day, perhaps two. The supply problems and lack of intelligence on the Siegfried Line's condition made General Hodges cautious. First Army's subordinate corps advanced toward Germany on widely separated avenues and a huge gap yawned between First Army and Patton's Third Army. Rather than smash through the border defenses on the run, Hodges ordered the V and VII Corps to pause two days before testing the Siegfried Line. On the other side of the border, the SS commanders felt immense relief for the brief respite. "It was an almost unbelievable stroke of luck that the Americans...halted their attack."[5]

Maj. Gen. Leonard Gerow, V Corps Commander, worried as much about the enormous frontage he had to cover as he did the supply problems. His three divisions had responsibility for a ninety-kilometer front between his northern flank with VII Corps and the Third Army to the south. He also drew the most difficult zone of action, the Ardennes-Eifel, where major obstructions limited mechanized mobility across the German frontier. Allied planners searched for avenues into enemy territory that offered relative freedom of movement for tanks and trucks, what they termed "mobility corridors." The Our, Sauer, and Moselle Rivers carved steep wooded gorges across the Luxembourg-German border except for an eight-kilometer mobility corridor between Vianden and Wallendorf. In the northern part of the corps zone, the Schnee Eifel, a densely forested ridge, ran twenty kilometers across the sector on a southwest-to-northeast axis. Vehicles could use a narrow road that ran along most of its crest but only one decent road crossed over the ridge. The V Corps' best avenue lay southwest of the Schnee Eifel. A twelve-kilometer plateau between the Our River gorge and Brandscheid, near the southern-western tip of the Schnee Eifel, provided a wide mobility corridor through the Siegfried Line. A suitable road network ran from the Belgian border east to the German cities of Prum and Pronsfeld. A third option, the "Losheim Gap," skirted the northern end of the Schnee Eifel on the corps' left flank.

General Gerow ordered the corps to attack on a broad front, rather than concentrate his forces against one of these mobility corridors. He gave each division a sector more than twenty kilometers in width. The corps assigned the 5th Armored Division the isolated Vianden-Wallendorf gap far to the south. Although Gerow had six infantry regiments gathered near the plateau southwest of the Schnee Eifel, he sliced the boundary between the two infantry divisions north of Brandscheid. This decision gave the 28th Infantry Division nearly all the Brandscheid-Habscheid plateau for maneuver, and channeled the 4th Infantry Division straight into the Schnee Eifel. Gerow used a cavalry group to screen the Losheim Gap. The official U.S. Army history correctly assessed this plan's weakness. "The V Corps attack thus began as three separate operations: the 4th Division on the Schnee Eifel, the 28th Division on the plateau southwest of the Schnee Eifel, and the 5th Armored Division far to the south."[6] (See Map VIII)

The Ivy Division had to attack a thickly forested ridge that only had military value as an obstacle. General Barton gave the 22nd Infantry Regimental Combat Team (CT 22) a narrow zone of action that included the only good east-west highway in the division zone that ran between Bleialf, Sellerich, and Prum along the division's southern boundary. Once through the Siegfried Line, CT 22 would move into open terrain behind the Schnee Eifel. Barton ordered CT 12 to punch through the Siegfried Line on the left side of CT 22. After the breach, the 12th Infantry would widen the gap by driving up the length of the Schnee Eifel. Barton kept the 8th Infantry and part of the 70th Tank Battalion in reserve to exploit any success. He set the attack for 1000 hours on September 14, which wasted four hours of daylight and left less time for any follow-through operations.[7]

Unlike Gerow, Barton planned a "penetration" despite the lousy terrain. Army doctrine for a penetration called for "three separate impulses": a break, a widening, and an exploitation. The division order did not specify a main effort, but CT 22 had a narrow zone along the best avenue. CT 12 had an apparent supporting role to maintain the shoulder and expand the breach, and the division retained a large reserve.[8]

Of the two lead regiments, CT 12 had the tougher mission to clear twelve kilometers of enemy pillboxes dotting the steep ridgeline. The dense woods of the Schnee Eifel gave the defenders ample concealment from Allied aircraft and forced the Americans into a series of localized fights. The cool, wet weather made the already marginal roads and trails even more treacherous. Colonel Chance planned to attack with the 1st

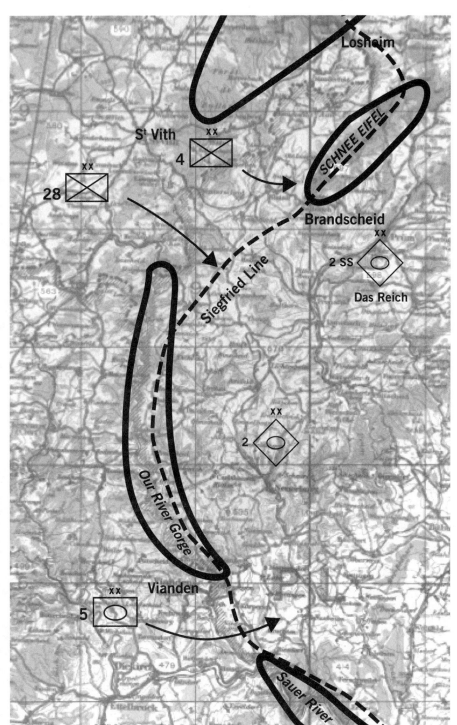

Map VIII

and 2nd Battalions abreast and the 3rd Battalion in reserve. The 2nd Battalion, on the regiment's right flank, would first seize Hill 697 where the Schnee Eifel's crest begins to descend toward its southwestern tip. Its next objective, the lone paved road crossing the Schnee Eifel, lay another six kilometers to the northeast. As with the division's order, CT 12's operations order did not designate a main effort but did reveal Colonel Chance's concerns about controlling movement through the Schnee Eifel. "[Battalions] upon reaching phase lines will halt, report location, reorganize and be prepared to continue the advance on order."[9]

The 2nd Battalion's operation kicked off the evening of September 13 with a platoon-size patrol led by the Assistant S-3, Lieutenant James Piper. Colonel Sibert directed Piper to infiltrate the Siegfried Line east of Radscheid and report on the state of enemy defenses. The patrol made it inside the enemy outpost line by midnight but had trouble spying on the enemy. The darkened forest concealed the pillboxes too well. The patrol had a brief skirmish then settled down to wait for dawn. When daylight arrived, Piper could see the Germans defended the line with a thin force. He contacted the lead elements of the battalion at 0930 hours on September 14 and asked them to pass this intelligence up to Colonel Sibert.[10] (See Map IX)

From Radscheid, the battalion had to cross three kilometers of open ground before hitting the forest edge masking the German fortifications. The battalion's avenue of advance aimed for the point of a pasture jutting into the forest. The attack launched at 1000 hours with F Company leading, followed by G Company. Bill's platoon stayed forward with the rifle companies. The open ground initially worried the Americans but a heavy fog provided concealment and a misty rain suppressed the noise of their movement. The battalion jumped a branch of the Alf River then pushed uphill toward the Schnee Eifel, going straight at the pillboxes on the far side of the fields. The infantrymen snuck forward through the drizzle, hoping to pounce on the unsuspecting Germans. Creeping, creeping, creeping, F Company neared the forest edge.[11]

Without warning the fog lifted, not in a gradual dissipation, but all at once, rising like a theater curtain. One second the Americans were

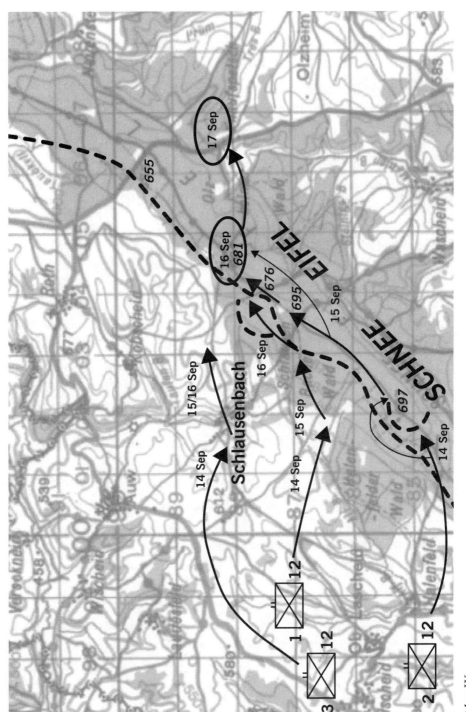

Map IX

cloaked in mist, the next they were standing naked in a field. Instinctively, they hit the ground.

A couple seconds later the startled German outposts opened fire, raking the open fields with machine gun fire. The riflemen got up and charged over the open ground in short rushes as Bill's squads put down suppressive fire.[12]

Luckily for the Americans, they had gotten close enough to the pillboxes to assault before the defenders could fully respond. The Germans had only a light screening force in the area and several bunkers had been left undefended. Those that were manned had only a few light machine guns among them. A few Germans rushed out of their bunkers to man nearby trenches but F Company overwhelmed them. Once the Americans rolled up the outside entrenchments the men inside the pillboxes gave up.[13]

With the initial line of bunkers cleared, F Company climbed northeast toward Hill 697, their initial objective. "The break-through was obviously too swift for the enemy who had abandoned equipment without destroying it." The charging Americans surprised more German troops who they found sauntering on their way to man the pillboxes the battalion had just seized. It took the Germans until early afternoon to organize a line of defense along the crest behind a handful of bunkers. Colonel Sibert reinforced F Company with one platoon of light tanks and another of Shermans and ordered them to pen the defenders inside the pillboxes. He then sent G Company with an equal force of tanks around the flank. The envelopment caught the Germans by surprise. "The attack was perfectly coordinated and the simultaneous heavy fire from front and rear demoralized the Nazis." The tanks fired at the bunker apertures while the infantry closed in. Troops crawled forward to place pole charges (satchels packed with TNT attached to a long pole) against the doors or embrasures, then blasted the openings. Once the pole charges went off, the Germans quickly surrendered. Resistance collapsed. "In approximately twenty minutes the attack cleared an area 200 yards wide by 1800 yards long containing seven pillboxes. One hundred and fifty prisoners were taken and approximately seventy-five enemy were killed."[14]

The battalion consolidated on Hill 697 by 1800 hours. "The C.P. was set up in a captured pillbox; the Siegfried Line was breached." Piece of cake. Bill spent the remaining daylight and evening hours positioning his machine guns to repel potential counterattacks. Back in the rear the intelligence staff sifted through the odd mix of *Hitler Jugend*, old men, *SS*, *Luftwaffe*, cadets, security, and artillery troops bagged by the battalion, evidence that the Germans were scraping the bottom of the manpower barrel.[15]

What did not happen late on September 14 had as great an impact on the battle as what did. Army doctrine for a "penetration" called for vigorous follow-up to any initial success. "In case of a break-through, armored units penetrate deeply into the hostile position and attack the enemy's reserves, artillery, and command and signal communication centers." No one chose to shove an exploitation force through the gap opened by 2nd Battalion. General Barton only expected CT 12 to secure the flank of a breach. Earlier in the day he had imposed a limit on its advance "until gas and ammo supplies are straightened out." Colonel Sibert seemed content to tie-in with the adjacent unit of CT 22, secure the battalion's forward position, and focus on the next day's advance.[16]

General Barton had reasons for not committing his reserve into the gap created by CT 12. The 22nd Infantry had not cleared Brandscheid and Sellerich, near the lone highway, and the forest trails in the 12th Infantry's sector were hardly suitable for an armored force. Yet, CT 12's quick puncture of the Siegfried Line convinced him that he only faced a thin German defense. Barton turned his attention north to the Losheim Gap, where open farmland bypassed the northern end of the Schnee Eifel and provided a quick route over the Kyll River headwaters. Rather than cram the 8th Infantry through the narrow Schnee Eifel gap, Barton sent it north. He then ordered CT 12 to continue attacking up the length of the Schnee Eifel and join CT 8 at its northern end. This order channeled the regiment up the long dimension of the fortified line, instead of crossing over and turning it.[17]

Colonel Chance expected September 15 to be a day of mopping up pockets of German resistance while taking out the line of bunkers on the

Schnee Eifel. Because the 1ˢᵗ Battalion held a position north of the 2ⁿᵈ Battalion, he chose to move it up to the crest road then turn it northeast to lead the attack. Colonel Sibert's battalion would follow the 1ˢᵗ in column. Chance kept the 3ʳᵈ Battalion in reserve near the town of Schlausenbach. The real chore fell to Company B of the 4ᵗʰ Engineers to demolish the captured pillboxes. The engineers learned through trial and error that it took four hundred pounds of TNT to completely destroy one bunker.[18]

Bill and his men got an early start. They moved out with the rifle companies by 0800 hours under a steady drizzle dripping from the leafy canopy. In this part of the Schnee Eifel, the crest road, little more than a dirt trail, turned to slop. The poor conditions of the lone supply route and dense woods kept the platoon's jeeps in the rear and forced the machine gun squads to carry all their ammunition. The gloomy forest limited fields of fire to only a few meters, so the machine gunners stayed upfront with the rifle platoons. The lead company had hardly deployed before word came back from the recon platoon. The early movement caught the enemy by surprise. The scouts captured a few Germans eating their breakfast.[19]

Despite the early success, the regiment's plan soon ran into trouble. The 1ˢᵗ Battalion, marching from the west, stumbled upon a defended pillbox before it gained the crest. Colonel Chance, not wanting to get bogged down, ordered the 2ⁿᵈ Battalion to take over the lead. Colonel Sibert sent G Company forward to the crossroads where the crest road intersected a narrow road coming from Schlausenbach (CR 695). Before they got to it, G Company hit a bunker held by sixty German infantrymen. The Americans quickly suppressed then flanked the enemy pillbox. The action did not significantly hold up the battalion but it triggered German artillery. Shells started raining on the narrow crest road, the battalion's critical supply route.[20]

G Company advanced beyond the crossroads and ran into another bunker only three hundred meters past CR 695. By now German artillery and mortar fire interdicted the crest road, preventing supply trucks and tanks from going forward. While G Company engaged the German pillbox, Colonel Sibert had F Company bypass the enemy pocket and lead the advance to the next crossroads (CR 676). Soon F Company started taking small arms and artillery fire. The incoming artillery shells, armed with quick fuses, exploded on contact with the treetops. These "tree bursts" showered the American infantry with shrapnel and splinters. Hemingway described the effect. "The tree bursts were like javelins in the half-light of the forest." By 1350 hours F Company had only made it halfway to CR 676, though they had captured thirty PWs during the short advance. With both G and F Companies tied up in sharp fights, Colonel Sibert realized that the battalion had a full-scale battle on its hands, not the mopping up operation he anticipated.[21]

A better intelligence picture began to emerge on September 15. CT 12 faced elements of the *Das Reich Division*, a unit that had been ground down to a fraction of its original strength. The Germans had slapped together a hodge-podge of replacements, including men recently discharged from hospitals, to fill the voids. These reinforcements had widely varying capabilities but they fought effectively under the command and control of *Battalion Weber*, part of the *3rd Panzergrenadier "Deutschland" Regiment.*[22]

Figuring the German defense centered on the crest of the Schnee Eifel, Sibert formulated a plan to envelop the enemy by sending E Company to seize the crossroads at Hill 681 (CR 681) in the Germans' rear. The 3rd Battalion had already sent K Company from Schlausenbach to seize CR 681 from the west but it had been stopped by a German counterattack shortly after noon. Sibert thought he could reach the crossroads by swinging around the east side of the ridge. Once E Company seized the intersection, he hoped to crush the defenders by trapping them between his forces at CR 676 and CR 681. To give the attack more firepower, the battalion pulled Bill's platoon from the front and attached it to E Company.[23]

First Lt. Martin MacDiarmid led E Company off the crest and down the eastern slope of the Schnee Eifel around 1600 hours. Once below the top of the ridge and out of the reach of enemy small arms fire, the company turned northeast. Staying on the slope, E Company and Bill's platoon walked the contour line past the German position. The infantrymen struggled to keep their feet through the damp woodland, especially Bill's crews who carried heavy-barreled guns and tripods. With only a few unmarked forest trails to guide them, the Americans hugged the slope and tried to stay on the same elevation. Around 1830 hours they hit a trail that led them uphill toward the crossroads. The men took turns bounding forward. One man watched while his buddy charged a few paces up the slope. The riflemen rushed from tree to tree, working their way to the summit. E Company swept over CR 681 with barely a shot fired.

Bill immediately deployed his squads to establish security on the objective and block German egress from CR 676. The crest road, in either direction, posed the greatest threat. The dirt road from Schlausenbach had to be guarded, too. A German force had already blocked K Company's advance along this road a few hundred meters to their west. Bill and E Company's light machine gun section leader had to coordinate the positions of the M1917A1s with the company's two M1919s. After a few minutes, E Company settled into its blocking position. Colonel Sibert's plan seemed to fall into place.

The other part of the plan, the push from the southwest, did not proceed as well. The German infantry, fighting from entrenchments next to the bunkers, held up the battalion's progress. The stands of spruce, oak, and beech prevented the Americans from concentrating firepower against the dug-in Germans. The poor roads and German artillery made it difficult to bring forward any heavier weapons or tank destroyers to blast the enemy positions. The battle turned into a close-quarters infantry action. F and G Company riflemen had to slither forward to points where they could fire into the German entrenchments from a few meters away or take them out with hand grenades. The German replacements fared poorly against the aggressive American riflemen. They usually gave up as soon as the Americans gained an advantageous position. The 2nd Battalion steadily advanced, but the close-in fighting slowed its pace to a literal crawl. The late afternoon light soon faded over the dank forest, leaving the battalion short of CR 676 and a full kilometer from E Company at CR 681.[24]

The enveloping movement had gone well. E Company set the anvil on which the battalion's hammer would fall...but the blow did not come. E Company had isolated the Germans at CR 676 but now they, too, were cut off at CR 681. Watching the daylight dim, Bill knew he was in for a difficult night.

Colonel Sibert took steps to support his isolated unit. More than anything, E Company needed ammunition for the machine guns. Bill's platoon only had the rounds they carried with them on the 1,200-meter hike along the slope of the Schnee Eifel. The ever-helpful Lieutenant Piper led a patrol that made several attempts to carry critical supplies to the company, but the enemy or the difficult terrain frustrated each one.[25]

E Company used the last hour of light to establish a 360-degree perimeter around the hilltop. Bill's four guns and the company's two machine guns provided the bulk of E Company's firepower. Bill prepared a defensive fire plan that integrated fires from all six guns and covered the principal avenues of approach: the crest road, the Schlausenbach road, and a forest trail. He positioned the guns to permit, at least, two of them to place interlocking fire on each of the six paths leading into the perimeter. That gave every gun a primary sector of fire covering one road and a secondary sector for an adjacent road. He planned FPLs along the perimeter. Working with the section sergeants and squad leaders, Bill trooped the line to point out directions of fire for all six gun crews. Riflemen from the company dug in close to the machine guns to provide additional security for them.[26]

The crews dug their positions and prepared for nighttime direct fire action. The gunners sighted the FPLs for traverse and QE then recorded the data on a range card. The assistant gunners pounded in an aiming stake on the gunner's line of sight close enough to be seen at night. The crews repeated the process for each target in their sector.[27]

Just as it did at Mortain, the *Deutschland Regiment* held its troops in place at CR 676. They were not about to abandon a defensive position just because of the American presence at CR 681. The Germans seemed more comfortable defending from isolated pockets than the Americans. While the forward troops kept the bulk of CT 12 tied up near CR 676, the Germans brought in reinforcements during the night to overwhelm the American infantry force in their midst.

The leafy canopy shrouded the forest floor around Hill 681. Everything turned black and silent. Tense soldiers sitting in hastily dug foxholes peered into the gloom and strained their ears. The time ticked by slowly until...*ta-ta-ta-ta-ta-tat*. Bright flashes from one of the machine guns lit up the woodland and tracers blazed magenta trails through the dark like shooting stars. Nearby riflemen began firing their M1s. Germans creeping up to the American position returned fire. The distinctive *Brrr-brrrp* sound from their MP 40 machine pistols echoed inside the forest. For a few horrifying minutes, the jarring sights and sounds of small arms fire pierced the darkened crest of the Schnee Eifel. Then all went quiet. An hour later another firefight erupted on a different trail leading into CR 681. Throughout the night German patrols struck the American perimeter at multiple points, trying to find a soft spot in E Company's perimeter through which they could assault and retake the crossroads.[28]

Bill scurried from one machine gun to the next inside the E Company position, low-crawling the last few meters. He sized up the crews to ensure they were awake and alert. Bill and the section sergeants reviewed sectors of fire with the crews. Darkness complicated fire control measures. The crews had to see their aiming stakes in the blackness and remember the traverse settings between known yet unseen targets. Bill looked for negative QE settings because the guns had to fire downhill. He talked with the gunners and squad leaders, making sure their range cards showed proper data to put fire on points of danger. After checking the squad's ammo status, he moved to the next gun. Once the Germans hit a section of the perimeter, Bill and the section sergeants redistributed ammunition. So long as the ammunition held out, E Company had a good chance of driving back an infantry assault. Before leaving a position, they gave a final warning. "Don't waste any rounds."

The Germans probed all night. They had enough strength to threaten the American position but, without tanks, they lacked the firepower to destroy it. The Germans clung to CR 676 and the Americans held CR 681. Stalemate.

The slow progress on September 15 and the rising casualties (forty men) frustrated Colonel Chance. He issued a memorandum to his subordinate commanders, admonishing them to make more use of supporting artillery, mortar, and machine gun fire if they could not power through enemy resistance on their own. His instructions showed a lack of appreciation for the close quarter combat his battalions faced. No one could call for artillery on a target within pistol range.[29]

CT 12, with its meager gains, still fared better than the rest of the Ivy Division. General Barton's bold move to send CT 8 through the Losheim Gap for what he assumed would be a fast dash to the Kyll River did not play out as planned. Stiff resistance at Losheim and Roth stopped CT 8 short of the Siegfried Line.

Barton had misinterpreted the spotty defense on the Schnee Eifel as an indication of overall German weakness across his entire sector. Now, the enemy situation became clearer. *Oberfuhrer* Otto Baum, commander of *Das Reich*, did not have the assets to defend his sector from the Losheim Gap to the Brandscheid-Habscheid plateau. He had left the Schnee Eifel lightly guarded, figuring that a breakthrough there would not jeopardize the German rear because the Americans would have trouble moving tanks over its poor roads. Instead, Baum concentrated his best troops and limited anti-armor weapons in the two mobility corridors, including the Losheim Gap.[30]

To his credit, once he realized his mistake, Barton moved quickly to correct it. He ordered CT 8 to halt its attack and regroup for an attack on September 16 aimed at a spot between CTs 12 and 22. The division CP had moved forward to Auw during the day in expectation of a rapid advance through the Losheim Gap. Once CT 8 pulled back, the CP stood unprotected, less than four kilometers from the enemy, and had to displace. The staff ruefully noted that this was the first time the division CP had retreated since the Carolina war games of 1941.[31]

Unfortunately for the Ivy Division, the Germans did not give the Americans a second chance to exploit the initial break in the Siegfried Line. *Oberfuhrer* Baum could see how the American tactical plan developed and fed reinforcements into the line to plug the holes in his defense.

He lacked well-trained formations but even low-quality troops could make a decent stand on the Schnee Eifel.

The operations order for September 16 provided no relief for CT 12. The division sent CT 8 to push east across the Schnee Eifel. To make room, CT 12's boundary shifted north. The new boundary put the roads and trails they had already cleared in CT 8's zone. The road crossing through CR 681 was the only one in CT 12's sector leading off the Schnee Eifel. Because of the confined terrain along the crest, CT 12 had to attack in column formation to relieve E Company, with 2nd Battalion again leading the charge.[32]

F Company moved out at 0745 hours from CR 695, heading northeast along the crest road to drive the enemy from CR 676. Within minutes they ran into severe small arms fire. A few minutes later German artillery and mortar fire came crashing down. Between the direct fire and the artillery rounds bursting in the trees, F Company's riflemen could barely move. The intense enemy fire alerted the Americans that the *Deutschland Regiment* had bolstered their defense during the night. The regiment now faced troops drawn from a security battalion, a light artillery battalion, and two infantry replacement battalions, all fighting as infantry.[33]

Colonel Sibert brought up a platoon of Sherman tanks by 0850 hours. The armor joined F and G Companies on the crest. The two infantry companies and supporting tanks took out one enemy entrenchment after another but the advance crawled and came at a stiff price. Incoming artillery and mortar fire chewed up the infantrymen and often forced the tanks off the road. At 1046 hours Colonel Sibert reported dismal news to Major Gorn, the regimental S-3. G Company was moving, but slowly. The enemy had F Company pinned down. E Company was still surrounded.[34]

E Company and Bill's platoon had a rough morning at CR 681. When daylight broke, they started taking fire from all directions. Lieutenant MacDiarmid, with help from Bill's platoon, organized an effective defense that broke up each enemy probe with machine gun and rifle fire. The position held but the situation remained tense. If anyone moved on the confined hilltop, he drew enemy fire. The prolonged fight during the night and morning had drained their ammunition supply. Without resupply, they could not sustain their position.

Colonel Sibert sent G Company in another flanking maneuver around the right (southeast) side of the crest with a platoon of M5 Stuart light tanks from Company D, 70th Tank Battalion. G Company and the smaller, more maneuverable Stuarts threaded through the stands of hardwoods and firs along the southeastern slope and began caving in the enemy flank.[35]

With the 2nd Battalion fully engaged, Colonel Chance decided to add weight to the regiment's attack. At 1255 hours he directed 1st Battalion to attack around the western flank of the German position. Another platoon of tanks came out of Schlausenbach to help.[36]

F Company continued its push up the crest road while the 1st Battalion organized for its attack. The rifle platoons drove the Germans back onto CR 676. The enemy responded by surging forward in a sudden counterattack, but these were not the hardened SS troops the battalion faced at Mortain. Staff Sergeant Leonard Pitman spotted the enemy leader and killed him with a rifle shot. The rest of the German troops withdrew. The enemy launched a second counterattack. Again, Sergeant Pitman dropped the enemy leader. The remaining German troops again lost heart. The Germans poured on more artillery fire but F Company's forward platoons were too close to the Germans' own positions. Most of the incoming rounds impacted behind the F Company riflemen. The indirect fire did succeed in interdicting F Company's efforts to resupply its own platoons. The infantrymen on the front line were down to only a couple clips of ammunition.[37]

The battle turned in the Americans' favor in the afternoon. A plucky sergeant, weighted down with bandoliers of .30 caliber rounds, braved the incoming artillery and mortar fire to deliver desperately needed ammunition to F Company's rifle platoons. A company from 1st Battalion with a platoon of tanks slammed into the enemy a short while later. "[T]he Germans were soon waving a white bed sheet and yelling 'Kamerad!' They marched into our line in a column of fours with their hands clasped on top of their heads."[38]

On top of Hill 681, E Company could hear the rumble of tank engines approaching up the southeastern slope of the Schnee Eifel. Coming from that direction, Bill and his men knew the tanks had to be friendly. The lead elements of G Company reached their isolated brethren at the crossroad by 1530 hours. E Company's ordeal at CR 681 ended. The time had come to make the Germans pay.[39]

The Americans had tanks on both CR 676 and CR 681 with German defenders trapped in between. The two armor platoons plowed toward each other down the crest road and crushed the demoralized enemy. The 2nd Battalion cleared the Schnee Eifel all the way to CR 681 while 1st Battalion mopped up five more pillboxes on its northwest slope. Farther west, L Company joined K Company at CR 636. Nearly all of CT 12 congregated around CR 681 by the end of the day. The regiment killed an untold number of Germans on September 16 and captured well over a hundred more. American losses climbed to fifty-eight, mostly from German artillery and mortar fire. The casualties were manageable, less than 4 percent, but the daily trend of increasing losses continued.[40]

Just as the fighting subsided, Colonel Luckett returned from leave and resumed command of the 12th Infantry. CT 12 had seven days of breathtaking advances and three days of dismal fighting during Colonel Chance's interim command. He would later return to the regiment.[41]

CT 12 accomplished little more than relieving E Company and clearing the Schnee Eifel to CR 681. It took the entire regiment to do that against a mishmash of German troops. Miserable terrain, miserable roads, and miserable weather had prevented it from doing more.

The rest of the division fared no better. CT 22 suffered heavy casualties fighting along the Bleialf-Sellerich-Prum highway. It did not capture Brandscheid and only pushed to the eastern edge of the Schnee Eifel forest near Sellerich and Hontheim. CT 8 spent the whole day shifting its battalions to the southeastern side of the Schnee Eifel between CTs 12 and 22.

General Barton lost his enthusiasm for breaking through the Siegfried Line. He recognized that the German defense had congealed. The days of rapid advances against weak resistance had come to an end. The division issued orders to continue the attack on September 17 but the mission statement emphasized cleaning up enemy resistance and pillboxes in zone rather than seizing deep objectives. The 2nd Battalion's direction of movement changed. Instead of driving up the Schnee Eifel crest, it would follow a forest trail east to Knaufspetsch. The tiny hamlet sat astride the Roth-Prum road, the only good road crossing the Schnee Eifel. The Germans had been using it to shift troops around and deliver supplies. The 1st Battalion was given the task of advancing up the crest road to CR 655 where the Roth-Prum road intersected the crest road. Once CT 12 had control over the vital road, the two battalions were to clear out German resistance from the headwaters of the Prum River.[42]

E and G Companies followed the Schlausenbach-Olzheim road off the crest to the east at 0900 hours on September 17. The battalion had a platoon of Stuarts attached but navigating the forested slopes of the Schnee Eifel was work for the infantry, not armor. The Germans pounded the 1st Battalion position on the crest with artillery just before its departure time. That forced 1st Battalion to delay its attack and re-organize. As Bill moved out, he felt the same uneasiness and dread he had at the San Francisco Airport and outside Montebourg. He knew something terrible was about to happen.[43]

Bill's platoon stayed with Lieutenant MacDiarmid's men. The attack through the Olzheimer Wald ruled out any long-range indirect fire for the machine guns. The crews again had to stay forward with the rifle platoons. E Company remained on the right-hand side of the battalion formation. Colonel Sibert put F Company in the rear after the grueling day they had fighting near CR 676.[44]

It did not take long for the Germans to discover 2nd Battalion's movement. Artillery and mortar fire started landing near the lead companies by mid-morning. The Germans brought up a *12cm Granatwerfer 42* heavy mortar that fired a thirty-four-pound projectile that delivered more punch than a 105mm artillery shell. Tree bursts from the mortar rounds splattered the infantrymen with shrapnel and splinters.[45]

The battalion's pace slackened. The intensity of the incoming artillery and mortar fire forced the troops to maneuver away from the bursting rounds that plastered the dirt road. At 1022 hours an 88mm or 75mm self-propelled gun began firing on them, ticking up the German bombardment another notch.

Pushing farther east, the Americans came across a clearing. The open ground lay on the far side of a creek. The field, only one hundred meters deep, stretched for a kilometer across the battalion's avenue of advance. The infantry spread out before moving forward. Bill's machine guns followed the E Company riflemen into the open area. The company had advanced part way across the clearing when a German machine gun opened fire.

Bill clung to the ground as a stream of bullets snapped overhead. The German machine gunner swept the open ground from left to right then back again. Bill spotted a small gully off to one side that offered cover. He waited until the machine gun's rounds passed overhead then jumped to his feet and ran for it. He had only taken a couple of strides when a nearby blast from a 120mm mortar round knocked him to the ground.

The enemy machine gunner continued his sweep of the clearing. Bill only had a few seconds to reach the protection of the gully. He jumped back to his feet, took a step, then crashed to the ground. His left leg did not move. Unable to run, Bill did the only thing he could to get out of the clearing—he started rolling his body toward the gully. Over and over he tumbled while the machine gun's bullets cracked closer and closer. Just as he reached the edge of the gully, a machine gun round slapped into his upper thigh only inches from where he had been hit by mortar shrapnel. Bill dropped into the safety of the low ground clasping his left leg.

E Company cleared the enemy machine gun by 1244 hours and secured the open area. As soon as the company declared the area safe, the medics who had attended Bill and stopped the bleeding evacuated him and the other casualties up the road to CR 681. From there, they had a twenty-kilometer ride to the clearing station in Belgium.[46]

The 2nd Battalion ended the day at Knaufspetsch, its objective. They set up a defensive position that severed the Germans' use of the Roth-Prum road over the Schnee Eifel. The battalion accounted for the division's only successful advance on September 17. The rest of the regiment remained stuck at CR 681. The Germans blocked all attempts by 1st Battalion to advance on the narrow crest. Elsewhere, CT 22 failed to take Brandscheid and had a company mauled by an enemy counterattack near Sellerich.[47]

Brig. Gen. George Taylor, the assistant division commander, traveled to V Corps HQ that night to explain the 4th Infantry Division's situation. All three regiments were bunched on the Schnee Eifel with entrenched enemy positions at Brandscheid and CR 655 blocking both ends. The weather, road conditions, and dense woodlands hindered the flow of supplies and limited tactical maneuverability. The division had exposed flanks, especially to the north where only a cavalry group screened the Losheim Gap. The V Corps staff canceled any further large-scale attacks against the Siegfried Line. V Corps had tested the enemy's defense and learned that, somehow, the Germans had restored their fragmented forces. The German Army proved fully capable of defending the Fatherland. To be successful, any offensive into Germany would need a well-planned, thoroughly resourced assault by a powerful force. In mid-September, the best hope for that was in Holland where Field Marshal Montgomery's 21st Army Group had just launched Operation Market Garden.[48]

Exhausted and disappointed, General Barton took extended medical leave on the same day Bill was wounded. Three different generals would command the Ivy Division during the seventeen days before Barton returned. The 12th Infantry would fight along the crest of the Schnee Eifel for another three days before adopting a defensive posture—as would the Germans.[49]

During the attack on and around the Siegfried Line, the regiment had done well. Time and again the regiment's infantrymen rooted out the entrenched enemy in close quarter combat, even though the Germans used their artillery more liberally than the Americans. The 2nd Battalion achieved excellent results and showed tactical skill when it enveloped the defenders on the Eifel's crest on multiple occasions.

The measly results of the assault on the Siegfried Line had more to do with the poor decisions and tactics of the American generals. The troubles began with General Hodges, who postponed any attack on the Siegfried Line until September 14. That forfeited a chance to punch through before the *Das Reich Division* had a chance to occupy their pillboxes. General Gerow's tactical plan failed to mass the 4th and 28th Infantry Divisions on the same mobility corridor, squandering an opportunity to overwhelm the Germans on terrain suitable for American armor. Gerow then directed the Ivy Division to take a useless piece of terrain and allowed it to get bogged down. Finally, the normally dependable Ray Barton held back his armor and reserve regiment after the breakthrough on September 14. He then committed his reserve into the untried Losheim Gap where it ran straight into a prepared defense. By the time he recovered from that mistake, the Germans had set their defense on the Schnee Eifel.

The battle of the Schnee Eifel proved that the battlefield prowess and fighting spirit of the men on the ground could not make up for the strategic and tactical errors of their leaders.

CHAPTER TWELVE

LUXEMBOURG

Bill began the journey of a wounded soldier, one that would take him three months to complete. The ambulance delivered him to the medical clearing station just outside Lommersweiler, Belgium, where the staff made sure his vital signs had stabilized. He then traveled to the division's field hospital for surgery to remove the bullet and shrapnel from his thigh. He convalesced there for a few weeks.[1]

Bill wrote to Beth at once to tell her that he had been wounded before she got one of the dreaded War Department telegrams. She wrote back to ask him where on his leg he was hit. He replied, "Two more inches and we would have had to adopt our children."[2]

While he sat in the hospital some good news arrived. His promotion to First Lieutenant came through. The Army issued the orders with an effective date of September 13, the day he had entered Germany. In October, General Barton came by the hospital to visit his wounded soldiers and award medals. To Bill's surprise, the general presented him the Silver Star. The citation lauded Bill's "gallantry in action" at Mortain.

The medal pleased Bill, a little. Naturally, he appreciated being recognized for his conduct in battle but he developed a diffident attitude about decorations. "I don't think much of medals because many are not given properly." He never considered his actions at Mortain to be any more heroic than in a dozen other battles and less so than several other occasions for which he received no official recognition. He knew of many others who never got noticed for courageous acts under fire that equaled or exceeded his own. Some of them did not live to see the final victory.[3]

The wounds to Bill's leg, though not as acute as the near fatal injuries he suffered in Normandy, did not mend as well. A nerve had been severed and his leg became paralyzed. For a few tense weeks, Bill worried that he might have been crippled. His condition forced the Army to evacuate him all the way to a hospital in England. Gradually, the nerve healed. He went through weeks of physical therapy that finally restored movement in his leg.

Bill's spirits got a boost on Thanksgiving Day. A packet of forty-three letters, twenty-five from Beth, finally caught up with him in the hospital. He stacked the letters, dated between May 19 and July 6, in chronological order, then pored through them.[4]

After his release from the hospital, Bill reported back to the 10th Replacement Depot. "Same old place as it was in Jan[uary] and July." Some of the same people, too. They told Bill he looked five years older. He shrugged it off. "They say I still can grin so I must be O.K." He noticed something about the men who hung back in England. "They have a soft life here. Strangely enough they are more afraid of being transferred to combat than any combat man is. Fear is one hell of a tough opponent but one's mind is one's strongest ally."[5]

Bill's letters to Beth revealed a subtle change in his motivations. Prior to D-Day, he burned with the desire to prove himself in battle. His performance in combat had answered that. Once he returned to the frontline in July, he felt compelled to do his share of combat duty, at least a bit more than the four days in the Cotentin Peninsula. Bill could have considered his obligations fulfilled after fighting another two months and getting wounded a second time. He did not. The idea of hanging back when others were fighting nagged at his self-worth. He occasionally wrote about taking an engineer assignment but, in his heart, he knew he could not leave the infantry while the war lasted. He could not identify with the soldiers in the rear area who fretted about drawing a combat assignment. "When I look at the soft job I turned down here and think of the job I have to go to I wonder at my sanity. If I get out O.K. my conscience will be clear and that means a lot. If I don't there will be no chance to regret it."

Delays frustrated Bill's efforts to get back to H Company. Instinctively, he had attached himself to the men in his unit as if they were a surrogate family. The other veteran lieutenants in his company, Jack Gunning, John Wandling, and Dave McElroy, had become solid friends after months of shared danger. He thought about spending Christmas with them but the red tape and bureaucracy vexed him. By the time he got notice to leave Lichfield, he realized he would not reach his battalion in time. "Guess I'll not be with the boys on x-mas. Damn it, I'd like to be there instead of here." Bill finally got his release orders with enough advance notice to take a forty-eight hour pass to London. He and another officer blitzed the tourist sites in the city and got teased by the prostitutes trolling Picadilly Square. He shipped out for the continent by December 18.

News of the Germans' Ardennes offensive greeted him when he arrived. Maps printed in the newspapers tracked the progress of the "Bulge" the Germans had pushed into the Allied front. Bill had no idea where the 4th Infantry Division was but he saw that the Germans had overrun the part of Belgium that he helped liberate in September. His thoughts went back to the little Belgian girl whom he promised would not see the Nazis again. The fear that the bastard SS officer might have come back to torment her and her mother plagued Bill.[6]

Anxious as he was to get back, Bill ran into confusion and frustration. The Army moved him by rail to the First Army replacement depot in Belgium. The personnel officers there advised him that they could not move him forward to his unit. The Ivy Division was fighting in Luxembourg on the opposite side of the "Bulge." Bill boarded another boxcar for the long ride back to France then east to the Duchy.

The closer Bill got to the battlefield, the more his nature changed. He admitted to Beth, "Sometimes I think this war is effecting [sic] me more than I like to admit...I have a 'faster' attitude than before." His justifications for welcoming a return to combat became tainted with resignation. "I, and everyone else knows that I will be wounded again maybe before Jan. is over. That fact does not frighten me. Instead of fear I feel a certain 'what the hell' attitude. If I am wounded it means a rest. If I am killed I'll never know it." Without saying or recognizing it, Bill had developed a warrior mentality. He belonged to the fight. He rejoined the regiment in Luxembourg on January 7, 1945.[7]

The Ivy Division and 12th Infantry had suffered through some terrible times during Bill's three-month absence. After the Schnee Eifel, the entire division occupied a peaceful portion of the front throughout October. "October was a dream," his friends told him. The easy time ended in mid-November when the First Army committed the division into the Hürtgen Forest battle. Once again, the 12th Infantry was attached to another division and badly mauled as it struggled against entrenched Germans and trenchfoot in the damp, chilled forest. The exhausted regiment came out of the Huertgen in December for a rest in a quiet sector of the front—the Ardennes. They quartered in a string of widely spaced company-sized outposts along the Sauer River in Luxembourg. On December 16, the German *Seventh Army* attacked. The enemy tried to capture Luxembourg City and form the southern flank of the Bulge. The *212th* and *276th Volksgrenadier Divisions* assaulted the area defended mostly by the 2nd Battalion. Enemy infantry infiltrated between the American outposts but the regiment held on. The stubborn American defense and the difficulty of moving armor through the thick snowdrifts foiled the German advance. The Ivy Division quickly sealed the enemy penetrations between the towns. The German *Seventh Army* failed to make any meaningful headway toward the capital city and the Americans held a firm shoulder against the enemy offensive. Sadly, the Germans surrounded 1st Lt. Martin MacDiarmid and E Company in the town of Echternach. MacDiarmid and his company fought for four days until they ran out of ammunition and had to surrender. The 12th Infantry ended December in positions along the bank of the Sauer River facing north against the German bulge.[8]

Bill's chain of command had turned over during the fighting in the Hürtgen Forest and Ardennes. Capt. Earl Enroughty, H Company Commander, was killed by a mine in the Hürtgen Forest. A Philadelphia native, Capt. Benjamin Compton, took his place.

The 2nd Battalion commander, Lt. Col. Franklin Sibert, received a slight wound in the Hürtgen Forest. He was evacuated and never returned. Maj. John W. Gorn, the regiment's S-3, became the battalion's fifth commander since D-Day. A native of Fond du Lac, Wisconsin, the boyishly handsome officer was noted for his "Pepsodent smile" and mild manner. He graduated from Ripon College's ROTC program and earned a commission in 1939. Gorn won rapid promotion during the Army's massive expansion, becoming a field-grade staff officer by the time the regiment landed in Normandy. Bill and Lieutenant Colonel Gorn (he would be promoted in January) would forge a lifelong friendship over the succeeding four months of combat.[9]

Col. James Luckett left the regiment, though not the division, after the Hürtgen Forest. The division did not publish the official reason for his leaving the 12th Infantry. Bill had his own theory. The steady loss of veteran officers and men chipped away at Luckett's spirit. "Over-identification with the men" was the customary term for this malady. The experience in the Huertgen, so similar to the horror of Mortain, might have proved too much for the veteran commander. Interestingly, Luckett went on to command the 80th Infantry Division's 318th Infantry Regiment in combat and saw more men fall, just not the ones he had served with since Normandy. Col. Robert Chance, the officer who took over when Luckett went on leave in September, returned to command the regiment for the remainder of the campaign in Northern Europe.

Maj. Gen. Ray Barton's health broke under the strain of the Ardennes battle. Just after Christmas, as soon as the division had stabilized its northern flank, he turned over the Ivy Division to his deputy, Brig. Gen. Harold Blakeley. Barton left the division and the European Theater. (See Fig. 5)

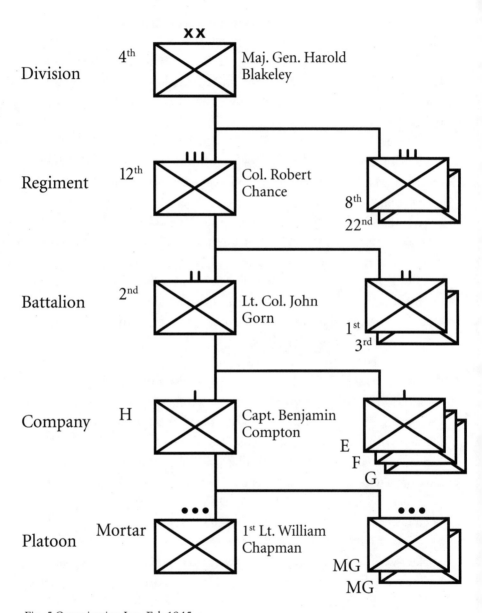

Fig. 5 Organization Jan–Feb 1945

Bill rejoined H Company in the little town of Consdorf, Luxembourg. Captain Compton assigned him to the heavy mortar platoon, but now as its platoon leader. He posed for pictures beside the town chapel. One of the veteran sergeants, Sgt. William Dahse, stood beside him while Lieutenant Gunning snapped the photographs.

During the first two weeks of January, Patton's Third Army and Hodges's First Army collapsed the German bulge west of Bastogne. General Bradley won approval from Eisenhower to follow up the elimination of the Bulge with an offensive to push the retreating enemy back into Germany, what he termed the "Hurry Up Offensive."

Meanwhile, the 12th Infantry concentrated on reconstitution. The number of officers in the regiment climbed back to 162 and the enlisted ranks swelled to more than 2,900 by mid-January. The regiment entirely replaced E Company with new faces and experienced infantrymen from other companies. The battalions were gradually reintroduced to the frontline, taking turns between forward outposts and rear positions a safe distance from enemy artillery. On January 9, the 2nd Battalion rotated forward to occupy high ground overlooking the Sauer River between Bollendorf and Berdorf, Luxembourg. "[T]he action was confined to patrol activity and reconnaissance of the enemy's defenses for a possible river crossing."[10]

The easy days could not last. Veterans like Bill figured that as soon as the regiment reached full strength and had rested for a few days, it would return to action. He prepared Beth in his letters for what was coming while girding his own spirit. His acceptance of his place on the battlefield showed in his scorn of a proposal floated by the journalist Clare Booth Luce. She suggested limiting American infantrymen to no more than 200 days in combat. "How can we afford to release men from the front who are capable of fighting?...Those of us in the infantry must realize there is no rest until the war ends." His letters also revealed a growing fatalism. "I don't want to be melodramatic but we both know I'm living on borrowed time—I've had my percentage of close calls."[11]

The 345th Infantry of the 87th Infantry Division relieved the 12th Infantry, in place, on January 17. The regiment had been designated as the corps reserve, so the troops moved by truck to the vicinity of Mersch, Luxembourg. The 2nd Battalion staff took that news as a bad omen. "Corps reserve hardly ever lasts a full day." The prophecy proved correct. The battalion reached its assembly area near Kehlen, Luxembourg at 0030 hours on January 18. New orders attaching them to a sister regiment, the 8th Infantry, arrived by 1425 hours. CT 8 had attacked across the Sauer River that morning and needed help mopping up the area. Bill and the rest of the battalion convoyed in the dark to Eppeldorf, arriving by 0300 hours on January 19.[12]

Once the men hopped off the trucks, they moved straight to the Sauer River. The rifle companies scampered across a footbridge downriver from Bettendorf, Luxembourg under the cover of darkness. Bill had to get his platoon across the river to provide immediate support for the rifle companies once they ran into the enemy on the north side. That meant displacing forward by sections. One section moved across the footbridge with the lead rifle companies. The remaining sections initially supported the attack from firing positions south of the river then moved quickly across the Sauer before daylight invited German artillery.[13] (See Map X)

Elements of the German *915th Regiment* of the *352nd Division* defended this portion of the Sauer River. They reacted to the battalion's attack with indirect fire, but darkness limited its accuracy and effect. By 0530 hours E Company was in Bettendorf and clearing it house-to-house. Bill's platoon set up nearby and surveyed in their mortar positions. When dawn arrived, F and G Companies attacked the high ground surrounding the town. Daylight allowed the observers who accompanied the riflemen to use hand-arm signals to call in mortar fire. After spotting the initial rounds, they signaled corrections in range and deflection until the mortar rounds hit their targets. The mortars, firing from the north side of the Sauer River, suppressed the German bunkers dug into the slopes. F Company secured its objective on the high ground by 1455 hours and G Company moved in alongside. They tied in with the 8th Infantry on the eastern flank. The next morning the 8th Infantry notified Colonel Chance that 2nd Battalion would return to his control.[14]

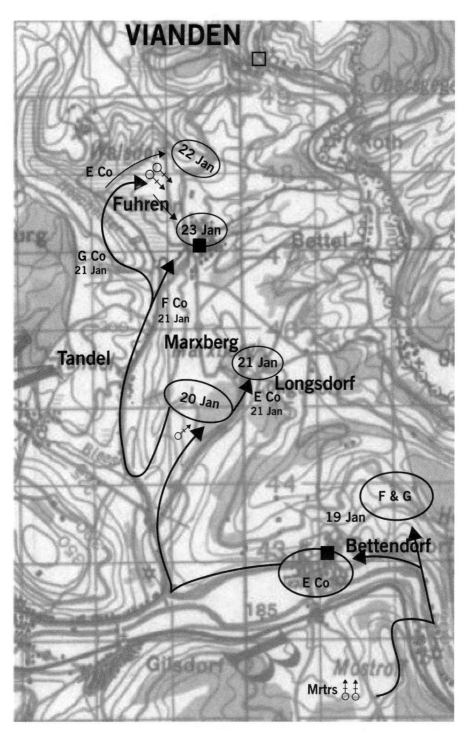

Map X

The division committed the rest of the 12th Infantry into the wedge of land between the Sauer and Our Rivers on January 20. While the 1st Battalion got trucked across the river below Bettendorf, the 2nd Battalion moved north along the Gilsdorf-Tandel highway. E and F Companies occupied positions held by a regiment of the 5th Infantry Division between the villages of Tandel and Longsdorf before dawn. H Company's mortars set up a short distance behind the rifle companies, preparing firing positions and planning targets against potential counterattacks. The 1st Battalion, CT 12's main effort, planned to attack through the 2nd Battalion then seize the spine of high ground between the Sauer and Our Rivers just north of Longsdorf.[15]

The brutal winter weather played against the regiment's plan. Deep snow restricted all vehicles to the roads. Trails and roads that had not carried traffic disappeared under the drifts. Heavy foot and vehicle traffic compacted the snow on the identifiable roads into rivers of ice. With chains on their tires, the mortar platoon's jeeps could gain traction but the tanks had more trouble. The pads on their tracks could not grip the icy surfaces. One tanker was killed when his tank slid over an embankment the day before. The sliding tanks also tore down wire communications strung along the sides of the roads. General Blakeley ordered them off the roads until engineers could spread gravel. His decision cost the 12th Infantry its tank support for the day.[16]

The infantrymen had to contend with bitter cold, too. One of the Midwestern troopers complained about the conditions. "I thought Iowa winters were bad but when someone is trying to kill you it is worse. I went days without taking off my combat boots." Bill handled the cold by layering his clothes. "I have a field jacket, an overcoat, scarf, gloves, and overshoes. My under-garments consist of 2 pr. of wool long-johns and 2 pr. of wool socks. In addition to that I have my O. D.s [olive drab woolen sweater] and a suit of fatigues. That gives me 6 sleeves on each arm. The overcoat is unnecessary if we are moving at all."[17]

The regiment ran into stiffer resistance on January 20. The attack across the Sauer River had caught the Germans off guard two days before. They pulled units from northern Luxembourg to shore up their defense along the Sauer River. The *2nd Battalion* of the *915th Regiment* dug in along the ridge north and east of the 2nd Battalion's position during the night. The Germans started the day by shelling Bettendorf in the hope of destroying the American crossing site.[18]

Company A of the 1st Battalion passed through E Company's position by 0845 hours. Just beyond the battalion's lines, they ran into small arms fire. Soon spot reports from the artillery FOs and 1st Battalion scouts identified German tank and infantry positions along the ridgeline. The 1st Battalion pressed ahead, but gained only a kilometer at a heavy cost. The Germans launched a counterattack from the east but a TOT strike from the American artillery broke up the attack.

In the meantime, E Company engaged enemy troops occupying the villages of Longsdorf and Marxberg, twin hamlets nestled in the draw between the 2nd Battalion's position and the German-held ridgeline. Bill's mortars targeted the enemy-occupied buildings but the Germans still held the town that night.

The 2nd Battalion drew the assignment to lead the attack the next day. The regiment gave Lt. Col. John Gorn two missions. F and G Companies would lead the main attack to seize the town of Fouhren. E Company had to stay behind and help 1st Battalion clear Longsdorf-Marxberg. The dual missions demanded that one of the 81mm mortar sections split off from the platoon to support E Company. The engineers had improved the treadway bridge over the Sauer River and spread gravel on the icy roads to give the tanks enough traction to join the fight. Colonel Chance attached a platoon from Capt. Francis Songer's B Company, 70th Tank Battalion and put a platoon of Company A, 91st Chemical Mortar Battalion in direct support to give the rest of 2nd Battalion more firepower. Colonel Gorn tasked Capt. Tallie Crocker's F Company to advance on Fouhren with G Company trailing.[19]

The German senior commanders considered the Our River crossing at Vianden vital for extricating their forces from the Ardennes. Long lines of tanks, trucks, staff cars, and horse carts snaked down the narrow roads leading into Vianden. To keep this escape hatch open, Lt. Gen. Baptist Kniess, commander of the *LXXXV Corps*, reinforced Fouhren with the *38th Engineer Battalion*, a *Panzergrenadier* company from the *2nd Panzer Division* and six Panther tanks. A nasty surprise awaited F Company.[20]

F Company shifted off the high ground into the Hoscheider Branch valley. Captain Crocker intended to bypass the *915th Regiment* defending the ridgeline and move F Company north along the Gilsdorf-Tandel-Fouhren highway that ran up the valley. The Americans launched their attack at 0915 hours. At first, the advance proceeded smoothly. The Shermans knocked out a German tank before F Company had moved past the village of Tandel. Farther north the stream valley narrowed, constricting the American avenue of approach. The Germans picked their defensive positions in Fouhren to take maximum advantage of this situation. They situated a few tanks and 88s to fire straight down the length of the road. The bulk of their machine guns and AT weapons sat in the high ground targeting the open space just north of the narrowest part of the valley. Once F Company pushed beyond the valley's choke-point, they caught the full brunt of "withering machine gun fire, mortar, and direct 88 fire." The enemy wiped out the FO team from the direct support artillery battalion in the first few minutes of the engagement. The defenders then dropped artillery and mortars along the road where the Americans were most confined.[21]

The F Company riflemen scurried for cover, and the Shermans, sitting ducks for the Panthers and 88s, pulled back. Casualties among the infantry mounted quickly. Tallie Crocker and his executive officer (XO) went down wounded, and two of the platoon leaders were killed outright. Bill and his observers had difficulty supporting F Company's attack with mortar fire. Blast waves rocked them off their feet and plastered them with debris and flying bits of steel. The stream valley turned aglitter with powder-laden ice crystals. The enemy fire forced Bill's observers to cover, just as it had the riflemen. They tried to bring fire on the enemy but the narrow approach up the valley limited their visibility to only what lay directly ahead. By mid-afternoon, Colonel Gorn called off F Company's attack.[22]

The attack had been completely predictable. The Germans knew that American tanks had poor off-road mobility in the snowy conditions, so they focused their firepower on the two roads leading into Fouhren. CT 12 had tried the Marxberg Road on the high ground the day before, then the one in the narrow valley this day. The Americans had sufficient firepower to bull their way to Fouhren but that required close coordination between artillery, suppressive smoke, tanks, and infantry—tactical expertise their leaders had not yet acquired.

Back in Longsdorf and Marxberg, enemy mortars hit E Company as soon as it started its advance into the draw. A Company of the 1st Battalion helped support E Company's attack by exchanging fire with the Germans in Longsdorf from the high ground north of town. E Company struck Longsdorf from the south. The Germans hung onto the two hamlets and shot it out with the two American forces.[23]

With German infantry fighting from buildings, the 81mm mortar section switched from the normal M43 high explosive (HE) round to the M45 round. The Army had designed this fifteen-pound munition specifically for demolition purposes. The crews set the fuses for delayed bursts that allowed the rounds to penetrate the depths of a building before exploding. The heavier round could only fire out to 1,200 meters—instead of the usual 3,000 meters—but the section was within that range.[24]

The 81mm mortars and the heavier 4.2-inch (106mm) chemical mortars (known as four-deuce) pounded Longsdorf while E Company's rifle platoons attacked across open ground from the south. Using fire and maneuver, the riflemen closed on the enemy-held houses. When the infantry got close enough to assault, the mortars shifted fire to the next enemy position. The infantrymen then charged and cleared the buildings. The German infantry had enough. Eleven of them surrendered. Just as E Company began securing the twin hamlets, the Germans brought up two tanks and a couple of self-propelled anti-tank guns, mostly likely to cover their withdrawal. The 4.2-inch mortars managed to suppress the tanks and AT guns with HE and smoke rounds. By 1610 hours the Germans abandoned

Longsdorf and Marxberg. E Company secured the villages "but found nothing but a big hole in the road."[25]

The battalion's main effort against Fouhren had been thwarted by enemy fire but Colonel Gorn did not give up. That afternoon, he ordered 1st Lt. Milford Quesenberry, commander of G Company, to continue the attack on a different, less obvious, route. Quesenberry found a draw leading into the high ground west of the valley and used it to envelop the Fouhren defenses. Taking advantage of cover and concealment, Quesenberry led his company off the high ground and back into the Hoscheider Branch valley west of the German positions. They popped out of the low ground late in the afternoon and seized the hill northwest of Fouhren. The American infiltration caught the Germans by surprise. G Company rounded up seventeen prisoners without a fight. Darkness brought an end to the fighting as the Americans remained reluctant to exploit G Company's success in the dark.

The 2nd Battalion only achieved half of its mission on January 21. E Company took Longsdorf but the Germans still held Fouhren, though Quesenberry's infiltration marked a step forward in American tactics. Nevertheless, while the Germans remained, the vital crossing site at Vianden stayed open. F Company suffered terribly but the fighting cost the Germans, too. Among the three companies the battalion captured thirty-seven Germans and destroyed two tanks and one anti-tank gun.[26]

The 2nd Battalion ended the day with its three rifle companies spread over three kilometers in separate, non-supporting positions. Colonel Gorn brought E Company back from Longsdorf that night to help consolidate the battalion near F Company. The records do not state where Bill had the mortar sections located. The logical location would have been behind F Company. They held the central position and had access to the roads. The platoon's jeeps could have resupplied the mortars with food and ammunition in that location.

The XII Corps Commander, Maj. Gen. Manton Eddy, and the division commander, Brig. Gen. Harold Blakeley, leaned on Colonel Chance to secure Fouhren. Chance maneuvered the recently returned 3rd Battalion west of the Hoscheider Branch, following the example of G Company. He wanted both battalions to seize the ridgeline on the northeast side of the Hoscheider Branch on January 22 to control the dominant ground above Vianden. The regiment directed 2nd Battalion to capture Fouhren and the ridge beyond it while 3rd Battalion passed through the town of Walsdorf. Again, Fouhren was the linchpin of the attack.[27]

Colonel Gorn could use two roads to attack Fouhren, one in the stream valley and another along the high ground from Marxberg. Intelligence showed *Panzergrenadieren* and engineers occupying Fouhren, supported by Panther tanks and anti-tank guns. Infantry from the *316th Volksgrenadier Regiment* of the *212th Volksgrenadier Division* showed up in Fouhren, too. Gorn knew the Germans would target the vehicle approaches, so he decided to make the main effort with infantry. He sent E Company to join G Company in an assault from the northwest while F Company and the attached tanks would make a supporting attack from the south.[28]

Shifting the battalion's main attack over to G Company's position meant that Bill had to move with two of his three mortar sections with E Company. The four gun crews humped the tubes, baseplates, bipods, and ammunition cross-country through the snow. Additional ammo bearers from the Ammunition and Pioneer Platoon helped haul more rounds. Besides the extra clothes, each man carried 80-100 lbs. of weapons and gear through the drifts. With each step, one foot sank up to the knee while the soldier struggled just to lift his other foot out of the snow.

E Company's movement did not go unnoticed. As soon as day broke, the Germans searched the Hoscheider Branch valley for signs of the Americans. Tracks in the snow alerted them to E Company's advance. The Germans had limited observation but they had a decent idea of where the American infantrymen were headed. Incoming artillery and mortar fire began falling along E Company's route. Shell bursts sent fountains of snow crystals and shrapnel skyward. The over-burdened troops plowed their knees through mounds of snow to get clear of the blasts. Between dodging the German artillery and furrowing through the snow, E Company made slow progress. Around 1000 hours, it got caught in a brief firefight with the Fouhren defenders but maneuvered clear of the enemy. They slogged through more drifts while crossing the valley farther upstream. When E Company and Bill's mortars finally reached G Company, they learned that Lieutenant Quesenberry's men had already had a busy morning, fighting back two pre-dawn counterattacks.[29]

CT 12 gave the 2nd Battalion an initial objective of clearing Fouhren and a final objective of seizing the ridge north of town that would give the Americans observation into Vianden. The threat of German counterattacks coming out of Vianden changed Colonel Gorn's plan. Instead of using E and G Companies to attack Fouhren from the northwest, he directed E Company to attack the final objective, first, to secure the battalion's flank. Gorn ordered F Company to make the main attack to seize Fouhren from the south. This time they would follow the high ground from Marxberg, instead of the narrow stream valley. This adjustment avoided some German defenses, but it also dissipated the battalion's combat power between two separate objectives, hindering its ability to accomplish its mission.[30]

The western slope of the high ground behind G Company provided the 81mm mortars excellent cover from German observers. From this defilade, they could fire southeast into Fouhren or north-northeast against the ridge E Company had to attack. Rather than split the two sections, Bill kept them together to maximize the fire against any given target. Firing against two different objectives forced the crews to lay out two sets of aiming stakes, each aligned with one of the designated directions of fire. Bill then dispatched a set of observers to both E and G Companies to spot targets.

At 1445 hours, E Company advanced northeast toward the ridgeline as the 42nd Artillery Battalion pounded Fouhren. Still concerned about a potential counterattack, Colonel Gorn told G Company to hold in place. Apparently, he wanted to keep them as a reserve force rather than have all three of his rifle companies engaged at the same time.[31]

The deep snow and steep incline (the men would climb seventy-five meters of elevation to reach the objective) slowed E Company's advance. Supported by Bill's mortars and H Company's heavy machine guns, the riflemen plodded uphill and seized the ridgeline above Fouhren. The rifle platoons quickly laid out defensive positions to secure the high ground. Bill set up OPs on the ridge to observe Vianden and select pre-planned targets. That gave the battalion more protection against a possible German counterattack.

South of Fouhren, F Company launched its attack on the town as soon as the artillery preparation lifted. They ran into another wall of rifle, machine gun, tank, 88, mortar, and artillery fire. The Germans covered every vehicle approach into Fouhren with withering direct fire. This time, the Americans made better use of their supporting fire. Friendly artillery took out two German tanks. B Company, 70th Tank Battalion pushed forward with F Company and managed to knock out another enemy tank. German mines on the road forced the tanks to halt until engineers could clear the way. The rifle platoons pushed to the southern outskirts of Fouhren by 1830 hours but without the attached tanks they lacked the firepower to capture the town. Once darkness set in, Colonel Gorn pulled them back to their starting position.[32]

Had Colonel Gorn not ordered G Company to remain in place, the attack on Fouhren might have succeeded. The town was simply too well defended for a single company to take. Gorn gave up on the idea of wasting infantry on the roads leading into Fouhren from the south. He ordered F Company to join G Company on the high ground northwest of town that night.

Bill and his platoon dug in for the night on the exposed hillside. Their defilade position shielded them from enemy fire but not from the bitter cold. To burrow out foxholes, they had to clear patches of snow, then chop through a layer of frozen soil—all with small entrenching tools. At least the digging got easier the deeper they dug. After Bill finished preparing the nightly defensive fire plans, he dropped into his muddy foxhole to catch a little sleep. Their isolated position kept the company from bringing forward sleeping bags, so Bill covered himself with his coat. He awoke a couple hours later to prepare for the next mission. When he tried to climb out, his legs could not move. He twisted and struggled but his feet were completely immobile. A moment of panic seized him. *Am I paralyzed?* He tried to clear his head and figure out what was wrong. He realized that, while he couldn't lift his legs, he could bend his knee and had sensation in his feet. *I'm not paralyzed—I'm stuck.* Bill pulled out his flashlight and shined it inside his foxhole. He found his boots shackled in frozen mud. He drew his bayonet and jabbed away at his frosty fetters. It took several minutes before he could break free.[33]

Colonel Gorn planned to hit Fouhren from the northwest with G Company and from the south with Captain Songer's company of tanks. E Company guarded the north flank against a potential counterattack and F Company remained in reserve. Gorn sent the battalion's Intelligence and Reconnaissance Platoon, known as the "Raider Platoon," to gain an infantry foothold in the town from the south and call in fire from the 4.2-inch mortars. A preparatory bombardment against Fouhren had already been scheduled from 0400 to 0600 hours.[34]

The Germans had held Fouhren for two days against the battalion's piecemeal attacks. They still had a strong force in town: two hundred infantrymen, four tanks, and several anti-tank guns. Over the previous days they built log shelters for their crew-served weapons and bunkers for their infantry. Even though the 2nd Battalion had positioned itself north, west, and south of the town, the Germans tried to hold on.

The battalion's attack started early. The Raiders left Tandel at 0100 hours on January 23. They used the diversion of the "four-deuce" mortar barrage to sneak into Fouhren. They had just entered a corner of the town around 0630 hours when one of the mortars' smoke rounds ignited a house. The blaze lit up that part of the village. The Raiders wore white snow capes to blend with the winter scenery but the Germans still spotted them. Machine gun and rifle fire poured from the houses and bunkers, forcing the Raiders to crawl to whatever cover they could find. The radio operator called back to the heavy mortars and adjusted their fire onto the machine guns. Under the umbrella of this fire, some of the Raiders managed to slink out of the kill zone. Others remained pinned down and had to wait for the main attack.[35]

On the hill above Fouhren, Bill coordinated his fire plan with Lieutenant Quesenberry. Having scouted Fouhren for two days, the observers had key enemy positions pinpointed on the ground and maps. The instrument corporal had time to survey precise measurements to the OPs and targets using an aiming circle and range finder. Bill then put his college surveying and math skills to work, validating precise firing data for the guns. The crews planned targets on anti-tank guns, machine guns, and any parked tanks. H Company's machine guns plotted direct fires from the high ground onto the German crew-served weapons and infantry bunkers.

Before G Company launched its attack, it got a welcome reinforcement. A platoon of tanks navigated its way up the snow-covered hill and joined the infantry. The battalion now had a combined arms force ready to smash Fouhren.[36]

Quesenberry started the attack at 0800 hours. The 81mm and 4.2-inch mortars dumped HE and smoke rounds on the pre-planned targets. While the gunners plastered key German weapons, the tanks and infantry started moving downhill. German 75mm and 88mm gun crews tried to adjust to the threat but the incoming mortar and machine gun rounds peppered them with shrapnel and bullets. Just as the infantry bore down on Fouhren, Captain Songer's Shermans charged up the Tandel road from the south. The dual American onslaught flushed the German tanks, and the Shermans knocked out two of them.[37]

German mortars managed to take out one of the American tanks, but the American combined-arms nutcracker crushed the German defense. The enemy fled in the only direction left for them—east. The 42nd Field Artillery Battalion blanketed that escape route, firing on four pre-plotted interdictory targets.[38]

G Company overran Fouhren by 1030 hours. They rounded up thirty-six prisoners and made a haul of abandoned German equipment: "two tanks, one 88mm gun, two 75mm guns and three multibarreled 20mm anti-aircraft guns." The tankers counted twenty-five dead Germans.[39]

The enemy did not make G Company wait long for the counterattack. Incoming artillery started impacting in Fouhren around 1320 hours. The strike alerted the Americans to the impending enemy assault. Shortly after 1400 hours, the hastily re-organized German force charged out of the low ground where they had sought refuge just three hours earlier. G Company reacted immediately and showered small arms fire on them. The mortars put fire across the German avenue of approach. The attached tanks, which had already withdrawn from Fouhren, were quickly recalled and joined the fight. The weak enemy counterattack never had a chance. An hour later, the regiment reassured the division that "everything is under control."[40]

Quesenberry notified the battalion that his company had cleared all the houses in Fouhren by 1730 hours. However, the Germans were not quite finished. That evening they snuck a force wearing snow suits into the southeast corner of town and surprised seventeen Americans who wore similar camouflage. Eight soldiers managed to slip away but the Germans still hauled off nine men.[41]

General Blakeley congratulated Colonel Chance for CT 12's tactical success at Fouhren and strategic success in closing the Vianden escape route. The heavy enemy losses helped the Americans overlook the fact that the Germans had held open the Vianden crossing for four days against the 2nd Battalion's attacks. Well-placed weapons blocked the Americans until the battalion infiltrated and hit the enemy from a less obvious direction. The Germans also made an uncharacteristic error by staying a day too long and allowed the battalion to inflict heavy losses.

The next day, January 24, Bill shifted his mortar platoon behind the steep ridge north of Fouhren. The new firing positions enabled the 81mm mortars to range the German side of the Our River opposite Vianden. G Company consolidated in Fouhren while Colonel Gorn held F Company in reserve on the high ground that G Company formerly occupied.[42]

The enemy clung to the slopes leading down to the Our River valley. Their artillery and heavy mortars fired on the battalion from positions on the far side of the river. The 12th Infantry swept up a few prisoners who, it learned, were from new German formations: the *57th Grenadier Regiment* of the *9th Volksgrenadier Division*, the *226th Grenadier Regiment* of the *79th Volksgrenadier Division* and a company of *Panzerjager* self-propelled anti-tank guns. At first glance, the enemy force looked imposing, but these units were woefully understrength. The scrambled enemy units provided a clue to the disorganization of the Germans escaping the Ardennes—and the chaotic nature of their retreat. The enemy organized another half-hearted counterattack against Fouhren, but even with a vigorous artillery and rocket bombardment, it failed to accomplish anything.[43]

German indirect fire continued to pound the Americans around Fouhren. With enemy artillery observers sitting on the bluffs across the river, the 2nd Battalion's men avoided moving beyond the top of the ridgeline. The battalion curtailed combat activity to nighttime patrols to prevent enemy infiltration.

For several days, Bill had endured frequent German artillery strikes. Each time, he cringed as the rising shriek of an incoming shell warned of imminent danger followed by the skull-rattling explosion. The momentary relief of not being hit was soon cut short by the high-pitched squeal of the next enemy shell. A single barrage might last only a few minutes, but the nerve-racking cycle of noise made it seem like hours.

Bill's mortar platoon and the two rifle companies on the hills above Fouhren needed protection from incoming indirect fire and the elements. Temperatures dropped to "the coldest it has been for 66 years." The regiment brought up construction materials and logs on two-and-a-half-ton trucks to help the troops build shelters.[44]

As his troops worked at putting up their shelters, Bill's mind began to wander. He started to imagine what the ideal house would look like. His engineering skills kicked into gear as he worked out the design in his head. The house would be underground, only accessible from a vertical shaft, so deep even the heaviest shells could not penetrate. He calculated the angles of the interior hallways to stop any potential ricochets. Once he had the design in his head he visualized himself burrowing into his well-protected home. Safely underground, he could ignore the pounding artillery and finally relax. Just as these comforting thoughts soothed his troubled mind, reality struck like a claxon. *Safely underground? Hell! That's living like a mole.*

Bill shook his head to clear the ridiculous notion. Just like a straggler in the desert running toward an imaginary oasis, he had hallucinated about escaping the pressure of constant danger.

Bill's battalion enjoyed another uneventful day on January 25 with one exception. Colonel Gorn and the battalion commander from the adjacent 3rd Battalion 10th Infantry went out to survey the defensive positions on the ridgeline west of Vianden. The commanders formed a small recon party with other staff members. While driving between infantry positions the party ran into an ambush set up by German infiltrators. The two colonels escaped, but the battalion's S-2, 1st Lt. William Anderson, was killed in the exchange of fire.[45]

Quiet times for the 12th Infantry never lasted. In the predawn hours of January 26 word came down to form a quartering party and an escort for another unit that was coming to relieve the regiment from its position. The move order arrived at 1700 hours. Peeking at the overlay, the officers realized they were in for a long ride. That evening the heavy mortars from the 1st Battalion of the 2nd Infantry took over Bill's position. H Company broke down its equipment and moved back to an assembly point where they mounted trucks. They moved south of the Sauer River and spent the night clustered around Stegen, Luxembourg, waiting their turn to commence an even longer motor march back into Belgium. The 12th Infantry was heading toward some painfully familiar terrain.[46]

CHAPTER THIRTEEN

BLEIALF

The 2nd Battalion's vehicle convoy rolled out early on January 27. The route meandered over slippery roads far to the west and south through Mersch, Sauel, and Attert. The convoy then turned north to Bastogne, Belgium. After passing through that demolished city, the trucks headed northeast along the Bastogne-Lonvilly highway. The vehicles passed scores of knocked out German and American tanks that gave mute testimony of the savage fighting around Bastogne. Late that afternoon, the men arrived at an assembly area near Bourcy, Belgium.[1]

The reason for the long motor march soon became clear. General Bradley had transferred the 4th Infantry Division to Maj. Gen. Troy Middleton's VIII Corps to give more impetus to the "Hurry Up Offensive." Bradley directed the VIII Corps to drive the retreating German forces through central Belgium and, he hoped, smash all the way to the Rhine.[2]

After a restful seventy-mile ride, Bill had enough energy to write to Beth that evening. "I sit here tonight in an abandoned, shell-torn house at my leisure. The past 10 or 12 days have been hell, but we are quiet today—tomorrow is another day." Bill thought back to his harsh transition from convalescence to winter combat. The memories of assaulting Fouhren and watching men like Tallie Crocker go down troubled him. "There have been hours when death seemed inevitable. During those hours I heard you say, 'Darling, I love you so much,' and somehow that knowledge kept me cool enough to maintain my command of men...The quick close calls of danger do not do more than startle a man; it is the sustained dangers that last for an hour or even as much as a day that crack a man. I am sure that you are the one that carried me through."[3]

Oral orders came down on January 28 to resume the motor march to an assembly area near Burg Reuland, Belgium. The regiment held the 2nd Battalion in reserve and placed them last in the order of march. The men remounted the trucks at 1800 hours but did not roll out until 2115 hours. Then it took almost nine hours to travel the forty kilometers to Burg Reuland. The delay and excruciating pace exposed the major problem with General Bradley's "Hurry Up Offensive." "On these last few days of January it seemed as though the entire American Army was trying to move down the Bastogne Highway...the highway from south of Bastogne to Trois Vierges was lined on both sides with a solid stream of vehicles." The snowbound countryside and clogged, icy roads doomed Bradley's offensive.[4]

General Blakeley passed down a new order directing the Ivy Division to pierce the Siegfried Line through the Schnee Eifel, ground it had fought over before. The division noted the irony. "It was thus one of the curious turns of fate that brought the division back to precisely the same battleground which it had originally fought over when it advanced to the Siegfried Line four and one half long months before." The veterans of that battle recalled the cramped, wet, gloomy ridge and the hard fighting along its crest. No one looked forward to attacking the Schnee Eifel in knee-deep snow.[5]

While Bill and the rest of 2nd Battalion settled at Burg Reuland, the 3rd Battalion led the regiment's attack on January 29. It ran into a strong enemy outpost holding the Our River defensive line. The 1st Battalion, in trail behind the 3rd, took the town of Bracht, Belgium. On January 30, the 3rd Battalion pressed its attack against the Our River under heavy German artillery, mortar, and rocket fire. The heavy snow and stiff enemy resistance made progress very slow, but it managed to gain a foothold on the east side of the river and seized the hamlet of Hemmeres, Germany. The 3rd Battalion then tried to envelop the town of Elcherath, Germany from the north but was stopped at a hill dubbed "Brussels B." On January 31, Colonel Chance passed the 1st Battalion through Hemmeres to seize Elcherath while 3rd Battalion eliminated the resistance on Brussels B.

Bill's battalion remained in reserve for these three days. On January 31, they moved up and occupied Bracht. Bedded down inside one of the houses, Bill wrote to Beth. "The snow changed to rain today, but I am inside so am quite comfortable. An occasional Jerry shell whines in but all in all it's a peaceful and quiet day." He also described the destruction in the Belgian town. Educated as an engineer to build rather than destroy, Bill felt sorrow about the devastation wrought by both sides in the conflict. "If we fight for a town for two days or more, few if any houses will have complete roofs. No windows will be intact, and wires will be strewn around the streets. A few fires will burn for another day and still a few civilians will remain through it all...The rooms in the houses are invariably filled with plaster, glass and the contents the Jerry left behind. There is no mess as complete as a war ravaged home."[6]

Over the next several months, as Germany's strategic situation turned hopeless, many people in the military and at home wondered why individual Germans continued to fight. In the letter, Bill made a comment that showed remarkable insight into what motivated the German soldiers. "Our soldiers realize what a horror it is to have war in your home. The Germans realize it so they fight on; we realize it so we will do all we can to keep war from our homes."

The regiment's initial order on January 28 identified seven objectives (OBJ 1 through 7) in its zone of action. OBJ 1, Elcherath, fell after three days of fighting. General Blakeley sensed that the Germans were performing a delay operation, a defensive tactic intended to trade space for time, so they could prepare the Siegfried Line fortifications. German delaying forces defended a series of outposts with enough strength to force the Americans to make a deliberate attack to take the position. Once the Americans gathered in strength and attacked, the Germans would pull back to the next delay position. The division commander decided to disrupt the Germans' timing. He ordered the regiment to launch an unusual night attack with 1st Battalion to seize OBJ 2, the village of Ihren. Blakeley wanted Ihren cleared in time to pass the 2nd Battalion through to take Winterscheid, OBJ 4, on February 1.[7]

Company C moved forward from Elcherath at 2300 hours on January 31. The enemy, so accustomed to the American habit of doing nothing at night, had not posted nighttime security. When the rifle company burst into Ihren, it caught the German defenders in their bunks. The 1st Battalion wasted no time following up this success, sending its scout platoon northeast to clear a critical road junction on a nearby hilltop, OBJ 3.[8]

The 2nd Battalion left Bracht in the pre-dawn hours of February 1 with G Company in the lead. Bill's mortar platoon followed behind them. He and the observers stayed abreast of the lead elements on foot but he likely kept the squads mounted on their jeeps. Cross-country movement through snow drifts while carrying mortars, bipods, and ammunition would have been exhausting.[9]

G Company crossed the rail line running through Ihren, the designated LD, at 0900 hours. They marched east up a stream valley, meeting no resistance. The slippery road conditions caused the most difficulty. A pattern of rain-thaw-freeze weather made them extremely treacherous. G Company followed the road out of the stream valley and approached Winterscheid from the south. Moving quickly, the riflemen overran the town before the Germans had a chance to react. By 1145 hours, G Company secured OBJ 4 and rounded up a dozen prisoners without a fight. The night attack and rapid advance on Winterscheid had the Germans off balance. The enemy did not respond until 1515 hours when machine guns fired across the stream valley into Winterscheid from Grosslangenfeld. The fire came from outside the regiment's zone but they still took a

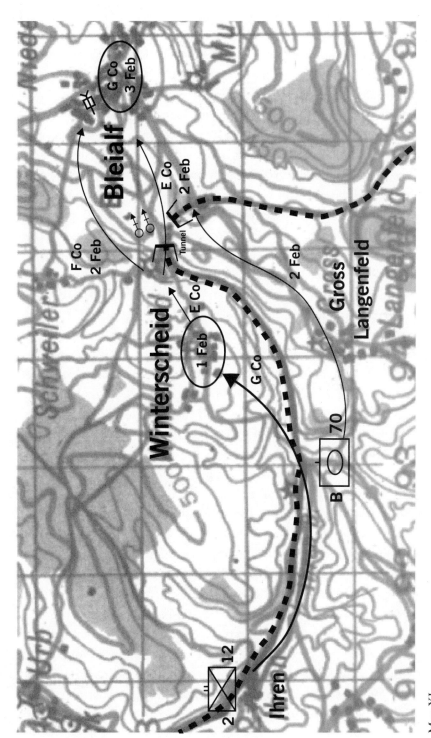

Map XI

few casualties. The record does not state how the Americans responded, but the machine guns across the little valley would have been easy targets for H Company's mortars and machine guns.[10] (See Map XI)

Colonel Gorn moved F Company into Winterscheid beside G Company and advanced E Company to a stream crossing six hundred meters closer to OBJ 7, the town of Bleialf. Meanwhile, 1st Battalion moved into Schweiler, OBJ 5, just north of Winterscheid. Both battalions sent patrols to investigate the enemy in Bleialf. While the patrols were out, prisoner interrogations helped intelligence develop the enemy situation. The regiment faced elements of the *326th Volksgrenadier Division*. The prisoners confirmed General Blakeley's suspicions when they revealed that the Germans intended to use Bleialf as their final delay position before withdrawing into the border fortifications. The patrols came back later that evening and reported seeing seventy enemy troops inside Bleialf armed with machine guns. Their reports confirmed the S-2's conclusion. Bleialf would be a tough nut to crack. Colonel Chance gave the mission to the 2nd Battalion. Because of the expected resistance, Chance attached two platoons of B Company, 70th Tank Battalion to Gorn's battalion. The extra firepower would come in handy because, during the night, the Germans reinforced Bleialf with another eighty men, a mortar section, a *Nebelwerfer* battery, and two tanks.[11]

Colonel Gorn planned to attack Bleialf with E and F Companies, augmented by the two tank platoons. A long, bare ridge ran from Grosslangenfeld to the northeast. Bleialf sat in a valley on the opposite side of that ridge from the battalion. E Company would start from its overnight position at the stream crossing east of Winterscheid. They would follow the general path of the Winterscheid road over the ridge and into the southern side of the objective. F Company would follow a draw heading farther northeast before popping over the ridgeline and attacking the western edge of Bleialf. Bill's mortars could support the battalion's attack from E Company's overnight position in the stream valley. However, the eight hundred-meter separation between the two assault companies might have forced him to detach one section to escort F Company.

Bill, at age fifteen, and his mother, Lucy, sitting next to the family car.

Bill and Beth's wedding portrait.

Bill and his parents strolling through Treasure Island, San Francisco in 1940.

Bill and his father standing in their uniforms outside their Oakland home after Bill enrolled in a West Point prep course.

Colonel Russell (Red) Reeder, commander of the 12th Infantry on D-Day, greeting General Montgomery, April 1944. *Courtesy of National Archives*

General Bernard Montgomery addressing the 12th Infantry Regiment during the pre-invasion train-up, April 1944. *Courtesy of National Archives*

American soldiers rehearse for Normandy landings at Slapton Sands on the Devon coast of England. *Courtesy of Library of Congress*

USS *Nevada* (BB-36) fires 14" shells on German positions behind Utah Beach. *Courtesy of U.S. Navy*

Troops and crew of an LCVP head to the beach on D-Day. *Courtesy of U.S. Navy*

Landing craft plowing through the surf off the Normandy beaches. *Courtesy of National Archives*

General Roosevelt (l) and General Barton (c) confer with Lieutenant Colonel Clarence Hupfer (r) behind Utah Beach. *Courtesy of 12ᵗʰ Infantry Regiment*

Bill's mortar platoon advancing over the inundated area behind Utah Beach (Note: the Signal Corps misidentified the unit as part of the 8ᵗʰ Infantry). *Courtesy of National Archives*

Bill's mortar platoon firing 81mm rounds in hedgerow country. *Courtesy of National Archives*

German crew in France preparing a *Nebelwerfer* for a launch of rockets. *Courtesy of Bundesarchiv*

U.S. infantrymen fighting in hedgerow country. *Courtesy of National Archives*

The Ivy Division's beloved General Teddy, Brigadier General Theodore Roosevelt, Jr. *Courtesy of National Archives*

German PWs marched to the rear by Ivy Division troops the day after the Allied bombing for Operation Cobra. *Courtesy of National Archives*

M4 Sherman tank with a "Rhino" attachment to break through hedgerows, passing an abandoned German 88mm *Flak* gun. *Courtesy of National Archives*

Column of M5 Stuart light tanks passes through a demolished French village during the breakout. *Courtesy of National Archives*

M1917A1 heavy machine gun crew supporting a rifle company in clearing a French town. *Courtesy of National Archives*

Ernest Hemingway and his driver talk with Robert Capa, photographer for *Life Magazine*, while traveling with the 4th Infantry Division after the breakout. *Courtesy of National Archives*

Knocked out German Mark V Panther tank and a dead crewman near St.-Pois. *Courtesy of National Archives*

Obersturmbannfuhrer Otto Weidinger, commander of the *Der Fuhrer Regiment* of the *2nd SS Panzer Division* at Mortain. *Courtesy of WW2gravestone.com*

German Mark VI Tiger tank and *Panzergrenadieren* of the *2nd SS Panzer "Das Reich" Division* in an attack. *Courtesy of Bundesarchiv*

12ᵗʰ Infantry mortar OP calling back target information to an 81mm mortar crew. *Courtesy of National Archives*

U.S. infantrymen attacking along a hedgerow during the Battle of Mortain. *Courtesy of National Archives*

U.S. infantrymen fighting behind a hedgerow during the Battle of Mortain. *Courtesy of National Archives*

Jubilant Parisians swarming Ivy Division vehicles on Liberation Day. *Courtesy of National Archives*

The darker side of liberation—public humiliation of women who consorted with German soldiers. *Courtesy of National Archives*

Ivy Division GIs enjoying the attention of joyous Parisians. *Courtesy of National Archives*

Citizens of Saint-Quentin, France celebrating their liberation by the 12th Infantry. *Courtesy of National Archives*

Ivy Division infantrymen riding an M10 tank destroyer through Belgium. *Courtesy of National Archives*

German Mark V Panther tank of the *1st SS Panzer "Leibstandarte Adolf Hitler" Division* cruising down a Belgian street. *Courtesy of Bundesarchiv*

CT 12 engineers repairing a bridge over the Huille River near Willerizie, Belgium. *Courtesy of National Archives*

Ivy Division infantrymen searching a Belgian town for snipers. *Courtesy of National Archives*

Ivy Division infantrymen working their way into a Belgian town. *Courtesy of National Archives*

12th Infantry column advancing through Belgium to the German border September 1944.
Courtesy of National Archives

General Barton, driving the "Barton Buggy," becomes the first U.S. general to enter Germany, September 12, 1945.
Courtesy of National Archives

Ivy Division heavy machine gun crew engaging the enemy along the Siegfried Line. *Courtesy of National Archives*

First Lieutenant Bill Chapman in Consdorf, Luxembourg, January 1945.
Picture by John Gunning, courtesy of Pat Gunning

Bill riding in one of the mortar platoon jeeps in Luxembourg, January 1945. *Picture by John Gunning, courtesy of Pat Gunning*

Ivy Division troops scampering across the Sauer River Bridge near Bettendorf, Luxembourg January 1945. *Courtesy of National Archives*

Brigadier General (later Major General) Harold Blakeley, commander of the 4th Infantry Division from December 1944 to the end of the war. *Courtesy of National Archives*

American mortar platoon advancing north of the Sauer River Valley through snow. *Courtesy of National Archives*

Bill tending one of his 81mm mortars in the Rhineland, February 1945. *Picture by John Gunning, courtesy of Pat Gunning*

Ivy Division soldier examining a juvenile German PW captured north of the Sauer River, January 1945. *Courtesy of National Archives*

Ivy Division 81mm mortar platoon firing amid rubble. *Courtesy of National Archives*

U.S. troops discover the frozen corpse of an American paratrooper killed during the Battle of the Bulge. *Courtesy of National Archives*

C-47s air-dropping supplies to the 12th Infantry because poor road conditions halted normal re-supply operations in February 1945. *Courtesy of National Archives*

H Company officers: (L-R) First Lieutenants Bill Chapman, David McElroy, Jack Gunning, and Captain Benjamin Compton, February 1945. *Picture by John Gunning, courtesy of Pat Gunning*

Bill standing next to a knocked out M4 Sherman tank near Brandscheid, Germany, February 1945. *Picture by John Gunning, courtesy of Pat Gunning*

Infantry officer receiving target data for a 81mm mortar section. *Courtesy of National Archives*

Ivy Division M1917A1 heavy machine gun crew engaging the enemy in the Rhineland. *Courtesy of National Archives*

Ivy Division M1917A1 heavy machine gun crew and an M36 tank destroyer supporting the attack near Prum, March 2, 1945. *Courtesy of National Archives*

Ivy Division rifleman digging in along the bluffs of the Prum River, March 1945. *Courtesy of National Archives*

M4 Sherman from the 70th Tank Battalion moving with infantry near Prum, February 1945. *Courtesy of National Archives*

Ivy Division troops advancing east of Prum under artillery fire. *Courtesy of National Archives*

Tanks of the 11th Armored Division and Ivy Division troops attack east of Prum, March 3, 1945. *Courtesy of National Archives*

Brigadier General James Rodwell, commander of Task Force Rhino and Task Force Rodwell. *Picture by John Gunning, courtesy of Pat Gunning*

Brigadefuhrer, later *Gruppenfuhrer*, Max Simon, who commanded the *XIII*th *SS Corps* in southern Germany. *Courtesy of Bundesarchiv*

Troops of the 12ᵗʰ Infantry boarding the SS *Sea Bass* at Le Havre. *Courtesy of National Archives*

U.S. anti-aircraft crew defending the Danube River Bridge at Lauingen, Germany, April 25, 1945. *Courtesy of National Archives*

Colonel John Gorn escorts President Kennedy and German Chancellor Konrad Adenauer while commanding the U.S. Army's ceremonial Old Guard in 1962. *Courtesy of White House Photographer*

Bill in uniform and Beth in her wedding dress at their belated wedding reception, June 26, 1983.

Bill, late in life, speaking to a convention of the American Society of Heating, Refrigerating and Air-Conditioning Engineers (ASHRAE).

The icy terrain complicated the battalion's plan. A rail line tunneled through the ridge halfway between Winterscheid and Bleialf. The tunnel was only three hundred meters long but the rail bed cut steep sides into the ridge on both ends. Each rail cut created an obstacle over two hundred meters in length. That left a maneuverable space of three hundred meters on the ridge above the tunnel. The Grosslangenfeld road traveled along the crest, then dropped off the east side of the ridge 1,400-1,800 meters short of Bleialf. It crossed the eastern rail cut on an overpass. The Germans demolished the overpass, leaving the snowbound crest trail above the tunnel as the only viable avenue from the south. The other road from Winterscheid climbed out of the stream valley on the far (north) side of the rail cut but intersected the crest trail directly above the tunnel before descending toward Bleialf. The lack of trees on the ridgeline meant that anybody crossing from west to east would be visible or "sky-lined" to German gunners on the other side. Any tank approaching Bleialf had to pass through the choke point above the tunnel, exposed to German anti-tank weapons.

Because of the poor state of the roads, B Company's tanks had remained behind in Burg Reuland. Bringing them forward proved to be a monumental task. The 4th Engineers had worked to exhaustion just keeping the roads open for wheeled supply vehicles. "Dozers had to be used to push aside roadblocks, destroyed vehicles, dead horses, blown bridges (railroad overpasses), as well as to plow snow from the roads. All types of mines had to be removed…Craters had to be filled." The depth of snow obstructed the Shermans' mobility and forced them to be road-bound for the attack. The tankers chose to take the road through Grosslangenfeld to Bleialf rather than following the 2nd Battalion's path through Winterscheid. The Grosslangenfeld road offered the tanks an avenue that stayed along high ground, as opposed to the Winterscheid road that had to cross a stream then go over a hill to the objective. The tankers soon discovered that simply climbing the hill to Grosslangenfeld posed a challenge. "The roads were so icy that infantry working at night, used entrenching tools to cut grooves to assist 70th tanks in going up a hill for the attack the next morning. In another case, all five 3d Platoon tanks had to be chained together to help get them up a hill." The tanks took so long to reach Gross-langenfeld that Colonel Gorn had to delay the 2nd Battalion's attack from 0900 hours to 1030 hours.[12]

Even that proved to be too optimistic. The tanks had not yet clawed their way up to Grosslangenfeld by the rescheduled start time. Gorn decided not to wait any longer and told the two infantry companies to begin moving toward the crest of the ridge. E and F Companies barely started across the stream valley before hitting a German outpost on the ridge. The two companies had to fight their way uphill. Bill's mortars started plunking rounds from their initial firing positions. That close to the targets, the mortar squad leaders could spot the rounds and adjust fire from the guns' positions. It was not until noon that the outpost was overrun and E and F Companies crossed the ridgeline that delineated their LD.[13]

The 42nd Field Artillery Battalion "prepped" the objective with HE rounds to help pave the way. E Company crossed the high ground above the tunnel where the roads converged with the crest trail. The enemy had this area targeted with machine guns and AT guns. Dodging shells and bullets, the troops pushed off the ridge toward Bleialf. To the north, F Company used the cover of the draw to gain a position six hundred meters from the northwest edge of Bleialf. They overwhelmed a German outpost and captured fifteen prisoners as they drove across the ridgeline. As they feared, the moment they crossed over the top, they caught fire from the German infantry and tanks in the town.

Bill and his observers could see targets inside Bleialf from the top of the ridge and called for fire. Soon the 81s began raining HE and smoke rounds on the German defenders. With the Germans firing from the protection of the buildings in Bleialf, the light HE rounds and smoke could only obstruct and annoy the enemy, not fully suppress them. The riflemen pressed ahead across open ground, supported by H Company's heavy weapons and their own machine guns. They charged in short rushes, hit the dirt, returned fire, then repeated the process. By minimizing their exposure to a few seconds of hasty charges, they made it difficult for the German gunners to score kills, but they could only creep forward.

B Company's tanks finally reached the scene of the battle where the Grosslangenfeld road began its descent from the top of the ridge. One of the tankers reported what he saw. "There was a lot of shooting going on. The infantry was being hit hard in the town, so we were sent down a hill just to draw fire from them." The lead platoon leader looked at the icy road leading to the railroad cut in full view of the Germans in Bleialf and objected to moving forward.[14]

Captain Songer radioed back, "You will go down that hill!"

"OK, here we go!"

The Germans knew the American tanks would be road bound and forced to attack over the railroad tunnel or the overpass. Their tanks and AT guns had the slope pre-targeted. The instant the Shermans began sliding down the icy road, they opened fire. One after another, the American tanks took hits. Four Shermans went up in flames within a couple of minutes. One American crew member jumped out of his burning tank and took cover behind it. His buddies watched in horror as "an 88 came in on the tracks and took his head right off his shoulders." The tankers could see that the bridge overpass had been demolished, trapping them single file on the slick road. Two of the remaining tanks turned off the road and slid out of control down the slope. One of them hit a mine at the bottom. The remnants of the two tank platoons pulled back.[15]

Without the tanks' firepower, the 2nd Battalion had to depend on its own resources to take Bleialf. Lieutenants Jack Gunning and Reuben Cuellar put direct fire on the town with their platoons' heavy machine guns. Bill needed to bring his mortars closer to Bleialf to effectively suppress the Germans. The platoon's jeeps could bring a section up the ridge to a point still on the west side of the crest but within 1,200 meters of the southwest corner of the town. At that range, they could hit the Germans defending from houses with the heavier M45 demolition rounds. Bill called the guns forward while he and the observers darted forward with the advancing rifle platoons.

The riflemen worked closer to Bleialf. E Company captured eight Germans, not far beyond the rail cut, but ran into more intense machine gun and 88 fire coming from the town. By 1430 hours E Company told the battalion they were pinned down.[16]

Getting pinned down was a frightful experience for an infantryman. If he did not crawl to cover or burrow into shallow ground, the next sweep of a machine gun could kill him. The slightest move might draw a fatal bullet. Anyone wounded in the open faced grim prospects.

While Bill and some of his observers scampered over some open ground the Germans sprayed them with rifle and machine gun fire. They hit the dirt immediately then crawled to the nearest cover. The Germans had a favorable firing position and shot at anyone who tried to move.[17]

Soon Bill heard one of his men calling for help. "Medic...Medic."

Bill shifted around to see who was wounded and to find a way to get help to him. He located the wounded soldier but the man had fallen in an exposed spot. Any medic trying to get to him would himself be shot.

To make matters worse, Bill recognized the soldier as one of the H Company old hands. Bill searched for any defilade approach that could be used to crawl out to the man but the enemy had every inch covered by fire.

"Medic...Medic." The wounded soldier kept pleading.

Other men wanted to dash out to the soldier but Bill ordered them to stay put. He made a tough call. No sense losing more men in a futile attempt to save one wounded soldier.

While the infantrymen exchanged fire with the Germans, Bill and his men could hear the wounded soldier's cries get fainter and fainter. "Medic...Medic."

The Americans, frustrated and angry, continued battling the Germans to clear them out of the way but the fight took too long. Finally, Bill heard the wounded man's last call for help. "Medic...Medic...Never mind...too late."

By the time they neutralized the enemy machine gun, the man had died. Bill and his men felt the pain of this casualty. The dead man was a stalwart veteran who had survived dozens of battles. His forlorn cries while he gradually faded away haunted the whole platoon, especially Bill.

The 81mm mortars began hitting the houses on the southern and western edges of town with the heavier demolition rounds once they settled into position on the ridge. While H Company's heavy weapons now suppressed the enemy more effectively, the hard work still had to be done by the riflemen. Even as German artillery joined the fray, the platoons kept inching forward. Regardless of how quickly the Germans saw off the road-bound American tanks, they could not stop the 2nd Battalion's aggressive infantrymen. The painstaking infantry assault finally reached Bleialf around 1630 hours. As the sun went down, E Company snagged a foothold on the southern edge of town and F Company seized a few buildings in the northwest sector.[18]

Rather than wait for daylight to take the rest of Bleialf, Colonel Gorn ordered G Company to attack that night—more evidence of the 12th Infantry's growing confidence in its tactical abilities.[19]

G Company moved forward from Winterscheid and passed through E Company's sector at 0215 hours on February 3. A rifle platoon from F Company and Lieutenant Reuben Cuellar's heavy machine gun platoon provided support. G Company's troops seized the center of Bleialf before first light after an intense but brief firefight. The Germans understood that once an enemy entered a town it could not be held. They left an outpost in Bleialf but withdrew the bulk of their forces. G Company cleared the town by 1020 hours and rounded up sixteen prisoners.[20]

February 3 marked another significant tactical development for the battalion. Company C, 610th Tank Destroyer (TD) Battalion knocked out two German tanks that morning a little southeast of Bleialf. The 610th had joined the 4th Infantry Division at the end of January and had just made its first appearance in the 2nd Battalion's area. The Ivy Division welcomed the addition of the 610th because it came equipped with the new M36 tank destroyer. The M36 mounted a 90mm gun that provided one vital tactical improvement—it could knock out the German Panther and Tiger tanks. For the first time, the Americans could take these tanks head-on and destroy them.[21]

After the capture of Bleialf, CT 12 reverted to defense. The 2nd Battalion set up positions around Bleialf, F facing northeast, G east, and E southeast. The 22nd Infantry passed through the 12th later that day to continue the division's attack to the Siegfried Line.[22]

Bill and his men did not realize that the switch to defense was more than a temporary tactical change. The attack against Bleialf coincided with a major strategic shift. On February 1, General Eisenhower ordered General Bradley to wrap up his "Hurry Up Offensive." Allied resources needed to flow to Field Marshal Montgomery's 21st Army Group for Operations Veritable and Grenade, aimed to clear the west bank of the lower Rhine. Eisenhower allowed Bradley leeway to conduct local offensive operations. The cancellation of his operation upset Bradley, but the offensive probably could not have produced a major victory. Bad weather and poor road conditions had robbed the 12th Army Group of any chance to exploit the German retreat from the Ardennes-Eifel.[23]

The 12th Infantry now endured their most wretched living conditions since the Channel crossing. Bleialf had been the scene of intense fighting in December. Heavy snows had subsequently covered the corpses of American and German soldiers, as well as the remains of draft horses, cows, hogs, and other livestock. The frigid winter had preserved the dead in their agonized, death-throe positions until the early February thaw, when the rain melted away the snow cover enough to reveal this grotesque refuse of war. The battalion called in a graves registration unit to recover the dead. The detail went about Bleialf lifting the contorted bodies out of the snow and ice. To get the twisted shapes loaded into trucks, they had to break limbs and flatten twisted corpses, much like busting up crates. Bill and his men watched the graves registration team go about their grisly work. No one admonished them for disrespecting the dead. Theirs was a nasty job that had to be done, just like the infantry. Still, the macabre scene had a sobering effect on the infantrymen. It reminded them how little a dead soldier was valued and that someday their remains might be given similar treatment.[24]

The rotting corpses scattered about Bleialf compounded another problem—disease. German soldiers had lodged in Bleialf's houses for several days of bitter cold, followed by days of severe fighting. The German army had demanding training and strict discipline but loose sanitation standards. While occupying Bleialf, the German soldiers preferred to answer nature's calls in the corners of their rooms rather than tramp outside in the snow and risk getting shot. When the battalion moved into any of the buildings, the indoors reeked of human waste. The stench of decay outside was no better.

The terrible living conditions disgusted Bill and his men. They had no choice but to occupy the same buildings and ground fouled by the retreating enemy. It only took a couple of days for dysentery to strike. Nearly everyone in the battalion suffered from the "runs." The sickness wearied the already tired soldiers and sapped their strength. Men struggled to perform the simplest tasks. Loading a truck or repositioning a crew-served weapon took twice the normal number of men to complete. Disease and fatigue got so bad, the companies began reporting half their actual numbers on the strength reports to reflect their true combat capabilities.

Bill was not immune to the ravages of dysentery. One night he woke up with his intestines in an uproar. He tried to get out of his bedroll to get to a latrine but the simple act of sitting up caused his bowels to burst. Weak and foul, he wriggled out of his sleeping bag. He picked up his entrenching tool and slipped away to find a secluded spot to clean himself. He limped through some trees searching for a suitable place when a sentry spotted him in the dark.

"Halt, identify yourself."

"It's Lieutenant Chapman. I've crapped my pants and I'm out here to bury my underwear." In the dark, Bill could hear the sentry chortle at his predicament.

"Okay, you can pass." No doubt, news of Bill's accident made the rounds of H Company's enlisted men by morning.

The Ivy Division continued to roll east while the 2nd Battalion stayed in Bleialf. The 22nd Infantry captured Brandscheid on February 5, the town at the southwest tip of the Schnee Eifel they failed to take in September. Their successful assault gave them a sense of satisfaction for the frustration they suffered five months earlier. Much like the 2nd Battalion had done in September, the 8th Infantry snuck through the enemy-held pillboxes on the Schnee Eifel and captured a large number of the unprepared defenders with only minor losses. Instead of driving up the length of the forested ridge, as the 12th Infantry had done in the fall, the 8th Infantry drove east through the hole it punched in the German line. The Germans, seeing that they could not mount a cohesive defense of the Siegfried Line, abandoned the fortifications on the Schnee Eifel and backpedaled toward the Prum River. The division's eastward progress finally relieved Bleialf from the irritating German artillery and rocket fire that had fallen on the town for several days.[25]

Bill received a letter from Beth, while stuck in Bleialf, telling him that two of the officers he knew from the 63rd Infantry Division at Camp Van Dorn had returned to the States as "psycho" cases. Bill remarked that one of the other officers from his old outfit had been killed, one sent home with nerves, and another refused orders to return to combat. "By God this war is tough at that…I don't razz these guys with 'nerves' though because every man does have a limit and I had some brave men go to pieces."[26]

By February 7, the 1st and 3rd Battalions moved forward to occupy portions on the Schnee Eifel they had seized in September while the 2nd remained in the filth of Bleialf. One small consolation was the arrival of a medical aid station that moved up near the sickly troops. The 12th Infantry rejoined the attack on February 9. The artillery opened the operation with a massive nine-battalion (162 guns) TOT strike against Nieder Prum and another six-battalion (108 guns) strike against Weins-feld. Stiff resistance from the *304th Panzergrenadier Regiment* of the *2nd Panzer Division* in the town of Steinmehlen stalled 1st Battalion, but the 3rd Battalion seized the high ground overlooking the city of Prum. Colonel Chance kept the sickly 2nd Battalion in reserve but brought them forward to Herscheid. Few regretted moving closer to the action as long as the advance got them out of the disease-ridden town. CT 12 continued its attack to secure bridges over the Prum River on February 10. They managed to push the Germans across the river but the enemy blew all the bridges before the Americans could capture them.[27]

The 4th Infantry Division's push ended at the Prum River, and it reverted to a defensive posture on February 11. Colonel Chance ordered the 2nd Battalion to relieve the 3rd and set up defensive positions on the high ground facing Nieder Prum.[28]

As had happened in the fall, the supply situation curtailed offensive actions. As early as February 5, the regiment had been forced to limit ammunition supplies. The daily allowance for Bill's mortars dropped to less than eleven rounds per tube. The road conditions continued to worsen, as noted by the Army's official history. "Not built for heavy military traffic, the roads of Belgium and Luxembourg had literally disintegrated under an alternate combination of freeze and thaw, daily rains and floods, and the coming and going of big tanks, trucks and guns." The regiment's S-3, Maj. John Meyer, offered to send infantrymen to help the 4th Engineers mend the roads. They replied, "Don't need men at present—main problem is hauling material." One of the adjacent regiments asked to use the roads in the 12th Infantry's sector for resupply because their main supply route had become impassable. The regiment gave its okay but advised that the roads could only support movement by jeeps. The deuce-and-a-halves simply could not haul bulk supplies over roads with the consistency of pudding. The Army turned to the Air Corps for help. On February 13, C-47 aircraft air-dropped supplies to the 12th Infantry near Bleialf. The battalions organized supply distribution parties using jeeps to deliver the rations, fuel, ammunition, spare parts, and medical supplies.[29]

The supply shortage kept the regiment on the defensive but that did not stop the action. Both the Americans and Germans patrolled the Prum River valley. Small parties crossed the river on footbridges or small watercraft to harass and ambush opposing troops or lay mines on the other side's roads. On February 12, an E Company patrol ran into a German raiding party on the west side of the river. The American patrol had to break contact but left a wounded man in the care of some sympathetic German civilians. The next night the battalion's Raider Platoon went back to retrieve the wounded man. They also evacuated the six German civilians who had watched over him.[30]

The two sides also exchanged indirect fire throughout the month. OPs reported movements of German infantry and armor across the river, giving Bill's platoon and the division's artillery an occasional target. The Germans replied with their own mortar, artillery, and rocket fire. Even with these limited engagements, the division's artillery could not maintain an adequate ammunition supply. Beginning February 16, the 610th Tank Destroyer Battalion began firing its 90mm guns in an indirect mode to interdict key crossroads and German positions. The M36 crews learned to achieve airbursts over exposed infantry with timed fuses on their HE rounds. This unorthodox use of the tank destroyers was suspended once their cache of HE rounds fell below basic loads.[31]

With the regiment in a static defense, Colonel Chance implemented a policy of rotating battalions off the front line for a rest. In the evening of February 16, the 1st Battalion took over the 2nd Battalion's positions, so Colonel Gorn's men could march back to a bivouac site near Herscheid. The men enjoyed showers, movies, and a day of relaxation. The H Company Commander, Capt. Benjamin Compton, decided to spend an afternoon away from the troops. He took Bill and 1st Lt. Jack Gunning with him for a short ride. Gunning brought along his camera and the three officers posed for pictures next to a knocked-out Sherman tank. The fun ended on February 18 when the battalion took over a sector held by the 358th Regiment of the 90th Infantry Division, after the 12th Infantry's zone got shifted south to cover Pronsfeld.[32]

Shortly after midnight, a platoon from E Company tried to move into a forward outpost on the west side of the river, opposite Pronsfeld. Before the platoon reached its OP, an enemy force occupying their intended position opened up with machine guns. The E Company platoon broke contact and set up its OP a short distance away. The enemy presence prompted Colonel Gorn to send the Raider Platoon on the afternoon of February 19 to drive off the enemy. The Raiders ran into more machine guns and a pillbox that forced them back. Based on the contact and prisoner statements, the S-2 determined that the Germans held the wooded bluff overlooking Pronsfeld and Pittenbach with at least a reinforced platoon. Gorn and his staff planned a more deliberate attack to eliminate the German pocket.[33]

G Company had the wooded bluff boxed on the north, west, and south sides. One platoon occupied the crest of the bluff only three hundred meters west of the woods where the German outpost had set up.

Gorn selected E Company, less the platoon manning the OP, to sweep the German position from south to north. The crest of the bluff gave H Company a perfect position to set up its mortars and machine guns at right angles from E Company's direction of attack. From this position, the observers could shift the mortar and machine gun fire simply by adjusting the azimuth to the targets as the infantry pushed north. The simplified fire control of the heavy weapons encouraged Gorn to make a night attack. He ordered E Company to strike in the pre-dawn hours of February 20.[34]

The attack began with artillery prepping the south end of the objective. Once E Company approached within "danger close" range, the artillery shifted its fire north. Bill's mortars and H Company's machine guns then opened fire. The mortar crews dropped rounds down the tubes at a steady clip. The entrenched Germans squirmed deeper into their foxholes while shrapnel, tree bursts, and .30 cal. rounds rained overhead. With the Germans suppressed, the American infantry closed on the southern end of the objective. The moment E Company was ready to assault, the observers signaled the mortars and machine guns to shift fire a few degrees north. The rifle platoons swept forward and seized the tip of the wooded bluff. E Company continued to advance behind the shifting artillery, mortar, and machine gun fire. The luckless Germans could do nothing other than keep their heads down in their foxholes. As soon as the overhead fire lifted, the American riflemen were on top of them. By 1030 hours it was all over. E Company cleared 1,000 meters of the wooded bluff and captured twenty-seven Germans while suffering only a few light casualties. They counted twenty-five dead Germans.[35]

The little engagement west of Pronsfeld demonstrated the growing tactical proficiency of the American infantry. The regiment made note of the battalion's excellent fire control. "The operation was especially successful because of coordinated use of artillery, mortar, rifle and machine gun fires."[36]

The fight also demonstrated the ineffectiveness and crumbling morale of the German army. In addition to the twenty-seven Germans captured by E Company, the patrols and forward companies netted a steady stream of prisoners and deserters. The Germans had withdrawn their panzer units from the area for re-fitting. The forces opposing the regiment appeared to be ad hoc units named after their commanders: *Kampfgruppen Geissel, Jung,* and *Kratzer.* These "thrown-together" units were so confused that some enemy commanders did not even know their own troop dispositions. The Germans limited their actions to aggressive patrolling and interdictory artillery, rocket, and 88 fire. General Blakeley and his senior staff officers champed at the bit given the disorganized German defense standing between the Ivy Division and the Rhine. Until the road conditions and supply situation improved, however, the Americans could only sit and wait.[37]

Bill's battalion had an uneventful time on the front line between February 20 and 23. The men manned the OPs, patrolled, set out trip flares, and improved their defensive positions. Besides the occasional German artillery or mortar fire, the scariest moments came when a flight of Air Corps P-47s strafed the battalion area. One P-47 dropped a bomb that, thankfully, injured no one. On February 23, the 1st Battalion relieved Gorn's men. The battalion marched back to a reserve position near Brandscheid where they took showers and watched movies. The men bunked in the old Siegfried Line pillboxes surrounding the town. During this rest period, the troops test fired their weapons, though the supply constraints prevented Bill's platoon from firing any live 81mm rounds.[38]

Colonel Chance called in his battalion and separate company commanders for a conference on February 26. The strategic situation had changed once more. The period of stagnation along the Prum River had come to an end.[39]

Before setting out on the new offensive, Bill turned his thoughts to Beth. That evening he wrote to her. He tried to prepare her for possible tragedy, in his own clumsy way, by urging her to keep focused on her own life. "Honey, please quit worrying about me. All you can accomplish is making yourself ill. If I am going to get hit there is nothing you can do about it."[40]

CHAPTER FOURTEEN

RHINELAND

Field Marshal Montgomery's 21st Army Group represented the Allied main effort in February and, consequently, absorbed the most resources. In Operations Veritable and Grenade, Montgomery's three armies—the Canadian 1st, British 2nd, and American 9th (which came under Montgomery's command during the Ardennes Campaign)—advanced toward the west bank of the lower Rhine River, a prerequisite for any assault into Germany. General Bradley, commander of the 12th Army Group, did not want his forces to stand idle, merely guarding Montgomery's southern flank. He drafted a plan called Operation Lumberjack that would clear the west bank of the Rhine between Cologne and Coblenz. Bradley planned to drive the First Army to the Rhine then turn it southeast along the west bank to meet Third Army's thrust through the Eifel. Bradley intended to crush the German forces remaining west of the Rhine between Hodges and Patton. General Eisenhower approved the plan but told Bradley to wait until Operation Grenade had progressed to the point that Hodges's First Army would no longer be required to secure Montgomery's flank. By late February, the U.S. Ninth Army, commanded by Lt. Gen. William H. Simpson, had punched through to the Rhine and the success of Grenade looked assured. Bradley issued orders to execute Lumberjack with a projected starting date of March 3.[1]

The 4th Infantry Division started a preliminary offensive on February 28 with CTs 8 and 22 leading the way. The division had to establish a bridgehead over the Prum River wide enough to allow the 11th Armored Division to pass through and roll to the Rhine. The German *5th Parachute Division*—many of its members newly recruited Hitler Youth who had never strapped on a parachute—faced the Ivy Division. The 12th Infantry stayed in reserve until the division secured the high ground on the east side of the river opposite the city of Prum. CT 12 got into the action on March 1. Colonel Chance ordered the 1st Battalion to pass through Prum, then take over a defensive position on the far bluff from the 22nd Infantry. The 2nd Battalion would follow the 1st Battalion through Prum then attack south, along the high ground, to seize Nieder Prum.[2]

Colonel Gorn's battalion started the day at 0800 hours in Brandscheid. The men marched eight kilometers along muddy roads toward Prum while their sister battalion cleared the city while under fire from rockets and an AT gun. By noon the 1st Battalion finished mopping up isolated enemy outposts inside the city and threw a footbridge across the river. The 2nd Battalion's rifle companies moved into Prum and waited for the 1st Battalion to complete its crossing.[3]

The men found temporary shelter in the piled rubble that was once a medieval town. Prum first came within range of American artillery back in September during the battle on the Schnee Eifel. From then until December the Americans periodically bombed and shelled the town to interdict the movement of German vehicles and supplies. The 22nd Infantry Regiment entered the city on February 12 after a heavy artillery preparation. The Germans, holding the high ground on the east side of the Prum River, had shelled the city ever since. The sustained pounding by both sides had demolished the place. Debris covered everything: homes, stores, yards, and avenues. Bill couldn't find two bricks lying atop each other in some sections of Prum. Parts of it had been flattened, desolation exceeding anything he had seen before.

At 1515 hours, E Company dashed across the narrow footbridge, followed by G Company. Bill positioned the 81mm mortars in defilade behind the Kalvarien Berg, the ridge overlooking Prum from the west. From this protected location, the mortars could strike targets along the bluffs east of the river on a 90 degree arc from Prum to Nieder Prum. The platoon's observers could view the battalion's entire zone of action from the top of the berg and still communicate directly with the gun crews. They also had the rare luxury of being able to set up the aiming circle and range finder to spot rounds and adjust fire during an attack.[4] (See Map XII)

E Company's rifle platoons began moving south along the face of the bluff under the concealment of a fir and beech woodland. The company advanced slowly as the riflemen tottered on the steep slope, slipping on the wet, leafy ground. The platoons emerged from the concealing woods and continued heading southwest on a grassy part of the bluff. Seven hundred meters past the footbridge the face of the bluff swelled slightly, just enough to mask the southern length of the slope. The minute E Company crossed this feature, streams of small arms fire from a patch of woods two hundred meters away ripped through its ranks, forcing the riflemen to the ground. The slight swell in the face of the bluff blocked the supporting fires from G and F Companies. E Company's infantrymen could only engage the defenders by moving past the swell into open ground. As the enemy paratroopers raked the slope, a self-propelled AT gun began shooting from a water mill near Nieder Prum.

Bill's mortars lit up the woods above Nieder Prum as soon as the call for fire came in, dropping rounds "as rapidly as accuracy in laying the mortar permit[ted]." The bombardment and suppressive fire from H Company's heavy machine guns made the enemy flinch but, protected by overhead cover, they still had the upper hand.[5]

E Company attempted to maneuver against the dug-in Germans but the enemy small arms fire proved too intense. The E Company Commander broke contact with the Germans then called back to battalion, telling Colonel Gorn that his company was stuck. With daylight waning, Gorn told E Company to stay put. That night, he and his staff put together a plan to seize Nieder Prum and bail out their forward company.[6]

Bill got called into Prum that evening for a meeting of H Company's officers. The ruined city made a depressing backdrop for the conference but a small gesture by one of Bill's friends helped boost spirits. Before the meeting started, the company mess team treated the officers to a meal. When Bill entered the makeshift officers' mess, he did a double take. He found a table arranged with complete place settings of china and crystal.

"Where did you get the china and crystal?" he asked.

One of the mess sergeants answered, "Lieutenant McElroy found it."

"Where?"

"In Prum."

"How the hell did he find anything left in Prum? The city's been completely destroyed."

"Don't know but he dug it up somewhere."

First Lt. David J. McElroy had already earned renown as a scrounger and someone who could get things done. This time he had outdone himself. Bill would've been astonished to have found an unbroken plate in the wreckage around Prum. To have found a complete china and crystal service seemed impossible.

A couple of weeks later the division HQ put out a request for a new aide-de-camp for the commanding general. Maj. Gen. Harold Blakeley wanted to select a combat officer from the division's ranks, and he asked the battalions to nominate a suitable lieutenant.

Bill knew the perfect man—Dave McElroy. "Tell division they can call off the search. I have the name of the guy they want." General Blakeley personally interviewed the candidates for the aide's position but as soon as he met with McElroy the interviews stopped. McElroy served as the general's aide-de-camp for the remainder of the war.

Colonel Gorn resumed the attack at 0500 hours on March 2 with E and G Companies moving abreast toward Nieder Prum. G Company

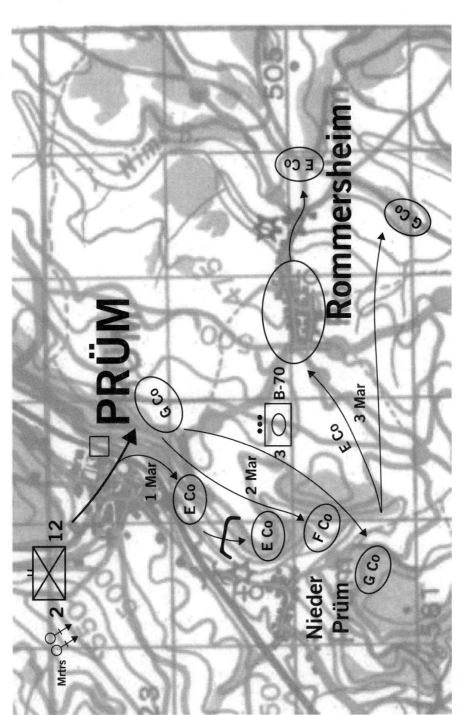

Map XII

moved along the top of the bluff while E Company stayed on the slope. Low clouds hung in the valley. Poor visibility forced Bill and the mortar observers to move with the rifle platoons and call back to the guns via radios or telephones. The 81mm crews had registered on the German positions the day before but the changes in weather affected the trajectory of the rounds. The observers had to get close enough to spot the impact of the rounds before the mortars could adjust fire onto their targets.[7]

Once again, E Company marched into severe small arms fire at the swell in the slope. The rifle platoons maneuvered forward but the company commander lost contact with two of them. E Company tried to regroup but the platoons discovered that a minefield separated them. By 0635 hours, the company commander still had not regained control of his platoons, and the attack stalled. Gorn committed F Company to relieve E and push the German paratroopers off the end of the bluff. G Company had more success on its advance over the high ground. By 0700 hours, it had crossed a ravine and driven to a second bluff due east of Nieder Prum. It took until 1000 hours before F Company tied in with E Company on the first bluff. The two companies finally drove the German paratroopers from the woods. By 1115 hours, they could look down into Nieder Prum from the ridge northeast of town.[8]

The battalion still had the mission "to capture Nieder Prum and the high ground south and east." The rifle companies already occupied the dominant ridges overlooking the town, so Colonel Gorn ordered F Company to push into Nieder Prum from the northeast while G Company attacked to seize the high ground south of the town. Gorn held E Company on the high ground to reorganize and, if need be, defend the battalion's rear.[9]

The afternoon attack did not proceed smoothly. F Company found its way into Nieder Prum littered with mines and booby traps. With so many obstacles, Gorn decided the town had no value for future operations. He got approval from Colonel Chance to leave the town for follow-on forces and concentrate on taking the high ground to the south. G Company attacked across a ravine to Hill 561 in the late afternoon. An enemy machine gun fired on them, but the men pressed forward and reached their objective by 1840 hours.

Assessing the day's actions, Colonel Gorn concluded that E Company's attack had lacked aggressiveness and tactical control. He put it down to its commander's lack of combat experience. Although a senior first lieutenant, the commander had only recently arrived in theater. Gorn decided that E Company needed a change of leadership to boost its fighting spirit.

Bill received a message to meet with Colonel Gorn in the battalion CP. Unsure of the purpose of the meeting, he reported to Gorn. The colonel explained the situation in E Company then asked Bill, "Do you think you can handle commanding a rifle company?"

"Hell, yes!" Bill answered.[10]

Gorn smiled. It was just the type of response he was looking for. "Okay, the job is yours."

Bill was not an obvious choice for the position. He had only been commissioned for twenty months and all that service had been in a heavy weapons company. Gorn chose to overlook this, and Bill's reputation for brashness, because of his solid performance as a weapons platoon leader and extensive experience fighting alongside rifle platoons.

The new assignment pleased Bill. Before, he thought the only way he could ever leave H Company was to transfer to the engineers or get killed. Company command meant future advancement in rank, more pay, and better career prospects. He now led 193 men, further confirmation that he had measured up. There was one major hitch. Because Bill had less "time in grade" and "time in service" than the minimum required for promotion, he stayed a first lieutenant. He had to hold a captain's slot for three consecutive months before the Army would bump him in rank. Bill had seen plenty of lieutenants take over companies only to be carried out on a stretcher or replaced by a newly arrived captain. Few made it to captain.[11]

Bill remained at the Battalion CP to attend the briefing for the next day's operation. The battalion was turning east to drive the Germans away from the Prum River and provide maneuver space for the 11th

Armored Division to unleash its tanks. The colonel wasted no time testing his newly assigned company commander. "E and G Companies will seize the town of Rommersheim and the ridge one kilometer east of the town." G Company would lead the movement by sweeping south of town. E Company would initially follow G then turn northeast to seize Rommersheim. After that, the two companies would advance east to higher ground.[12]

After the briefing, Bill worked his way, in the dark, over the brushy slopes to E Company. He immediately called in the platoon leaders. As soon as they assembled at the company CP, Bill announced that he had taken command and immediately issued his operations order for the next day's attack. He began by reviewing the enemy situation and the battalion's overall plan. The mission for E Company, he told them, was to seize Rommersheim then the high ground beyond it. He explained the details for the company's plan of attack. The new commander went over the "scheme of maneuver" and the "plan for fire support." He designated the roles each platoon would play in the attack. He told the company's key leaders how supplies were to be distributed and the wounded evacuated. Bill closed the order by passing out the radio frequencies, call signs, and the new chain of command.

The order followed the classic format of the Army's five-paragraph field order, just as Bill had learned it at Fort Benning. Its detail and thoroughness also mirrored his principles for doing things the proper way and sticking with tactical doctrine. After he dismissed the platoon leaders, one of the experienced officers, 1st Lt. Patrick Tuohy, approached him. "You know, sir, that's the first time I've heard a five-paragraph field order since I arrived in Europe." Bill nodded. Tuohy's statement was tacit affirmation of the new standard for E Company. The two officers formed a professional bond in that moment.

Rommersheim lay east of two small, barren hills that protected the little town from the ridges overlooking Prum and Nieder Prum. Rather than defend the exposed hilltops, the Germans defended the eastern or reverse slope. A "reverse slope" defense is a tactic that sets up positions on the back side of a ridge or hill rather than its crest. The defender sacrifices observation and wide fields of fire but gains other advantages. The attacker must cross over the hill and expose his leading elements before he can engage the defender, thereby losing the ability to mass supporting fires from the units trailing the lead elements. A careless attacker, still in column formation, who stumbles into a "reverse slope" defense runs the risk of feeding his subordinate units into the defender's kill zone, one at a time. Colonel Gorn's plan avoided this trap by swinging around the hill instead of marching down the road from Prum or straight east from Nieder Prum.

G Company started movement at 0900 hours on March 3. E Company shifted south, behind them, before crossing the LD. The two infantry companies advanced slowly up and over the high ground south of Rommersheim. G Company continued straight east through a draw south of town. Bill reoriented E Company to the northeast. By early afternoon, the company advanced toward Rommersheim, guiding along a road that entered the town on its southwest corner. Bill used a slope of the southern hill to mask his approach and provide cover for the rifle platoons to within three hundred meters of town. He also deployed the platoons on line to present maximum firepower forward. The platoons opened suppressive fire then, using fire and maneuver, individual rifle squads attacked. The Germans stood their ground and a sharp firefight brewed up. Bill called on H Company's heavy machine guns and mortars for support, and the latter began hitting the enemy with the heavier M45 rounds. A platoon of tanks from B Company, 70th Tank Battalion popped over the hilltops and fired into Rommersheim, adding even more firepower to the assault. With tanks firing from one direction and infantry assaulting from another, the Germans gave up and pulled out of Rommersheim. E Company seized the town by 1630 hours, rounding up fifteen prisoners and counting ten dead Germans.[13]

While the enemy had not defended Rommersheim in strength, the successful and well-organized attack served as a tonic to the men of E Company after the frustration of the previous two days. Keeping his feelings to himself, their new commander quietly rejoiced that he had taken his first objective.

E Company did not have time to celebrate—the mission continued. The rifle platoons took an hour to clear the buildings in town before they proceeded east. Elements of the *14th Parachute Regiment* had withdrawn to defend the high ground on the far side of Nims Branch, a creek that ran north-to-south just east of Rommersheim. G Company had already run into heavy small-arms fire a kilometer south of E Company. Bill's rifle platoons crossed Nims Branch and started moving uphill to their final objective. By 1835 hours, E Company hit the German defenses. The attack pushed the paratroopers back five hundred meters, to a point where several roads intersected. With darkness falling, there was not enough time to coordinate a more deliberate attack up to the top of the hill. Both E and G Companies dug in on the southern extension of the high ground.[14]

While 2nd Battalion was busy at Rommersheim, CCB of the 11th Armored Division passed through the 4th Infantry Division and assembled on the open ground north of Rommersheim. From that spot VIII Corps launched it into the Rhineland. CT 12 would spend the next few days trailing the armor and mopping up bypassed defenders.[15]

The crossing of the Prum River, the capture of Rommersheim, and the presence of the 11th Armored Division forced the Germans to abandon their defense of the rolling farmland east of Prum. They fell back to the next defensible terrain, the Kyll River, leaving behind scattered delaying forces. CT 12's mission became clear—advance rapidly behind the armor all the way to the Kyll River.[16]

The 2nd Battalion led with two combat patrols at 0200 hours on March 4. Its scouts secured a position five hundred yards to E Company's front. G Company moved out early and, by dawn, had advanced several hundred meters. E Company moved forward at 0645 hours, reaching the scout position by 0830. Bill then sent a patrol to reconnoiter the route another six hundred meters ahead.[17]

By 1000 hours, the lack of contact with the Germans convinced Colonel Chance that the enemy had withdrawn. He told Colonel Gorn to keep E Company advancing on foot and send F Company into Fleringen to relieve part of the 1st Battalion. Chance turned his sight to the next objective. At 1125 hours, he ordered G Company to mount on the attached tanks and tank destroyers for a rapid dash to Wallersheim. Word came down from division that CCB had already bounded forward to Budesheim. At 1230 hours, Chance called Colonel Gorn to urge him forward. "Have F Co. move right thru Fleringen...Get the whole Bn moving. Keep in contact with the armor."

Bill pushed E Company forward in the direction of Wallersheim. The sustained movement, known as an "approach march," gave Bill an opportunity to control the tactical movement of his rifle platoons. By doctrine, rifle companies had to move forward in dispersed formations that provided protection from enemy artillery and small arms fire yet still allowed the company commander to control his platoons. These competing goals required the men to spread out for protection but remain grouped for easier communication. Much depended on the terrain. "Consequently, platoons will be separated laterally, or in depth, or both. On open terrain, platoons may be separated by as much as 300 yards. In woods, distances and intervals must be decreased until adjacent units are visible, or, if the woods are dense, connecting files or groups must be used between platoons." Bill gained some needed experience controlling E Company as it repeatedly drew in then extended as it encountered woods, farmland, ravines, and hills.[18]

G Company, riding the attached tanks and tank destroyers, breezed into Wallersheim at 1435 hours. E and F Companies tramped into town a short time later. Colonel Chance gave them little time to rest. He wanted to gain more ground. At 1600 hours, he issued orders to continue the advance. E and F Companies marched another two kilometers to occupy Hill 631, wooded high ground due east of Wallersheim. Colonel Chance, still not quite satisfied, directed 2nd Battalion to send a patrol forward to block a road 1,800 meters beyond E Company. G Company obliged, dispatching a platoon to establish the outpost after dark.[19]

After securing his own defensive position on Hill 631, Bill bedded down his tired troops in the woods. The men had advanced seven kilometers. Although they had almost no enemy contact, the company had marched steadily in tactical formation the whole day.

The 2nd Battalion enjoyed a quiet day on March 5. Most of the action occurred north of their sector. Before CCB could charge to the Kyll River it had to pass through the town of Oos and cross a bridge over the Oos River, a minor tributary of the Kyll. C Company set out early on March 5 to seize the crossing for the armor. Just as it approached the town, the Germans blew the bridge, and paratroopers, fighting from hills on the far side of the river, put small arms fire on Oos. The 1st Battalion joined the 2nd Battalion of the 22nd Infantry in a vicious battle against the German paratroopers that lasted into the night. It ended with the enemy getting wiped out. Meanwhile, CT 12 ordered Gorn's Battalion to consolidate in Budesheim as the regiment's reserve.[20]

The 1st Battalion cleared the way, and the engineers bridged the Oos River overnight. CCB jumped the river at 0700 hours on March 6. The tankers drove north past marshy ground then swung east. They passed over high ground northeast of Roth and surged to the Kyll River valley. By 1020 hours CCB reached the town of Niederbettingen. The armored force had covered seven kilometers before lunchtime.[21]

The 2nd Battalion started the day in Budesheim as the regimental reserve. The rapid armored advance prompted Colonel Chance to order them forward to Oos at 0940 hours. When the men arrived at 1220 hours, they were greeted by an incoming artillery barrage that sent Bill and his men ducking for cover.

General Blakeley and Colonel Chance wanted to keep the infantry as close behind the 11th Armored Division as possible. All three battalions of CT 12 pressed forward with 2nd Battalion advancing to Roth.

The 11th Armored stopped at the Kyll. It had to establish crossing sites and a bridgehead before its tanks and halftracks could get over the river. On the east side of the river, a tank ditch, backed by infantry trenches, sprawled between Bolsdorf and Dohm. The 55th Armored Infantry Battalion of CCB forced crossings at Oberbettingen and Niederbettingen. Bad road conditions delayed the arrival of bridging equipment, so the engineers improvised. They created a ford by dropping a bridge span into shallow water. However, the tankers did not consider the crossing suitable.[22]

Farther downstream, the armored infantry forded the river at Dohm. CCB wanted to drive east but it ran into the extensive tank ditch that cut the road between Dohm and Lammersdorf, also covered by infantry in nearby trenches. Until they could drive off the German infantry, CCB was stuck in Dohm.

The 4th Infantry Division needed to break the German obstacle belt to get the rest of the 11th Armored over the Kyll River. CT 12 ordered Colonel Gorn to assist CCB in Niederbettingen. General Blakeley called Colonel Chance forty minutes later to work out more details for the river crossing. They decided to have two companies of the battalion assault across the river from Niederbettingen to Bolsdorf. They tasked E Company to relieve the armored infantry at the Dohm fording site.[23]

Bill kept his men moving well into the evening. They reached the fording site near midnight. Squad by squad, the infantrymen slid off the bank into the frigid river. The men teetered under their loads, stepping rock to rock, guided by the light from a waning moon. They made it safely across but emerged soaked and chilled. (See Map XIII)

E Company took over from two companies of the 55th Armored Infantry and settled into Dohm for the night. With no chance to change or dry their clothes, Bill and his men fought against the wet and cold the rest of the night. Upstream, F and G Companies waded the river under equally harsh conditions.

E Company's mission for March 7 presented Bill with his biggest challenge since taking command. While the rest of the battalion would attack Bolsdorf, his company had to dislodge an entrenched German force on its own. Bill could call on an 81mm mortar section and a platoon of heavy machine guns from H Company but, to assault the objective, he only had his own weapons platoon and three rifle platoons to "close with the enemy by a combination of fire and movement." His first task, according to doctrine, was reconnaissance. Aided by a detailed map over-printed with the German fortifications, Bill scouted the enemy position "to determine where enemy guns and men…might be located [and] the routes or areas where the enemy's observation or fire [was] most hampered by the nature of the terrain."[24]

Bill followed tactical doctrine by drafting a "scheme of maneuver" that took "advantage of every accident of the terrain to conceal and protect the company...while in movement." As usual, the Germans had cleverly positioned their defenses. From a farm on a gently rising hill northeast of Dohm, German gunners had observation over the tank ditch and the approaches all the way down to the river. The defense did have one significant weakness. The hill naturally bowed out toward the river. That meant the gunners defending the north side of the position could not fire to the south and vice versa. The Germans compensated by digging trenches that allowed them to shift men from one sector to the other. Bill also noticed that the buildings in the little town of Dohm would offer some cover for his infantry as it approached the southern side of the trenches.

Bill's experience in H Company paid dividends as he prepared his plan of fire support. He could use the 81mm mortar section and E Company's own section of three 60mm mortars to drop rounds inside the trenches at certain points and prevent the enemy from shifting troops into a threatened sector. The Germans dug their trenches in a zig-zag pattern. By using high-angle indirect fire, the heavy machine guns could target sections of the trench that aligned with the long axis of their plunging fire. Where the heavier weapons were not firing, Bill's own M1919 machine guns and the platoons' rifle fire would force the enemy to keep their heads down.

Bill briefed his key leaders on his plan of attack in the early hours of March 7. "The men and my platoon leaders were dubious about jumping due to the Jerry['s]...tactics and his superior positions." The other lieutenants wanted to hold off making the attack until the rest of the battalion could help. Bill later confided to Beth his anxiety. "At that time I had a tough decision. I was new to the company and the company plan was my own. If it failed the men would lose a lot of confidence in me and it was a tough job." After listening to his subordinates' objections, Bill elected "to override my 5 officers and jump as planned."[25]

The 2nd Battalion began the operation with F and G Companies attacking to seize Bolsdorf and a knoll just north of that town. The

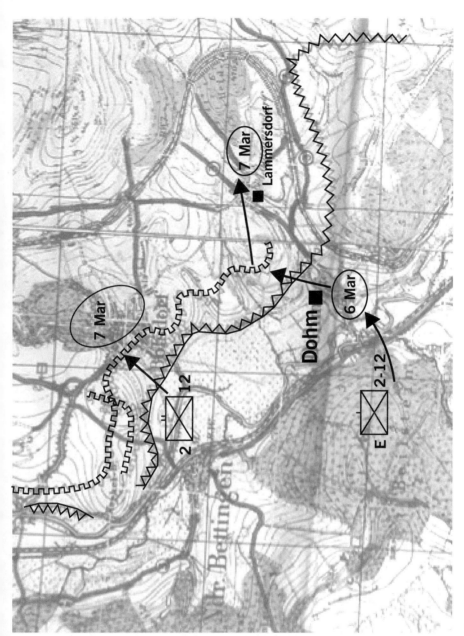

Map XIII

Germans resisted fiercely from the buildings. Both companies spent the morning trying to dislodge German paratroopers, taking thirty casualties. The heavy fighting in Bolsdorf meant that E Company would have no help. The junior lieutenants again objected to the attack but Bill held firm.[26]

At Bill's signal, the supporting machine guns and mortars opened fire. Before any infantry could advance, the enemy gunners had to be pinned inside their positions. Bill motioned for the lead platoon to advance once the volume of suppressive fire on the trenches reached its peak.[27]

Infantry companies did not charge German defensive positions in a single rush. Instead, they bounded their rifle platoons forward one at a time. The majority of riflemen had to remain busy firing at the enemy in order for a handful to rush forward—the greater the enemy fire, the fewer men moving. As Army doctrine put it, "This combination of fire and movement enables attacking rifle elements to reach positions from which they can overcome the enemy in hand-to-hand combat."[28]

The riflemen clawed their way up the gentle incline in a series of short, quick dashes. Bill stayed forward with the rifle platoons where he could best control the attack. When they closed on the trenches, he signaled the supporting mortars and machine guns to lift fire for the final assault. As soon as they did, the American infantrymen leaped into the trenches and killed those who did not immediately surrender.

E Company still had more terrain to seize. Besides the trenches, one hundred enemy soldiers in Lammersdorf blocked the road leading east from Dohm. Bill and his men had to drive them out before the bridgehead could be secured. This time, E Company had some help. The 3rd Battalion had forded the Kyll at Dohm and seized the high ground south of town. From that position, 3rd Battalion could bring some of its heavy weapons to bear on Lammersdorf. Bill conferred with the sister battalion around 1515 hours to secure their help.[29]

Bill's plan of attack exploited the capture of the trenches. The town sat in low ground. The Germans could block the road but with E Company occupying the trenches above Dohm, they did not have a secure defense. Bill planned to maneuver into terrain that could dominate the little town. He also coordinated with the artillery to pound Lammersdorf in advance of the assault.

The attack began in the late afternoon. With artillery blasting the town and small arms fire pouring in from multiple directions, the Germans abandoned Lammersdorf. The 3rd Battalion reported enemy troops dashing out of one side of Lammersdorf as E Company entered from the opposite end. The company finished the day by occupying the wooded hill just beyond the town.[30]

The action of March 7 gave E Company a big boost in morale. It had overrun an enemy trench line, driven the Germans from Lammersdorf, and captured sixteen enemy soldiers while suffering only two casualties. The regiment applauded the company's performance, calling it "a brilliant attack." Bill wrote to Beth, "Thank goodness we made it so now the men feel very tough and capable." Back at the battalion CP in Niederbettingen, someone else felt justified by E Company's success. Colonel Gorn noted that the young lieutenant he picked to command the company had restored its fighting spirit in less than a week.[31]

Late in the day, Colonel Chance ordered 1st Battalion to pass through the 2nd Battalion and carry the attack farther east. The 2nd reverted to regimental reserve.[32]

On March 8, the division formed Task Force (TF) Rhino by putting the 8th Infantry on trucks and combining elements of the 70th Tank, 610th Tank Destroyer, 4th Engineers, and 29th Field Artillery Battalions with the 4th Recon Troop. Under the command of the Assistant Division Commander, Brig. Gen. James Rodwell, TF Rhino roared across the Rhineland, advancing twenty-five miles and capturing 1,541 prisoners in twenty hours. Even at that breakneck pace they could not keep up with the collapsing German defense. By the time TF Rhino completed its run, on March 9, the 4th Armored Division closed on Koblenz and the Rhine River. Two days earlier, the 9th Armored Division captured a bridge over the strategic river at Remagen. Operation Lumberjack culminated with the Germans evicted from the Rhineland and the Americans holding a bridgehead over the Rhine.

The 12th Infantry remained in place for a few days, giving the troops a chance to clean up and rest. The only contact they had with the enemy came on March 11 when a lone German soldier drifted into Lammersdorf to surrender. He explained that he had wandered the countryside for a week but none of the German civilians would feed or shelter him. He finally gave up and turned himself in.[33]

Things got even better on March 12. The battalion's troops rode trucks from Niederbettingen to Bleialf where they hopped on rail cars for a long move to a rest area around Portieux la Verrerie, France. The new area, near the Moselle River in the region of Lorraine, offered billets for all the soldiers as well as showers, clean clothes, and hot chow. Bill shared the news with Beth. "We are in a rest area now! Can you believe it, the 4th Div. in a rest area!!...It is the first time I have not heard the roar of a cannon since 7 Jan." The men were not entirely idle. Colonel Chance insisted on a training program to ensure all soldiers knew how to operate key weapons and their rifles. The battalion started rotating officers on a schedule of three-day passes to Paris. Bill drew his pass on March 16.[34]

Bill enjoyed his short holiday in the French capital but he noticed that the euphoria of August had gone. The warmth and affection for American soldiers had been cooled by a slight chill of resentment. He noticed some Parisian merchants skinning a few extra dollars off ignorant GIs.

Bill also saw that the debris of war remained weeks after the campaign had passed. The French appeared to accept the disorder left by the fighting. He had seen something different in Germany. German civilians worked quickly and diligently to repair the damage left by the combatants the moment the frontline swept beyond their homes.

The Germans earned Bill's grudging admiration for their industry, just as they had for their fighting ability. Despite his personal suffering at their hands, Bill never made deprecating comments about the Germans. He certainly condemned the Nazis and abhorred Germany's war atrocities, but that did not seem to diminish his overall opinion of the German people. These feelings contrasted with his attitude toward his allies. Bill inherited his mother's Irish animosity against the English. His time in England and Field Marshal Montgomery's fighting record failed to improve his view of them. As for the French, their warmth and joy seemed to slip into disdain and arrogance after the glow of liberation faded.

Shortly after Bill returned from Paris, the 2nd Battalion moved to the hamlet of Kriegsheim, outside Hagenau, France. In this assembly area, the men had to wear helmets and shoulder their weapons. The familiar tank, tank destroyer, and artillery battalions rejoined them in the assembly area. The regiment transformed back to CT 12. The men still enjoyed movies, recreation, and showers, but they knew their down time would not last much longer.[35]

CT 12 moved into the plains of the upper Rhine Valley on March 26. As the troops trucked across the German border, they saw numerous displays of white bed sheets hanging from windows, what they termed "the new German national flag." The regiment occupied an assembly area around Ellerstadt, a few kilometers east of Bad Durkheim. With an impending offensive deep into German territory, the battalion issued a general policy governing interactions between the troops and the German civilian population. The S-2 cautioned the men about "the order prohibiting fraternization between soldiers and civilians." The men also learned that the 4th Infantry Division had been transferred to XXI Corps, commanded by Maj. Gen. Frank Milburn. The XXI Corps served in Lt. Gen. Alexander Patch's 7th Army under Gen. Jacob Devers's 6th Army Group. If any of the men wondered why they had been moved from Bradley's command down to the southern army group, the reason became clear when they heard that the 7th Army had forced a crossing over the Rhine River at Worms. Four days later, CT 12 was ordered to cross the Rhine at Worms to re-enter the fight.[36]

The upcoming campaign into the heart of Germany would present Bill with severe challenges of both a military and moral nature as the American Army brought the ravages of war to the doorsteps of the German people.

CHAPTER FIFTEEN

SIMMRINGEN WOODS

In the fall of 1944, a handful of news correspondents in Europe began speculating on desperate measures the *Third Reich* might take to prolong its survival. One idea the writers floated was the creation of an *Alpenfestung*, literally "Alpine Fortress," where well-armed and well-supplied Nazi fanatics could hold out indefinitely within an inter-connected ring of mountaintop bunkers. This speculation received scant attention from Allied intelligence until the Battle of the Bulge. Hitler's bold gamble in the Ardennes set the G-2s to wondering what else he might do to delay the inevitable. Allied planners considered the construction of a "National Redoubt" in the Alpine region the most worrisome option. Once they latched onto that dubious theory, intelligence staffs had no trouble finding facts and random bits of evidence to support it. By the beginning of January 1945, Propaganda Minister Goebbels got into the act by falsely promoting Allied fascination with the National Redoubt.[1]

As early as January 1945, the concern about an *Alpenfestung* began to influence Allied strategy. Eisenhower wanted to finish the war in Europe as quickly as possible so America could shift resources to the war in the Pacific. A stubborn defense of some sort of Alpine fortress could delay final victory for months, even years.

The collapse of German resistance west of the Rhine, the capture of the bridge at Remagen, and the advance of the Red Army into eastern Germany caused a simultaneous shift in Allied thinking. Berlin diminished as an objective in Eisenhower's calculations. After the capture of the Ruhr, preventing a Nazi withdrawal into the National Redoubt became the next most important strategic goal.

Eisenhower announced his plans for the final push into the German hinterlands on March 28. After crossing the Rhine, Montgomery's 21st Army Group would drive northeast to cut off Denmark from Red Army encroachment. The U.S. First Army and Ninth Army, now back under Bradley's command, would encircle and reduce the Ruhr. Patton's Third Army would guard First Army's flank until the Ruhr fell, then charge east-southeast toward Leipzig. Patch's Seventh Army, under Devers's 6th Army Group, would exploit its Rhine bridgehead to the east then hook sharply south to turn the German *First* and *Nineteenth Armies* that defended the upper Rhine Valley. Patch would continue driving south across the Danube River to overrun the National Redoubt before the German Army could occupy it in strength.[2]

General Milburn's XXI Corps surged east from the Worms bridgehead with the 12th Armored Division in the lead. The tankers forced their way through the Odenwald, the forested highlands east of the Rhine. Milburn ordered the 4th Infantry Division to follow. On March 30, CT 12 crossed the Rhine at Worms.[3]

The regiment had problems getting underway. Their own vehicles and attached motorized units drove across the bridge as scheduled and occupied an assembly area southeast of Heppenheim. However, the trucks to haul the foot soldiers did not arrive on time. The deuce-and-a-halves showed up the next day then had to play catch up, chugging their way through multiple traffic jams. The convoy made a tempting target for an aerial attack but the Air Corps provided ample cover, much to the relief of Bill and his men. "Thank God we have an Air Force!"[4]

While passing through Worms, the men got their first glimpse of a sight that would become both disturbing and common. A long column of "displaced persons" (DPs) walked and bicycled in the opposite direction, heading home after years of enslaved service to the *Reich*. In August 1944, 7.6 million foreign laborers, most of them conscripted, constituted 25 percent of Germany's work force. With the Allies and Red Army breaking into the Fatherland, these people began spilling out of Germany in droves.[5]

The truck convoy finally caught up with the rest of CT 12, and the entire combat team gathered in an assembly area on the night of March 31. The 2nd Battalion centered around the hamlet of Airlenbach. The regiment picked up sixteen German prisoners during the movement who had either deserted or surrendered while home on leave.[6]

CT 12 remained in division reserve on April 1 and made another road march to Hardheim, using the invaluable trucks to shuttle the march serials forward—and collecting another fifty-four PWs. The 2nd Battalion assembled that evening near Erfeld, a small village south of Hardheim. The day had been quiet until a German jet dropped a single bomb in the battalion area. The bomb caused no damage, but the attack reminded the Americans that the war was not over yet.[7]

The regiment stayed put on April 2 while the rest of the Ivy Division pushed east to the Tauber River. Bill and his men spent most of their time cleaning weapons and equipment. The only serious event occurred near evening. A dozen ME 109s swooped in to strafe Erfeld and drop a bomb. The battalion suffered no losses but the aerial attacks proved how sensitive the Germans had become to the XXI Corps thrust. A little before noon the next day, the regiment issued new movement orders. The 2nd Battalion moved to Herchsheim, another thirty-four kilometers to the east. The movement put them close to Ochsenfurt on the Main River. This time, the troops dug in a defensive perimeter.[8]

By now, the 12th Infantry had gone nearly a month without serious contact with the enemy. It had used the time wisely. The rest period in

France had rejuvenated the spirits of the veterans and given the new recruits time to fit in. Everyone got refresher training on weapons and tactics. Unlike the brutal days in Normandy, the squad leaders acquainted the replacements with the dangers of combat and showed them how to fight the Germans. Two of Bill's officer friends, Jack Gunning and Ben Compton, left for new assignments. First Lt. Frank Hackett replaced Compton in command of H Company. Bill's battalion stood primed for action and ready to unleash a swift campaign to finish off what appeared to be an already defeated enemy.

The eastward surge of General Patch's Seventh Army had driven a wedge between the German *First* and *Seventh Armies*. The *XIII SS Corps*, on the *First Army's* right, had a huge gap on its eastern flank where it had lost contact with the *Seventh Army*. The corps commander, *SS Gruppenfuhrer* Max Simon, tried to shore up his defense by turning the corps to face north. He deployed the *212th Volksgrenadier Division* (actually a division HQ commanding an assortment of spare organizations and training units) along a series of woodlands south of Tiefenthal, anchored on the Tauber River in the west. This "division" defended the open plain southwest of Wurzburg and Ochsenfurt. Simon stiffened the backbones of these troops by infusing their formations with cadres of fanatic *SS* troops. The 116th Cavalry Squadron located the *212th Volksgrenadier Division* and alerted General Blakeley to its presence. The German position denied the Americans use of the highway passing through Tiefenthal. The Ivy Division commander decided to send the 12th Infantry to destroy this makeshift defensive line.[9]

CT 12 passed the order to the 2nd Battalion to eliminate the Germans located in the woods next to the hamlet of Simmringen. The regiment beefed up the battalion with ten tanks and four tank destroyers. Lt. Col. John Gorn gave E Company the mission of leading the attack into the Simmringen Woods. Rather than charge into the forest, he instructed Bill to make initial contact with the enemy then determine where they set up their "kill zone."[10]

Bill briefed his officers and sergeants on his plan of attack. He wanted the scouts well forward to locate the enemy defenders without getting the whole company pinned down. Before the meeting broke up, one of the platoon sergeants asked, "Who do you want on the BAR?"

The Browning Automatic Rifle provided the rifle squads with their heaviest firepower. It fired a standard .30 caliber cartridge in automatic mode from a twenty-round magazine. The BAR fired at a high rate but frequent magazine changes reduced its volume of fire. Its chief advantage came from the fact that a gunner could fire the BAR from a prone position or sling it over his shoulder while walking. That gave the squads an automatic weapon in the assault.

Most of the BARs had been assigned to veteran infantrymen but the recent reorganization meant that a few had to be given to new men. Bill thought for a moment then recalled one soldier who had just joined the company. The kid had the bravado of someone who had never been under fire. The first thing out of his mouth was "When do I get a chance to kill Germans?" While the regiment remained in reserve or in a forward assembly area, he complained about not seeing any action. His bluster annoyed the company's veterans, including its commander, who had long since forgone their zeal for shooting it out with the Germans.

"Let the new hot shot kid take one. Let's see what he can do," Bill answered.

The battalion moved out by 1300 hours. An hour later, E Company assumed its attack formation and passed through Tiefenthal where the LD had been drawn. G Company followed on their left (east) flank. As they approached Simmringen Woods, the scouts started taking fire. Bill could see that the fire only came from a German forward outpost, nothing that a little supporting fire from the mortars and tanks could not handle. He continued pressing ahead. As E Company neared the edge of the woods, Bill perceived that the German commander had set his defense inside the woods rather than along its edge. The enemy chose to sacrifice good observation and long fields of fire from the tree line, so his men would not be easily targeted by the American tanks, mortars, and machine guns. After conferring with Colonel Gorn, E and G Companies advanced into Simmringen Woods.[11] (See Map XIV)

The rifle platoons and squads compressed their formations once the company entered the woods, otherwise the limited visibility would complicate command and control. Bill brought all three platoons on line to present maximum firepower forward. Platoons tied in with each other's flanks and connected with G Company on the left. As soon as the company was lined up to Bill's satisfaction, he gave the signal to advance. An attack in thick woods called for cautious movement and close supervision to maintain control. Bill and his command group adhered to doctrine and followed closely behind the platoon at the center of the line.[12]

E and G Companies barely got started before the Germans opened fire from a series of bunkers. The men hit the dirt. Bill shouted to his men to return fire, and E Company responded with a massive volley of small arms fire. Just as the Americans got the upper hand in the volume of fire, the new soldier with the BAR stepped away from the cover of the tree that protected him, leveled the BAR from his hip, and started to spray .30 cal. rounds into the dirt.

Bill watched in horror as a German machine gun instantly shifted in the direction of the BAR and fired a quick burst. The kid fell dead, taking the BAR out of action. "Dammit!" Bill shouted. The eager recruit lasted less than a minute once the shooting started.

Bill turned his attention from the lost man back to the battle. He searched for a weak point to attack while his platoons traded shots with the enemy. The collective fire from the rifles and two light machine guns helped suppress the defenders' fire and took out some of the enemy. The riflemen crawled through the underbrush but the attack moved forward slowly.

Bill brought up a platoon of tanks but the woods were too dense for them to be of much use. Bill scouted up and down the line looking for a gap in the German entrenchments. He found none. To E Company's left, 1st Lt. Clarence Dunn, G Company commander, found no gaps farther east, either. The two lieutenants reported back to Colonel Gorn that they faced a cohesive enemy front stretching from one side of the Simmringen Woods to the other. Their report and the interrogation of prisoners revealed the full scope of CT 12's situation. It faced an enemy

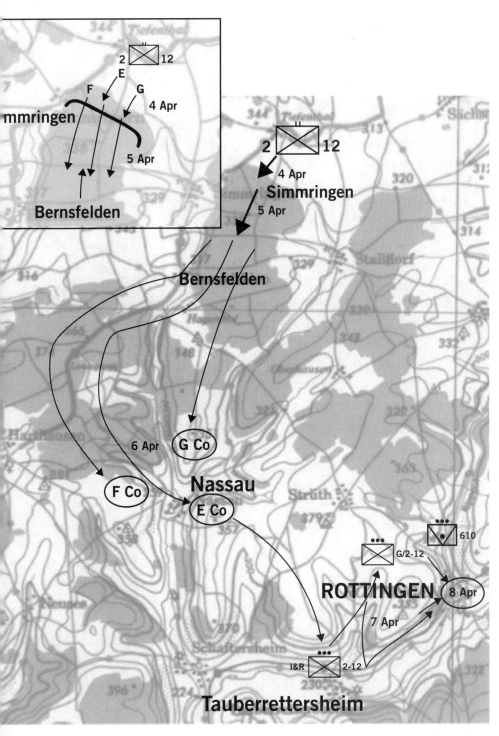

Map XIV

force of equivalent size with companies bolstered by platoons of *SS* troops.[13]

Given this information, Colonel Gorn and Colonel Chance agreed to halt the attack and prepare for a more deliberate assault on April 5. The 2nd Battalion prepared a hasty defense for the night. Bill and Lieutenant Dunn tied their two companies together to prevent any German infiltration. Working with the two forward companies, the H Company Commander, Lieutenant Hackett, set his machine guns to cover the frontline with FPLs. Bill positioned his own M1919 machine guns to fill the gaps in his front. E Company had only pushed a few hundred meters into the woods, so the men had to dig foxholes with only a couple hundred meters separating them from the Germans. Everyone spent a sleepless night watching and listening.

After bedding down the troops, the battalion staff and company commanders planned the next attack. Colonel Gorn decided to slide F Company into the woods on E Company's right. He wanted the full force of the battalion to drive the enemy from the woods. The battalion now had two platoons of Sherman tanks and one platoon of Stuart light tanks attached. Earlier in the day, the thickness of the woods had kept the tanks out of the action. During his recon Bill noticed that four narrow logging trails ran north to south through Simmringen Woods. These trails could accommodate the American tanks. Gorn organized the tanks into four columns, one per logging trail. He also split the rifle companies between the trails—G on the left (east), F on the right (west), and E in the center. The Ammunition & Pioneer (A&P) Platoon distributed satchel charges to the infantry companies to help them take out the enemy bunkers. All three company commanders coordinated plans to stay linked during the attack.[14]

At 0730 hours on April 5, E Company's riflemen rose from their foxholes and formed on line. Bill ordered them forward, keeping the platoons in tight formation. He wanted to deliver highly concentrated fire when they hit the enemy defense. F and G Companies moved out at the same time. The scouts crept forward ahead of the platoons. E Company hit the enemy first. The Germans opened fire with machine guns and rifles from bunkers and foxholes only two hundred to three hundred meters deeper in the woods.[15]

Bill crawled forward to spot the enemy positions. He located a German bunker close to a logging trail. That would be his first target. He crawled back to the nearest rifle platoons and brought them forward. The platoons advanced using "assault fire." As Army doctrine explained it, "Automatic riflemen and riflemen, with bayonets fixed, all taking full advantage of existing cover such as tanks, boulders, trees, walls, and mounds…fire as they advance at areas known or believed to be occupied by hostile personnel. Such fire is usually delivered from the standing position and is executed at a rapid rate." In this case, Bill ordered the platoons to crawl forward rather than charge the bunker upright but he told them to keep up the same rate of fire. The platoons responded with a full fusillade of .30 cal. rounds. Bullets tore through the underbrush like a horizontal rain shower, forcing the defenders' heads down.[16]

Bill scurried over to the logging trail and escorted one of the medium tanks forward. He pointed to the location of the bunker then let the tank maneuver into a firing position. A German *Panzerfaust* could knock out the Sherman but the torrent of bullets made it impossible to use one. The tank fired its main gun into the bunker, killing the machine gun crew. With the machine gun out of action, one of the American soldiers worked his way to the side of the casemate and tossed in a satchel charge. Seconds later a huge explosion blew out the bunker's interior and killed the Germans inside.

The infantrymen then opened fire on the next fortification in the line. With the Germans pinned inside, the tanks moved up without worrying about a *Panzerfaust*. As soon as it got close enough to sight the breastwork, it fired a round through its opening. Quickly, an infantryman tossed a satchel charge into the second bunker.

By this time, the light machine gunners had to pour water from their canteens over their barrels to cool them. Continuing to use the same techniques it had against the first two bunkers, E Company took out a third then a fourth position.

Lieutenant Touhy, Bill's XO, kept calling for more ammunition to fill the company's insatiable demand. To meet it, the battalion loaded two-and-a-half-ton trucks with crates of .30 cal. ammunition, some in belts for the machine guns, others loose for the M1 rifles, and sent them to the edge of the woods. The A&P Platoon unloaded the trucks, broke down the crates, and crammed loose rounds into eight-round magazines. The ammo bearers draped bandoliers stuffed with magazines over their shoulders and hefted green ammo cans filled with belted rounds. They ran forward to the platoon sergeants and dropped off the ammo. The platoon sergeants broke open the ammo cans then sent runners back and forth to the squads and machine gun crews to deliver the bandoliers and belts. Over and over it went.

Bill pressed the attack down the line. Riflemen, machine gunners, tank crews, and the soldiers carrying satchel charges worked together to suppress then destroy each bunker in turn. Instead of pinning the Americans down inside the woods, the German commander's force was pinned inside its fortifications. The enemy force could not stop E Company from overwhelming it one position at a time.[17]

At 1045 hours, the terrain got too thick for the Shermans. The smaller Stuart tanks came forward to assist E Company. The attack progressed beyond the first line of bunkers but "was stopped time and time again because of the dense woods which caused the units to lose contact and to allow gaps to appear in our lines." At one point resistance built up on E Company's right flank. Later a buildup of Germans on the left stalled the attack. Nevertheless, Bill's rifle platoons and those of F and G Companies continued to push deeper into the woods.[18]

The German defense crumbled under the relentless onslaught and methodical destruction of its entrenched positions. "Around noon the enemy began to surrender," Bill reported. The German commander resorted to desperate measures to keep the battle from slipping away entirely. "At 1330 Jerry launched a counterattack at the crossroads with a force of 150 men. E and F Companies and the tanks fired continuously for ten minutes and stopped the attack." The enemy assault amounted to a suicide charge straight into a storm of American fire. Bill later counted eighty-five enemy bodies near the crossroads.[19]

The battle raged into the late afternoon. The sound of the infantry "assault fire" rattled through the woods like snare drums at dress parade. The place reeked of spent ball propellant. Light machine gun crews switched barrels back and forth. Ammo bearers passed out more .30 cal. rounds. The enemy tried to form another counterattack but Bill called in mortar rounds on them and broke up the attack before it could get organized. The tanks stood nearby, ready to move up under the infantry's intense protective fire and blast another bunker.

Word filtered up the chain of command that 2nd Battalion had a major fight on its hands. General Milburn, XXI Corps Commander, stopped at the regimental CP at 1440 hours to get a briefing. Late in the day, the CP called Bill back to meet with a different senior officer. He worked his way to a spot away from enemy fire where he found a jeep carrying the 4th Infantry Division's Ammunition Officer.

The lieutenant reported to the staff major. "Sir, what do you need?"

"Lieutenant, I'm here to find out what the Hell is going on."

"Sir, we're taking out a line of enemy bunkers inside the woods."

"I see that but why do you need all that ammo?"

"We're using suppressive fire to keep the Germans buttoned up while we take out their bunkers. Is there a problem?"

The major shook his head. "No. I was just curious about where all that ammo was going."

"We're putting it to good use."

"That's fine, Lieutenant, but do you know that you've exhausted the entire division's stock of small arms ammunition?"

Bill shrugged then returned to the fight. The battle ended as darkness began descending over the woods. The company picked up a few prisoners late in the day. Bill pulled one of his soldiers to march the Germans back to the battalion collection point. The soldier he selected happened to be a Native American armed with a submachine gun. Bill told the soldier where to take the prisoners and ordered him to return as quickly as possible.

The soldier took charge of the prisoners and started marching them to the rear down a forest trail. A minute later, Bill heard a burst of fire from the submachine gun. Alarmed, he ran to the sound of the gunfire. He found the soldier standing over the German bodies a short distance down the trail. Steam hissed off the submachine gun's barrel.[20]

"Why'd you shoot them?" Bill asked.

"They tried to escape," the soldier replied.

Bill looked at the dead Germans. They had all fallen evenly spaced along the side of the trail. "What do you mean 'tried to escape'? They're all still in line."

The Native American soldier shrugged. "They started to run, so I shot 'em."

Bill fumed. This looked like an obvious case of murdering prisoners but he had no way of disproving the soldier's lame excuse.

Incidents of frontline retribution were not common but not unknown. Soldiers, still flush from battle, who had charge over prisoners sometimes chose to avenge lost buddies rather than send the prisoners back to sit out the rest of the war in a camp. Some commanders chose to look the other way. Why charge a soldier with murder for killing the enemy? Bill did not share that sentiment. He still saw the German soldiers as people, even in the heat of battle. He had no way of prosecuting the soldier but he made up his mind never to trust him with prisoners, again.

As he walked away Bill looked back at the dead Germans and the Native American soldier. A question popped into his head. *Did those Germans die for Hitler or Custer?*

Measured by distance covered, the attack of April 4–5 accomplished little, just a few hundred meters. In terms of comparative losses, the battle of Simmringen Woods had been one of the battalion's most successful engagements. E Company only had four men killed in action, including the over-eager replacement with the BAR the day before. Over the two days, it had killed well over a hundred Germans and captured dozens more. In the process of inflicting those losses, the 2nd Battalion rooted out a large, entrenched enemy force from terrain that favored the defender. What a difference from the bloody days in the Cotentin Peninsula when dead GIs marked every few meters of advance. Bill would later regard April 5 as one of his best days in command.[21]

The men spent another anxious night next to the enemy. They had driven back every German defender they had faced but only cleared the first of their four objectives. The question remained: how tough would the fight be on April 6?[22]

The answer came shortly after the attack resumed at 0630 hours. The scouts pushed ahead of the company's main body to locate the enemy front. They snuck forward but made no contact. By 0830 hours the company had advanced four hundred to six hundred meters without "meeting anything." Colonel Gorn, guessing that the Germans had abandoned the woods, re-directed E and F Companies to Bernsfelden. F Company seized the town at 1100 hours while E Company overran Hagenhof, a small hamlet farther south. The two companies aligned on the Tiefenthal-Harthausen highway at noon. With E Company on the left side and F Company on the right, the two rifle companies marched southwest in attack formation. They swept the woods en route to Harthausen, meeting no resistance. Air reconnaissance had reported 200–300 enemy fleeing south from the town earlier that morning. In mid-afternoon, the S-2 learned from prisoner interrogations that a German force had withdrawn to Nassau, the battalion's final objective. Colonel Gorn ordered his rifle companies to change direction and proceed to Nassau. Bill reoriented his attack formation to the southeast and marched his company through more woods. By nightfall, it entered the town with F and G Companies positioned on the flanks. The German force had already pulled out. E Company covered seven kilometers on April 6, about ten times the progress of the day before. The lack of resistance proved that the Germans had fallen back to establish a new line along an east-west bend of the Tauber River.[23] (See Map XIV)

Colonel Chance wanted to break through this new defensive barrier before the Germans could prepare it. He issued orders for the 2nd and 3rd Battalions to clear the zone north of the Tauber River while sending only one reinforced company from each battalion to seize seven crossing sites. Chance warned both battalions to be ready to attack in force across the river on short notice. Colonel Gorn tapped E Company to capture the three sites in the battalion's sector: Tauberrettersheim, Rottingen, and Bieberehren.[24]

The regiment's tactical plan had major shortcomings and did not comply with Army doctrine. River crossing operations called for "boldly and rapidly executed crossings," the establishment of "local bridgeheads, and the crossing of follow-on units." Colonel Chance planned for two companies to capture seven crossing sites spread over a sixteen-kilometer front. Even if Bill's company could seize three separate river crossings in a day, he could only hold them with platoon-size forces—never mind establishing bridgeheads. The timid plan to capture just the crossing sites, without establishing bridgeheads on the far side, indicated that the division and regiment did not intend to attack over the Tauber River just yet. Colonel Gorn altered the plan in his zone by sending the regiment's Raider Platoon and one platoon from G and F Companies to Tauberrettersheim, Rottingen, and Bieberehren, respectively. E Company would then relieve each platoon in succession or help drive out any Germans the platoons encountered.[25]

The patrols departed at 0700 hours on April 7. E Company moved south from Nassau shortly thereafter. They climbed the hill south of town then followed the contours of a ravine down to the Tauber River valley. Meanwhile, the Raider Platoon entered Tauberrettersheim by 1150 hours. The scouts found the bridge destroyed but discovered a serviceable ford in the same area. E Company approached the town ninety minutes later. All went well until a German 20mm anti-aircraft gun opened fire from the hill to their east. Bill may have had troubles orienting himself that morning. He reported his position on the hill above Shaftersheim while he was actually one hill farther east, above Tauberrettersheim. Fortunately, the German 20mm gun withdrew. The records do not say why, but the company likely returned fire with machine guns and mortar fire. E Company entered Tauberrettersheim and freed the Raider Platoon to continue its scouting mission.[26]

Bill left one of his platoons to guard the fording site then marched the rest of the company east, up the river valley, toward Rottingen. An elongated ridge, Hill 355, stood between Tauberrettersheim and Rottingen. The road between the river towns traveled up the southwestern slope of Hill 355. Bill used the hill to mask the company's advance from the enemy occupying high ground across the river from Rottingen. On the way, they met the platoon from G Company that had been sent to seize the crossing site. The platoon had been driven back from the objective by German small arms fire from the town and the hills south of the river. Bill took control over the loose platoon to replace the one he left at Tauberrettersheim. Examining the town and enemy positions from Hill 355, he spotted a rail line running along the valley floor. German engineers had built an embankment to elevate the rail line coming into Rottingen from the southwest. The quick recon gave Bill an idea for attacking the town.

At 1508 hours, Bill requested an artillery strike on the Germans across the river. He brought forward an attached platoon of tank destroyers from the 610th TD Battalion at the same time. Their guns joined the 105mm guns of the artillery in pounding Rottingen and the enemy lurking in the woods south of town. He sent the G Company platoon around to the north side of Hill 355 where they could fire on the enemy inside the town. E Company's remaining two platoons slipped down into the valley and moved northeast toward Rottingen. Bill had the men scrape the railroad embankment with their right shoulders as they advanced, shielding them from enemy observers on the opposite bank.

Around 1720 hours, the lead elements ran into German small arms fire. The G Company platoon replied with covering fire on Rottingen as Bill pushed his platoons forward. The lead rifle platoon stormed Burg Brattenstein on the southwestern edge of town. As the company got a toehold in Rottingen, some of Bill's troops jerked a German soldier out of a nearby culvert. The prisoner told Bill that a company of SS troops, armed with two *Panzerfausten* apiece, occupied Rottingen. E Company pushed ahead in the dwindling daylight, going house-to-house to root out the enemy. The inexperienced Nazi troops failed to impress Bill with their fighting skills. "In the battle for the town the krauts used their panzerfausts as mortars shooting them up in the air with a total result of two dead chickens."

Back in the regimental CP, Colonel Chance received a call from General Blakeley. The general said he wanted to give the troops a chance to rest before the next big push and cautioned against any further coordinated attacks. Blakeley's guidance showed that he did not feel ready to launch a major offensive south of the Tauber River. Bill received word not to press the fight too hard. He halted the house-to-house fighting, figuring he had better chances to use supporting fire the next morning.[27]

Before the word got out, Private Max Gartenberg of New York City, who knew a little German, pounded on the door of a house. He demanded that the residents let him and a few other soldiers inside. A middle-aged man appeared at the door. "*Wir sind anti-Nazi*," he said raising his hands. The family welcomed the Americans into their home.[28]

The troops were about to enjoy some German hospitality when another soldier ran in and announced, "The captain said we're not to flush any more houses. This town is full of Jerries, and we're not going to do anything more until the morning." The disappointed troops said farewell to their hosts and rejoined the rest of the company on the west side of Rottingen.

The next morning, Colonel Gorn sent Lieutenant D. Smith's platoon of Sherman tanks from B Company, 70th Tank Battalion to E Company. Bill used them to escort the infantry through the streets of Rottingen, providing the riflemen with extra firepower as they cleared the houses. Block by block, E Company ground its way through the town against light resistance. By mid-morning they had possession of most buildings.[29]

That morning, the company CP summoned Private Gartenberg to serve as a translator. "Inside an officer and a noncom were sitting with a big map stretched out between them. Opposite them sat a civilian. It was none other than my German host from the night before. He recognized me, too, and greeted me warmly.[30]

"What he was trying to say, I told the officers, was that in a stone house beside a stream there were SS men. My new friend pointed out the spot on the map."

With the information from the civilian, Bill orchestrated the rest of the battle to clear the SS from Rottingen. He positioned crew-served weapons to cover the stone building then plotted artillery fire on the building and beyond to cut off the enemy's line of retreat. On his order, the 105mm guns opened fire.

Private Gartenberg witnessed the rout. "Suddenly, the door opened, and men in dark uniforms started running out. A machine gun opened up out of nowhere, and men fell like berries shaken off a bush. There were at least a dozen I could see wounded...dying."

Bill watched the action, too. "At 1000 the enemy could be observed withdrawing across the open fields to the east. One group ran directly into a prepared artillery barrage. A kraut fleeing from Rottingen dashed madly up a draw. A mortar barrage fell and he dove into a hole; one shell appeared to land directly into his hole and exploded. Miraculously, he had escaped death and he jumped out of his hole and raced out of sight."[31]

Bill reported that E Company had finished clearing Rottingen shortly after noon. During the morning, Colonel Chance had pulled the rest of the 2nd Battalion off the line and replaced them with the 1st Battalion. B Company took over responsibility for Rottingen. Deuce-and-a-half trucks picked up E Company then drove them back to an assembly area near Stalldorf, seven kilometers back from the Tauber River.[32]

By the time Bill's battalion pulled off the front, the regiment held most, but not all, of the seven crossing sites over the Tauber River. The five-day drive did not gain much ground. CT 12 had pushed the line a little more than ten kilometers south from the Simmringen Woods. In terms of attrition, the scales tipped markedly in CT 12's favor. The 12th Infantry smashed the north-facing defensive line the *XIII*[th] *SS Corps* had tried to form, and *Gruppenfuhrer* Simon had only hastily organized *Kampfgruppen* left along the Tauber River. Besides the heavy casualties it inflicted, the regiment swept up 493 prisoners. One soldier in the 1st Battalion made a huge haul on his own. He fell asleep on patrol one night in an enemy-held town. During the night, the German garrison woke him up to surrender. He brought in ninety-three prisoners the next day by himself. The rear detachments collected nearly as many loose German soldiers roaming the countryside as the three rifle battalions. By comparison, the regiment had only modest losses.[33]

The 2nd Battalion spent the next two days resting and taking care of their equipment. The tough fighting in early April came as a severe shock and disappointment to the veterans in the outfit. Men who had survived the Normandy bloodbaths or struggled through the Ardennes—twice— had hoped for an easy drive through Germany. The savage fighting in the Simmringen Woods dispelled that notion. There were still plenty of chances to be killed. With the war now drawing tantalizingly close to an end, many of the old hands began dwelling on their own survival, something they had not allowed themselves to do earlier.

Bill, still haunted by the premonition that he would never return home, steadfastly did his duty. Others chose a different course. Two of Bill's veteran non-coms calculated that, if they deserted then were caught, the Army would throw the book at them. Normal punishment for desertion was thirty days of confinement. The prospect of waiting out the last month of the war in jail looked like a safer bet than risking death on the front line. The two slipped away from the company assembly area and spent a couple nights carousing in a nearby town. Just as they planned, the Military Police rounded them up and hauled them back to E Company.[34]

Bill saw through the sergeants' plan. He could not tolerate non-coms deserting. Their infraction called for stern punishment, yet he did not want to lose two experienced soldiers. Besides, he hated to give them exactly what they wanted, confinement in the stockade safely tucked away from combat. Bill's solution delivered punishment without rewarding the offenders. Instead of court-martialing them, he issued administrative punishment under Article 15 of the Uniform Code of Military Justice. He busted each sergeant down to the rank of corporal and docked both a month's pay. One of the sergeants had a previous infraction, so Bill court-martialed him on the lesser charge of stealing government property. The two sergeants got the worst of both worlds. They would return to combat but would fight without earning any pay. The word spread quickly within E Company. There was no point deserting under Bill's command.

While resting in Stalldorf, Bill found time to write a letter to Beth, his first in almost a week. The latest campaign weighed on his mind. "Really had a tough week this time...Some of my decisions have been difficult and some have been easy, but all in all it was a damn tough job." The responsibility of commanding men in combat crept into his thoughts. "Made a few mistakes and probably have a few more lives on my hands— but that is an officer's usual task." Bill's mind gravitated to reason and rational thinking. He used those faculties to manage the stress of ordering men to their deaths. "I really don't feel guilty about some of the boys that have died doing the accomplishment of my orders, but I'll always wonder if there could have been fewer losses." He accepted that losses among his men were inevitable. As he noted once, *A guy can get hurt out here.* As long as he believed that his actions and decisions served a purpose and he had exercised sound judgment, Bill could bear the emotional strain without sliding into self-reproach. The ability to dissuade emotions and fear through rational thought was one of the traits that made him so suitable for combat command.[35]

CHAPTER SIXTEEN

MARCH THROUGH FRANCONIA

The eastward thrust of the U.S. Third and Seventh Armies ripped open the seams of the German Western Front in the early days of April 1945. The German *Army Group G*, under the command of Lt. Gen. Friedrich Schultz, lost control of its *Seventh Army* when the American offensive forcibly detached it from his control. Separated from Berlin, Schultz did his best on his own to protect Bavaria and Baden-Wurttemberg from the Allied flood. He bent *Army Group G* at a 90-degree angle. The German *First Army* defended an east-west defensive line across northern Bavaria, loosely anchored between the Neckar and Reynitz Rivers. The *Nineteenth Army* tried to hold the north-south line along the upper Rhine valley.

Already, the First French Army and the U.S. VI Corps had turned the *Nineteenth Army's* northern flank and unhinged the joint between the two German armies, leaving the German *First Army* with two exposed flanks. On its eastern flank, *Gruppenfuhrer* Max Simon, commander of the *XIII SS Corps*, had responsibility for defending the broad plains of Middle Franconia east of the Tauber River. As he had with the forces smashed in the Simmringen Woods, Simon formed his defense with a patchwork of units from the *Wehrkreis* (the German replacement army), officer schools, the *Luftwaffe*, and anti-aircraft battalions, then implanted *SS* troops within them. Despite the increasingly dire strategic situation, the *XIII SS Corps* remained a determined, sometimes rabid, fighting force.[1]

The strategic situation for the German *First Army* quickly became more difficult. General Patch's Seventh Army redirected its attack south to avoid getting pinched out by Patton's Third Army. This new direction of attack threatened to outflank the German defense of the upper Rhine. The southern thrust by Patch had the added benefit of thwarting the potential formation of the feared *Alpenfestung* in Bavaria. Allied intelligence had already noted the disturbing fact that the Germans had drawn 65–75 percent of their *SS* and *Panzer* divisions into southern Germany and Austria. General Milburn's XXI Corps, including the 4th Infantry Division, began its southward drive against the German *First Army* front on April 11.[2]

The corps may have re-oriented to the south, but E Company's orders for April 11 pointed it east. Bill and his men had to relieve a cavalry unit near the town of Baldersheim to help open a new zone of action for the regiment. The division wanted to advance south-southeast down the length of the Tauber River, with CT 12 east of the river and CT 22 on the western side. *Battalion Furth* and *Kampfgruppe Busse* defended a defensive line behind the east-west section of the Tauber River and a tributary flowing from the northeast, Gollach Creek. Before the regiment could move into its new zone, the 1st and 3rd Battalions had to clear Germans out of the high ground south of Rottingen and Weikersheim. F Company and much of H Company were attached to the 1st Battalion for that job. Meanwhile, E and G Companies would move into the new sector facing Gollach Creek.[3]

Trucks picked up E Company in Stalldorf that morning. They dropped the company off at Gelcheim, two and a half kilometers north of Baldersheim, because German mortars had the main road into

Baldersheim targeted. E Company relieved the cavalry troop and settled into the high ground southwest of town. They kept an eye on the woods across Gollach Creek where a couple hundred German soldiers were reported.[4]

German civilians still occupied Baldersheim, and Bill had to get them out of the way. He brought his runner with him to speak with the towns-people. The runner, a German-born Jew, had fled Germany with his family in 1938. The nineteen-year-old hated the Nazis. He enlisted in the U.S. Army in 1944, itching to get back at them. Bill found the kid "invaluable" in these situations. He had his men round up all the residents then gave concise orders to the German civilians. "You have thirty minutes to leave town." The townspeople listened with downcast eyes and hunched shoulders as the runner passed Bill's demand to them in German. The harsh edict, coming from the lips of a juvenile Jew, drove home the point of how low they had been brought down by the war. None of them said a word. With heads bowed, the procession of old women and children shuffled out of Baldersheim. Standing before them, stone-faced, Bill showed no sympathy as they left, but the sight tugged at his heartstrings. He had not come as a conqueror or an oppressor. Nevertheless, the town had to be cleared.[5]

Bill turned his attention to the enemy. He needed a better idea of what he faced, so he sent patrols into the woods. One of them returned with a prisoner who told Bill that as many as four hundred enemy soldiers occupied the woods on the other side of the creek.[6]

Before he could prepare an attack, Bill received word that a Seventh Army psychological warfare expert was on his way. Senior officers had given their blessing to a psychological appeal to induce German soldiers to surrender. They chose the enemy position near Baldersheim for the experiment. Bill may have been skeptical but he cooperated with the expert who set up a loudspeaker at one of the company's outposts. The expert blasted out his message in German to the enemy soldiers across the creek. "Throw down your weapons! Your situation is hopeless. Hitler is doomed. Don't let yourselves be killed for no reason. Give yourselves up to the Americans. We'll give you plenty of food. You can spend the rest of the war safe in a camp...We'll give you a few minutes to come out. After that we'll shell the woods."[7]

No one came out. To add incentive, the Americans fired a five-minute artillery barrage into the woods. Bill made note of the result. "Out came four krauts." He did not dismiss the effectiveness of the psychological warfare effort, but he remarked that a heavier artillery barrage would have been more persuasive.

With firm intelligence of at least two hundred enemy in the woods, E Company prepared to clean them out. Bill planned an evening attack. No longer could the Germans relax at night, free from worries of an American attack. E Company stormed across Gollach Creek at dusk. The riflemen entered the woods but drew no fire. Instead of running into *Kampfgruppe Busse*, they discovered piles of German uniforms. The German soldiers had swapped their uniforms for civilian clothes and deserted, preferring to pose as non-combatants rather than surrender.[8]

E Company finished clearing the woods the next morning. Meanwhile, G Company carried the main attack on April 12. Riding on attached tanks, G Company attacked through Biereberehren and crossed Gollach Creek. After capturing Buch, it turned northeast and took Waldmannshofen. E Company joined them at the end of the day and occupied Hill 343 outside the town. First Battalion, fighting on the right (west) flank of CT 12, advanced across the Tauber River and moved alongside the 2nd Battalion. Colonel Chance now had all of CT 12 in its zone east of the river.[9]

The battalion advised Bill that E Company would go to battalion reserve on April 13. With this in mind, Bill took a few moments to write a letter to Beth. He devoted much of it to lamenting the emotional burden of command. The job of company commander carried more responsibility than ever before. Companies captured towns by themselves with kilometers separating them from the nearest friendly unit. Bill had to face ethical issues about the conduct of war in an enemy's land. He felt uneasy about his role in bringing devastation to Germany's homeland. He also was concerned about the war's effect on his own personality. He warned Beth. "Darling, I know you won't like the changes in me. War has made all of us cruel and mean."[10]

Bill had to deal with civilians and make combat decisions that either spared or destroyed their communities. The warrior in him demanded relentless prosecution of warfare against an enemy that had embroiled the world in conflict. "I must admit however, I actually want the chance to destroy their towns and order the artillery observers to burn the buildings...The people are now receiving a taste of the carnage of war, but it has to be done if the soldiers persist in fighting from towns." He cited the case of Rottingen. "[W]e sent an ultimatum to the town and told them to evacuate or we would give 'em hell. Well, they stayed and so we blasted the place." Yet, Bill still felt a tingling of remorse for the fate of German civilians. "Unfortunately, the church [in Rottingen] was burned to the ground. That is one thing I hate—I try to spare shrines...It seems different to out-smart the Jerry into a position where you can slaughter him, but when you deliberately burn his homes it does seem cruel."

After Simmringen Woods, E Company's battles differed from previous campaigns when battalions and regiments fought shoulder to shoulder and rifle companies were mere formations within larger attacks. The colonels maneuvered companies like pieces on a vast chessboard. Field orders showed numbered objectives corresponding to the hamlets and towns within the regiment's zone of action. Battalions defined company avenues of advance by assigning a series of objectives, usually towns, they had to pass through.

F Company's turn to lead the battalion attack came on April 13. They advanced to Frauental and Weidenhof against scattered opposition. Across its zone CT 12 gathered 245 prisoners even though they had inflicted only eighteen combat casualties on the Germans.[11]

The battalion enjoyed another uneventful day on April 14. E Company followed F Company's advance. Bill's men tramped twelve kilometers down roads and over German countryside. The troops breezed through Frauental, Equarhofen, Klein-Harbach, and Gross-Harbach. They ended the day at Gickelhausen. The enemy made almost no effort to slow the battalion's advance. G Company received some artillery fire near Ohrenbach at the end of the day but no one reported any losses. F Company ran into some small arms fire as they occupied Gumpelshofen. The F Company infantrymen noticed that the enemy fire corresponded with the movements of a civilian who walked around in a nearby field. Finally, a rifleman shot the civilian and the small arms fire stopped. They discovered the man wore German officer's boots. The most excitement for Bill's men came when someone found thirty German aircraft abandoned in the woods outside Gross-Harbach. The regiment ordered part of the reserve battalion to stand guard over the planes until the Air Corps could haul them off.[12]

CT 12 continued its attack in a southeasterly direction on April 15 to clear its zone of action. Colonel Gorn started leapfrogging E and F Companies to lead the 2nd Battalion's main attack. Bill's troops passed through F Company at Gumpelshofen then marched on Reichelshofen with the scouts well out front. G Company, under the command of 1st Lt. Richard Cook, made a supporting attack abreast of E Company 1,500 meters to the east with Endsee as its objective. The enemy had been scarce for the past few days, but Bill approached Reichelshofen with caution, clearing the woods west of the town before he moved in. As the lead platoon neared the edge of Reichelshofen, the Germans opened fire with rifles and machine guns. Gauging the volume of fire, Bill concluded that E Company confronted only a small outpost. Rather than assault with infantry, he ordered his attached platoon of tanks to return fire. The Shermans made quick work of the German outpost with their 75mm main guns. The rifle platoons followed up and secured the town by 1000 hours.[13]

Civilians informed Bill that as many as one hundred German soldiers had fled Reichelshofen shortly before E Company attacked. They also pointed out a minefield just south of town, which fit into a picture of a stiffening German defense. Bill sent a patrol to scout Ellwingshofen, the next objective on the line of march. F Company was scheduled to bound forward to Ellwingshofen and he wanted to give it an idea of the objective's defenses. Two hours later, the patrol started taking fire from the town. Around 1400 hours, Bill handed over the platoon of attached tanks to 1st Lt. Raymond Gilge, F Company Commander. F Company seized Ellwingshofen a short time later with the help of the tanks. Farther east G Company lost two men in a minefield as it approached Endsee. Lieutenant Cook had his men clear lanes through the minefield but they started taking small arms fire. G Company pulled back, then maneuvered into Endsee using the cover of woods.[14]

Colonel Gorn took note of the heavier small arms fire and presence of minefields on both avenues of advance. He decided to continue the attack into the late afternoon with E Company going to Steinsfeld and G Company to Hartershofen. He also tried to coordinate the attack by having E Company "support by fire" G Company's assault on Hartershofen, then using G Company to support E Company's attack on Steinsfeld.[15]

Gorn's plan failed to unfold as he planned. G Company cleared the woods south of Endsee but got caught in a firefight as they emerged into the open fields. At 1820 hours, they were still 1,500 meters short of Hartershofen. Gorn signaled Bill at 1900 hours to launch his attack on Steinsfeld without G Company's help.[16]

Steinsfeld sat in a shallow bowl carved by the Steinbach Branch, a small tributary of the Tauber River. Low, bare hills boxed in the town on all sides. E Company had to cross over the short, rounded hill that separated Ellwingsofen from Steinsfeld. The scouts moved over the top and started heading downhill without trouble but, when the lead platoon advanced within sight of Steinsfeld, the little valley erupted in machine gun fire. The riflemen hit the ground and started returning fire. Enemy rounds cracked overhead and pitted the dirt around them. The enemy positioned machine guns east and west of town that pinned down the Americans with "inter-locking fire." If a soldier turned to face one way, he exposed his flank to the machine guns firing from the other direction. To make matters worse, the gently rising ground allowed the Germans to achieve "grazing fire" as the bullets arced slightly uphill.

Bill was on the verge of bringing his other platoons into the fight when Colonel Gorn called and told him to halt the attack. He feared E Company would get slaughtered if it pressed ahead alone. Pulling the men back from Steinsfeld was no easy task. Colonel Gorn ordered Lieutenant Cook to shift G Company over to provide additional supporting fire on Steinsfeld. Bill finally got all his men extricated after dusk. The company dug in for the night on the north slope of the hill between Ellwingshofen and Steinsfeld.[17]

Colonel Gorn called his company commanders back to the 2nd Battalion CP in Gumpelshofen for a midnight conference. According to the S-2, the Germans had somehow put together a new "main line of resistance" (MLR) in the regiment's zone. The Germans' western flank was anchored on the Tauber River near the town of Bettwar. The line ran east to Steinsfeld then northeast along the Steinbach Branch, ending at the forested hills next to Urphershofen. The division faced the same assortment of SS, cadets, replacements, and Hitler Youth organized under the *212th Volksgrenadier Division, Alpenland Division*, and *Kampfgruppen Dirnagel* and *Reinwald*. Bill did not welcome the prospect of fighting more SS men. He had already complained to Beth about it. "They always slap this division in the hardest sector. The only sector with SS troops is the 7th Army sector." The men of the Ivy Division looked ruefully at the rapid gains made by other Allied armies in northern and central Germany while they battled die-hard Nazis in Bavaria.[18]

Colonel Gorn planned to penetrate the newly discovered German line at Steinsfeld by attacking in a column of companies. E Company would make the main attack on Steinsfeld along the same path they had just taken. Gorn gave Bill nine tanks from B Company of the 70th Tank Battalion to add weight to the infantry assault. Bill and his men would assault the objective when the artillery preparation lifted. Once through Steinsfeld, E Company would hook right (west) to seize Gattenhofen. F Company would follow through the penetration then turn left (east) toward Hartershofen. Last in column, Lieutenant Cook's G Company would attack straight through the gap to seize the deeper objective, Schweinsdorf.[19]

This plan put a huge burden on E Company. It would take the full brunt of the enemy's fire as it created the penetration. The tanks and artillery would help, but his men still would cross open ground in the face of interlocking machine gun fire. Bill gathered his lieutenants to go over his plan for the assault in the predawn hours of April 16. The situation did not lend itself to an elegant tactical solution: E Company would make a frontal attack to break the German line. The company would bound forward, a platoon at a time, during the artillery preparation. Bill wanted all three rifle platoons to get as close to Steinsfeld as possible while the artillery suppressed the German guns. The moment the artillery stopped, the rifle platoons—joined by the attached tanks—would have to fight their way into the town and beyond.

The lieutenants howled in protest. Considering the machine guns they had encountered the day before, the mission looked suicidal. They asked Bill to go back to Colonel Gorn and beg him to call off the attack. Bill insisted that the company comply with the battalion's order. When he asked which platoon would lead the attack, none of the platoon leaders volunteered. Bill passed over the platoon that took the heat on the previous attack and selected one of the other rifle platoons. When that platoon leader protested, again, Bill quashed his complaints. The attack would proceed as ordered. He sent the lieutenants back to their platoons then spent the few hours before dawn fretting about the coming attack. He did not feel the odd sensation that preceded the times he was wounded near Montebourg and the Schnee Eifel, but his experience told him that he and his men could be torn to pieces once they crossed the hill separating them from Steinsfeld. He later described the decision to go forward with the attack on Steinsfeld as his most difficult of the war.

E Company assembled in the early morning dark of April 16. The infantry platoons snuck forward to a line just short of the top of the low hill where they remained just out of sight of Steinsfeld. The nine B Company tanks formed on line behind the infantry. Bill crawled forward a few extra meters to observe the objective. The show started at first light. Two battalions from the division artillery opened fire on Steinsfeld. Thirty-six guns rained destruction on the German town. The bursting rounds shot plumes of dust and debris skyward like geysers.[20] (See Map XV)

Bill did a time check. The artillery prep would last thirty minutes. The company had to use some of that time to cross the five hundred meters of open ground to close on Steinsfeld. If they failed to get on top of the objective by the time the artillery lifted, the German machine gunners would slaughter them. The company's only chance was to spring on the enemy before they lifted their heads out of their foxholes. Bill counted down the seconds to his "jump off" time. His heart thudded in his chest with each tick of the watch. He had never felt this level of tension before. Every second that went by brought him closer to the dreadful moment when he had to launch the attack. The instant his watch hit the designated mark, Bill gulped down his trepidation and rose to his feet. He waved to the lead platoon to move out.

Bill turned toward Steinsfeld and began marching downhill to the objective, leading the way for his men. He advanced a short distance then turned around to check the lead platoon's movement. The only person he saw was his own radio operator. The two of them stood by themselves on the forward slope. Nobody else had followed.

Cowardice! Mutiny! Insubordination! Furious, Bill strode straight for the lieutenant in charge of the lead platoon. As he approached, he pulled his pistol from its holster and chambered a round. Bill planted himself in front of the lieutenant and shoved his .45 into the reluctant officer's face. "Get your men moving or, so help me, I'll blow your head off!"

The lieutenant looked at the muzzle of the .45 cal. pistol that loomed as large as a howitzer. His eyes grew to the size of hubcaps. Suddenly more afraid of Bill than the Germans, he jumped to his feet and flapped his arms at his men to get them off the ground. The platoon's enlisted men hurried to their feet. The rest of the company showed no hesitation in following, after witnessing the tense altercation between the officers.

E Company moved downhill toward its objective. The German gunners held their fire as the tanks and infantry approached. Bill assumed the artillery had forced them down into their foxholes. He pushed the platoons forward more rapidly to close on the town while the enemy machine guns remained quiet. Every two seconds, an artillery shell burst over Steinsfeld. A cloud of dust and smoke hung in the air above the American infantry. The riflemen crept within seventy-five meters of the

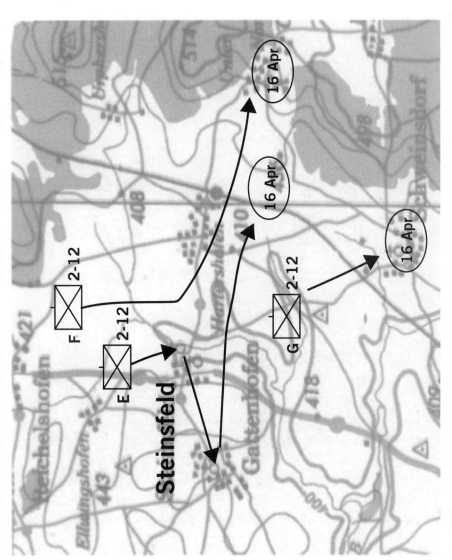

Map XV

impacting rounds, as close as they dared. Blast waves buffeted their faces, and they could see the shrapnel kick up dust a few feet to their front. The tanks rumbled behind the platoons, ready to open fire on any targets that appeared. Bill's radio operator relayed a message from the artillery, "Last shot out!" A few seconds later, he called out the message Bill had been waiting for. "Splash!" One last *boom* rocked Steinsfeld.

Bill ordered the company to open fire then motioned to the lead platoon to launch its assault. The platoon bounded forward using "assault fire." Nothing more than a smattering of rifle fire greeted the Americans. The dreaded German machine guns failed to engage. The tanks immediately blasted the few defenders who dared to fire and the assault force overwhelmed their positions. The Americans rolled into Steinsfeld. Soldiers barged into the wrecked houses to root out any defenders. Street by street, the riflemen pushed through town but found few remaining Germans, much to everyone's relief.

Nobody felt more relieved than Bill. It took his leadership and courage to get the attack started. Thankfully, the operation became a cakewalk. He did not have to think about more lives lost "doing the accomplishment" of his orders.

The 2nd Battalion took advantage of the sudden capture of Steinsfeld. E Company hurried past the village. Bill turned the company formation to the right and advanced over the low hill west of Steinsfeld. By 0945 hours, the lead platoon walked into Gattenhofen, their secondary objective. F Company followed Bill's men through Steinsfeld then attacked Hartershofen from the west and south with the help of one of the tank platoons. F Company continued rolling southeast and captured their secondary objective, the town of Unter Nordenberg, but a well-defended roadblock halted its advance short of Ober Nordenberg. With the gap opened wide, Colonel Gorn shoved G Company to the deep objective, Schweinsdorf. It had to fight its way into Schweinsdorf against direct fire from a German 88 but it took the town. Bill relinquished control of Gattenhofen to the 3rd Battalion and marched east to occupy Hartershofen, where Colonel Gorn located the battalion CP. The rifle companies seized all of their objectives and completed movement by 1445 hours. Bill and his men ended the day in Hartershofen as the battalion reserve. The hard punch by the 2nd Battalion and the advance of the 1st Battalion on the right flank brought CT 12 up to its next major objective—Rothenburg.[21]

Rothenburg ob der Tauber (the city's full name) sat on a high bluff dominating the Tauber River valley. The city dated back to the Middle Ages and had been declared a Free Imperial City by the Holy Roman Emperor in 1274. A formidable wall surrounded the old section of the city that last fell to the Emperor's army during the Thirty Years' War. Since then Rothenburg grew little but retained its medieval architecture and romantic charm. In the preceding week, the Assistant Secretary of War, John J. McCloy, received a briefing from the 6th Army Group Commander, General Devers, about the upcoming attack on the city. Devers laid out a plan to demolish the city with artillery before making any attempt to assault its fortifications. McCloy had visited Rothenburg in his youth and recalled its medieval beauty. He remarked to Devers that it would be a shame to destroy such an ancient relic this late in the war. The general took the comment to heart and issued instructions to avoid damaging Rothenburg.[22]

The 12th Infantry's commander, Colonel Chance, worked out a plan to take the medieval city peacefully, but to do so would require Germans cooperation. On April 16, he instructed the 1st Battalion to send a patrol into Rothenburg under a flag of truce. The American patrol would offer to occupy the city without firing on it, provided the German garrison agreed to vacate the city beforehand. The Germans granted the patrol safe conduct, and the garrison commander met with the Americans. Fortunately, he was a Wehrmacht major, not an SS officer. The major listened to the American ultimatum then replied that he wanted to preserve the city, too, but he could not surrender without higher-level approval. Because of communications problems, he elaborated, it would take four hours to get confirmation. The Americans protested. The patrol had to return to American lines immediately. After the German commander repeated that he had to await confirmation, the patrol returned to the 12th Infantry CP. They relayed the German commander's comments but mentioned that he seemed willing to leave the city open to the Americans.[23]

Colonel Chance conferred with General Blakeley, who decided to wait. The two senior officers spoke again at 2130 hours after hearing nothing from the Germans. Blakeley figured that the German commander could not accept terms without risking reprisal but would likely comply with the Americans' terms. The general told Chance to move into Rothenburg in the morning but not to use any artillery unless the Germans defended the city. The 1st Battalion entered through the gates of the medieval fortification early on April 17 and rounded up fifty-six prisoners. By 0845 hours they passed on the good news that the Germans had vacated and declared Rothenburg to be an open city.[24]

The news that Rothenburg had been spared the destruction of war pleased Bill. He appreciated the beauty and culture of Germany, and it saddened him to see so much of the country devastated. He remembered Prum. Bill felt a sense of relief that the beautiful city had been preserved. Yet duty called him to deliver more destruction on the very day Rothenburg had been saved.

While CT 12 took possession of Rothenburg, the 2nd Battalion continued pushing southeast. A heavily forested slope separated F Company in Unter Nordenberg and G Company in Schweinsdorf. Colonel Gorn decided to insert E Company between them and drive southeast with all three companies abreast. E Company left Hartershofen in the early morning and pushed uphill through the woods. Within the forest, the men moved cautiously but found no enemy. They emerged from the woods a little before 1000 hours. Bill spread out the company formation as it reached the top of the high ground. There they discovered a man holding a white flag by the side of a road. He identified himself as the mayor of Linden, their next objective. The lead element brought the mayor over to Bill and his German-speaking runner. At first, the mayor mistook the dirty unshaven American for a private but Bill's translator assured him that he was standing before the company commander. The mayor greeted the American officer with a smile.[25]

Bill wanted to know the situation in Linden. "Are there any German troops in the town?"

"No, the soldiers left. You can march right into the town without worry."

That answer seemed a little too inviting. Bill suspected an ambush, so he decided to call the mayor's bluff. "That's good. We'll move in right away…but if anyone fires on my troops, I'll shell the town."

The instant the translator gave Bill's warning in German, the mayor blanched and his eyes widened. A moment later, he started to shake.

Bill leaned in toward the terrified mayor. "Are you sure there aren't any German soldiers or SS in the town?"

The mayor trembled so much he could barely speak. Finally, he squeaked out an answer. "No…no German soldiers…in town."

The mayor's act fooled no one. The artillery FO with Bill started to chuckle at the sight of the quaking mayor. Without waiting for instructions, he called up the artillery fire direction center (FDC). "Redleg 1 this is Redleg 4, fire mission over."

"Redleg 4 this is Redleg 1, fire mission over."

"Target, enemy infantry defending in houses." The FO gave the coordinates of the town. "Six rounds of HE quick. Fire on my command, over."

"Roger Redleg 4, fire on your command, standing by, out."

Bill listened as the FO scheduled the mission. When the FO nodded that the artillery battery was ready, Bill motioned to the scouts to move forward.

The scouts barely got started before they drew small arms fire from a handful of defenders in Linden. Shaking his head at the mayor's stupidity, the FO called back to the FDC. "Redleg 1 this Redleg 4, commence fire, over."

"Redleg 4, this is Redleg 1 roger out." A minute later the FDC called back. "Redleg 4 this is Redleg 1, shot, out."

Within seconds Bill, his command party, and the terrified mayor heard the screeching of artillery shells passing overhead. *Crump! Crump! Crump!* Houses, trees, fences, livestock, and wagons blew apart as the rounds impacted in the small town. With tears in his eyes, the mayor watched his and his neighbors' homes disappear under the rising cloud of dust. The artillery pounded the little village for six minutes.

Bill motioned to the scouts to resume the advance. He then turned to the distraught mayor. "You should've told the truth."

The few German defenders fled as soon as the shells started hitting Linden. The Americans walked into the town without incident, just as the mayor promised—only there was no town there anymore.[26]

From Linden, E Company turned south and re-entered the forested high ground. They captured seven prisoners and an 88 nearby, possibly the one that had been firing at G Company the day before. One of the prisoners alerted the Americans to eighty Germans dug-in deeper in the wooded high ground. E and G Companies pushed past the reported position without making contact but farther south G Company got into a running small arms fight with a delaying force. E Company plowed through the center of the woods and ended the day by capturing Gunsendorf. G Company settled into Steinbach, and F Company took up a position a few hundred meters to the northeast of Gunsendorf. The battalion netted another forty prisoners with only slight casualties for the day.[27]

CT 12 changed directions on April 18. Instead of heading southeast, the regiment now headed almost due south. The 2nd Battalion attacked on the left (east) flank of the zone. The 3rd Battalion assumed the role of the 1st Battalion and attacked on the right (west) flank. The 1st Battalion followed as the regimental reserve.[28]

This put the 2nd Battalion in a tough spot. The battalion's initial move shifted southwest. E Company seized Aidenau while G Company had to cross a wooded ridge to take Sodelbronn. The battalion then advanced south with its lead companies split on opposite sides of a forested ridge. Luckily, the Germans had so few forces in the area that they could not take advantage of the situation.[29]

E Company rolled south against almost no opposition, ticking off objectives like a grocery list in an uncontested ten-kilometer march: Aidenau, Breitenau, Speirhof, Schonbronn, Neuweiler. Bill took advantage of woods and hills to mask the company's movement from enemy artillery observers. Nothing happened until they passed Neuweiler, where enemy observers spotted them from their OP on the high ridge at Schillingsfürst, farther south. Rather than proceed directly down the road to the next objective, Wohnbach, Bill moved his platoons up the slope of a ridge and kept them concealed in woods as they maneuvered east of the town.[30]

Once E Company advanced to the edge of the woods overlooking Wohnbach, Bill ordered a halt so he could plan how to take the objective. A minute later, the troops heard the whistling of approaching German artillery rounds. The men hit the dirt until they heard the rounds impacting a few hundred meters away. Relieved, Bill went back to planning the attack.

A few minutes later, the German artillery fired again, and the shells landed a couple hundred meters farther up the ridge from the first target. The Germans shifted the artillery to a third target. This time the rounds landed at the edge of the woods closer to E Company.

Bill figured out what they were doing. The enemy artillery observers in Schillingsfürst were trying to flush E Company from the woods. He called his platoon leaders over for a quick conference.

"The Germans can't see us," he explained. "They're shifting their artillery until they finally hit our position. They'll shift their fire higher up the ridge in a few minutes. After that they'll target this spot. The next time they shift fire I want everyone in the company to run as fast as they can to the town. Tell your men to take cover in the basements of the houses. If we move quickly, we can get everyone under cover before the artillery observers can shift fire on us." He sent the platoon leaders back to spread the word among their men.

Just as Bill predicted, the Germans lifted their artillery fire after a few more rounds. The entire company sat in silence, waiting for the next salvo. Before long the men heard the familiar whistle of incoming rounds then the *crump* of the artillery blasting the new target higher up the ridge.

The whole company got up and dashed for Wohnbach. The men of E Company covered the short distance in a couple of minutes. Inside the town, Bill watched his men scurry for cover in the houses and shops.

When he felt satisfied that his troops had found shelter, he ducked inside one of the houses himself. He found a dozen of his men hiding in the basement and sat down at the top of the steps to catch his breath after the sprint from the woods.[31]

The German observers spotted the Americans and adjusted fire onto Wohnbach. The first round hit next to the house where Bill hid. The blast rattled his senses and sent a huge chunk of shrapnel through the top step of the staircase. Bill looked at the step and saw a hole just inches from his seat big enough to put his boot through. He dove to the bottom of the steps.

The Germans plastered the little town with artillery but without any effect. E Company survived the enemy fire with no casualties.

After the artillery lifted for good, Lieutenant Touhy, the company XO, confronted Bill. "Sir, you took an awful chance. What if the Germans had a machine gun in town? We could've been mowed down running out of the woods."

"Naw, I knew there weren't any machine guns here."

"How did you know that?" Touhy asked.

"Their gunners would've seen us moving on the ridge and they would've adjusted their artillery right on us, instead of shifting fire all around."

"Maybe they didn't have communications with the artillery observers?"

"The Germans wouldn't put machine guns here unless they were defending the town. If they planned to defend the place they'd have communications, too. Besides, the Germans wouldn't defend here."

"How could you be sure?"

"They always follow good tactics. The Germans wouldn't defend here because we had a good approach into town and their line of retreat would be over open ground. They always set their defense where they can catch us on exposed terrain and where they can pull out when they have to."

Months of fighting the Germans taught Bill a lot about German tactics. "They always did the right thing," Bill noted. Germans stayed true to their doctrine and training. Their leaders seldom made tactical mistakes. Invariably, they defended ground overlooking choke points in the Americans' avenues of approach. In earlier campaigns, mines, anti-tank guns, machine guns, infantry, and artillery would have been tied together to put maximum fire at the points the Germans wanted to defend. Once their positions were penetrated or turned, they would counterattack to re-establish their defense. If the counterattack failed, they would fall back to more favorable terrain. At this stage of the war, the Germans lacked the ability to put together cohesive defensive lines or make strong counterattacks. Nevertheless, they gave ground grudgingly, but would abandon a losing position before the Americans overwhelmed them.

Bill's problem-solving skills helped him see the vulnerabilities in German tactics. Their disciplined adherence to doctrine and training made their tactics predictable. The Germans would analyze the terrain, see the logical way for the Americans to attack—and the best way to defend against it. Knowing what the Germans anticipated, Bill searched for ways to hit them where they did not expect. "You can always fool the Germans," he told his men. "They always look for the tactically sound option. Avoid the obvious avenue of approach. Use surprise to beat them."

E Company moved into Wohnbach the same time Lieutenant Cook's G Company flushed a large number of enemy troops from Bellershausen. Friendly artillery and H Company's heavy weapons fired on Bellershausen, paving the way for G Company's successful attack at 2000 hours. The battalion called it a day with all three companies abreast between Bellershausen and Wohnbach.[32]

Looking south, Bill saw an impressive castle sitting atop the next ridge. The Schloss Schillingsfürst, ancestral home of the Hohenlohe dynasty, had been the residence of Prince Chlodwig zu Hohenlohe-Schillingsfürst, who became German Chancellor four years after Bismarck left office. In April 1945, Prince Franz Josef zu Hohenlohe-Schillingsfürst and his wife Princess Aglae shared the *Schloss* with the headquarters of the *XIII SS Corps*. The German HQ fled shortly before the 12th Infantry's arrival but a few

SS remained to take advantage of the fact that the castle's magnificent views in all directions made it a perfect OP. It had to be taken the next day.[33]

The war had entered an irrational and brutal stage by mid-April of 1945. Only the most ardent Nazis held out hope that somehow, some way, Germany could still win the war. Most Germans understood the war had been lost. German resistance in central and northern Germany could not stop the Allied armies, and Berlin began to gird itself for an onslaught by the Red Army. The commander of the *212ᵗʰ VG Division* summed up the effect that the obvious absurdity of continued fighting had. "The apparent uselessness of these battles virtually crushed the will to resist and sense of duty of the German troops." Growing numbers of Germans now deserted or threw down their arms rather than fight to the death.[34]

The Fuhrer thought the German people had failed some great test and, more precisely, had failed him—and so deserved to go down in flames along with his *Reich*. He demanded that everyone fight to the last and ordered a "scorched earth" policy across Germany to leave nothing for the triumphant Allies, or for the war's survivors. Throughout southern Germany, *SS* men spent much of their energy enforcing Hitler's nihilistic policy. They threatened to punish any civilian who failed to resist the American advance or, in other ways, committed *wehrkraftzersetzung*, that is, "undermining the war effort." Some civilians cooperated with the *SS*, such as the mayor of Linden. Those who defied the *SS* risked immediate and brutal retribution. During the battle of Simmringen Woods, for instance, a priest had raised a white flag from his church tower to safeguard his place of worship but had to pull it down when the *SS* threatened to shoot him on the spot. As the war dragged into its final weeks, the German people saw for themselves what so many other nations had learned while the conflict raged in their lands: "One fears the *SS* like the devil."[35]

Schloss Schillingsfürst played a role in a sordid case that illustrated the brutality and fanaticism of the *SS*. On the morning of April 7, the same day E Company attacked Rottingen, a gang of Hitler Youth under the leadership of an *SS* corporal sent four boys armed with *Panzerfausten* and rifles to patrol the town of Brettheim, a nearby village. The armed teenagers had a run in with locals, who scolded the boys for their juvenile bravado. One of the local farmers went so far as to disarm and chase them off. He then dumped their weapons into a pond. The sulking teens reported the incident to their corporal who, in turn, called the *XIIIth SS Corps*, headquartered at the *Schloss*. *Gruppenfuhrer* Max Simon sent one of his staff officers to Brettheim to clear up the matter. The officer convened a summary court martial that quickly convicted the farmer of *wehrkraftzersetzung*. However, two members of the court, the mayor and the local Nazi Party boss, declined to impose the death penalty favored by the *SS* officer. On April 10, the *SS* officer brought the matter to *Gruppenfuhrer* Simon who convened an expanded court martial against the farmer for his actions and the two local officials for their refusal to sentence him to death. The court found all three guilty. Simon signed the verdict and added a note to "hang them." The *SS* strung up the three men on a linden tree outside the Brettheim cemetery and left them dangling several days as an admonition to the locals. The *SS* hung around Brettheim long enough to fire on the lead elements of an American force. Their fire triggered an American aerial bombardment that blew the town to bits along with many of its citizens, thereby compounding the tragedy.[36]

Across Bavaria and Baden-Wurttemburg, this scenario repeated itself. *SS* units terrorized civilians into mounting hopeless fights against the Seventh Army offensive or sniped at Americans then retreated before the Americans blasted the towns and villages. Their cruel treatment of the people they were supposed to protect echoed the perverse nature of the Nazi regime and Hitler's own thoughts: "We can no longer afford to concern ourselves with the population."[37]

The 2nd Battalion began its attack on Schillingsfürst at 0800 hours on April 19. E Company advanced with an attached platoon of tanks. Scanning the *Schloss* and town, Bill could see no white flags. As they had moved across Germany, the Americans had dropped propaganda leaflets warning all German civilians to display white flags or sheets from prominent windows to indicate their desire to surrender. American forces respected the "new German national flag" and avoided firing on towns or homes that put one out. Inside Schillingsfürst, the SS diehards threatened everyone with immediate execution if they put out a white sheet. As the Americans approached, one of the tanks fired a warning shot from its main gun into the north face of the *Schloss*. Taking matters into their own hands, Princess Aglae and a Red Cross worker yanked white tablecloths from the dining areas and draped them from the windows. That prominent display ended any attempt by the Germans to defend Schillingsfürst or the *Schloss*.[38]

Bill and his men hustled forward the instant they spotted the surrender flags. They wanted to take the castle quickly and peacefully before the SS changed anyone's mind. After riding up the steep hill on a tank, Bill hopped off and crossed an arched bridge to the castle's front entrance. Bill approached the elegant iron gate, backed by the tank. Standing in the courtyard, Prince Franz Josef greeted Bill, then announced that the *Schloss* was at the Americans' disposal. E Company rounded up ten German stragglers and took possession of the town and castle. Except for the SS, both sides felt relieved that the magnificent residence was captured without a fight. The Americans gained a key terrain feature with no losses. The town was spared destruction and the prince and princess saved their home, a priceless example of baroque architecture.[39]

E Company continued to the adjacent village of Frankenheim while others took advantage of the castle. Colonel Gorn, Capt. Tallie Crocker (now on the battalion staff), and several artillery FOs settled into the lavish upper rooms of Schloss Schillingsfürst. From their vantage point, they could see ten kilometers in every direction. Almost at once, they spotted a large column of enemy vehicles trying to escape down a highway. The FOs of two artillery battalions called in 105mm rounds onto the fleeing vehicles.[40]

Colonel Gorn decided to combine his attached armored vehicles with one of his infantry companies to form a single combined arms force. He wanted to attack deep into the battalion's zone in one bold, armored thrust. F and G Companies were busy pushing past the wooded hilltops southwest of Schillingsfürst, but E Company was handy. Bill's men climbed aboard four M4 tanks, four M36 tank destroyers, and three halftracks. Bill mounted the tank platoon leader's vehicle to control the force. While the combined arms force formed, a general officer joined Colonel Gorn and Captain Crocker to watch the impending attack from the battalion's richly appointed OP. At 1600 hours, Task Force Chapman moved out.[41]

The road south from Schillingsfürst passed through a narrow choke point formed by the wooded hills to the west and a creek bed meandering through the valley. Beyond the choke point the valley opened into a broad plain. A German infantry company defended a finger-ridge next to Wornitz, south of Frankenheim. The position blocked both the road coming from Frankenheim and the Rothenburg highway coming from the northwest. Two kilometers farther to the southwest, a platoon-sized reserve force occupied a bald hill dominating the towns of Erzberg and Harlang.

Bill planned to punch through one part of the German defensive position at Wornitz, bypass the other half of the enemy position, then launch an attack on the hill to the south. The attack required some fancy maneuvering with the tanks, so Bill coordinated the movement and signals with the leaders of the mechanized platoons.

TF Chapman rolled toward Wornitz with infantrymen clinging to the hulls of the armored vehicles. The narrow valley south of Schillingsfürst forced the vehicles to move in a column of platoons until it passed the choke point of the valley.

The general, observing from the upper floor of the *Schloss*, became concerned about the column formation. He turned to Colonel Gorn. "That company better get out of column before they start taking fire."[42]

As if reading the general's mind, Bill ordered the tank platoon to slow down then signaled the following platoons to move forward on line with the lead element. The task force quickly switched from a column to a line formation.

Bill directed the task force to concentrate on the eastern half of the enemy position. The armored formation rumbled toward the enemy and opened fire. The 90mm and 75mm main guns with the added fire from the machine guns and rifles smothered the Germans. The enemy infantry had nothing to match and no way to stop the charging combined arms force. As the task force approached, the Germans ran for cover or held up their hands in surrender. TF Chapman pushed up toward the enemy position. They routed half of the German defense but the other half remained on their flank.

Watching from the castle, the general became concerned once again. "That company commander better watch out. He's bypassing the other position with his flank exposed."

At the same moment, Bill signaled the platoons to change from a line to an "echelon right" formation as they bypassed the remaining enemy. The tank on the far left became the lead vehicle. Every other vehicle spaced itself back from the vehicle to its left. The new formation allowed the tanks to orient all their guns to their right. As soon as the vehicles re-formed into an echelon right, they opened fire on the bypassed German position. The entire enemy line gave way. The Americans rolled up the enemy flank and blasted the few die-hards with heavy direct fire. Those who weren't killed or wounded stampeded to the rear.

Bill watched the panicked enemy soldiers running for their lives from the top of his tank. His interpreter raised his rifle and started shooting at them. Bill shouted. "Quit it. Can't you see they're running?"

"But sir, they're Germans."

"They're men. We don't shoot men in the back."

TF Chapman drove past the demoralized Germans. Most of them gave up as the armored vehicles swarmed past. The attack formation roared south toward the final German position on the hill near Erzberg.

Seeing the task force approaching the hill, the general again voiced his concern. "That company needs to get back on line before it attacks that hill."

Down in the valley, Bill signaled the vehicles to change formation once again. The platoons adjusted their speed to bring the entire task force back into line formation. With maximum frontal firepower, the Americans charged. The Germans holding the hill had watched the forward line collapse and knew what they were in for. TF Chapman overwhelmed the enemy, who barely put up a fight.

The general lowered his field glasses when the task force seized the Erzberg hill. Colonel Gorn grinned from ear to ear as he looked at him. The general nodded to Gorn, acknowledging the skill and aggressiveness of the 2nd Battalion's attack. He then departed Colonel Gorn's sumptuous OP, pleased by what he had seen.

The day had not quite finished for the rifle companies. TF Chapman remained at Erzberg long enough to support F Company's attack on Harlang then moved to seize Grub and Arzbach before daylight gave out. Bill and his men had completed an exhilarating day of swift, violent combat. They had surged forward ten kilometers, captured a castle, and destroyed an enemy company.[43]

With the general out of his hair, Gorn had time to think about Bill's success leading a tank-infantry team. E Company's swift attack reinforced Gorn's opinion of Bill that had been growing since he gave him command of E Company back in the Rhineland. The battalion commander knew he had found his "go-to guy" for any tough assignment down the road.

CHAPTER SEVENTEEN

TASK FORCE RODWELL

On April 20, E Company enjoyed a relatively easy day in reserve as
F and G Companies led the battalion's attack south, sweeping
aside dispersed enemy delaying forces and clearing numerous towns.
Bill's men began the day clearing Erzberg then marching behind G
Company to Leukershausen and Waldmannsberg. The battalion
advanced a healthy thirteen kilometers that day, but that was not
enough to satisfy General Blakeley. After watching the adjacent 12th
Armored Division rack up more impressive gains on its way to the
Danube River, Blakeley decided the division could not limit its advance
to the speed of foot soldiers.[1]

At 2050 hours, the Assistant Division Commander, Brig. Gen. James
Rodwell, visited the 12th Infantry's CP and told the regiment to hold in
place, pending a new mission. That meant E Company could stand down
while the divisional and regimental staffs worked out a new plan.[2]

The 12th Infantry awoke on April 21 to discover that, overnight, the
division formed a new fighting organization that would be entirely

motorized: Task Force Rodwell. Commanded by General Rodwell, the task force combined the 70ᵗʰ Tank Battalion, a company of the 610ᵗʰ TD Battalion, the 4ᵗʰ Engineer Battalion, a reconnaissance troop, two artillery battalions, and the 12ᵗʰ Infantry Regiment. The trucks necessary to carry the infantrymen came from the corps artillery. E Company would initially serve as the task force's rear guard.[3]

TF Rodwell planned to race thirty-five kilometers south, through Crailsheim and Ellwangen, to the industrial city of Aalen in a single day. It would continue farther south, all the way to the Danube River, at the same swift pace. Expecting only scattered remnants of the *19ᵗʰ Volksgrenadier, 212ᵗʰ Volksgrenadier,* and *Alpenland Divisions,* and trusting in the task force's strength and mobility, General Rodwell intended to use momentum to collapse enemy resistance and reach the Danube before the Germans could organize a river line defense.

The task force assembled into an elongated column near Rudolfsberg. At 1040 hours, a platoon of light tanks led the movement toward Crailsheim. The column bypassed the city on the east to avoid a roadblock but ran into a blown bridge three kilometers beyond the city. After an hour-long delay, the march proceeded to a river crossing near Jagstheim where the Germans bombarded the column with mortars, artillery, and rockets. General Rodwell decided the task force could make better time by staying off the main highway, and shifted the column over to secondary roads east of the Jagst River Valley. The column snaked through the countryside before running into another blown bridge and road craters at Stimpfach. The engineers repaired the bridge and used a bulldozer to fill the craters. The lead elements crossed the Jagst River to the west side then stopped for the night outside of Jagstzell.

E Company and a platoon of AT guns protected the task force's rear while the over-stretched column moved out. In typical "hurry-up-and-wait" fashion, the company had to sit around until 0130 hours the next day before they started moving.[4]

On the morning of April 22, the task force advanced on secondary roads through wooded terrain, rather than the main highway, but this route proved difficult, too. The retreating Germans felled trees, threw up roadblocks, and blew craters at constriction points. The exhausted engineers pushed, blasted, and dozed their way through these obstacles. Farther back in the formation, the 2nd Battalion rode past several columns of dispirited German PWs slowly tramping in the opposite direction. The men paid little attention to the now familiar sight until someone noticed that the prisoners had no guards.

The 70th Tank Battalion and the 1st Battalion, at the front of the task force, had a sharp fight with a German force in Neuler, losing one tank to a *Panzerfaust*. After wiping out several dozen stubborn defenders the column continued south and overran a number of towns before stopping just short of Aalen for the night.[5]

Friendly civilians tipped off the Americans that five hundred German soldiers defended Aalen. The German commander had pressed the local *Volkssturm* (Nazi militia) into service as well as any able-bodied teenage boys and old men. Expecting a tough fight, General Rodwell and Colonel Chance planned a deliberate attack to seize the city. The 1st and 3rd Battalions, each with an attached tank company, would attack abreast into Aalen from the north. Rodwell kept 2nd Battalion in reserve to guard the task force's rear in Wasseralfingen, a reasonable precaution given that TF Rodwell had advanced fifteen kilometers ahead of the rest of the division.[6]

The two battalions jumped off by 0615 hours on April 23 and pushed into Aalen. Whenever the enemy fired from a building, the Shermans and infantry platoons blasted the spot. The Germans could not match the Americans' firepower but gave ground slowly. The enemy played some of their old tricks, such as letting tanks go by then popping up behind them to resume fighting. This forced the American infantry to clear each building. As the two battalions approached the city center, the resistance intensified and enemy tanks joined the fight.[7] (See Map XVI)

The spirited fight in Aalen gave General Rodwell an idea. He saw an opportunity to trap the enemy force inside Aalen by maneuvering his reserve around the city and sealing off any escape route. At 1200 hours he warned Colonel Gorn to get ready for a motorized attack and attached

B Company, 70th Tank Battalion to 2nd Battalion. Gorn assembled his attached tanks, tank destroyers, and halftracks, then ordered Bill to mount his men on the tracked vehicles. The rest of the battalion boarded trucks.[8]

E Company's armored formation and the battalion's trucks followed the 4th Reconnaissance Troop out of Wasseralfingen, swinging around the north side of Aalen. Near Unt-Rombach, the battalion offloaded the trucks and formed for the attack. At 1455 hours, E Company moved south then east to encircle the city. G Company followed Bill's force and set up a blocking position to seal the southwest exit of the city.[9]

As E Company moved around to Aalen's south side, it started taking artillery fire. The mounted force maneuvered out of the impact area but the artillery followed it. Given its accuracy, Bill suspected that the Germans had an observer spotting the rounds. Scanning the area with his binoculars, he spied a tower on an adjacent ridge more than 1,000 meters away.[10]

Bill tapped the shoulder of the tank commander. "Hey, I think we're being spotted by an artillery observer."

"Yes, sir. Do you know where he is?" the tanker asked.

"I see a tower on the next ridgeline. I bet he's sighting us from there."

The tanker pulled out his binoculars and searched for the tower. "Yeah, I see it."

"Can you take him out?"

"Sure." The tank commander made a quick estimate of the target's range. He decided to override his gunner's controls to fire a spotting round then let his gunner adjust onto the target. With his eyes locked on the distant tower the commander elevated his tank's 75mm main gun. When he was satisfied that he had a good initial range, he hit the turret motor to turn the gun toward the target. The instant the turret swiveled onto the right azimuth the tank commander simultaneously stopped the turret's rotation and fired.

A second later, the shell scored a direct hit on the tower and blew it to pieces.

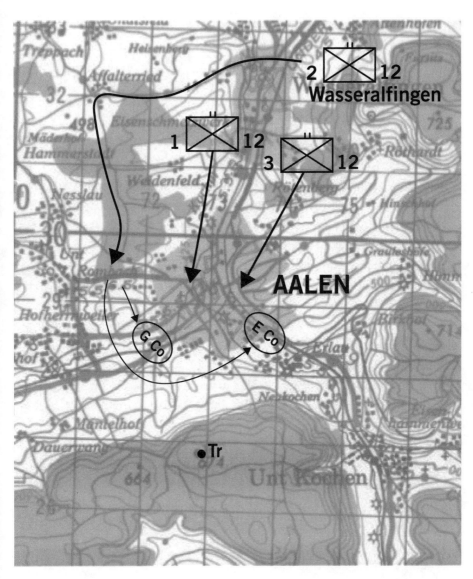

Map XVI

"Damn! What a shot," Bill shouted while the other tank commanders cheered their comrade's amazing dead-reckoning aim. The enemy artillery stopped a minute later.

Now free of the vexing artillery, E Company rolled toward the southeastern corner of Aalen. One kilometer short of their objective (the highway heading south toward Unt-Kuchen), they spotted a column of German troops and vehicles fleeing east out of the city. The infantrymen jumped off the armored vehicles to let the tanks and tank destroyers engage. Within seconds, 75mm and 90mm shells slammed into the enemy vehicles and machine guns raked the retreating German column. E Company's foot soldiers charged toward a paper mill next to the highway. A small group of German infantrymen opened fire on the advancing Americans. The rifle platoons pressed the assault. The M4s and M36s, finished with the fleeing German column, then began firing on the paper mill.[11]

As E Company closed on the objective, 75mm shells exploded in their midst. Two German tanks appeared in Neukochen, a small town a kilometer to the southeast. The American tanks and tank destroyers immediately reacted, jockeying for position to get clean shots. The uneven fight did not last long. An M36 knocked out one of the German tanks, and the other one bugged out.[12]

Bill's infantrymen, supported by the tanks and tank destroyers, steamrolled the enemy defending the paper mill and moved to block Aalen's southern exit. Bill had his men place mines on both sides of the highway and position weapons to cut off any potential line of retreat. This encirclement took the heart out of the Germans. A short time after dark, the forward platoons of the 3rd Battalion reached E Company, ending the battle for Aalen.[13]

The regiment hauled in over three hundred prisoners from Aalen. The success validated General Rodwell's maneuver tactics. It also proved that isolated German defensive positions, even ones embedded in urban areas, could not stop the highly mobile Americans.[14]

Task Force Rodwell had to slim down on April 24 because the XXI Corps Artillery recalled its trucks. General Rodwell decided to advance with just one infantry battalion and one artillery battalion, plus the armor. Colonel Chance left the 1st and 3rd Battalions in Aalen and ordered Colonel Gorn to move with the task force. Once again, Gorn chose E Company to lead the attack mounted on the tanks and TDs.[15]

Overnight reconnaissance showed that the Germans had blocked the main highway passing through Unt-Kuchen at numerous sites. Rather than attempt to bull through the roadblocks and blown bridges along the highway, General Rodwell chose a new route along roads that ran south through a series of towns on the high ground east of the Kocher-Brenz River valley. Forests covered the high ground but each village was surrounded by farmland forming a chain of clearings.[16]

The combined arms team turned east from Unt-Kuchen and climbed the steep wooded slopes out of the valley. After three kilometers of winding through the forest, E Company emerged onto an open plateau. Bill formed the M4s and M36s into a spread attack formation and moved south through Ebnat and Niesitz.

The farmland ended against a wooded ridge south of Niesitz. In woods, an unseen enemy soldier with a *Panzerfaust* could ambush a tank, so the infantry dismounted and led the advance into the forest. E Company's riflemen hustled to clear the wooded terrain for the tanks while the rest of TF Rodwell waited for the column to pick up speed.

The Germans used these narrow patches of woods to throw up roadblocks. A German engineer unit left behind more sophisticated obstructions than the haphazard clump of fallen trees the Americans usually encountered and reinforced them with anti-tank mines. As soon as the leading infantry discovered an abatis, they secured the area and called up the engineers who reduced the obstacle and disarmed any mines.

By 1055 hours, the company had covered two kilometers through woods to the next clearing with the town of Grosskuchen in the middle. Bill ordered his men to remount the tanks. The combined-arms force resumed its spread formation and plunged ahead through three more towns before coming to another wooded ridge. The infantry again took the lead for the next two kilometers.[17]

As the force crossed one ridge, scouts located an 88 behind the ridge's south slope. In that position, the Germans could pick off the American tanks, one by one as they crested the high ground on the road.

Bill and the lead tank's commander crept forward to observe the German position. Normally, the infantry would maneuver against the gun and force it to withdraw, but the tank commander had another idea. "I can take him out."

"You sure you want to shoot it out with an 88?" Bill asked.

"Yes, sir. I think we can get the drop on him."

The tank commander went back to the column and brought forward his tank, stopping short of the crest. The tank commander and his crew dismounted and examined the enemy position. Returning to the tank, the crew repositioned it off the road and aligned it in the direction of the 88. The tank gunner depressed his tube a few degrees to minimize the time he would need to adjust to the target.

Bill could see the German gun crew. Their apparent agitation signaled that they could hear the tank but were not certain where it would appear. The duel came down to which crew could acquire, aim, and shoot first. The unfolding shootout mesmerized Bill and the scouts.

Calling into his intercom, the tank commander ordered the driver forward. The Sherman roared up the last few yards of the incline then burst over the top pointed straight at the German 88. The instant the gunner spotted the target he bellowed, "Stop!" The driver slammed on the brakes. The tank had already aligned itself with the target, it was all up to the gunner.

The German gun crew cranked the 88's traversing mechanism for all they were worth. Bill could see the big gun's muzzle turn toward the Sherman.

Boom! The tank gunner fired. *Crump!* The German gun position blew apart as the 75mm HE round hit home.[18]

After congratulating the daring tank crew, Bill ordered the column to continue over the ridge. German resistance notched up at Nattheim. A handful of defenders fired on E Company as it approached the town. A few minutes later German artillery began landing near the column.

Bill sent the rifle platoons into Nattheim to clear the houses while the tanks overwatched.[19]

During the brief halt, he climbed onto the turret of the lead tank to confer with the tank company commander, who was standing in his hatch.

Ping! A bullet bounced off the rim of the tank's hatch an inch below Bill's exposed stomach. Bill and the tank commander both flinched. A German sniper had them in his sights. The tank commander dropped into the tank, slamming the hatch cover as he did. Bill barely saved his hand from getting chopped off by the hatch cover before he dove behind the vehicle. The American officers moved so fast the sniper had no chance for a second shot.

Bill restarted the column shortly after 1330 hours. The combined arms team hurdled another wooded ridge before reaching Oggenhausen, where they caught up with some retreating Germans. The Americans unleashed a heavy barrage on the south part of town that blocked the enemy's line of retreat. The rest of E Company then moved in, seizing the town and rounding up sixty-two prisoners.[20]

Among the captured Germans was an *SS-Obersturmbannfuhrer* (equivalent in grade to a lieutenant colonel), who identified himself as Karl Weigel. *Obersturmbannfuhrer* Weigel was not typical of the *SS* officers Bill normally encountered. Weigel did not serve in the *Waffen SS*, the military arm of the *Schutzstaffel*. Instead, he was the director of the *Pflegesttate fur Schrift und-Sinnbildkunde* (Promotional Center for the Study of Inscriptions and Symbols) that was part of Nazi Germany's *Ahnenerbe*, a foundation to research ancient Aryan heritage. The organization had the mission of fulfilling Heinrich Himmler's intellectual fantasy that the Nazis could trace their roots back to pre-historic Germanic tribes. Weigel earned Himmler's gratitude for interpreting ancient runic symbols in a way that connected them to Nazi ideology. Through Himmler's influence, Weigel landed a prestigious assignment to the faculty of Gottingen University, much to the chagrin of its legitimate historians. When Patton's Third Army threatened Gottingen, Weigel had fled south, winding up as Bill's prisoner.[21]

After greeting Bill, the *Obersturmbannfuhrer* unbuckled his pistol belt and ceremoniously handed him his Walther P38. "Sir, I surrender to you and present you with my pistol."

Bill took the P38 and then ordered one of his men to search Weigel. The pat down turned up a small .25 cal. pistol hidden in the German's boot. The soldier who frisked him handed the pistol to Bill.

"Wait, that is my personal firearm," Weigel complained.

"I don't care. You're not keeping any weapons."

"You do not understand. I use that only for my personal protection. I would never use it against you."

"That doesn't matter. You're not keeping it." Bill stuffed both pistols into his jacket.

The arrogant *SS* officer huffed but had to bear the indignity of being as defenseless as the rest of the prisoners.

TF Rodwell roared two more kilometers south before hitting one last wooded ridge near Schratenhof. Bill's column followed the now familiar routine as it moved through the woods. The riflemen took the lead while the engineers knocked down obstacles and removed mines to open the way for the task force's vehicles. Once past the forested ridge, they moved across an open bowl of farmland to a low bare hill, 1,500 meters short of their next objective, the city of Giengen. In the last hour of daylight, the Americans got their first glimpse of the city.[22]

An ad hoc mix of a few hundred *Volksgrenadieren* and *SS*, backed by artillery, defended Giengen. As soon as the Americans appeared on the ridgeline above the city, the enemy artillery began firing.

The task force dodged the Germans' preplanned artillery concentrations. Bill got a hold of his artillery FO and ordered a counter-strike against Giengen. Under the cover of artillery and heavy machine guns, Task Force Rodwell bounded forward. Without tanks or 88s, the defenders had no chance of stopping the attack and quickly gave up the fight. Two hundred of them fled the city before TF Rodwell stormed in at dark.[23]

The general decided to halt the column and bed the troops down for the evening. Despite the easy capture of Giengen, the troops had an uneasy night. Enemy troops remained in the area and German machine guns on the other side of the Brenz River kept up an annoying fire.

It had been an exhilarating day for TF Rodwell and E Company. Bill's combined arms team had moved more than thirty kilometers, overrun nine German towns, and captured more than 150 prisoners while losing only one KIA and fifteen wounded.[24]

By this time, Bill had been in command of E Company for nearly eight weeks. In that time, he had developed a comfortable relationship with his lieutenants, sergeants, and men. He kept tight discipline and made quick, sound tactical decisions. The company had performed superbly and, consequently, the men gained confidence in themselves and their commander. They had even given Bill the nickname "Little Caesar." As someone explained it to him, it stemmed from his "reputation for bringing so much firepower on an objective." Of course, it may have had other connotations. Regardless of the innuendo, Bill liked the moniker so much that he asked his driver to stencil it on his jeep.[25]

Little Caesar and the rest of TF Rodwell motored out of Giengen the next morning at 0800 hours. They followed the Brenz River valley toward the Danube—against no resistance. That changed after they drove through Hermaringen.[26]

Boom! A single artillery round impacted off to one side of the column. A second shell landed on the opposite side of the company a few minutes later. The experienced soldiers realized the Germans were trying to "bracket" them with spotting rounds. Once they had done so, they would "fire for effect" with all the guns in their battery. Each time a spotting round landed, Bill shifted his column to get outside the bracket. But the spotting rounds followed the Americans' every movement. Bill figured the German observer had them sighted from an excellent vantage point.

Bill pulled the column into the woods to keep it out of sight. Using his binoculars, he scanned the horizon for the observer's likely position. A tall church steeple appeared in the distance.

The best way to confound an observer was to throw smoke on his position and blind him. Bill called up the four-deuce mortar platoon to request a 4.2-inch round loaded with white phosphorous (WP). The WP rounds—which everyone in the Army called by their phonetic acronym "Willie Pete"—burned with extreme intensity and threw off a dense white cloud that could obscure a target. Bill gave the church's coordinates to the mortars then ordered, "One round Willie Pete, will adjust, over."

"Roger, one round, Willie Pete, out."

A couple minutes later, the section called back. "Shot out."

Bill lifted his field glasses and focused on the church steeple. Once the spotting round landed, he intended to adjust the next round to bracket the church before calling "fire for effect."

Several seconds went by as the round soared overhead. They called again to alert Bill of the impending impact. "Splash, over."

As Bill stared at the target, the Willie Pete round hit the top of the cross on the top of the church steeple. Plumes of smoke rolled in waves down each side of the steeple completely covering the target. Within seconds, a fire broke out inside the church.

A single mortar round, with its high-arcing trajectory, had hit a target only a couple of inches wide—an impossible shot.

The mortars called back, disturbing Bill's moment of wonder. "Do you have an adjustment, over?"

"Negative, target destroyed, out."[27]

Bill led the task force into Brenz, where they were greeted by an incongruous sight. The town's residents stood by the roadside and waved at them, as if the American troops were on parade. The column passed through Brenz then turned toward the city of Gundelfingen, nestled within the Danube Valley. The Ivy Division's soldiers crossed the same broad, fertile plain where Marlborough and Napoleon had triumphed. Elements of the 12th Armored Division greeted them as they entered the city. The linkup with the tankers fulfilled the mission of Task Force Rodwell and completed the division's charge to the Danube. With the arrival of the 4th Infantry Division, the XXI Corps could now launch a full-scale offensive across the Danube River.[28]

The 2nd Battalion offloaded their vehicles in Gundelfingen. From there, they marched two kilometers south to Petersworth while trucks brought up the rest of the 12th Infantry. At 1600 hours on April 25, the regiment notified Colonel Gorn that Task Force Rodwell had been dissolved. General Rodwell resumed his normal duties and Colonel Chance once again reported directly to General Blakeley.[29]

For five days, Task Force Rodwell led the division on a dash to the Danube River that had covered ninety kilometers, inflicted heavy casualties, and swept up hundreds of prisoners.

The Germans could do little more than slow down the charge with roadblocks and occasional blocking positions. When they chose to fight at Neuler, Aalen, and Giengen, the Americans overwhelmed the pitiful defense they offered.

Bill and his men—as well as many other Allied soldiers—must have wondered what purpose any further fighting served. So too many Germans. A staff officer of the *XIII*th *SS Corps* remarked, "In an increasingly vocal way the question was being asked, what did we hope to achieve with this senseless fighting?"

Yet, for many reasons—fanatical devotion to Hitler, hope in some miraculous change in fortune, or the promise of a "wonder weapon"— the pointless fight continued. American troops would risk their lives, more Germans would die, and more towns would be demolished—all to fulfill the death wish of a deluded dictator.[30]

CHAPTER EIGHTEEN

DRIVE TO VICTORY

The 12th Armored Division had captured the bridge over the Danube at Dillingen on April 22. Soon afterward, the engineers threw up another crossing site at Lauingen. The Ivy Division wanted to get CT 12 across the river quickly to reinforce the 12th Armored's bridgehead and dash any thoughts the Germans might have had of building a defensive line along the Danube. As a result, after being released from TF Rodwell, the 2nd Battalion's first order of business was to march back to Gundelfingen then to Launingen. The troops undoubtedly grumbled about back-tracking while humping their gear. After a brief traffic jam waiting on the 8th Infantry to go by, Bill and the rest of 2nd Battalion walked across the bridge in the twilight. One of the staff officers observed, "The Danube River was found wide, straight and beautiful."[1]

The battalion trudged another ten kilometers across the flat plain of the Danube Valley, reaching its assembly area near Weisingen twenty minutes before midnight. The exhausted infantrymen prepared defensive positions in the off chance the Germans counterattacked during the

night. Bill and his subordinate leaders spent the next few hours of darkness planning for the next day's mission.[2]

On April 26, the battalion and its attached armor pressed up the
gentle slope immediately south of Weisingen. They moved southeast out
of the Danube flood plain into the rolling Bavarian hills with E Company
on the right flank and F Company to its left. After passing between the
towns of Altenbaindt and Holzheim, the men entered a wood line. E
Company had pushed three hundred to four hundred meters into the
woods when rifle and machine gun fire erupted. As the lead infantrymen
returned fire, scouts reported to Bill that the company had run into a
line spanning the breadth of the wooded high ground. F Company ran
into the same defensive line between Holzheim and Ellersbach.[3]

Just like the battle of Simmringen Woods, the German commander
established a defensive position inside the forest to negate the Americans'
firepower advantage. The Germans had a chance in a small arms fight
at close range. Just as he had done in the Simmringen Woods, Bill put
the rifle platoons on line and told them to open "assault fire" on the
enemy. American .30 cal. rounds snapped over the Germans' heads and
ricocheted off the trunks of trees. The enemy soldiers pressed their faces
into the dirt, smothered by the volleys flying their way. Colonel Gorn
committed G Company on E Company's right to help crush the defenders. The attached Shermans and tank destroyers crept forward and fired
their main guns at nearly point-blank range, blowing holes in the German line.[4]

The old men and young boys that filled the enemy ranks lacked the
stomach and the skills to deal with overwhelming American firepower,
and the German line gave way. E Company seized twenty prisoners who
could not or would not leave their foxholes. Some of the enemy tried to
set up another line farther back in the woods, but E and G Companies
kept shoving the outgunned Germans back. On the left, F Company
broke into open ground and attacked Ellersbach. With help from the
tanks, they took the town and seized forty more prisoners. F Company
kept going, capturing three towns in rapid succession. After negotiating
a weak bridge, it pulled up in Eppishofen.[5]

E and G Companies pushed the Germans out of the forest by late afternoon. After breaking up another hastily concocted defense on the far side of a clearing near Bairshofen, G Company drove to Unt Schoneberg and E Company took up a position south of Altenmunster.[6]

In a day of almost continuous contact, the 2nd Battalion had driven the Germans back ten kilometers and nabbed two hundred prisoners. The records made no mention of the number of enemy killed. The battalion's own losses amounted to a few men wounded.[7]

It was much the same throughout the Seventh Army's zone of operations. The Americans had swept up or slaughtered countless German soldiers but had yet to locate the feared *Alpenfestung*. The German war machine that had scored brilliant successes from 1939 to 1942 had dissolved. Any attempt by the depleted German Army to resist the muscular American offensive only resulted in more casualties. Across the shrinking *Third Reich*, losses mounted sharply as its soldiers turned to cannon fodder. One-fourth of Germany's total military losses for the entire war occurred in 1945. Civilian losses soared as well in April as the tide of conquest swept the Fatherland.[8]

To the veterans of Normandy and the Siegfried Line, this campaign barely resembled their idea of warfare. Bill described the situation in a letter to Beth. "The war is very peculiar these days and should have ended this month...We have rolled along to beat hell lately, but still the war was hot for a few." And the war would remain "hot for a few" more, as long as the Nazi regime refused to acknowledge defeat.[9]

Bill also wrote Beth with news about another one of his abiding concerns—promotion. "Bad news, dear, an officer came back today with rank of captain. I'm afraid I'm out of luck for promotion now...It means that I have to duck just a bit longer now—my gamble is greater. Probably never will get [promoted] 'cause more captains are apt to come in. Hell, no use crying though." Much to Bill's surprise, he stayed put. Apparently, Colonel Gorn placed a high value on his abilities and left him in command of E Company.

While he kept his company, Bill lost his XO, 1st Lt. Pat Touhy. The Seventh Army assigned him to administer civilian areas under U.S.

military control. "Sent one of my best officers to AMG [American Military Government]. I'll miss that Irishman."

Colonel Chance decided to give 2nd Battalion a break on April 27. Colonel Gorn's men had been leading the attacks of TF Rodwell and CT 12 since taking Aalen. The regiment committed the 1st Battalion into the attack alongside the 3rd Battalion and put the 2nd in reserve.[10]

The regiment's two other battalions forged ahead on April 27 against very light resistance. The 1st Battalion vaulted the small Schmutter River and reached Strassberg on the Wertach River. The 3rd Battalion consolidated near Anhausen, eight kilometers farther north.[11]

Colonel Gorn's men "were all set for a well-deserved rest" but CT 12 told them to follow behind the other battalions and clear pockets of Germans already bypassed. After moving by truck to a new assembly area near Adelsried, they started clearing towns around the nearby autobahn.[12]

The pesky job of sweeping enemy troops from towns showed that, despite the German collapse, the missions could still be dangerous. One southern German village proved that point. It looked like many others E Company had passed through on its way south. As a precaution, Bill sent scouts ahead to detect any ambush. When they neared the edge of town, a single enemy rifleman opened fire. Bill quickly determined that the company faced a lone sniper, not an organized defense. He deployed spotters and supporting machine guns to pinpoint and suppress him. The infantrymen in the forward platoon then moved in, using available cover and short rushes to keep the sniper from acquiring a target.

The sniper fired a couple more times but did not hit anyone. Once the Americans had a foothold in the town, the sniper fire ended. The forward platoon reported back to Bill that the town was empty.

In the center of the village, Bill encountered a lone German civilian, a man of military age dressed in plain clothes. Bill walked up to him.

The man smiled as he greeted the American officer. "*Guten tag, Herr Leutnant.*"

Bill knew at once the German was no civilian. He wore street clothes but his appearance and demeanor indicated that he had been a soldier, perhaps only minutes earlier.

The German complimented the American lieutenant, through the translator, on the fine work of his company. The man said he was impressed with how well the Americans had maneuvered their way into town.

Bill was convinced that this man had been the one shooting at his men. Without finding a gun or a uniform on him, he had no choice but to treat him as a non-combatant. Bill left the man where he stood. The German may have gotten away with taking shots at the Americans but, at least, he was out of the war.[13]

Bill's battalion enjoyed another restful day of reserve duty on April 28, following the rest of the regiment by truck. Ordered to secure the near shore of the Lech River and search for a potential crossing site, the 1st and 3rd Battalions swept southeast to the broad river ten to twenty kilometers south of Augsburg under minor harassing fire. Each made fascinating discoveries along the way. The 1st Battalion came across six operational, though abandoned, jet aircraft. Troops from the 3rd Battalion found nineteen 88s. The Germans apparently ran out of ammunition for them and abandoned the dreaded guns after removing their breechblocks.[14]

CT 8 secured a crossing over the Lech River at Schwabstadt on April 27 and the engineers threw a Bailey Bridge over the river. General Blakeley decided to exploit this bridgehead with all three of his combat teams. He directed CT 22 to cross the Lech in the early morning of April 29 with CT 12 following immediately behind. After motoring from its assembly area near Bergheim, the 2nd Battalion marched by foot to the east side of the Lech followed by the other two battalions. Once across the river, CT 12 moved east.[15]

The 2nd Battalion hiked northeast to Winkl where it formed for another attack. From there, F and G Companies marched seven kilometers east to Dunzelbach. An impressive advance, but Colonel Gorn had his eyes on an even deeper objective—thirteen kilometers deeper. The regiment's zone of action brushed the northern tip of the sixteen-kilometer long Ammer See. The large lake drained into a five-kilometer long marsh at its northern end before emptying into the Amper River. A bridge crossed the Amper River just north of the marsh at the town of Grafrath. The regiment needed a bridge to get around the Ammer See, so Gorn pooled his armored assets and gave them to Bill with orders to capture the Amper River Bridge. E Company's riflemen climbed aboard four Shermans, four tank destroyers, and six halftracks. An engineer squad riding in a deuce-and-a-half filled out the team.[16] (See Map XVII)

Bill's team rumbled out of Winkl, passed through G Company in Dunzelbach, and took the lead in the battalion's attack. With so much firepower against wilting resistance, Bill concentrated on the distant objective with no regard for secure flanks. Sixty Germans surrendered in the column's first encounter at Eismerszel. Bill dropped off a token force to guard the PWs and resumed the charge. Seven kilometers later, the team forced its way into Kothgeisering and hauled in thirty more prisoners. The expanding bag of PWs—and the fact that one in eight of them were officers—provided more evidence of the enemy's collapse.[17]

The column then skirted the northern end of the marshland and dashed for the bridge at Grafrath. Bill and his men could see the bridge still stood as they swarmed the crossing site. But, upon closer examination, they saw that a German demolition team had damaged its underpinnings enough to render it useless. They had to find another crossing.[18]

The map showed another bridge about a kilometer downstream at Wildenroth. Bill immediately dispatched a small force of tanks and infantry under 1st Lt. Charles Christensen to secure it.[19]

A few minutes later, Christensen's platoon stormed into Wildenroth, where they caught German engineers standing on the bridge, wiring it for demolition. The American riflemen and tanks opened fire and chased off the enemy engineers before they could detonate the charges. One of the tanks rushed across the bridge to secure its far end. The sudden appearance of the Americans overawed the Germans. More than one hundred of them surrendered to Christensen's reinforced platoon, a force half their size. The rest of Bill's team arrived at the bridge a short time later. Bill radioed back to the battalion CP to let them know that E Company had captured a bridge intact. He then deployed his force across the river, firmly establishing a bridgehead.

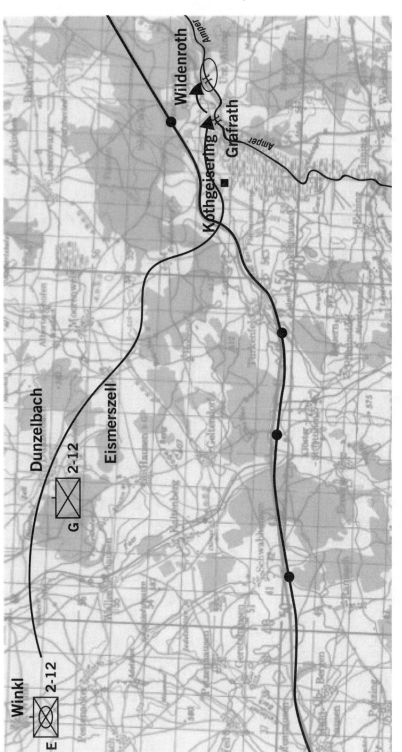

Map XVII

Overnight, CT 12 ordered 2nd and 3rd Battalions to exploit the Wildenroth bridgehead. Mounted on tanks, TDs, and trucks, the 3rd Battalion crossed the Amper River (compliments of E Company) and attacked to the southeast with the Reconnaissance Company of the 610th Tank Destroyer Battalion screening ahead of the formation.[20]

The 2nd Battalion attacked on the 3rd Battalion's left flank. The U.S. Army configured infantry companies to attack like pawns, one square at a time, but Colonel Gorn started bounding his companies forward like knights. Bill's company began the battalion's attack on foot, pushing forward two kilometers to Mauren. The battalion then launched G Company toward Unt-Brunn. First Lt. Milford Quesenberry mounted his troops on tanks and halftracks and raced thirteen kilometers to his objective. Along the way, Task Force "Quiz" overtook groups of German soldiers, all of whom surrendered the moment the Americans appeared. G Company dismounted then foot-marched south to capture Ob-Brunn while the halftracks sped back to Mauren to pick up F Company. The halftracks and attached tanks drove F Company to Unt-Brunn, where they off loaded and moved east then south to take Leustetten. Bill's company, riding trucks, followed F to Leustetten. From there, E Company advanced dismounted southeast to Wangen, picking up fifty prisoners on the way.[21]

The 2nd Battalion had already gained an impressive twenty-two kilometers but Colonel Gorn wanted to keep pace with 3rd Battalion that was pushing all the way to the Isar River. G Company remounted the halftracks to race farther southeast and, after passing through E Company in Wangen, headed toward Icking. Shortly before it arrived, Allied fighters strafed a German convoy outside the town. When the Germans returned to their burning vehicles, they met G Company, who dispersed them in a brief firefight.

F Company moved to Wangen on trucks. After dismounting, its men advanced through two kilometers of woods toward the town of Neufahren. There, F Company troops stumbled on a German major rolled up in his sleeping bag. At first, the officer tried to shoo away the soldiers who kicked at him, refusing to believe that the Americans could be so close. Sergeant Carl DeBoer finally convinced him by forcibly yanking the major out of his bedroll.

The trucks hauled Bill's company forward in the late afternoon to Neufahren where they off-loaded. E Company walked through falling snow two kilometers to the town of Irschenhausen on the Isar River. Bill established a defense for the night along the river's bank. Later, F Company rode in trucks to Zell. The 2nd Battalion finished April 30 with all three rifle companies along the Isar River.[22]

The dazzling movement of CT 12 outpaced the Germans' ability to slow it down. The Reconnaissance Company of the 610th TD Battalion captured a pair of bridges over the Loisach and Isar Rivers within the city of Wolfratshausen just as a German major rigged one for demolition.[23]

At the beginning of April, the 12th Infantry had to fight its way through entrenched enemy defenses. By mid-April, TF Rodwell spent most of its time pushing through roadblocks. Now, as the month closed, the Germans could not even slow the American advance across their rivers.

CT 12 and the rest of the Ivy Division had driven to within sight of the Austrian Alps. It had scooped up abandoned enemy aircraft, heavy weapons, and munitions—the materiel needed to establish the dreaded *Alpenfestung*—and collected thousands of prisoners. Just after the battle of Mortain, Bill had predicted the Germans would fight to the "end" but this campaign seemed beyond even that.[24]

On May 1, with the 2nd Battalion in reserve, 1st and 3rd Battalions charged southeast, guiding on the east bank of the Isar River. Driving through cold, snowy weather, they wiped out a couple pockets of resistance and advanced another fourteen kilometers.

Two days earlier, as the 12th Infantry reached the Amper River southwest of Munich, elements of the 45th Infantry Division liberated the Dachau concentration camp a little north of the city. In the massive complex, the Americans discovered thousands of emaciated internees from across occupied Europe, plus hundreds of corpses loaded on boxcars.

The appalling conditions at the concentration camp outraged Allied soldiers. A few of the liberators shot a handful of the camp's guards.

The massive number of internees created a problem for Allied commanders. The internees could not be set free. Almost none of them could care for themselves. Besides, where would they go? They decided to keep the internees locked up to make it easier to supervise their feeding and medical care.

This decision did not sit well with the starved internees. Who could feel liberated when they remained locked up inside the place where so many of their friends and loved ones had perished?

Seventh Army HQ became concerned about security at Dachau and its satellite camps and assigned spare combat units to contain the internees and prevent any riots, especially over food. E Company drew one such assignment.

Bill and his men rode trucks to one of the camps of the Dachau complex in CT 12's zone at Föhrenwald, a suburb of Wolfratshausen. I. G. Farben originally set up the Föhrenwald camp in 1939 to house workers in nearby munitions plants. The Nazis converted it to a slave labor camp during the war.[25]

The veteran soldiers had seen more than their share of horror and savagery in the preceding eleven months but the sights of Föhrenwald unveiled a new level of cruelty. A mess sergeant with the 70th Tank Battalion described the situation. "At the sight of hundreds of people dressed in prison garb, everything else was inconsequential. These long-suffering prisoners pressed in close as we off-loaded cases of rations for them. Glassy eyes stared out of deep-set sockets as tightly drawn skin revealed the facial structure beneath. Heads were shaven, and arms and wrists looked like sticks, hanging loosely beside distended bellies. German guards had left no more than an hour or so before, but there were no cheers, no animated demonstrations of joy, only unabashed weeping and wide smiles by those alive enough to know that their ordeal was over."[26]

Bill deployed his men to secure the compound and oversee the internees, but one look at the former prisoners convinced him the mission made no sense. "The prisoners were starved and helpless. They barely had the strength to stand up, much less riot."

He immediately called division HQ and explained there was no need for an infantry company at the camp. HQ called back a little later saying that trucks were on the way to return them to division reserve in Wolfratshausen.

In the meantime, the company handed out boxed rations to the troops. Bill pulled out the cigarettes to trade for chocolate bars because he never smoked then dumped his K ration on a mess plate. He sat down just outside the compound with his back to the barbed wire fence. Most soldiers, Bill among them, detested K rations. As he poked at his meal, he felt a sensation, as he had one time in Normandy, that someone was staring at him. Bill turned around to see one of the internees behind the fence with his eyes ballooning out of his head. The internee fixated on the plate of processed pork and cheese Bill held in his hand.

Bill looked at the internee then back at his meal. He gestured with the plate and asked, "Do you want this?"

The man bobbed his head like a dog begging for a treat. Bill passed the plate through the fence. The internee lifted the plate to his mouth then dumped the contents into his gullet in one pass.

The man's act startled Bill. He sat amazed, watching the starved man lick and pick the remaining crumbs from the plate. Bill called over to another soldier who had no interest in his meal, either. "Hey, watch this." Bill handed the second plate to the internee. Again, the man dumped the food down his throat without bothering to chew, although this time it took him two passes to empty the plate.[27]

A handful of MPs relieved E Company a short time later. Bill's men boarded the trucks and moved to Wolfratshausen where they remained for the night.[28]

Bill only shared this one semi-humorous episode about his experience at Föhrenwald. Strangely, he never displayed a visceral reaction to the horrors of the camp. Perhaps what he saw there was just one more in a long series of gory sights he had witnessed leading all the way back to that first dead German soldier behind Utah Beach.

CT 12 rolled farther southeast on May 2. The 3rd Battalion swept to Greiling, a small town near Bad Tolz. The 1st Battalion pushed to the Tegern See. They fought a brief action against a few *SS* troops supported by artillery in Gmund. The Americans rounded up forty more prisoners but suffered one KIA in the fight. After being released by the division, Bill's company rejoined the 2nd Battalion at its reserve position in Ascholding.[29]

Bill did not make that journey because of the pressing demands of paperwork. The U.S. Army may have been a strong, mobile fighting force, but it was also a vast bureaucracy that required regular feedings of mundane paperwork. Much of this "administrivia" needed the signature of the company commander. Under normal operating conditions, the company's administration section stayed with the regiment's adjutant in a rear CP. First Sergeant John Cromwall made regular visits to the company CP during lulls in the fighting to go over administrative issues with Bill and get his signature on documents.

The 12th Infantry had moved so quickly and so far in the last weeks of April that the admin section fell behind. The typists and clerks spent too much time tearing down, loading, moving, unloading, and setting back up just to keep up with the frontline troops. This created a backlog of paperwork. E Company's clerks had not linked up with the fighting elements since April 27 in Altenmunster. They stayed there four days to whittle down the buildup of orders, reports, and requisitions. In that time, the rest of the company had marched all the way to the Isar River.[30]

After six days without seeing the company commander, the clerks had a mound of documents the size of a manure pile waiting for Bill's signature. Company clerks were usually very skilled in the art of forgery but some documents related to disciplinary actions, pay, and property could only pass with a genuine signature. There was no way around it— Bill had to go back. As no one had arrived to replace Pat Touhy as company XO, Bill turned over command to his senior platoon leader then hopped into a jeep for the one hundred-kilometer trip to the rear CP.[31]

The roads were clogged with people on foot: liberated prisoners, displaced people, PWs, and German deserters. Truck convoys and long lines of support vehicles jammed the few standing bridges over the waterways. After an hours-long journey, Bill reunited with his admin section. First Sgt. Cromwall immediately placed the intimidating stack of papers in front of him. As Cromwall explained the purpose of each document, Bill signed away and passed his guidance on other matters. After signing his last form, Bill hopped back in the jeep for another drive that consumed the rest of the day.

With no forewarning the division stepped off the gas pedal on May 3. At 0750 hours, CT 12's southern boundary shifted to their current positions along the line from Bad Tolz to the Tegern See. General Rodwell stopped by the regimental CP to tell Colonel Chance that offensive operations had been suspended in their sector. Despite the order not to advance, the regiment still gathered over 2,300 German soldiers who were eager to surrender to the Americans. The 2nd Battalion actually moved backwards about ten kilometers at the end of May 3 from Sachsenkam to an assembly area at Petershofen. From there, E Company occupied a spot next to the Isar River at Tattenkofen.[32]

The next day, Colonel Chance received word that the 327th Glider Infantry Regiment of the 101st Airborne Division would relieve the regiment in place and that the 12th Infantry would move to an area around Sulzbach in the Upper Palatinate (Oberpfalz) district of Bavaria— two hundred kilometers to the north. The regiment's combat mission had transformed into occupation duty.[33]

The troops loaded on deuce-and-a-halves at 0800 hours on May 5 for the long road march. Before it began, there was a moment of excitement. Twelve truckloads of German soldiers made a sudden appearance. These men—including many from the SS—were not looking for a fight, just the opportunity to surrender. This late in the war, many German soldiers deliberately fled west so they could surrender to American or British forces, rather than the Soviets. After disposing of these Germans, the 12th Infantry motored onto the autobahn, speeding past Munich, Ingolstadt, and Neumarkt. The troops saw the carcasses of numerous German planes discarded or destroyed along the sides of the autobahn. Some sections of the highways had been used as runways. DPs lined the roadways everywhere they looked. Some stepped in eager anticipation of homecomings, some shuffled with their heads hung in despair—most toddled toward an uncertain future. The men marveled at the enormous destruction wrought on the major urban areas by Allied bombing. The devastated cities and countryside left the men of the 12th Infantry to wonder if the people of Central Europe had the spirit to rebuild their ruined cities and culture after the dual ravages of Nazism and war.[34]

The 2nd Battalion arrived at Altdorf that evening. The regimental CP opened in Sulzbach while the Ivy Division stood up its CP in Amberg. The opening of the new CPs marked the division's transfer from the Seventh Army back to Patton's Third Army.[35]

While the Ivy Division was on the road, important events took place in their former command. Generals Devers and Patch met with Lt. Gen. Hermann Foertsch, commander of the German *First Army* and official representative of *Army Group B* at an estate outside of Munich to negotiate the surrender of all German forces in Bavaria. When Devers explained that the only terms on offer were nothing less than unconditional surrender, Foertsch stiffened. He struggled with his emotions then confessed, "I can assure you, sir, that no power is left at my disposal to prevent it." Devers asked Foertsch how many men he had left to surrender. His answer of around a quarter of a million men stunned the American generals. The Sixth Army Group had amassed 600,000 German PWs in the previous three weeks. This claim that the Germans still had 250,000 men in their ranks seemed hard to believe. With such a huge number of troops, Devers and Patch wondered, why had they not established the feared *Alpenfestung*? Not until the war ended did the Allies learn that the "National Redoubt" had been a work of fiction.[36]

Colonel Chance called his battalion and separate company commanders to Sulzbach for a meeting on May 6. He designated battalion areas of operations and issued guidance on their new duties. Personal cleanliness and vehicle maintenance took top priority, at least until the command got a better understanding of what occupation duty entailed. Chance stressed that the regiment "is now in a semi-garrison status" to help with "readjustment of the troops." The 12th Infantry settled into a routine of patrolling its zone around Sulzbach-Rosenberg. The infantry relieved other units in the area at German military installations, refugee centers, and critical facilities. The veterans considered the duty easy after the strains of combat, although it had been nearly ten days since E Company's last pitched battle.[37]

The accommodations improved, too, as the regiment requisitioned housing. No more sleeping on the ground. The 3rd Battalion took over Herman Goering's castle in Neuhaus and used it as their HQ.[38]

On May 7, the division instituted a leave policy. Soldiers were prioritized for leave rotations based on their rank, days overseas, and decorations. Bill fell short of the cutoff because his days in the hospital did not count. Colonel Gorn qualified and promptly departed for the States. Before he left, he made a few personnel changes. Maj. Glenn Zarger moved from XO to acting commander. Capt. Tallie Crocker, the acting S-3, took Zarger's place as XO. Gorn surprised everybody when he tapped Bill to fill the S-3 slot. The Battalion Operations Officer was the senior staff captain, one step below a major's billet. Bill still needed another month before he could even qualify for promotion to captain because of the Army's "minimum 90 days in duty position" rule for officers who fell below normal "time in grade" requirements. Bill had only nine months' "time in grade" as a first lieutenant. The move to S-3 meant he had leapt over several more senior officers to get the job. Gorn pulled Bill aside to explain that he made the move as a reward for Bill's performance as a company commander. Lieutenant Touhy returned from his military government duties to take over E Company.

Bigger news soon filtered into the battalion. Word that Germany had signed surrender documents at SHAEF HQ in Reims earlier that day leaked out to the press. Bill reacted to the news with as much astonishment as joy. He sent a hurried letter off to Beth. "Today the radio announced that all German resistance had ended. In other words I lived through the war in Europe—eleven months of doubt is now over!!" He then noted the timing of his elevation from company command to battalion staff. "Every day of this war I spent in a line company and on the first day of peace I become a staff officer. Well Dear, at least I can say that I did my part—nobody can say I ever asked for relief or rest. There is no officer in this battalion with as much time on the line as your husband, not <u>one</u>!"[39]

The troops greeted the announcement with only muted celebrations. For many, memories of fallen comrades made VE Day bittersweet. One sergeant on the battalion staff recorded the general mood. "VE Day didn't create much enthusiasm, but it was good news."[40]

For Bill, too, the memory of those who were not there to share the victory tempered his relief that the fighting had ended. He thought back to his mortar crews that landed on Utah Beach; few remained. Staff Sergeant Luther Conarty made it but 1st Sgt. John Mashlar and Technical Sergeant Max Solomon died in Normandy. Bill remembered his officer buddy, Sam Kyle, who was wounded and never returned; officers he respected, like Earl Enroughty and Warren Clark, who died; and Martin MacDiarmid and Paul Dupuis who were captured. A few had moved on like Dave McElroy, who served as the general's aide-de-camp, and Jack Gunning, who had been sent stateside a month earlier to train recruits. Of the thirty-five officers in the battalion on D-Day, only four remained. One of the other three, Capt. Tallie Crocker, H Company Commander on D-Day, now ended the war as the battalion XO.

The fierce fighting in Normandy, the Hürtgen Forest, the Ardennes-Eifel, and Rhineland had chewed through the battalion's lieutenants and captains several times over. In total, 180 officers had served in the 2nd Battalion of the 12th Infantry. Thirty-eight of them died in combat, more than the number the battalion landed on D-Day.

CHAPTER NINETEEN

RETURN TO PEACE

Bill began his duties as S-3 helping Major Zarger split up the battalion area of responsibility into company sectors and issuing move orders. The staff passed instructions to all soldiers in the unit on garrison duty and policies against fraternization. Unlike company orders, most battalion directives had to be written, copied, and distributed. As the S-3, Bill had to review and put his name on all orders. He tolerated the tedium, reminding himself that at least no one was shooting at him anymore.

While E Company settled in the nearby town of Berg, Bill lugged his personal belongings to quarters in Altdorf where HQ and H Company stayed. He shared a room with 1st Lt. Frank Hackett, his friend from H Company.[1]

Bill and Frank bedded down that first night of peace in a house with mattresses and a roof, rare comforts for infantrymen. The two officers enjoyed a restful few hours until Lieutenant Hackett was awakened by the noise of Bill walking around their room. He thought Bill might have gotten up to relieve himself but he noticed that Bill moved about aimlessly. It took Frank a minute to realize that Bill was still asleep.

Frank jumped out of bed. "Bill! Wake up. Wake up." He finally roused Bill by shaking him. Bill looked around in the darkened room in a confused state. "Bill, you were asleep." Frank maneuvered Bill back to his bed.

Once Bill sat back on the bed, Frank thought about the incident. "Holy shit. Did you know you walk in your sleep? How the hell did you make it through all that fighting?" The danger had passed but Frank was still shaken. The idea that his buddy, an experienced infantry officer, walked in his sleep struck him as bizarre and frightening. Luckily, Bill's subconscious or his guardian angel kept him from sleepwalking during the months he spent in combat.

For the next six days, 2nd Battalion maintained "law and order" in its zone east of Nuremberg. The regiment issued "Operations Memo 1" on May 9 that spelled out responsibilities for civil service and security within its area. The men guarded vital facilities: telephone exchanges, bridges, factories, and ammunition dumps. Roving patrols kept a lid on criminal activity. Camps required supervision and DPs needed safeguarding at the rail stations and on the roads. It seemed to the Americans that half of Europe was moving in different directions. SHAEF estimated that it had responsibility for over six million DPs just within its occupation zone. German soldiers marched to PW camps. Russian prisoners filed east toward the Red Army—and, for some, eventually, the Gulag. Slave laborers and Holocaust survivors shuffled to camps for processing and rehabilitation. Freed internees walked home, if their homes still stood. People packed every train whichever way it headed. Millions traveled in search of loved ones lost in the war's turmoil. The bulk of central Europeans coped with some degree of sorrow as they journeyed, in contrast to the happy-go-lucky troops who crisscrossed the countryside in jeeps and trucks.[2]

Bill stayed busy tasking companies for guard duty, sending detachments to MP training, posting security at radio towers, arranging work details for German prisoners, and organizing billeting parties for new sectors. A few security matters cropped up, enough to keep the unit on its toes. One day the regiment went on the lookout for a fugitive German general and a Vichy government official.[3]

Some security issues posed more direct threats. As the curtain came down on the *Third Reich*, Propaganda Minister Josef Goebbels issued a proclamation exhorting German civilians to unleash guerrilla warfare against the Allied occupation forces, as if the population had not suffered enough. Goebbels urged them to adopt the identity and manner of the "Werewolf" to terrorize both the occupiers and German "traitors." He relished using the mythical creature for its ability to strike terror and noted that the Werewolf "is not tied by limitations of bourgeois methods of warfare." The 1st Battalion arrested five civilians suspected of being "werewolves" in its sector but the widespread guerilla warfare promised by Goebbels turned out to be as mythical as its mascot.[4]

The duties of a staff officer kept Bill busy but not stimulated. Three days into his staff job, he wrote to Beth and dropped a bombshell. "As soon as my captaincy comes in I am going to volunteer for the Pacific Theater." Apparently, while there were bad guys left to fight, Bill felt duty bound to fight them. "I hate to leave the Div. but this life is not for me. I'll get a chance to get another company if I'm a captain…I'm uncomfortable and restless here. Not only that I'd be more useful over there." Despite earning a reputation within the battalion as an officer who could make snap decisions under pressure, he confessed self-doubt to Beth about becoming over-cautious. "Wonder how much slower I am than when I hit the beach? Several times I've noticed a difference and frankly, it bothers me." Then he made a jaw-dropping statement that left Beth stunned and bewildered. "Guess I'll always doubt if I've got guts."[5]

On May 12, 1945, the War Department announced a point system, the Advanced Rating Service Score, to prioritize soldiers for demobilization. The point system was based on time in service, time spent overseas, the number of campaigns, decorations earned, and the serviceman's number of young dependent children. A score of eighty-five or higher could earn an enlisted man an early discharge and quick transport back to the United States. The system worked a little differently for officers.

The scoring was the same but the officer's efficiency reports and the ever present "need of the service" influenced how quickly he could go home.

Bill had one of the highest scores among his peer group of junior grade officers. Few lieutenants or captains could match his total of two Purple Hearts, a Silver Star, five campaigns, and seventeen months in the European Theater. He had enough points to seek an early discharge but he stayed put for the time being. He needed to remain in the S-3 slot three more weeks to qualify for promotion.

The 12th Infantry moved to a new area west of Nuremberg on May 14. The 2nd Battalion established a military government in Uffenheim, a town in Middle Franconia only twenty-five kilometers east of the Simmringen Woods. Its sector stretched twenty kilometers from Seinsheim in the north to Burgbernheim in the south. The troops stayed busy with mundane occupation duties and refresher training. The regiment's chaplains and medical officers delivered Sex Morality Lectures warning of the dangers of fraternizing with German women. The lessons were a hard sell, especially given the attitude of the local women. Bill noticed how eager they were to please the American soldiers. "[The women] always dress up when an army unit moves in. I've noticed they even wear shoes when men are around. When we move into a town no woman has shoes."[6]

Each battalion took over the operation of PW and DP camps in its sector, processing five hundred PWs a day. Intelligence sections sifted through the massive number of German soldiers and officials to segregate Nazis and high-ranking officers. Ordinary prisoners performed routine labor on numerous infrastructure projects. DPs had to be cataloged, housed, and fed until their futures could be determined. The American authorities eliminated Nazi injunctions against religious practice, so many Jews openly worshipped in the DP camps for the first time in years.

The strategic situation in the Pacific Theater forced a change in the division's occupation duty. By early June, the Pentagon had developed preliminary plans for the anticipated invasion of Japan that involved two major invasions of the Japanese home islands. The first landings, Operation Olympic, were scheduled for the fall of 1945 on the southern island of Kyushu. The Pentagon drew resources for Olympic from forces already in the Pacific Theater.

The second set of landings targeted the main island of Honshu. Operation Coronet would use two powerful armies to cut off and over-whelm Tokyo. The scale of Coronet required more time to assemble combat units and more naval lift capacity than the invasion of Kyushu and exceeded the available force in the Pacific Theater. Planners projected Coronet for the spring of 1946.

Operation Coronet dictated a massive redeployment of forces from the continental United States and Europe, among them the 4th Infantry Division. Under the plan, the Ivy Division would not take part in the initial landings but would reinforce the invasion a month later.

Before its redeployment, the War Department decided the division needed an extended period of stateside rest, recuperation, and retraining. It notified the Ivy Division to forgo occupation duties and prepare for redeployment. Without requesting a transfer, Bill got his wish—the Army would return him to combat.

On June 10, the 12th Infantry Regiment received orders to move to a transit zone near Bamberg, Germany, where it was housed in a huge tent city. There, Bill and his men suffered nearly two weeks of soaking rain. One bright spot for Bill came when he received orders promoting him to captain. He beat the odds and held a captain's slot for the minimum ninety days. He had jumped from second lieutenant to captain in slightly less than two years.[7]

Three days after arriving in Bamberg, the Ivy Division bade farewell to the enlisted men with eighty-five or more points and took in an equal number of "low point" men from other units to refill the vacancies. On June 15, Colonel Chance paraded the regiment for a review by General Blakeley. The division commander enjoyed the review so much, he decided to stage his own parade on June 18. With the 8th, 12th, and 22nd Infantry Regiments, division artillery, and divisional troops standing in mass formation, Maj. Gen. Harold Blakeley passed in review, standing in the rear of a halftrack. Snapping a salute before each standard, he paid his respects to the units that helped conquer Germany and would help finish off Japan.[8]

The 12th Infantry moved to Le Havre, France in two groups beginning on June 21. Most of the troops loaded boxcars and rode the rails to Camp Old Gold near the French port. Bill stayed behind to help manage the 2nd Battalion's motor convoy. The battalion's wheeled vehicles departed Bamberg on June 22 with Major Zarger in command.

The journey was a far cry from the tension-filled moves during combat when wrong turns had deadly consequences and troops had to remain alert for any appearance by the *Luftwaffe*. MPs marked the route and manned critical points to ensure none of the convoy's serials got lost. The vehicles stuck to the specified route but Bill became concerned about the pace. Major Zarger, in the lead vehicle, set a slow march speed to prevent gaps from forming in the middle of the convoy. Riding in the second jeep, Bill looked back to see vehicles and their impatient drivers bunched up behind him. With too slow a pace the convoy ran the risk of missing its time checks.

Bill decided to act. He jumped out of his jeep then ran forward to Zarger's vehicle. Bill was no sprinter but the convoy moved slowly enough that he overtook the lead vehicle. Pumping his arms and legs, he got alongside the major's jeep.

Bill's sudden appearance running beside the jeep startled the major. "Sir," Bill said, "I think we need to pick up the pace." Major Zarger got the point. As soon as Bill hopped back in his own jeep, the major increased the convoy's speed.

It took five days to reach Le Havre. For Bill and the men, the time passed agreeably. Quarters were arranged for overnight stays and meals were served at the stops. Of course, young men could not resist the many opportunities for a little mischief. One soldier in the convoy described some of the hijinks. "Picture this: A long convoy of various army vehicles traveling through a city. Regardless of its size, the lead vehicle would spot a pretty girl walking down the sidewalk. The driver would drive right up onto the sidewalk, and the occupants would all stick their arms out trying to pat the young lady on the derriere and each vehicle following would do the same. I think some ladies liked it, for no one ran; they would just wave and smile. The GIs would throw them chocolate bars or cigarettes, which we had plenty of."[9]

On June 26, the men dropped off the regiment's wheeled vehicles at the terminal and reported to Camp Old Gold, thirty miles outside Le Havre. They joined the rest of the regiment in packing equipment and processing for redeployment. The troops moved by truck on July 3 to Le Havre's port. After meandering through the wreckage of the port facilities, Bill boarded the SS *Sea Bass* along with the rest of the regiment. The transport stood out to sea at 1615 hours and the men bid adieu to the European continent. Once underway, the acting regimental commander, Lt. Col. John Meyer, called the battalion and separate company commanders up to the forward B Deck for a short ceremony. The 12th Infantry normally celebrated its organization day on July 3, and Meyer had a special announcement. Colonel Red Reeder, the regiment's D-Day commander, had telegraphed word that the Secretary of the Army had awarded the 12th Infantry the Presidential Unit Citation for its campaign in Luxembourg. The colonel handed out the badges to the commanders, who went below decks to pin them on all the troops.[10]

The *Sea Bass* had a slow, uneventful voyage. Heavy fog in the North Atlantic delayed the ship's arrival by a day but New York City made up for it. "The New York Fire Department had all their boats out spraying streams of water. Fire engines on the dock all had their sirens blowing and lights flashing." The 12th Infantry made a proud entry into the harbor on July 12. Two gigantic canvas banners hung from the *Sea Bass's* starboard railing, one showing the 4th Infantry Division insignia and the other painted with the regiment's coat of arms. New Yorkers showered the troops with cheers and hospitality. "Amidst the accompaniment of band music and happily waving crowds the men of the 12th Infantry stepped once more upon the shores of the United States." "As we exited the boat Red Cross and Salvation Army gals distributed doughnuts and coffee. They made sure we felt welcomed."[11]

The Army shuttled the regiment to nearby Camp Shanks where the men went through two hectic days of "out-processing" then were cut loose with instructions to report to Camp Butner, North Carolina, thirty days later. Bill was not among them. The regiment had formed an advance party to travel to Camp Butner, and he volunteered to go with it. He explained to Beth that the trip would only delay his homecoming by a couple days but give him first crack at securing housing at the rural post. A couple extra days of duty seemed like a fair trade for the benefit of decent quarters.[12]

Bill's decision provides a clue about his emotional state. His stated reason for delaying his reunion with Beth may have been sensible, yet most soldiers in his place would have let their emotions overrule logic. Perhaps, with a conflict in Japan looming in his future, he could not let go of his warrior temperament. His feelings had to remain subservient to rational thought—he could not let his guard down. With the business of fighting and killing unfinished, Bill's psyche may not have been fully ready for a homecoming.

As promised, Bill scarfed up one of the few available rental houses in Durham, the closest city to Camp Butner. Once the advance party finished its work sectioning off the post and organizing the HQ, Bill started his thirty-day leave. He called Beth to let her know that he was on his way then hop-scotched across the country on various military and civilian flights. The couple planned to rendezvous in Sacramento where she taught school and maintained an apartment.

As in most military operations, things did not work out as planned. Bill missed his connecting flight from Los Angeles to Sacramento. He caught a flight for San Francisco, instead. Once the plane pulled up to the terminal, Bill stepped down to the same tarmac that he departed from two and a half years before. If he pondered the troubling premonition that had haunted him while in combat, he never mentioned it.

Being in the Bay Area, Bill knew he could not bypass his mother, Lucy, who still lived in Oakland, no matter how anxious he was to see Beth. He called Beth and told her to meet him at Lucy's home. Beth raced to the Sacramento bus terminal and jumped on the next bus to Oakland.

The joyful reunion fell a bit short of the romantic idyll the young couple hoped for. Beth made better time than Bill expected and arrived while he was still shaving. After nineteen months of separation, they finally embraced, with Bill half-shaven and his mother looking on.

Bill and Beth stayed with Lucy for a few days but felt a little awkward. After all, they had a year and a half of conjugal time to make up. Happily, friends of Beth agreed to let the couple stay at their beach house on Lake Tahoe.

The couple took a bus to Oakdale to visit Beth's family and borrow her mother's car. As Bill climbed out of the cab in front of the Hartley home, a pretty young woman threw her arms around his neck and started kissing him. At first, the girl's wildly affectionate greeting startled him. It took Bill a few seconds to recognize Beth's younger sister Lois Ann. The last time he had seen her she had been a gawky thirteen-year-old.

Beth's parents graciously loaned the couple their second car. Bill and Beth headed into the High Sierra the next day. They finally enjoyed time by themselves in the dreamlike setting of a brilliant blue lake surrounded by tall mountain peaks. The cozy beach cottage at Lake Tahoe gave them a long-delayed honeymoon free from the pressures of family and war.

After a day or two at the cottage, the mid-summer weather turned warm and Bill decided to test the lake's waters. He never learned to swim, but Tahoe's crystal-clear waters looked too inviting to pass up. He slipped on a pair of swimming trunks and walked out to the end of the pier. Even if he could not swim, he figured he could jump off the dock and dog paddle around. Taking a deep breath, he plunged into the lake.

"Aaaiiah!" What seemed to be a million needles stabbed his skin. Bill had failed to notice that snow, melted off the Sierra Nevada Mountains, filled Lake Tahoe. He struggled to keep his head above the surface of the frigid water while his body contorted. Panting and wiggling, he barely made it back to the pier. His stiff, frozen hands had just enough strength to grasp the steps on the pier. He dragged his body out of the water then ran back to the cabin to warm up.

While at Lake Tahoe, Bill and Beth took time to visit Beth's maternal grandfather, William Simmonds. Grandfather Simmonds, born in England eighty years earlier, ran away from home as a teenager and took passage to Canada. He eventually worked his way to the United States where he settled down and raised his family. He still served as a local meteorologist and tended the dam on the Truckee River.

Bill and the old Englishman failed to hit it off. As Bill discussed the victory in Europe, the old man cut in. "The only reason you beat the Germans was because you could hide behind the English Navy."

Beth gasped and Bill fumed. *Count to one hundred.* Somehow, he kept his half-Irish temper under control and avoided making a scene, but he boiled like a teakettle inside.

Grandfather Simmonds invited Bill and Beth back for dinner on the night of August 6. This time Beth's Aunt Ethel and cousin Beryl came along. Their presence kept things congenial despite the latent tension between the two men. After eating, the family adjourned to the living room and listened to the radio.

A news flash interrupted the radio program. President Truman came on the air and announced that America had just dropped a massive new bomb on the Japanese city of Hiroshima. The bomb, using atomic power, had the equivalent blast effect of 20,000 tons of TNT. The president solemnly told the world that this one weapon had destroyed the city. He went on to warn the Japanese people that America would obliterate Japan, a city at a time, until it surrendered.

At first, the thought that the country had converted atomic energy into a bomb amazed Bill. Then he marveled at the immense magnitude of the device. As an engineer, he wondered about the properties and design of this new wonder weapon. A few seconds later both Bill and Beth began to consider its implications.

Wonder turned to joy when the couple realized that the atomic bomb meant Japan's certain defeat. There would be no invasion of Japan. Bill would not have to deploy to the Pacific. He would not have to return to combat. His war was over.

Although victory in the Pacific seemed assured, Captain Chapman still had to return to Camp Butner when his leave expired. Bill and Beth decided to buy a car in California and drive to North Carolina. That would give them handy transportation while stationed at Camp Butner.

After stopping by Oakdale, they traveled to the Bay Area to find a suitable vehicle.

With a 3,000-mile trip in front of them, the couple concentrated on finding a car with one particular feature—tires good enough to make it to the East Coast. They found a decent set of tires underneath a Chrysler Airflow. After plopping down cash for the car, Bill and Beth started their cross-country trip. They drove at night to spare the tires as much wear as possible, better to avoid the heat of the day.

Japan's formal acceptance of surrender, announced on August 14, allowed Bill to finally let go of his warrior spirit and the addictive rush of combat command. That burning self-doubt about proving himself worthy in the face of danger no longer mattered. He could rest on his laurels.

Bill turned his attention to his future life as a civilian and family man. He contacted his old professor, Dr. Frank Hutchinson, who had accepted a full professorship at Purdue University. Hutchinson had stayed in touch with Beth throughout Bill's combat tour. He let her know that he wanted Bill to join his thermal engineering program at Purdue. When Bill wrote to him, the professor offered Bill a research fellowship and pulled strings to get him accepted into Purdue's graduate school of engineering in the 1945 fall semester. When Bill showed the acceptance letter back at Camp Butner, the Army put him on terminal leave. The Chapmans hopped in the Airflow and sped to Lafayette, Indiana in time for Bill to start classes. Bill's official separation from the Army came through with an effective date of December 12, 1945.[13]

The transition to civilian life came relatively easily to Bill. He held the psychological trauma of war in check. Lucy later claimed that the war had made Bill testy and profane, but Beth did not see much difference from the earnest young man she dated at Berkeley. He would, at times, display the reflexes he had developed under fire, like the time he dove into a snow bank when a snapped power line made a whistling noise similar to incoming artillery. Still, he managed to leave combat behind him as he concentrated on his engineering classes and growing family. Beth became pregnant in early 1946.

The war and combat might have receded into his past but Bill still valued military service. His practical mind considered the advantages of earning pay and a retirement from the military to supplement his civilian income. Bill took a reserve commission, although he transferred out of the infantry and joined the Corps of Engineers, finally aligning his professional and military careers. Prospects for promotion to field grade looked more promising in the Engineers, too.

In 1947 Bill earned his master's degree and took a job with the National Tube Division of U.S. Steel. Bill, Beth, and their son Bruce moved to Pittsburgh to start his long and successful career as an engineer and business executive.

A year after graduating, Captain Chapman reported to a nearby VA hospital for his quadrennial physical, a routine requirement for reserve and active soldiers. He went through all the stations and tests without any problems. The last station in the physical was an appearance in front of the Army physician who had to sign each soldier's medical file.

The doctor examined Bill for the usual mobility and flexibility tests. He checked for heart rate and breathing problems. Bill bent over for the customary prostate exam. Everything seemed in order.

Bill started to get dressed, already anxious to be done and on his way. Meanwhile, the doctor sat behind his desk and scribbled his last few observations in Bill's medical record. While dressing Bill glanced down at the doctor's summary exam sheet. The doctor had just checked the box next to the "Unfit for General Duty" rating.

Bill stiffened. *Unfit?* A medical classification of "unfit" would result in a medical discharge. Alarmed and confused, Bill confronted the doctor. "Doc, why'd you check the unfit box?"

"Because you're not physically able to perform field duty."

Count to one hundred. "Sure, I can. There's nothing wrong with me. Why would I be unfit?"

"On account of your wounds."

"My wounds?"

"Yes, your wounds make you unfit to serve."

"Doctor, you don't understand. I fought in combat for four months after getting wounded. Hell, I served as a rifle company commander with these wounds and even earned a promotion."

The doctor, in no mood to argue with the captain, folded his arms and scowled. "We needed you then."

ACKNOWLEDGMENTS

This book could never have been written without three essential foundations: Bill Chapman's oral history, his letters to his wife, Beth, and painstaking research into the combat history of the 12th Infantry Regiment.

The whole Chapman family got into the act of recalling and recording my father's war stories. Three generations contributed anecdotes, facts, and memories—the heart of the book. We shared what we remembered and jointly clarified details of things my father had said over the years. The family compiled over one hundred specific stories and verbal accounts that make this book a meaningful personal history. All deserve to be mentioned by name: my mother, Beth; my wife, Mary; my brothers, Dean and Brian and his wife, Nancy; and Bill's grandchildren, Jennifer, Paul, Thomas, Daniel, Abigail, Rebecca, and Anne.

Special thanks go to my mother, who graciously turned over my father's wartime letters. Due to censorship, these letters shed minimal light on the combat action, yet they yielded a treasure trove of insight into Bill Chapman's state of mind—what I call the soul of this book. Instead of the composed, fatherly figure I knew growing up, I discovered a determined and adrenalin-addicted young man struggling to keep his emotions in check while dealing with the moral, psychological, and physical challenges of combat.

Others contributed firsthand information. Two surviving members of Bill's battalion, Jack Port and Morgan Welch, shared their own personal stories to help build the narrative. Pat Gunning, the daughter of one of Bill's closest friends, Lieutenant Jack Gunning, turned over the only photos we have of Bill during his combat tour and an unpublished account by one of Bill's fellow officers in Normandy. Martin MacDiarmid III also provided information about his father, who is featured in the story.

The heavy work involved unearthing the movements and actions of Bill's company, battalion, and regiment—something necessary to place Bill's war stories into the context of the fighting that swirled around him. Gerden Johnson's fine *History of the Twelfth Infantry Regiment in World War II* provided an excellent starting point, but I knew I had to drill down deeper to get the perspective of an infantry company officer. That meant searching the archives. I must "tip my hat" to the many dedicated and helpful historians and archivists who have preserved and cataloged the precious documents in our nation's archives. Dr. Timothy Nenninger, Chief of the Textual Reference Staff, and his folks at the National Archives and Records Administration (NARA) in College Park, Maryland deserve recognition for the amazing work they do with the vast collection of modern military records. Coincidently, Tim and I had crossed paths in our younger days at the University of Wisconsin. The NARA staff, including those with the Cartographic Services and Still Pictures Branch, pointed me to the journals, maps, photos, reports, field orders, overlays, and casualty lists that enabled me to track the precise movements of Bill's battalion. Lori Miller of Redbird Research assisted by locating and copying morning reports in the Personnel Archives at NARA's St. Louis facility.

Another archive worthy of mention is the World War II Topographic Map Series held by McMasters University in Hamilton, Ontario. The university has made available digital copies of the U.S. Army's maps on their website. Historians can see the terrain as the soldiers saw it in 1944–45. Without these contemporary maps, the overlays in the archives would be useless. The university has kindly permitted me to reprint the maps to illustrate the tactical movements of my father's battalion and company.

The Combined Arms Research Library at Fort Leavenworth, Kansas and Ray Merriam of Merriam Press provided contemporary government publications and manuals that explained the U.S. Army's organization and tactical doctrine of that era.

Finding the files in the archives is one thing, going through the documents for the relevant information is an even bigger task. Fortunately, I had help. My wife and my two sons, Paul and Tom, made trips with me to College Park to comb through boxes of documents. We even discovered a five-page deposition made by my father about the campaign in southern Germany. No one in the family knew the deposition existed until we fished it out of the 4th Infantry Division's archive. It is one of the few accounts written by my father about the war and, by far, the most extensive.

With research in hand, I launched into writing my father's wartime experiences. I have to thank my literary friends, Skip Dyer, Ilia Davidovich, Paul Crockett, and Tom Burns, who helped me mold my initial manuscript into presentable form through their helpful critiques. My editor, Scott Belliveau, worked tirelessly to help my father's story emerge from a fact-laden manuscript. The editorial staff at Regnery History, especially Alex Novak, Maria Bonvissuto, and Joshua Taggert, earned my thanks for pulling together the narrative, photos, and maps to make this book a complete package. Also, I need to recognize Greg Johnson, for showing faith in this project and assisting me in bringing my father's wartime journey to the reading public.

This war biography fulfills a long-held dream and filial obligation by preserving, in print, the oral history of a soldier. My thanks to everyone who pitched in to make this book a reality.

BIBLIOGRAPHY

Oral History of William P. Chapman

Correspondence:
William P. Chapman to Mrs. William P. Chapman, 1943–5.

Family Documents:
Separation Qualification Record, WD AGO Form 100. Chapman, William P. 12 Dec 45.

Military Record and Report of Separation – Certificate of Service, WD AFO Form 53–98. Chapman, William P. 12 Dec 45.

Remembrances of D-Day—June 6, 1944, William P. Chapman, May 30, 1994.

Silver Star Citation, handwritten transcription.

Government Documents:

70th Tank Battalion. After Action Reports, 1 Aug–30 Nov 44, 1–31 Mar and 1–31 May 45. Combined Arms Research Library, Fort Leavenworth, Kansas.

70th Tank Battalion. *Soixante-Dix, A History of the 70th Tank Battalion.* Combined Arms Research Library, Fort Leavenworth, Kansas.

746th Tank Battalion. After Action Report 1 – 30 Jun 44. Combined Arms Research Library, Fort Leavenworth, Kansas.

Adair, L. R. Captain, U. S. Army, et al. *The Battle of Mortain.* Fort Leavenworth, KS: Combat Studies Institute, 1983.

Bailey, Claude E. Captain, U. S. Army. *Operations of Company "I" 8th Infantry (4th Infantry Division) East of Olzheim, Germany 28 February–1 March 1945.* Fort Benning, GA: General Subjects Section, Academic Department, The Infantry School, 1949.

Campbell, William R. Major, U. S. Army. *Tanks with Infantry.* Fort Knox, KY: Military Monograph, The Armored School, 1947.

Doubler, Michael D. Captain, U. S. Army. *Busting the Bocage: American Combined Arms Operations in France, 6 June–31 July 1944.* Fort Leavenworth, KS: U. S, Army Command and General Staff College, 1988.

Folsom, Charles D. Captain, U. S. Army. *Hedgerow Fighting Near Carentan.* Fort Know, KY: Military Monograph, The Armored School, 1948.

German Order of Battle, Normandy—13 June 1944. Fort Leavenworth, KS: Combined Arms Research Library.

Graduation Program, Twenty-Fifth Company, Second Student Training Regiment, Fort Benning, Georgia, June 1943. (Courtesy of Pat Gunning)

Miles, Otha G. Major, U. S. Army, et al. *The Battle of Schnee Eifel.* Fort Leavenworth, KS: Combat Studies Institute, 1984.

National Archives and Records Administration, College Park, Maryland. Office of the Adjutant General. Record Group 407: File 304-INF, records of the 4th Infantry Division, including File 304-INF(12), records of the 12th Infantry Regiment; File 330-INF, records of the 30th Infantry Division.

National Personnel Records Center, St. Louis, Missouri. Morning Reports, 12th Infantry Regiment, 4th Infantry Division.

Order of Battle of the German Army–1 Mar 45. Fort Leavenworth, KS: Combined Arms Research Library.

OSS Section, 7th Army. *Dachau*. Fort Leavenworth, KS: Combined Arms Research Library.

US Army, Table of Organization & Equipment 7–15, Infantry Battalion, February 26, 1944.

US Army, Table of Organization & Equipment 7–16, Headquarters and Headquarters Company, Infantry Battalion, February 26, 1944.

US Army, Table of Organization & Equipment 7–18, Infantry Heavy Weapons Company, February 26, 1944.

War Department, Infantry Field Manual 7–5, Organization and Tactics of Infantry: The Rifle Battalion, October 1940.

War Department, Infantry Field Manual 7–10, Rifle Company, Rifle Regiment, June 1942.

War Department, Infantry Field Manual 7–15, Heavy Weapons Company, Rifle Regiment, May 1942.

War Department, Infantry Field Manual 7–20, Infantry Battalion, October 1944.

War Department, Infantry Field Manual 7–40, Rifle Regiment, February 1942.

War Department, Field Manual 23–55, Browning Machine Guns, Caliber .30, M1917A1, M1919A4 and M1919A6, July 1945.

War Department, Field Manual 23–90, 81mm Mortar M1, April 1943.

War Department, Field Manual 100–5, Operations, June 1944.

War Department, Field Manual 101–5, Staff Officers' Field Manual: The Staff and Combat Orders, August 1940.

Zarger, Glenn W. Major, *Defense of Little Switzerland*. Carlisle Barracks, PA: Military Monograph US Army Military History Institute, 1948.

Pamphlets:

The Beachhead, The Official Journal of the U. S. Committee for the Battle of Normandy Museum. Washington, DC, Summer 1990.

Periodicals:

Blakeley, Harold W. Maj. Gen., U. S. Army. "Artillery in Normandy." *The Field Artillery Journal* 39, no. 2 (Mar–Apr 1949): 52–54.

Hemingway, Ernest. "The G. I. and the General." *Collier's*. (Nov. 4, 1944): 11 and 46.

———. "War in the Siegfried Line." *Collier's*. (Nov. 18, 1944): 18 and 70.

Segel, Robert G. "The Model 1917 Browning Water-Cooled Machine Gun." *Small Arms Defense Journal* (Fall 2009): 60–69.

Newspapers:

Taylor, Michael. "Liberating France Hemingway's Way/Following Author's 1944 Reclaiming of the Ritz Hotel." *San Francisco Chronicle*, August 22, 2004. Available online at www.sfgate.com/travel/article/Liberating-France-Hemingway-s-way-Following-2731590.php.

Unpublished Works:

McGrann, Roy T. Captain, U. S. Army. "The 610th Tank Destroyer Battalion: Apr. 10, 1942–Dec. 7, 1945". N. P., N. D.

Rousek, Charles E. Major, U. S. Army. A Short History of the 38th Cavalry Reconnaissance Squadron (Mechanized). N. P., N. D.

Slaymaker, William H. 1st Lt. U. S. Army, "Invasion: Personal Notes of 1st Lt. W. H. Slaymaker." N.P., N. D.

Interviews:

Chapman, William P. Video interview by Mike Kearney. *Leadership Recall.* American Society of Heating, Refrigerating and Air-Conditioning Engineers (ASHRAE), June 13, 1990. Available online at www.ashrae.org/society-groups/leadership-recall/william-p-chapman.

Foreign Military Studies: Manuscript Department, William R. Perkins Library. Duke University. Durham, NC. Interviews identified by name and MS#. National Archives and Records Administration, College Park, Maryland. Interviews identified by name and MS#. *World War II German Military Studies*, vols. 1–24. New York: Garland Publishing, 1979. Interviews identified by name and MS#.

Port, Jack. Phone interview by Craig S. Chapman. February 27, 2014.

Reeder, Russell P. Jr. Colonel, U. S. Army. Interview by Forrest C. Pogue. October 18, 1960. Transcript. George C. Marshall Foundation. Lexington, VA.

Welch, J. Morgan. Phone interview by Craig S. Chapman, March 21, 2014.

Books:

Administrative History of U. S. Naval Forces Europe 1940–46. vol V. London: Historical Section, COMNAVEU, 1946. Available online at www.history.navy.mil/library/online/comnaveu.htm.

Ambrose, Stephen E. *Citizen Soldiers: The U. S. Army from the Normandy Beaches to the Bulge to the Surrender of Germany June 7, 1944–May 7, 1945.* New York: Simon & Schuster, 1997.

Atkinson, Rick. *The Guns at Last Light: The War in Western Europe, 1944–1945.* New York: Henry Holt, 2013.

Babcock, Robert O. *War Stories: Utah Beach to Pleiku.* Baton Rouge: St John's Publishing, 2001.

Balkoski, Joseph. *Utah Beach: The Amphibious Landings and Airborne Operations on D-Day, June 6, 1944.* Mechanicsburg, PA: Stackpole Books, 2005.

Beevor, Antony. *D-Day: The Battle for Normandy.* New York: Penguin, 2009.

Bessel, Richard. *Germany 1945: From War to Peace.* New York: HarperCollins, 2009.

Blumenson, Martin. *Breakout and Pursuit.* Washington, DC: Office of the Chief of Military History, Department of the Army, 1961.

Blumenson, Martin. *Liberation.* Alexandria, VA: Time-Life Books, 1978.

Bradley, Omar N. General of the Army, U. S. Army and Clay Blair. *A General's Life: An Autobiography by General of the Army Omar N. Bradley.* New York: Simon & Schuster, 1983.

Bull, Stephen, Ph.D. *World War II Infantry Tactics: Company and Battalion.* Oxford, England: Osprey Publishing, 2005.

Cole, Hugh M. *The Ardennes: Battle of the Bulge.* Washington, DC: Office of the Chief of Military History, Department of the Army, 1965.

Desch, John. "The 1941 German Army/The 1944-45 U.S. Army: A Comparative Analysis of Two Forces in Their Primes." In *Hitler's Army: The Evolution and Structure of German Forces*. Conshohocken, PA: Command Magazine, 1996.

Dow, James R. and Hannjost Lixfeld. *The Nazification of an Academic Discipline: Folklore in the Third Reich*. Bloomington, IN: Indiana University Press, 1994.

Dwyer, William M. *So Long for Now: A World War II Memoir*. Bloomington, IN: Xlibris, 2009.

Eisenhower, David. *Eisenhower at War 1943–1945*. New York: Vintage Books, 1986.

Featherston, Alwyn. *Saving the Breakout: The 30ᵗʰ Division's Heroic Stand at Mortain, August 7–12, 1944*. Novato, CA: Presidio Press, 1993.

Fritz, Stephen G. *Endkampf: Soldiers, Civilians and the Death of the Third Reich*. Lexington, KY: The University Press of Kentucky, 2004.

4ᵗʰ Infantry Division, 12ᵗʰ Infantry Regiment. Baton Rouge: Army & Navy Publishing Company, 1946.

Harrison, Gordon A. *Cross-Channel Attack*. Washington, DC: Office of the Chief of Military History, Department of the Army, 1951.

Hastings, Max. *Armageddon: The Battle for Germany, 1944–1945*. New York: Vintage Books, 2004.

Hastings, Max. *Overlord: D-Day and the Battle for Normandy*. New York: Simon & Schuster, 1984; New York: Vintage Books, 2006.

Howe, G. B. Lieutenant, U. S. Navy. *Skill in the Surf: A Landing Boat Manual*. Coronado, CA: Department of the Navy, 1945. Available online at www.history.navy.mil/library/surfskill.htm.

Hutton, Christopher. *Linguistics and the Third Reich: Mother-tongue Facism, Racism and the Science of Language.* London: Routledge, 1999.

Jensen, Marvin G. *Strike Swiftly: The 70th Tank Battalion: From North Africa to Normandy to Germany.* Novato, CA: Presidio Press, 1997.

Johnson, Gerden F. Colonel, U. S. Army. *History of the Twelfth Infantry Regiment in World War II.* Boston: National Fourth (Ivy) Division Association, 1947.

Knapp, George W. Rev. *A Chaplain's Duty: Letters Home from a WWII Chaplain.* Edited by Gayle E. Knapp. Marietta, GA: Deeds Publishing, 2011.

Liddell Hart, B. H. *History of the Second World War.* New York: Putnam, 1971.

MacDonald, Charles B. *The Last Offensive.* Washington, DC: Office of the Chief of Military History, Department of the Army, 1973.

MacDonald, Charles B. *The Siegfried Line Campaign.* Washington, DC: Office of the Chief of Military History, Department of the Army, 1963.

Marshall, S. L. A. Colonel, U. S. Army. *Men Against Fire: The Problem of Battle Command in Future War.* Gloucester, MA: Peter Smith, 1978.

McManus, John C. *The Americans at Normandy: The Summer of 1944—The American War from the Normandy Beaches to Falaise.* New York: Tom Doherty Associates, 2004.

Pyle, Ernie. *Ernie's War: The Best of Ernie Pyle's World War II Dispatches.* Edited by David Nichols. New York: Random House, 1986.

Reardon, Mark J. *Victory at Mortain: Stopping Hitler's Panzer Counteroffensive.* Lawrence, KS: University Press of Kansas, 2002.

Roberts, Charles C., Jr. *Armored Strike Force: The Photo History of the American 70ᵗʰ Tank Battalion in World War II*. Mechanicsburg, PA: Stackpole Books, 2016.

Ruppenthal, Roland G. Major, U. S. Army. *Utah Beach to Cherbourg (6 June–27 June 1944)*. Washington, DC: Historical Division, Department of the Army, 1947.

Ryan, Cornelius. *The Longest Day, June 6, 1944*. New York: Simon & Schuster, 1959.

Shields, David and Shane Salerno. *Salinger*. New York: Simon & Schuster, 2013.

Speer, Albert. *Inside the Third Reich: Memoirs by Albert Speer*. New York: MacMillan, 1970.

Stafford, David. *Endgame 1945: The Missing Final Chapter of World War II*. New York: Little Brown, 2007.

Stodghill, Dick. *Normandy 1944: A Young Rifleman's War*. Baltimore: PublishAmerica, 2006.

Thornton, Willis. *The Liberation of Paris*. New York: Harcourt, Brace & World, 1962.

Vannoy, Allyn R. and Jay Karamales. *Against the Panzers: United States Infantry versus German Tanks, 1944–1945*. Jefferson, NC: McFarland & Co., 1996.

Weidinger, Otto. *Comrades to the End: The 4ᵗʰ Panzer-Grenadier Regiment "Der Fuhrer" 1938–1945*. Translated by David Johnston. Atglen, PA: Schiffer Publishing, 1998.

Wilson, George. *If You Survive*. New York: Ballantine Books, 1987.

Winton, Harold R. *Corps Commanders of the Bulge: Six American Generals and Victory in the Ardennes*. Lawrence, KS: University of Kansas Press, 2007.

Websites:

"Geschichte," Schloss Schillingsfurst, December 17, 2103, schloss-schil-lingsfuerst.de.

"Battalion Organisation during the Second World War," March 17, 2015, bayonetstrength.150m.com.

"Discours de l'Hotel de Ville de Paris, 25 Aout 1944," June 16, 2016, charles-de-gaulle.org.

"Glider Landings" and "talliecrocker_utah," June 2014, normandy.secondworldwar.nl.

"Gorn_J," September 10, 2015, Memorial.thetasigmatau.org.

"Units," June 6, 2015, tankdestroyer.net.

"World War II Topographic Maps," June 6, 2015, digitalarchive.mcmaster.ca. This website is a gem. Viewers can search through contemporary 1:100,000 scale maps of the European Theater.

NOTES

Prologue

1.   Colonel Gerden F. Johnson, *History of the Twelfth Infantry Regiment in World War II* (Boston: National Fourth (Ivy) Division Association, 1947). Calculation based on the indexed list of officers assigned to the battalion. Johnson's book is one of the best regimental histories of World War II and provides an excellent accounting of the 12th Infantry's operations (hereafter cited as Johnson).

2.   National Personnel Records Center, St. Louis, Missouri. Morning Reports, 12th Infantry Regiment, 4th Infantry Division (hereafter cited as Morning Report), May 7, 1945.

Chapter 1

1. Family oral history is a major source of the information contained in this work. In most cases, the reader will easily see that certain facts and descriptions come from personal recollections by family members, most notably from William P. Chapman (hereafter cited as WPC). Rather than repetitively cite oral history notes, personal recollections will only be cited to clarify potentially confusing situations.

2. Separation Qualification Record, WD AGO Form 100. Chapman, William P. 12 Dec 45 (hereafter cited as Chapman Form 100).

3. Chapman Form 100.

4. William P. Chapman, video interview by Mike Kearney, *Leadership Recall*, American Society of Heating, Refrigerating and Air-Conditioning Engineers (ASHRAE), 13 June 1990 (hereafter cited as ASHRAE Interview). Available online www.ashrae.org/society-groups/leadership-recall/william-p-chapman/.

5. Chapman Form 100.

6. Lieutenant William P. Chapman letters to Mrs. William P. Chapman (hereafter cited as Letter), March 29, 1943.

7. Letter, March 29, 1943.

8. Graduation Program, Twenty-Fifth Company, Second Student Training Regiment, Fort Benning, Georgia, June 1943. The poem printed in the program has ten stanzas.

9. Letter, March 29, 1943.

10. Letter, June 14, 1943.

11. Letter, June 14, 1944; Military Record and Report of Separation—Certificate of Service, WD AFO Form 53-98. Chapman, William P. 12 Dec 45 (hereafter cited as Chapman Form 53-98); Letter, March 1, 1944.

12. The author heard the account of that day's tragedy from Bill's mother, Lucy.

13. Letters, January 1 and 10, 1944.

Chapter 2

1. Letter, January 19, 1944; Chapman Form 53–98.

2. Letter, January 31, 1944.

3. Letter, February 4, 1944.

4. Letter, February 6, 1944.

5. Letter, March 7, 1944.

6. Letter, March 14 and 15, 1944.

7. John Desch, "The 1941 German Army/The 1944-45 U.S. Army: A Comparative Analysis of Two Forces in Their Primes," in *Hitler's Army: The Evolution and Structure of German Forces* (Conshohocken, PA: Command Magazine, 1996), 83 (hereafter cited as Desch); Max Hastings, *Overlord: D-Day and the Battle for Normandy* (New York: Vintage Books, 2006), 166–7 (hereafter cited as Hastings); S. L. A. Marshall, Colonel, U. S. Army, *Men Against Fire: The Problem of Battle Command in Future War,* (Gloucester, Mass.: Peter Smith, 1978), 15 (hereafter cited as Marshall).

8. Morning Report, Mar. 27, 1944; Letter, March 19, 1944.

9. Colonel Russell P. Reeder, interview by Forrest C. Pogue, George C. Marshall Foundation, Lexington, Virginia, 18 October 1960, transcript.

10. Ernie Pyle, *Ernie's War: The Best of Ernie Pyle's World War II Dispatches,* David Nichols ed. (New York: Random House, 1986), 329 (hereafter cited as Pyle); Antony Beevor, *D-Day: The Battle for Normandy* (New York: Penguin, 2009), 215 (hereafter cited as Beevor).

11. Morning Report, Mar. 27, 1944.

12. 1st Lt. William H. Slaymaker, *"Invasion: Personal Notes of 1st Lt. W. H. Slaymaker"* (N.P., N.D.) (hereafter cited as Slaymaker); US Army, Table of Organization & Equipment 7-18, Infantry Heavy Weapons Company, February 26, 1944 (hereafter cited as TO&E 7-18).

13. War Department, Infantry Field Manual 7-15, Heavy Weapons Company, Rifle Regiment, May 1942, 3–4 (hereafter cited as FM 7-15); War Department, Field Manual 23–90, 81mm Mortar M1, April 1943, 2 (hereafter cited as FM 23-90).

14. Letter, April 10, 1944.

15. Letter, May 12, 1944.

16. FM 23-90, 71–112.

17. FM 23–90, 71 and 77–80.

18. Johnson, 50.

19. Johnson, 50–1; Hastings, 57–8. The negative comments based on WPC.

20. Johnson, 51; National Archives and Records Administration, College Park, Maryland, Office of the Adjutant General. Record Group 407 (hereafter cited as NARA), File 304-INF(12)-0.3, After Action Report April 1944 (hereafter cited as 12th AAR); COMNAVEU, *Administrative History of U. S. Naval Forces Europe 1940-46.* vol V (London: Historical Section, 1946), 365 (hereafter cited as COMNAVEU); Letter May 1, 1944.

21. COMNAVEU, 365.

22. Johnson, 52.

23. Letters, May 17, 1944.

24. Johnson, 52; NARA, File 304-INF(12)-3.7, Maps (hereafter cited as Maps).

25. Colonel Russell P. Reeder, letter to Chief of Military History, May 23, 1966, found in NARA, File 304-INF(12)-0.3.

26. Johnson, 52-4; NARA, File 304-INF(12)-3.7, Aerial Photos; NARA, File 304-INF(12)-3.9.1 Field Order #1 (hereafter cited as Field Order); NARA, File 304-INF(12)7-3.9.1, Second Battalion Field Order; Letter, May 24, 1944.

27. Hastings, 36, 146, and 152; General of the Army Omar Bradley and Clay Blair, *A General's Life: An Autobiography by General of the Army Omar N. Bradley* (New York: Simon & Schuster, 1983), 234 (hereafter cited as Bradley); Stephen E. Ambrose, *Citizen Soldiers: The U. S. Army from the Normandy Beaches to the Bulge to the Surrender of Germany June 7, 1944–May 7, 1945* (New York: Simon & Schuster, 1997), 18-9 (hereafter cited as Ambrose); War Department, Infantry Field Manual 7-5, Organization and Tactics of Infantry: The Rifle Battalion, October 1940, pp. 43-6 (hereafter cited as FM 7-5); Desch, 89.

28. Letter, May 1, 1944.

29. COMNAVU, 496; Johnson, 54. Johnson gives the date as June 4, but naval records show that Force U put to sea late on the third.

Chapter 3

1. Johnson, 54; COMNAVEU, 305, 400 and 499; NARA File 304-INF(12)-0.10. D'Avino's artwork is kept in a special file at the National Archives.

2. Johnson, 54; COMNAVEU, 397 and 493–6; Major Roland G. Ruppenthal, *Utah Beach to Cherbourg 6 June– 27 June 1944* (Washington, DC: Historical Division, Department of the Army, 1947), 13 (hereafter cited as Ruppenthal).

3. COMNAVEU, 433–42 and 497–506; Ruppenthal, 13.

4. Johnson, 55.

5. COMNAVEU, 464–76; Hastings, 86–7.

6. COMNAVEU, 409 and 503; Ruppenthal, 43; Cornelius Ryan, *The Longest Day: June 6, 1944* (New York: Simon & Schuster, 1959), 231–3, (hereafter cited as Ryan).

7. Slaymaker; "talliecrocker_utah," 6 June 2014, normandy. secondworldwar.nl, .

8. See "talliecrocker_utah," 6 June 2014, normandy. secondworldwar.nl,. This may have been the same artillery round.

9. William P. Chapman, Remembrances of D Day—June 6, 1944 (hereafter cited as Remembrances).

10. NARA, File 304-INF(12)-0.3.0, Unit History, Invasion of France (hereafter cited as Invasion of France); COMNAVEU, 503–4; Slaymaker.

11. Remembrances.

12. Thousands of 4th Infantry Division troops received a personal greeting from General Roosevelt as they left Utah Beach. See Ryan, 231 and 286.

13. See Beevor, 118 for confirmation about Roosevelt's appearance.

14. 14 Field Order #1; TO&E 7-18; Morgan J. Welch, Interview with author, March 21, 2014 (hereafter cited as Welch Interview). Welch confirmed that the battalion's vehicles had not been offloaded for the first few days in Normandy.

15. David Shields and Shane Salerno, *Salinger* (New York: Simon & Schuster, 2013), 15 (hereafter cited as Salinger). Bill was not the only one to think about a firetrap. Colonel Reeder had been alerted to the potential danger of fuel being ignited in the inundated area but no course of action was ever prepared to deal with that threat.

16. Slaymaker; Hastings, 88; Colonel Russell P. Reeder, *The Beachhead, The Official Journal of the U. S. Committee for the Battle of Normandy Museum*, (Washington DC, Summer 1990).

17. Johnson, 60–2; Gordon A. Harrison, *Cross Channel-Attack* (Washington, DC: Office of the Chief of Military History, Department of the Army, 1951), 147 (hereafter cited as Harrison); Ryan, 134; Ruppenthal, 6.

18. NARA, File 304-INF(12)7-3.9.1, 2nd Battalion Field Order; FM 23–90, 2.

19. Invasion of France; Johnson, 62.

20. Slaymaker.

21. Invasion of France; Johnson, 62.

22. Johnson, 63; NARA, File 304-INF(12)-0.9 Unit Report #1 Overlay (hereafter cited as Unit Report).

23. FM 7-15, 175-7; FM 23-90, 133-5.

24. Invasion of France; Johnson, 64; Slaymaker; Robert O. Babcock, *War Stories: Utah Beach to Pleiku* (Baton Rouge: St John's Publishing, 2001), 115 (hereafter cited as War Stories); "Glider Landings," 6 June 2014 normandy.secondworldwar.nl.

25. War Stories, 115.

26. Bradley, 248–9; COMNAVEU, 493 and 503–6.

Chapter 4

1. Bradley, 233.

2. Ruppenthal, 61; NARA, File 304-INF(12)-0.7, Journal, June 6, 1944 (hereafter cited as Journal).

3. Ruppenthal, 59, image of captured German map; NARA, File 304-INF(12)-1.6, Proposed Citation (hereafter cited as Proposed Citation); Unit Report #2, overlays.

4. FM 23-90, 6–10 and 64–5.

5. Proposed Citation; Invasion of France.

6. Bill did not specify which day this incident occurred but the circumstances suggest June 7. For an example of this German recon tactic, see Ambrose, 60–1.

7. Journal, June 7, 1944; Johnson, 66; Slaymaker. Johnson stated the counterattack occurred at 1900 hours, but that would've been well before sunset.

8. Harrison, 545.

9. Captain Michael D. Doubler, *Busting the Bocage: American Combined Arms Operations in France, 6 June–31 July 1944* (Fort Leavenworth, KS: U.S., Army Command and General Staff College, 1988), 28 (hereafter cited as Doubler).

10. Marvin Jensen, *Strike Swiftly: The 70th Tank Battalion: From North Africa to Normandy to Germany* (Novato, CA: Presidio Press, 1997) 154 (hereafter cited as Jensen); Doubler, 22–3; Ambrose, 35.

11. Ruppenthal, 103; Johnson, 67–8; Proposed Citation; NARA File 304-INF(12)-0.3 After Action Report-Notes on Emondeville, June 1944 (hereafter cited as Notes on Emondeville); Maj. Gen. Harold W. Blakeley, "Artillery in Normandy," *The Field Artillery Journal* 39, no. 2 (Mar–Apr 1949): 52-54.

12. Notes on Emondeville; Ruppenthal, 103.

13. FM 7-15, 149.

14. Johnson, 72–3; Hastings, 188; Ambrose, 62.

15. Notes on Emondeville. Luckett surmised that the German counterattack and rocket barrage may have been intended to hit the 3rd Battalion in the rear but ran into the 2nd Battalion by surprise.

16. Notes on Emondeville; Slaymaker.

17. FM 23-90, 71; Major William R. Campbell, *Tanks with Infantry*, Military Monograph, The Armored School, Fort Knox, Kentucky, February 25, 1947, 5; Harrison, 284; FM 7-15, 195; TO&E 7-18.

18. Johnson, 68-9; Proposed Citation; Ruppenthal, 103. The killing of Lieutenant Everett may have been deliberate. See Beevor, 160.

19. Johnson, 69; Slaymaker.

20. Johnson, 69–71; Proposed Citation.

21. Slaymaker; FM 7-15, 174–8.

22. Ruppenthal, 103; To get an idea of how badly Colonel Reeder wanted tank support see Journal, June 8, 1944.

23. Journal, June 9, 1944; Johnson, 71.

24. Hastings, 188; Casualties in H Company rose sharply starting June 8. See NARA, File 304-INF(12)-.03, After Action Report, H Company Casualty List, June 1944.

25. Slaymaker; 746th Tank Battalion, After Action Report, 1–30 Jun 44. Combined Arms Research Library, Fort Leavenworth, Kansas (hereafter cited as 746th AAR).

26. Johnson, 72; Ruppenthal, 103; 746th AAR; Proposed Citation; Slaymaker. Whenever the 12th Infantry had attached units, especially tanks and tank destroyers, it identified itself as Combat Team 12 (CT 12) instead of the 12th Infantry Regiment. Throughout the narrative I will interchange the terms "regiment," "12th Infantry," "Combat Team 12," and "CT 12" when tanks or tank destroyers are attached to the regiment.

27. Ruppenthal, 103; Johnson, 72–3.

28. Dick Stodghill, *Normandy 1944: A Young Rifleman's War* (Baltimore: PublishAmerica, 2006), 140 (hereafter cited as Stodghill). See also Max Hastings, *Armageddon: The Battle for*

Germany, 1944-1945 (New York: Vintage Books, 2004), 85 (hereafter cited as Armageddon).

29. WPC. Bill did not specify the exact time and place of this close call, just that it happened in hedgerow country, but the situation closely matches the engagement outside of Joganville.

30. 746th AAR.

31. 746th AAR; Johnson, 72–3. Johnson incorrectly identifies the 70th Tank Battalion, the unit habitually attached to the 4th Infantry Division throughout the campaign in Europe. For the first few days after D-Day the 746th Tank Battalion was also attached to the division and they fought alongside the 12th Infantry on June 9, 1944.

32. WPC; Morning Report, June 9, 1944.

33. Letter, June 13, 1944.

34. Proposed Citation; Johnson, 77–80; Slaymaker. The last statistic comes from WPC.

35. Unit Report, #2-4; Ruppenthal, Appendix D; Beevor, 114.

36. Ruppenthal, 59.

37. David Eisenhower, *Eisenhower at War 1943-1945* (New York: Vintage Books, 1986), 285–7 (hereafter cited as Eisenhower).

Chapter 5

1. Letter, June 17, 1944.
2. Letter, June 13, 1944.
3. Letters, June 13 and 20, 1944.
4. Letter, June 26 and 27, 1944.
5. Letter July 1, 1944.
6. Letter, July 1944.
7. Letter, July 1944.
8. Morning Report, July 22, 1944; Unit Report #47, overlay.

9.   See Johnson, 73–132 for a description of this campaign; Martin
     Blumenson, *Breakout and Pursuit* (Washington, DC: Office of
     the Chief of Military History, Department of the Army, 1961),
     175 (hereafter cited as Blumenson); Eisenhower, 355–6; Bradley,
     272.

10. War Department, Field Manual 100-5, Operations, June 1944,
     111-7 (hereafter cited as FM 100-5); Stephen Bull, Ph.D., *World
     War II Infantry Tactics: Company and Battalion* (Oxford,
     England: Osprey Publishing, 2005), 14 (hereafter cited as Bull).

11. Blumenson, 130; Morning Report, July 20, 1944; Johnson 131-
     2.

12. Robert G. Segel, "The Model 1917 Browning Water-Cooled
     Machine Gun," *Small Arms Defense Journal* (Fall 2009): 60-69;
     FM 7-15, 134.

13. Blumenson, 180; Bradley, 272; NARA, File 304–0.3, 4th Infantry
     Division After Action Report, July 1944 (hereafter cited as 4th
     AAR).

14. Blumenson, 228-9.

15. Stodghill, 226-9.

16. Field Order #34; Rev. George W. Knapp, *A Chaplain's Duty:
     Letters Home from a WWII Chaplain*, ed. Gayle E. Knapp
     (Marietta, GA: Deeds Publishing 2011), 107 (hereafter cited as
     Knapp); Journal, July 25, 1944; Unit Report #50. Johnson and
     Stodghill state that the regiment moved south of le Hommet-
     d'Arthenay days before. The unit reports, journals, and field
     orders indicate the move from Le Desert to the southern
     assembly area occurred after the bombing on the twenty-fifth.

17. Blumenson, 235-8 and 243; Pyle, 337; Jensen, 190; Journal, July
     25, 1944.

18. Bradley, 280; Eisenhower, 381; Rick Atkinson, *The Guns at Last Light: The War in Western Europe, 1944–1945* (New York: Henry Holt, 2013), 144 (hereafter cited as Atkinson); Hastings, 255.

19. Journal, July 25, 1944; Stodghill, 231; WPC. Both Bill and Stodghill recalled running across German prisoners still in a state of shock after the bombing, yet official unit records clearly state that the 2nd Battalion, 12th Infantry remained in an assembly area four kilometers back from the highway.

20. Journal, July 25, 1944; Blumenson, 246; Atkinson, 145-6; Hastings, 255-6.

21. Journal, July 25-6, 1944, Field Order #35-6.

22. FM 7-15, 90-3.

23. Stodghill, 232; FM 7-15, 95-9; Journal, July 26, 1944, Unit Report #51, overlay.

24. Journal, July 27, 1944; Field Order #37; Stodghill, 233.

25. Journal, July 27, 1944, Unit Report #52, overlay; 4th AAR July 1944; 70th Tank Battalion, *"Soixante-Dix": A History of the 70th Tank Battalion* (Combined Arms Research Library, Fort Leavenworth, Kansas), 248 (hereafter cited as Soixante-Dix). The narrative for late July appears to be off by one day.

26. WPC did not state the exact date of this incident. Journal, July 27, 1944.

27. Jensen, 162; Allyn R. Vannoy and Jay Karamales, *Against the Panzers: United States Infantry versus German Tanks, 1944–1945* (Jefferson, NC: McFarland & Co., 1996), 15 (hereafter cited as Vannoy); Stodghill, 133.

28. War Department, Field Manual 23-55, Browning Machine Guns, Caliber .30, M1917A1, M1919A4 and M1919A6, July 1945, pp. 106-7 (hereafter cited as FM 23-55).

29. 29 FM 23-55, 169-70, 206-20 and 270-87.

30. Journal, July 27, 1944.

31. Journal, July 27, 1944; Field Order #38, Johnson, 135; Stodghill, 233.

32. Journal, July 28, 1944.

Chapter 6

1. Stodghill, 238–9; Journal, July 28, 1944.

2. Journal, July 28, 1944; Field Order #39; 12th AAR July 1944.

3. FM 7-15, 31; Stodghill, 247–8 shows that company machine guns were also loaded on their carriers for this move.

4. Johnson, 135–6; Journal, July 28, 1944, Unit Report #53; NARA, File 304-INF-0.3, Special Operations Report, St. Lo Breakthrough (hereafter cited as Special Report—St. Lo); Stodghill, 249; FM 7-15, 18.

5. Journal, July 29, 1944; Unit Report #44; FM 23-55, 200.

6. Unit Report #54 (mislabeled as #44); Special Report—St. Lo; Journal, July 29, 1944; Stodghill, 252–3.

7. Journal, July 29, 1944; Johnson, 137; FM 7-15, 74; FM 23–55, 163–70 and 182–3.

8. WPC. Bill never identified the French town the tank unit passed through but the circumstances fit Hambye. See also, Stodghill, 253.

9. Blumenson, 273–81.

10. Field Order #40; Stodghill, 257.

11. Field Order #40; War Department, Field Manual 101-5, Staff Officers' Field Manual: The Staff and Combat Orders, August 1940, 51; FM 100-5, 135.

12. Beevor, 242; WPC. Bill never identified the company commander by name but his description closely matched those in Stodghill, 141.

13. Special Report—St. Lo; Journal, July 30, 1944; Blumenson, 296; Unit Report #55; Otto Weidinger, *Comrades to the End: The 4th Panzer-Grenadier Regiment "Der Fuhrer" 1938–1945*, David Johnston trans. (Atglen, PA: Schiffer Publishing, 1998), 322–3 (hereafter cited as Weidinger).

14. FM 23-55, 143.

15. Special Report—St. Lo; Unit Report #55, overlay.

16. Journal, July 30, 1944; Special Report—St. Lo.

17. Special Report—St. Lo.

18. Desch, 91.

19. Special Report—St. Lo; Johnson, 138–9; Unit Report #55.

20. Hastings, 168.

21. Armageddon, 87; Lt. Gen. Guenther Blumentritt, MS# B-683, Foreign Military Studies, Manuscript Department, William R. Perkins Library, Duke University, Durham, NC, 6 (hereafter cited as Blumentritt, MS# B-683).

22. FM 7-5, 84–8; War Department, Infantry Field Manual 7-20, Infantry Battalion, October 1944. 155; FM 100-5, 241.

23. Field Order #41; Journal, July 31, 1944

24. Journal, July 31, 1944; Unit Report #56.

25. WPC. There is no way to substantiate the exact night during the Normandy campaign this incident occurred.

26. Field Order #42; Blumenson, 308.

27. Field Order #42. The order was contradictory. The written order specified that the 2nd Battalion follow the First but the overlay showed a separate route. The Journal reported the battalion following CCB.

28. Journal, August 1, 1944.

29. Johnson, 139. As the principal player in this battle, Johnson's book provides the best firsthand account.

30. FM 23-55, 101–3 and 206–12.

31. Journal, August 1, 1944; Special Report—St. Lo;

32. FM 23-55, 217–20; Johnson, 139.

33. Journal, August 1, 1944.

34. Johnson, p. 139, Journal, August 1, 1944; Special Report—St. Lo.

35. Special Report—St. Lo; FM 23-55, 68–71.

36. Journal, August 1, 1944. The journal does not explicitly state that this was a summary execution.

37. Johnson, 139; Unit Report, August 1, 1944 overlay; Journal, August 1, 1944. Stodghill, 268, describes a heavy engagement for G Company along a blacktop highway on August 1. The highway seems to match the Hambye–Villedieu highway but no one else mentions any fighting in the new assembly area.

Chapter 7

1. 4th AAR, August 1944; Weidinger, 344.

2. Field Order #43; Journal, August 2, 1944; Special Report—St. Lo.

3. Welch Interview.

4. Charles C. Roberts Jr., *Armored Strike Force: The Photo History of the American 70th Tank Battalion in World War II* (Mechanicsburg, PA: Stackpole Books, 2016), 164 (hereafter cited as Roberts); Johnson 142; Special Report—St. Lo.

5. Journal, August 2, 1944.

6. FM 7-15, 30–5.

7. Journal, August 2, 1944; Special Report—St. Lo; Johnson, 142.

8. Special Report—St. Lo; 70th Tank Battalion, After Action Reports, 1 Aug–30 Nov 44, 1-31 Mar and 1-31 May 45. Combined Arms Research Library, Fort Leavenworth, Kansas (hereafter cited as 70th Tk AAR).

9. Special Report—St. Lo; Johnson, 142.

10. Journal, August 2, 1944.

11. Stodghill, 280.

12. Johnson, 143.

13. Special Report—St. Lo.

14. Johnson, 143; 4th AAR, August 1944.

15. Journal, August 3, 1944; Johnson, 143–4; Special Report—St. Lo.

16. Stodghill, 282.

17. Beevor, 258; Marshall, 16; Ambrose, 273–86; Special Report—St. Lo.

18. Marshall, 47.

19. Special Report—St. Lo; Letter, February 26, 1945.

20. Field Order #44 and Change 1.

21. WPC. The town in Normandy was not identified but Bois-Yvon is one of the few villages that the 2nd Battalion liberated that had its own church.

22. WPC. Bill did not mention the specific day of this incident but the circumstances fit the situation of August 3, 1944.

23. Johnson, 143–6; Special Report—St. Lo; Journal, August 3, 1944.

24. Special Report—St. Lo.

25. Special Report—St. Lo.

26. Journal, August 3, 1944; Special Report—St. Lo; Stodghill, 283.

27. Stodghill, 284–5; Special Report—St. Lo; Johnson, 147–8.

28. Journal, August 4, 1944; Blumenson, 447; Roberts, 166.

29. Field Order #46, Journal, August 4, 1944.

30. WPC. Bill did not identify the precise day of this incident, just that it occurred during the drive through Normandy.

31. Special Report—St. Lo; Johnson, 148.

32. Journal, August 4, 1944; 4th AAR August 1944.

33. Special Report—St. Lo; Johnson, 149; Stodghill, 289.

34. Ernest Hemingway, "The G. I. and the General," *Collier's* (Nov. 4, 1944), (hereafter cited as G. I. and the General); Stodghill, 290.

35. WPC; Stodghill, 291.

36. Special Report—St. Lo; Johnson, 148–9

37. G. I. and the General, 11 and 46.

38. Journal, August 4-5, 1944.

39. Special Report—St. Lo; Johnson, 149.

40. Journal, August 5, 1944; Special Report—St. Lo; Johnson, 149.

41. Journal, August 6, 1944.

42. Blumenson, 447–8; Field Order #47; NARA File 304-INF(12)-0.3, After Action Report, Exploiting the Breakthrough, 1-6 August 1944.

Chapter 8

1. Journal, August 7, 1944; Johnson, 154.

2. Journal, August 7, 1944.

3. For information on the German strategic planning for Mortain, see Eisenhower, 390-4; Blumenson, 455-60; Hastings, 283-5; Donald Detwiler, Charles Burdick, and Jürgen Rohwer eds., *World War II German Military Studies* (New York: Garland Publishing, 1979) 1–21; Maj. Gen. Rudolph von Gersdorff, MS# A-921, *Avranches Counterattack, Seventh Army (29 Jul–14 Aug 44)* (hereafter cited as Gersdorff MS# A-921); Alwyn

Featherston, *Saving the Breakout: The 30th Division's Heroic Stand at Mortain, August 7–12, 1944* (Novato, CA: Presidio Press, 1993), 47–56 (hereafter cited as Featherston); Mark J. Reardon, *Victory at Mortain: Stopping Hitler's Panzer Counteroffensive* (Lawrence, Kansas: University Press of Kansas, 2002), 44–64 (hereafter cited as Reardon).

4. For information on the attack against the 30th Infantry Division on August 7, see Featherston, 75–143; Gersdorff MS# A-921, 21–6; Weidinger, 323–6; Blumenson, 460–5; Captain L. R. Adair, et al., *The Battle of Mortain* (Fort Leavenworth, KS: Combat Studies Institute, 1983), Sec. IV 11–7 (hereafter cited as Adair); Hastings, 285–7; Atkinson,155–7.

5. Blumenson, 464–5 and 481–6.

6. Journal, August 7, 1944; Oral Order August 7, 1944; Johnson,154. The Oral Order misidentified the attached tank Company. B Company 70th Tank Battalion was attached to the 12th Infantry, not C Company.

7. Johnson, 154, Journal, August 8, 1944; NARA File 304-INF(12)-0.3, After Action Report-The Mortain Stand: 7-14 August 1944 (hereafter cited as Mortain Stand).

8. NARA File 304-0.3.0 Special Operations Report—The Attack into Belgium Sept 1944: Interview August 18, 1944 (hereafter cited as Special Report—Mortain) [This report appears misfiled within the 4th Infantry Division archive, probably because the 12th Infantry was detached during the battle of Mortain]; Journal August 8, 1944; Field Order #48; Reardon, 185–6; Johnson, 155.

9. Special Report—Mortain; Journal, August 8, 1944; Johnson, 155–6.

10. Journal, August 8, 1944; Special Report—Mortain; Weidinger, 325–6.

11. Mortain Stand; Journal, August 8, 1944; Johnson, 156.

12. Johnson, 156; Reardon, 188.

13. Knapp, 100; NARA, File 304-INF-1.13, 4th Infantry Division, General Order #80, 29 Oct 44, Award of Silver Star to 2nd Lt. William P. Chapman and handwritten transcription of citation (hereafter cited as Silver Star Citation); Journal, August 8, 1944. The 1944 Army maps appear to have switched labels on the la Pourcerie and la Tourbelere farms. For the reader's sake, the narrative remains consistent with the maps.

14. Special Report—Mortain; Weidinger, 325–6; Reardon, 188; Journal, August 8, 1944; Unit Report #64; 30th Division Journal, August 8, 1944; Johnson, 156; Stodghill, 295-7.

15. Journal, August 8, 1944; Unit Report #64; Reardon, 188.

16. Special Report—Mortain.

17. Hastings, 190–5 and 289; Vannoy, 15; Bull, 44–5.

18. Special Report—Mortain; Unit Report #64; Journal, August 8, 1944; NARA File 330-3.2, Journal (hereafter cited as 30th Division Journal) August 8, 1944; Johnson, 156–7; Silver Star Citation.

19. Johnson, 165–6.

20. Johnson p. 157; Jensen, pp. 193-4.

21. Special Report – Mortain; Salinger, p. 116; Reardon, p. 228.

22. Johnson, p. 157.

23. Journal, August 9, 1944; Special Report – Mortain; Johnson, p. 157; Reardon, p. 189. Colonel Johnson did not explicitly state when he issued the order to withdraw. Reardon states that the battalion completed its withdrawal across the stream by 0200

hours but the unit journal and special report clearly show that the 2nd Battalion pulled back across the stream the next morning.

24. Silver Star Citation.

25. Special Report – Mortain; Journal, August 9, 1944; Johnson, p. 157; Mortain Stand.

26. Journal, August 9, 1944; 30th Division Journal, August 9, 1944; Silver Star Citation.

27. Special Report – Mortain.

28. Journal, August 9, 1944.

29. Special Report – Mortain; Journal, August 9, 1944.

30. NARA File 304-INF-0.3 Daily Operations (hereafter cited as 4th Daily Ops), August 9, 1944

31. Reardon, pp. 162-4.

32. Journal, August 9, 1944; Unit Report #65.

33. Special Report – Mortain; Journal, August 10, 1944.

34. Special Report – Mortain; 30th Division Journal, Letter of Instruction August 9, 1944; Unit Report #66.

35. Special Report – Mortain; Journal, August 10, 1944.

36. Journal, August 10, 1944; Reardon, p. 247.

37. Journal, August 10, 1944.

38. Journal, August 10, 1944; Special Report – St. Lo, Interview with Captain Dunbar Whitman; Johnson, pp. 158-9. Working from memory, Lt. Col. Gerden Johnson conflated the actions of August 11 and 12 when he wrote the regiment's history. The 1st Battalion crossed the 2nd Battalion's path on the tenth when neither unit had supporting tanks.

39. Journal, August 10, 1944; Weidinger, p. 326; Unit Report #66. American 1:25,000 maps show the farm's name as la Dainie.

40. Unit Report #66.

41. Journal, August 10, 1944; Special Report - Mortain.

42. Special Report – Mortain; 30th Division, August 8, 1944.
43. WPC. This event cannot be ascribed to a specific date or location.
44. Journal, August 10, 1944; Unit Report #66.
45. Journal, August 10, 1944.
46. Journal, August 10, 1944.
47. Journal, August 10, 1944.
48. Journal, August 10, 1944; Unit Report #66.
49. Journal, August 10, 1944.
50. Weidinger, p. 326; Journal, August 10, 1944.
51. Special Report – Mortain; Reardon, p. 256. Reardon puts this incident on August 11 when the Germans counterattacked E Company with several tanks. In the special report Lieutenants Anderson and Piper state that Burik engaged the German tank on the night of August 10. Although the unit journal does not record any tank engagements that evening, I see no reason to doubt the date they gave. They described the incident as a solitary tank probing at night,which could easily have occurred on the tenth.
52. Journal, August 11, 1944.
53. Reardon, p. 255.
54. Journal, August 11, 1944; Special Report – St. Lo, Interview with Captain Dunbar Whitman; Unit Report #67; Special Report – Mortain. The regiment did not issue a new operations order for August 11.
55. Journal, August 11, 1944; Johnson, p. 158; Reardon, pp. 254-5.
56. Reardon, p. 254; Johnson, p. 159.
57. Journal, August 11, 1944; Reardon, p. 254; Johnson, pp. 158-60.
58. Johnson, p. 159.

59. Journal, August 11, 1944; Special Report – Mortain. The two
     staff lieutenants, Anderson and Piper, who gave the interview for
     the special report, related this story as happening on August 10
     but the halftracks did not cross the stream until August 11.

60. Welch Interview.

61. Jensen, p. 195.

62. Reardon, p. 255.

63. Reardon, p. 255; Johnson, pp. 159-60; Special Report –
     Mortain; Journal, August 11, 1944; Mortain Stand; Unit Report
     #67. Johnson's book says he was wounded by a mortar round,
     but Reardon relates that German tank fire caused the casualties.
     It is difficult to contradict the author's own version of how he
     was wounded but Reardon's account is based on the firsthand
     testimony of Major Lay and corroborated by Lieutenants
     Anderson and Piper in the Special Report. Johnson may have
     been too seriously wounded to know how he was struck.

64. Journal, August 11, 1944; Special Report – St. Lo, Interview
     with Captain Dunbar Whitman.

65. Weidinger, p. 326; Gersdorff, MS# A-921; Reardon, p. 260.

66. Special Report – Mortain; Armageddon, p. 87. Hastings
     discusses the lack of American nighttime patrols and attacks.

67. Field Order #50; Special Report – Mortain. Field Order #50
     shows the battalion west of the highway with the mission of
     moving behind the 1ˢᵗ Battalion to a position south of RJ 278 on
     August 12. Field Order #51 shows the battalion occupying the
     ridgeline near la Sablonniere on the morning of August 13. The
     journals provide further evidence that events overtook the
     guidance in FO #50 and the battalion never attempted to shift to
     the south of RJ 278.

68. Mortain Stand; Johnson, p. 163; Special Report – Mortain; Unit Report #68; Reardon, p. 261.

69. Special Report – Mortain; Reardon, p. 263.

70. Journal, August 12, 1944; Unit Report #68; Mortain Stand; Special Report – Mortain.

71. Journal, August 12-3, 1944.

72. Journal, August 13, 1944; Field Order #51 and #52.

Chapter 9

1. Field Order #52.

2. NARA File 304-INF(12)7-0.3, 2nd Battalion Unit History (hereafter cited as 2nd Bn History).

3. Johnson, 168; Special Report – Mortain.

4. NARA File 304-INF-0.3.0, Special Operations Report – Movements of 4th Div. St. Pois to Paris (hereafter cited as Special Report – St. Pois to Paris); 4th AAR, August 1944; Journal, August 14-6, 1944.

5. Special Report – St. Pois to Paris.

6. 2nd Bn History; 12th AAR, August 1944.

7. Blumenson, 523.

8. Field Order #53; 2nd Bn History, August 14-17, 1944.

9. 4th AAR, August 1944; NARA File 304-INF(12)-0.3 After Action Report – The Liberation of Paris, August 1944 (hereafter cited as Liberation of Paris).

10. Journal, August 18, 1944.

11. Journal, August 18-23, 1944; 2nd Bn History; Special Report – St. Pois to Paris; Field Order #54; 4th Daily Ops, August 22, 1944.

12. Eisenhower, 416; Blumenson, 602-10.

13. Journal, August 23, 1944; Field Order #55; Special Report – St. Pois to Paris; 2nd Bn History.

14. 2nd Bn History; Journal, August 24, 1944, Liberation of Paris;

15. War Stories, 236-7.

16. 2nd Bn History, Journal, August 24, 1944; Liberation of Paris; Blumenson, 611-2; 4th AAR, August 1944; Willis Thornton, *The Liberation of Paris* (New York: Harcourt, Brace & World, 1962), 177 (hereafter cited as Thornton); Field Order, Overlay 24-Aug-44.

17. Journal, August 24, 1944; 4th Daily Ops, August 24, 1944; Jensen, 205.

18. Journal, August 24, 1944; Liberation of Paris; Second Bn History.

19. Liberation of Paris; Blumenson, 613-4; Martin Blumenson, *Liberation* (Alexandria, VA: Time-Life Books, 1978), 140 (hereafter cited as Blumenson Liberation).

20. Liberation of Paris; 4th AAR, August 1944; Journal, August 25, 1944; War Stories, 237; Roberts, 181.

21. Liberation of Paris; 2nd Bn History.

22. Thornton, 186-9; Blumenson, 616; Liberation of Paris.

23. Johnson, 169; Liberation of Paris; Thornton, 189.

24. Thornton, 189-91; Blumenson, 616-7.

25. Liberation of Paris; Blumenson, Overlay XIV.

26. Thornton, 187-8 and 193; Liberation of Paris.

27. War Stories, 240; George Wilson, *If You Survive* (New York: Ballantine Books, 1987), 64–5; Roberts, 181; Salinger, 117.

28. Michael Taylor, "Liberating France Hemingway's Way/Following Author's 1944 Reclaiming of the Ritz Hotel," *San Francisco Chronicle*, August 22, 2004; Beevor, 513; Salinger, 109.

29. Blumenson Liberation, 156.

30. Field Order #57; Journal, August 26, 1944.

31. "Discours de l'Hotel de Ville de Paris, 25 Aout 1944," June 2016, charles-de-gaulle.org; Beevor, 512.

32. 2nd Bn History; Liberation of Paris; War Stories, 238. The regiment's AAR gives the time of 0930 hours for the Mass but that was thirty minutes after the movement to the Bois de Vincennes started. The Battalion history states the Mass was held before the movement. That makes more sense.

33. Jensen, 211; 2nd Bn History.

34. Journal, August 26, 1944; Unit Report #82; 2nd Bn History.

35. Ibid; WPC never mentioned whether or not his heavy machine gun platoon escorted G Company on this mission.

36. Liberation of Paris; 2nd Bn History.

37. Journal, August 27, 1944.

38. Disposition Overlay, August 27, 1944.

39. Journal, August 28, 1944; 2nd Bn History.

Chapter 10

1. War Stories, 239.

2. Journal, August 28, 1944; Disposition Overlay, August 28, 1944; 2nd Bn History.

3. Overlay to Oral Order, August 29, 1944; Journal August 29, 1944; Disposition Overlay, August 29, 1944; 2nd Bn History. The battalion history misidentified the objective on August 29 as Levignen.

4. Eisenhower, 411-2; Bradley, 310-3; B. H. Liddell Hart, *History of the Second World War* (New York: Putnam, 1971), 561 (hereafter cited as Liddell Hart); Blumenson, 658.

5. Eisenhower, 416-20; Bradley, 313-4; Atkinson, 224.

6. Eisenhower, 420-3; Bradley, 314-6; Atkinson, 224-5; Liddell Hart, 562; Blumenson, 659-60.

7. Bradley, 317.

8. Field Orders 58, 59, 60 with Change 1; Journal, August 30 and 31, 1944; Unit Report #87; Disposition Overlays.

9. NARA File 304-INF(12)-0.3 After Action Report – Dash for Germany (hereafter cited as Dash for Germany); 2nd Bn History. The battalion history is off by a day.

10. Field Order #61; Journal, September 1, 1944; Dash for Germany; NARA File 304-INF-0.3.0 Special Operations Report – Pursuit thru Belgium (hereafter cited as Pursuit thru Belgium); Blumenson, 661-4 and 671-4.

11. Pursuit thru Belgium; Field Order Strip Map, September 2, 1944; 4th Daily Ops September 2, 1944; Journal, September 2, 1944; 2nd Bn History; Johnson, 178.

12. Jensen, 221.

13. 2nd Bn History; Jensen, 222.

14. Jensen, 221-2.

15. Blumenson, 680-2; Journal, September 3, 1944.

16. Eisenhower, 438-9; Bradley, 321-2; Blumenson, 686. The British promoted Montgomery on September 1.

17. Eisenhower, 436-7; Atkinson, 249-50; Blumenson, 700. Von Rundstedt's successor and predecessor, Field Marshall von Kluge, committed suicide during the retreat from Falaise.

18. Field Order #63; Journal, September 5, 1944.

19. Journal, September 5, 1944; 2nd Bn History; Johnson, 179; Foreign Military Studies, National Archives and Records Administration, College Park, Maryland. Interviews identified by name and MS#, *Obergruppenfuhrer* Georg Kepler MS#

B-155 I SS Panzer Corps (14 August–18 October 1944), (hereafter cited as Keppler MS# B-155).

20. Journal, September 5, 1944; Charles E. Rousek, Major, U. S. Army. A Short History of the 38th Cavalry Reconnaissance Squadron (Mechanized). N. P., N. D., 6 (hereafter cited as Rousek).

21. 2nd Bn History; Journal, September 5, 1944; Rousek, 6.

22. Dash for Germany; 2nd Bn History; Johnson, 179.

23. Ernest Hemingway, "War in the Siegfried Line," Collier's (Nov. 18, 1944): 18 and 70 (hereafter cited as Hemingway, "War in the Siegfried Line").

24. Field Order #64; Dash for Germany; 2nd Bn History; Journal, September 6, 1944; Unit Report #93; Roberts, p. 185; Rousek, 6.

25. 2nd Bn History; Johnson, 179; Dash for Germany; Journal, September 6, 1944; Unit Report #93 and Disposition Overlay; Rousek, 6-7; Keppler, MS# B-155.

26. Weidinger, 338; Blumentritt, MS# B-683, 10. Weidinger's quote applies to the general situation in the retreat across Belgium, not specifically to the action near Gedinne.

27. FM 100-5, 152; FM 7-5, 52.

28. Journal, September 6, 1944.

29. Pursuit thru Belgium; Weidinger, 337.

30. WPC did not identify the village. Morgan Welch reported a very similar, if not the same incident.

31. Field Order #65; 2nd Bn History; Unit Report #94; Johnson, 180; Journal, September 7, 1944.

32. Field Order #66; 4th Daily Ops, September 9, 1944; Rousek, 7; Unit Report #95; 2nd Bn History.

33. Field Order #67; Journal, September 9, 1944; Rousek, 7.

34. Rousek, 7; Johnson, 181; 2nf Bn History; FM 23-55, 185.

35. Journal, September 9, 1944; FM 23-95, 182-3; Pursuit thru Belgium; Knapp, 212; Johnson,181; 2nd Bn History.
36. Letter, December 24, 1944. The battalion lost one of the escorting resistance fighters but no one from the unit.
37. 2nd Bn History.
38. Letter December 24, 1944.
39. Letter December 24, 1944. Whenever recounting this story, Bill identified the town as Houffalize, a similar town about seventeen kilometers southeast of La Roche-en-Ardenne. Bill confused the two towns on the Ourthe River. The 12th Infantry did not pass through Houffalize. His description of the town and the action closely match La Roche.
40. Field Order #68; Journal, September 10, 1944; 2nd Bn History; Unit Report #97.
41. Field Order #69; 2nd Bn History; Journal September 11, 1944; Johnson, 181-2; Disposition Overlay, September 11, 1944.
42. Weidinger, 338; Field Order #70; Journal, September 12, 1944.
43. 2nd Bn History; Weidinger, 338-9.
44. 4th Daily Ops, September 12 and 13, 1944.
45. Field Order #72; Charles B. MacDonald, *The Siegfried Line Campaign* (Washington, DC: Office of the Chief of Military History, Department of the Army, 1963), 36-8 (hereafter cited as MacDonald).
46. Journal, September 13, 1944; 2nd Bn History.
47. 4th Daily Ops, September 9, 1944.
48. 2nd Bn History; Johnson, 183-4; MacDonald, 49.

Chapter 11

1. NARA File 304-INF-0.3.0 Special Operations Report – Penetration of the Siegfried Line (hereafter cited as Special Report – Siegfried

Line), Documentation of the Siegfried Line (hereafter cited as Documentation – Siegfried Line); MacDonald, 31-5.

2. Lt. Gen. Erich Brandenberger, MS# B-730, Foreign Military Studies, Manuscript Department, William R. Perkins Library, Duke University, Durham, NC, 65-6; Weidinger, 347-8.

3. Armageddon, 16; Bradley, 459

4. Keppler, MS# B-155.

5. Maj. Otha G. Miles, et al, *The Battle of Schnee Eifel* (Fort Leavenworth, KS: Combat Studies Institute, 1984), 19-20 (hereafter cited as Miles); MacDonald, 37; Weidinger, 349.

6. MacDonald, 41, 44 and Map III.

7. Miles, 21-3 and 47.

8. FM 100-5, 115; Miles, 22.

9. Field Order #73.

10. NARA File 304-INF(12)-0.3 After Action Report – The Siegfried Penetration (hereafter cited as Siegfried Penetration); Johnson 186; Special Report – Siegfried Line; 2nd Bn History; Unit Report #101.

11. 2nd Bn History; Special Report – Siegfried Line; Siegfried Penetration; Journal, September 14, 1944.

12. WPC. Bill did not specify the date of the incident with the fog but his story perfectly matches the events of September 14.

13. 2nd Bn History; Documentation – Siegfried Line.

14. 2nd Bn History; Siegfried Penetration; Documentation – Siegfried Line; Special Report – Siegfried Line; Unit Report #101. The interview within the Special Report states that combat action was minimal but other sources indicate a serious, though lopsided, fight.

15. Journal, September 14, 1944; 2nd Bn History; Unit Report #101; Keppler, MS# B-155.

16. FM 100-5, 146; Journal September 14, 1944.

17. MacDonald, 52; Miles, 53.

18. Field Order #74; Documentation – Siegfried Line.

19. Journal, September 15, 1944; 2nd Bn History.

20. Special Report – Siegfried Line; Siegfried Penetration; 2nd Bn History; Journal, September 15, 1944; Unit Report #102.

21. Ibid; Hemingway, "War in the Siegfried Line."

22. Miles, 13-5; Unit Report #102. The poor records of the *2nd SS Panzer "Das Reich" Division* make it difficult to sort out the German dispositions. Miles indicates that the *4th Panzergrenadier "Der Fuhrer" Regiment* defended the northern half of the Schnee Eifel and Losheim Gap but Weidinger's descriptions make reference to engagements south of Brandscheid. The unit reports on 14 and 17 September mention confronting the *3rd Panzergrenadier "Deutschland" Regiment.*

23. Special Report – Siegfried Line; Siegfried Penetration; 2nd Bn History; Journal, September 15, 1944; Unit Report #102.

24. Special Report – Siegfried Line; Siegfried Penetration.

25. 2nd Bn History; Siegfried Penetration.

26. FM 7-15, 106-13.

27. FM 23-55, 199.

28. NARA File 304-INF(12)-1.6 Commendations (hereafter cited as Commendations), Commendation for Meritorious Service Company E, 12th Infantry, October 2, 1944. WPC noted in his copy of Johnson's regimental history that his platoon was attached to E Company for this battle.

29. Special Report – Siegfried Line; NARA File 304-INF(12)-3.9.1, Memorandum, September 15, 1944; Miles, 54; Unit Report Overlay, September 15, 1944.

30. Brandenberger, MS# B-730, VII. MacDonald in *The Siegfried Line Campaign*, 51, incorrectly identifies *Brigadefuhrer* Heinz Lammerding as commander of *Das Reich* but Baum held command between July and October 1944.

31. Miles, 54; Special Report – Siegfried Line.

32. Field Order #75.

33. Journal, September 16, 1944; Unit Report #103.

34. Journal, September 16, 1944; Siegfried Penetration; 2nd Bn History; Unit Report #103.

35. 2nd Bn History.

36. Journal, September 16, 1944; Unit Report #103; Special Report – Siegfried Line.

37. Johnson, 188.

38. Ibid.

39. 2nd Bn History; Siegfried Penetration; Journal, September 16, 1944; Unit Report #103.

40. 2nd Bn History; Siegfried Penetration; Special Report – Siegfried Line.

41. Journal, September 16, 1944.

42. Field Order #76.

43. Journal, September 17, 1944; Unit Report #104. WPC claimed that he knew beforehand that he would be wounded on both occasions.

44. 2nd Bn History. There is no direct evidence that Lieutenant Chapman's platoon was attached to E Company. That is inferred by the fact that G Company suffered almost no casualties on September 17 while Bill described an intense direct fire engagement and was, himself, wounded.

45. Journal, September 17, 1944; Unit Report #104; 2nd Bn History; Siegfried Penetration.

46. Journal, September 17, 1944; Unit Report #104; Chapman Form 53-98; Field Order #76.

47. Special Report – Siegfried Line; Miles, 57-9.

48. MacDonald, 55.

49. *4th Infantry Division, 12th Infantry Regiment* (Baton Rouge: Army & Navy Publishing Company, 1946), 16 (hereafter cited as Division History); Special Report – Siegfried Line.

Chapter 12

1. Field Order #76.

2. Letter, 1944.

3. Morning Report, September 20, 1944; Silver Star Citation; Letter, January 27, 1945.

4. Letter, November 24, 1944.

5. Letters, December 3, 4 and 18, 1944.

6. Letter, December 23, 1944.

7. Letter, December 23, 1944; Morning Report, January 7, 1945.

8. Hugh M. Cole, *The Ardennes: Battle of the Bulge* (Washington, DC: Office of the Chief of Military History, Department of the Army, 1965) 238-58; Johnson, 230-300.

9. Welch Interview; "Gorn_J," September 10, 2015, Memorial. thetasigmatau.org.

10. Bradley, 372-3 and 386; Unit Report #222; NARA File 304-INF(12)-0.3 After Action Report, January 1945 (hereafter cited as AAR – Jan 45); 2nd Bn History.

11. Letter, January 10 and 13, 1945.

12. FO #112; 2nd Bn History; Unit Report #226; Journal, January 18, 1945.

13. 2nd Bn History; Journal, January 19, 1945; FM 7-15, 60-3.

14. Unit Report #229; Journal, January 19, 1945; Second Bn
    History; FM 23-90, 88.

15. 2nd Bn History; Field Order #113; FM 7-15, 150; Journal,
    January 20, 1945.

16. Field Order #113; Soixante-Dix, 201; Journal, January 20, 1945;
    Roberts, 218.

17. War Stories, 353; Letter, January 4, 1945.

18. Johnson, 301; Journal, January 20, 1945; Unit Report #229;
    Charles B. MacDonald, *The Last Offensive* (Washington, DC:
    Office of the Chief of Military History, Department of the Army,
    1973) 48 (hereafter cited as Last Offensive).

19. Field Order #114; FM 7-15, 146.

20. AAR – Jan 45; Johnson, 301; Unit Report #230.

21. Journal, January 21, 1945; Jensen, 280; Soixante-Dix, 202; AAR
    – Jan 45; Roberts, 218; Commendations, 12th Infantry, 24
    January 1945; 2nd Bn History. The 2nd Bn History has confused
    some of the dates.

22. Journal, January 21, 1945; Soixante-Dix, 202; Johnson, 303;
    AAR – Jan 45; Commendations, 12th Infantry, 24 January 1945;
    Unit Report #230; 2nd Bn History.

23. Journal, January 21, 1945; Unit Report #230; 2nd Bn History;
    Johnson, 301-3.

24. FM 23-90, 2, 25 and 28.

25. 2nd Bn History; Unit Report #30; Johnson, 301-3; Journal,
    January 21, 1945.

26. Journal, January 21, 1945.

27. Unit Report, Operation Overlay, January 22, 1945.

28. Unit Report #231.

29. Journal, January 22, 1945; Unit Report #231; AAR – Jan 45.

30. Operation Overlay for 22 January 1945; Unit Report #231.

31. Journal, January 22, 1945.

32. Journal, January 22, 1945; Unit Report #231; 2nd Bn History; AAR – Jan 45; Jensen, 281; Roberts, 218.

33. WPC did specify the exact day this incident occurred.

34. Unit Report #232; 2nd Bn History, Journal, January 22, 1945.

35. 2nd Bn History.

36. FM 23-90, 179-207. No mention was made of how this tank platoon reached G Company's position but the journal and AAR state that tanks attacked Fouhren from both directions.

37. 2nd Bn History; Journal, January 23, 1945; Unit Report #232; AAR – Jan 45; Johnson. 303; Jensen, 281. Soixante-Dix, 202; Roberts, 218.

38. Journal, January 23, 1945; Jensen, 281; Soixante-Dix, 202.

39. Journal, January 23, 1945; Commendations, 12th Infantry Regiment, 24 January 1945; Jensen, 281. Sources disagree on the precise numbers of German tanks and guns destroyed. I quoted the inventory from the letter of commendation.

40. Journal, January 23, 1945.

41. 2nd Bn History; Journal, January 23, 1945; Johnson, 304.

42. Unit Report Disposition Overlay, January 24, 1945.

43. Unit Report #233; Journal, January 24, 1945.

44. Knapp, 224.

45. Johnson, 304-5; Journal, January 25, 1945. Johnson gives the date of January 24 for this incident but the journal shows that it happened on the twenty-fifth.

46. Journal, January 26, 1945; Unit Report #235 and disposition overlay; Field Order #115.

Chapter 13

1. Field Order #115; Journal, January 27, 1945; Unit Report, Disposition Overlay; 2nd Bn History.

2. Bradley, 390; Last Offensive, 55-7.

3. Letter, January 27, 1945.

4. Johnson, 306; 2nd Bn History; NARA File 304-INF-0.3.0 Special Operations Report - Second Penetration of the Siegfried Line (hereafter cited as Second Penetration).

5. Field Order #116; Second Penetration.

6. Unit Report #240; Letter, January 31, 1945.

7. Field Order #116 and #117; Journal, January 31, 1945.

8. Unit Report #241; NARA File 304-INF(12)7-0.3 After Action Report, February 1945 (hereafter cited as AAR – Feb 45); Second Penetration; Johnson, 307-8.

9. Journal, February 1, 1945; Unit Report #241.

10. Journal, February 1, 1945; Unit Report #241; AAR – Feb 45; Johnson, 308.

11. Unit Report #241 and Disposition Overlay; Field Order #118; Unit Report #242.

12. Second Penetration; Jensen, 287; Roberts, 218; Journal, February 2, 1945.

13. Journal, February 2, 1945; Unit Report #242; AAR – Feb 45. The regimental overlay did not show the battalion's LD but it was most likely the crest of the ridge.

14. Jensen, 287.

15. Jensen, 176 and 287; AAR – Feb 45; Unit Report #242; Second Penetration; Johnson, 308. Johnson seems to imply that the tank attack preceded the infantry crossing of the LD but the testimony of the tankers indicates that the infantry assault was well under way by the time the tanks came on the scene.

16. Journal, February 2, 1945.

17. WPC. This story cannot be matched to this exact date but fits with the circumstances of this day's action.

18. Journal, February 2, 1945; Unit Report #242; AAR – Feb 45; Johnson, 308.

19. Journal, February 2, 1945.

20. Journal, February 3, 1945; Unit Report #243; AAR – Feb 45; Johnson, 308-9.

21. Journal, February 3, 1945; Captain Roy T. McGrann, "*The 610th Tank Destroyer Battalion: Apr. 10, 1942 – Dec. 7, 1945*" (N. P., N. D.), 73 (hereafter cited as McGrann).

22. Journal, February 3, 1945; AAR – Feb 45.

23. Eisenhower, 643-5; Bradley, 392; Last Offensive, 67.

24. Second Penetration; Welch Interview.

25. Second Penetration; Last Offensive, 86.

26. Letter, February 2, 1945.

27. AAR – Feb 45; Journal, February 7-10, 1945; Unit Report #247-50 with disposition overlay; Johnson, 308-9.

28. Field Order #122.

29. Journal, February 5, 11 and 13, 1945; Last Offensive, 96; AAR – Feb 45; Johnson, 311.

30. Journal, February 12 and 13, 1945.

31. McGrann, 78-9.

32. Journal, February 16 and 18, 1945; AAR – Feb 45; Field Order #123.

33. Journal, February 19, 1945; Unit Report #259; AAR – Feb 45.

34. Disposition Overlay, February 19, 1945.

35. Journal, February 20, 1945; Unit Report #260; Johnson, p. 311; AAR – Feb 45.

36. AAR – Feb 45.

37. Unit Report #258-61.

38. Journal, February 21-5, 1945; Unit Report #260-5.

39. Journal, February 25-6, 1945; Unit Report #266.

40. Letter, February 26, 1945.

Chapter 14

1. Eisenhower, 671; Bradley, 400-1; Last Offensive, 185.

2. Field Order 124 and 125; Second Penetration; NARA File 304-INF(12)-0.3 After Action Report – March 1945 (hereafter cited as AAR – Mar 45).

3. 2nd Bn History; Journal, March 1, 1945.

4. Journal, March 1, 1945; 2nd Bn History; Unit Report Disposition Overlay.

5. FM 23-90, 116.

6. Journal, March 1, 1945; 2nd Bn History; Unit Report Disposition Overlay.

7. Journal, March 2, 1945; AAR – Mar 45; 70th AAR Mar 45.

8. Journal, March 2, 1945; AAR – Mar 45; Unit Report #270; 2nd Bn History; Johnson, 314.

9. Field Order #125; Journal, March 2, 1945; AAR – Mar 45; Unit Report #270; 2nd Bn History.

10. Letter, March 7, 1945. In his letter Bill said he answered "Yes, sir." However, as he related the story he always claimed his answer was "Hell, yes."

11. US Army, Table of Organization & Equipment 7-15, Infantry Battalion, February 26, 1944.

12. Field Order #126.

13. Journal, March 3, 1945; Unit Report #271; 2nd Bn History; 70th Tk AAR Mar 45; Roberts, 229. The 2nd Battalion disposition overlays normally did not show the H Company positions but the

situation at Rommersheim was ideal for involving the heavy weapons platoons from firing positions west of town.

14. Journal, March 3, 1945; Unit Report #271 with Disposition Overlay.

15. Second Penetration; AAR – Mar 45; Journal, March 3, 1945; Last Offensive, 197.

16. Unit Report #272; Field Order #127.

17. Journal, March 4, 1945.

18. War Department, Infantry Field Manual 7-10, Rifle Company, Rifle Regiment, June 1942, 15-6 (hereafter cited as FM 7-10).

19. Journal, March 4, 1945.

20. Field Order #128; Second Penetration; AAR Mar 45; Journal, March 5, 1945; 2nd Bn History; Unit Report #273.

21. Journal, March 6, 1945.

22. Maps; Second Penetration; Journal, March 6, 1945.

23. Last Offensive, p. 199; Journal, March 6, 1945; 2nd Bn History; AAR – Mar 45.

24. FM 7-10, 26-7; Maps.

25. Letter, March 7, 1945.

26. Journal, March 7, 1945; 2nd Bn History.

27. FM 7-10, 37.

28. FM 7-10, 38.

29. Journal, March 7, 1945.

30. Journal, March 7, 1945; Unit Report #275; 2nd Bn History; Johnson, 316.

31. Journal, March 7, 1945; Johnson, 316; Letter, March 7, 1945.

32. Field Order #129; Journal, March 7, 1945; AAR – Mar 45.

33. Johnson, 317; Unit Report #279.

34. Unit Reports #280-2; 2nd Bn History; Letter, March 14, 1945.

35. Unit Report #287-90; 2nd Bn History; Johnson, 318.

36. Unit Report #284, AAR – Mar 45; McGrann, 86; 2nd Bn History; Johnson, 318; Field Order #133. The 4th Infantry Division had been sent south in March as a reinforcement for Operation Undertone, the Seventh Army push to the Rhine River. See Bradley, 403-4. The assignment to Seventh Army came after Undertone was finished.

Chapter 15

1. Stephen G. Fritz, *Endkampf: Soldiers, Civilians and the Death of the Third Reich*, (Lexington, KY: The University Press of Kentucky, 2004), 1-9 (hereafter cited as Endkampf); David Stafford, *Endgame 1945: The Missing Final Chapter of World War II* (New York: Little Brown, 2007), 254-8 (hereafter cited as Stafford); Atkinson, 590-3; Eisenhower, 628-9; Last Offensive, 340.

2. Eisenhower, 729; Bradley, 418-21; Last Offensive, 421.

3. Last Offensive, 413.

4. AAR – Mar 45; Field Order #134; 2nd Bn History; Unit Report #298; Johnson, 318; Once again, the 2nd Battalion History is off by a day in its narrative.

5. 2nd Bn History; Richard Bessel, *Germany 1945: From War to Peace* (New York: HarperCollins, 2009), 54 (hereafter cited as Bessel).

6. Unit Report #299; 2nd Bn History; Johnson, 318.

7. Field Order #135; 4th AAR – Apr 45; NARA File 304-INF(12)-0.3 After Action Report – April 1945 (hereafter cited as AAR – Apr 45); 2nd Bn History; Journal, April 1, 1945; Unit Report #300.

8. AAR – Apr 45; 2nd Bn History; Journal, April 2 and 3, 1945; Unit Report #301 and 302; Field Order #136.

9. Last Offensive, 413-4; Endkampf, 71-2; Journal, April 4, 1945 (sketch map); 2nd Bn History.

10. Field Order #137.

11. Journal, March 4, 1945; NARA File 304-INF-0.3.0 Special Operations Report - Second Penetration of the Siegfried Line, interview with Lt. William Chapman (hereafter cited as Chapman Interview). After VE Day the division historical staff interviewed Bill about the campaign across Southern Germany. He made a five-page statement. This interview has apparently been misfiled within the division archive. It can be found in the "Second Penetration of the Siegfried Line" folder even though it is labeled "East of the Rhine." Bill never mentioned this interview to anyone in the family. The family did not know of its existence until it was discovered in the division archive while researching for this book.

12. FM 7-10, 60-1.

13. 2nd Bn History; Journal, March 4, 1945.

14. Chapman Interview.

15. Journal, April 5, 1945; Unit Report #304; Chapman Interview.

16. WPC; FM 7-10, 142.

17. WPC.

18. Journal, April 5, 1945; Chapman Interview.

19. Chapman Interview; Endkampf, 92.

20. WPC. Bill did not give the precise date of this incident but the circumstances correspond with the battle of Simmringen Woods.

21. WPC.

22. Field Order #167. Objective #4 - north end of Simmringen Woods, #5 – Hills 366-374, #6 – Harthausen, #7 – Nassau.

23. Journal, March 6, 1945; Chapman Interview; Unit Report #305 and Disposition Overlay.

24. Field Order #138.
25. FM 7-40.
26. Chapman Interview; Journal, April 7, 1945.
27. Chapman Interview; Journal, April 7, 1945; Unit Report #305; AAR – April 45;
28. War Stories, 369.
29. Chapman Interview; Journal, April 8, 1945.
30. War Stories, 369-70.
31. Chapman Interview.
32. Chapman Interview; Unit Report #307; AAR – Apr 45.
33. 4th AAR April 1945; Unit Reports #303-7; Johnson, 323.
34. WPC; Letter, April 13, 1945.
35. 2nd Bn History; Letter, April 9, 1945.

Chapter 16

1. Last Offensive, 418-21; *Endkampf*, 92.
2. Last Offensive, 420-1; *Endkampf*, 15.
3. Field Order #139; 4th AAR – Apr 45; Unit Report #310 and Enemy Disposition Overlay.
4. Journal, April 11, 1945; 2nd Bn History; Chapman Interview.
5. Letter, April 13 and 20, 1945.
6. 2nd Bn History.
7. Chapman Interview; 2nd Bn History.
8. Chapman Interview.
9. 2nd Bn History; Journal, April 12, 1945; Unit Report #311; AAR – Apr 45.
10. Letter, April 13, 1945.
11. Journal, April 13, 1945; Unit Report #312; AAR – Apr 45; 4th AAR – Apr 45.

12. Chapman Interview; 2nd Bn History; Journal, April 14, 1945; Unit Report #313; AAR – Apr 45.

13. Field Order #140; Chapman Interview; 2nd Bn History; Journal, April 15, 1945; Roberts, 234.

14. Journal, April 15, 1945; Chapman Interview; 2nd Bn History; Unit Report #314; AAR – Apr 45.

15. Journal, April 15, 1945.

16. Journal, April 15, 1945; Chapman Interview.

17. Chapman Interview; Disposition Overlay, April 15, 1945.

18. Chapman Interview; 2nd Bn History; Unit Report #314; 4th AAR – Apr 45; Letter, April 13, 1945.

19. Chapman Interview; 2nd Bn History.

20. Chapman Interview.

21. Chapman Interview; 2nd Bn History; Journal, April 16, 1945; Unit Report #315.

22. William M. Dwyer, *So Long for Now: A World War II Memoir* (Bloomington, IN: Xlibris, 2009), 119-20 (hereafter cited as Dwyer); Journal, April 16, 1945.

23. The patrol's trip into Rothenburg is described in detail in Dwyer, 118-31 and reprinted in Johnson, 326-37.

24. Journal April 16 and 17, 1945.

25. Journal, April 17, 1945; 2nd Bn History.

26. WPC. Bill did not identify the name of the town but entries in the regiment's journal and 2nd Bn History correspond to his story.

27. Chapman Interview; 2nd Bn History; Journal, April 17, 1945; Unit Report #316 and overlay.

28. Field Order #141.

29. Journal, April 18, 1945.

30. Journal, April 18, 1945; Chapman Interview; 2nd Bn History; Unit Report #317; AAR – Apr 45.

31. WPC. Bill retold this story many times but did not mention the town by name. However, the circumstances of the story fit with E Company's capture of Wohnbach.

32. Journal, April 18, 1945; 2nd Bn History; Unit Report #317; AAR – Apr 45.

33. "Geschichte," December 17, 2013, schloss-schillingsfuerst.de. Schloss Schillingsfürst, 2009. (hereafter cited as Schillingsfurst).

34. National Archives and Records Administration, College Park, Maryland. Interviews identified by name and MS#, Major General Max Ulich MS# B-795 *The Last Battles of the 212th Volksgrenadier Division (1-26 April 1945)*.

35. *Endkampf*, 91, 136 and 179; Bessel, 45; Albert Speer, *Inside the Third Reich: Memoirs by Albert Speer* (New York: MacMillan, 1970), 401 and 447; Journal, April 6, 1945.

36. *Endkampf*, 132-6; Schillingsfurst.

37. Speer, p. 439.

38. Journal, April 19, 1945; Schillingsfürst.

39. WPC; 2nd Bn History.

40. 2nd Bn History; Journal, April 19, 1945; Unit Report #318.

41. Chapman Interview; 2nd Bn History; Journal, April 19, 1945.

42. Colonel Gorn related his discussion with a senior officer in the *schloss* during TF Chapman's attack. Bill did not give the senior officer's name but General Rodwell is the likeliest candidate. The unit journal did not mention the visit of any general to the regimental CP at that time but that would not preclude a visit by Rodwell to the 2nd Battalion CP.

43. Johnson, 339; 2nd Bn History.

Chapter 17

1. 2nd Bn History; Journal, April 20, 1945; Unit Report #319 and Disposition Overlay. From April 21 to the end of the month the 2nd Bn History was off by one day.

2. Journal, April 20, 1945.

3. Field Order #142; 4th AAR – Apr 45; AAR – Apr 45; Johnson, 340; Roberts, 235.

4. Journal, April 22, 1945.

5. Johnson, 340-1; Jensen, 314-7; 4th AAR – Apr 45; 2nd Bn History.

6. Jensen, 317; Confirmation of Verbal Order, 222300 April 45; Bessel, 22-3.

7. Journal, April 23, 1945; Unit Report #322; AAR – Apr 45; 4th AAR – Apr 45; Jensen, 317-8; Johnson, 341.

8. Journal, April 23, 1945; Chapman Interview; 2nd Bn History.

9. Chapman Interview; 2nd Bn History; Johnson, 341-3.

10. WPC. Bill never mentioned the location of the tank shot. However, the elements of the story, the tanks, the incoming artillery, and the presence of a tower, match the situation at Aalen.

11. Chapman Interview; 2nd Bn History.

12. Chapman Interview; McGrann, 91.

13. Chapman Interview; 4th AAR – Apr 45; AAR – Apr 45; Unit Report #322.

14. Unit Report #322.

15. 2nd Bn History; AAR –Apr 45; Chapman Interview; Unit Report #323; Johnson, 343.

16. Johnson, 343; Roberts, 237.

17. Journal, April 24, 1945. Sources do not give a clear picture of the time TF Rodwell began movement that morning. Johnson and the 2nd Bn History say 1000 hours. The regiment's AAR says

0700 hours. The first definitive time check by the journal places the task force west of Grosskuchen at 1055 hours, ten kilometers from the initial point.

18. WPC. Bill never stated the exact date or location of the tank-88 duel but the circumstances strongly suggest that it occurred somewhere along TF Rodwell's line of advance on this day.

19. Journal, April 24, 1945.

20. Journal, April 24, 1945; Johnson, 343.

21. Johnson, 343; James R. Dow and Hannjost Lixfeld, *The Nazification of an Academic Discipline: Folklore in the Third Reich* (Bloomington, IN: Indiana University Press, 1994), 65, 257. Bill did not state the exact date and location where Weigel surrendered to him nor do any biographical sketches of Weigel. The only clue is Johnson's comment that someone of his rank was captured at Oggenhausen, where Bill was present to accept his surrender.

22. Journal, April 24, 1945.

23. Chapman Interview; Johnson, 343-4.

24. Unit Report #323.

25. Letter, May 8, 1945.

26. Chapman Interview; 2nd Bn History; Johnson, 344. Johnson mistakenly claimed the regiment backpedaled to Oggenshausen. He confused TF Rodwell's march from Giengen with the forward movement of the 1st and 3rd Battalions that had consolidated at Oggenhausen overnight.

27. WPC. Bill claimed that the church steeple was in the city of Ulm but that was incorrect. Ulm was more than twenty kilometers out of TF Rodwell's sector. Possibly, Bill recalled that he was working off the "Ulm" map sheet when the incident occurred.

28. 4th AAR – Apr 45; 2nd Bn History.

29. 4th AAR – Apr 45; AAR – Apr 45; 2nd Bn History; Johnson, 344.

30. Jensen, 319; Endkampf, 179.

Chapter 18

1. Field Order #144; AAR – Apr 45; Chapman Interview; 2nd Bn History.

2. Journal, April 25, 1945; Unit Report #324.

3. 4th AAR – Apr 45; AAR- Apr 45; 2nd Bn History; Unit Report #325.

4. 2nd Bn History; Chapman Interview.

5. AAR – Apr 45; Unit Report #325; 2nd Bn History.

6. 2nd Bn History; Chapman Interview.

7. Unit Report #325.

8. Bessel, 11; *Endkampf*, 191-2.

9. Letter, April 27, 1945.

10. Unit Report #326

11. Unit Report #326.

12. 2nd Bn History.

13. WPC. Bill did not give a precise date or location for this incident.

14. Field Order #145; AAR – Apr 45; Journal, April 28, 1945; Unit Report #326.

15. Field Order #146; AAR - Apr 45.

16. 2nd Bn History; Chapman Interview.

17. 2nd Bn History; Unit Report #328.

18. 2nd Bn History; Chapman Interview.

19. Chapman Interview; NARA File 304-INF(12)7-0.3, Handwritten Journal of 1/Sgt. Edgar Weber (hereafter cited as Weber Journal). The Weber Journal was one day off for the first days of May, similar to the error of the 2nd Bn History in late April.

20. Field Order #147; McGrann, 92.

21. Weber Journal.

22. Weber Journal. Unit Report #329 and AAR – Apr 45 incorrectly state that the 2nd Battalion only progressed to Unt-Brunn.

23. McGrann, 92-3; Unit Report #329; AAR – Apr 45.

24. Unit Reports #325-30.

25. Weber Journal; Stafford, 484-5. WPC did not give a specific date or location of the camp but Weber's Journal clearly states that E Company had "law and order" duty on May 1 and Föhrenwald was the nearest slave labor camp.

26. Jensen, 320. Likewise, Jensen does not identify the precise date or site of this anecdote but Föhrenwald is the likeliest camp to be served by his mess team. Also, see Knapp, 286-7.

27. WPC. Bill's seeming act of kindness was actually ill-advised. A starving man should only be fed gradually under close medical supervision. Unfortunately, Bill did not know this at the time.

28. Weber Journal; Journal, May 2, 1945.

29. Weber Journal; Journal, May 2, 1945; Unit Report #331; AAR – May 45.

30. Morning Report, April 27 – May 3, 1945.

31. Weber Journal.

32. Weber Journal; Unit Report #332; AAR – May 45.

33. Weber Journal; Johnson, 347.

34. Weber Journal; Knapp, 289.

35. Weber Journal; Journal, May 5, 1945; Unit Report #334; AAR – May 45; Johnson, 347.

36. Last Offensive, 472; Atkinson, 618; *Endkampf*, 22.

37. Journal, May 6, 1945; Unit Report #335.

38. Johnson, 347.

39. Bessel, 131; Letter, May 7, 1945.

40. Weber Journal.

Chapter 19

1. Weber Journal.
2. 12th AAR – May 45; Bessel, 256.
3. Journal, May 9-13, 1945.
4. *Endkampf*, 198, Journal, May 13, 1945.
5. Letter, May 10, 1945.
6. Journal 23, May 1945; Knapp, 312; Letter, May 18, 1945.
7. 12th AAR – Jun 45; Journal, June 10, 1945; Weber Journal.
8. Journal, June 13-8, 1945; Weber Journal; Division History, 48-9; Knapp, 325.
9. Weber Journal; War Stories, 417-8.
10. Weber Journal; War Stories, 418; 12th AAR – Jun 45; Knapp, 329.
11. War Stories p. 418; 12th AAR – Jun 45.
12. Weber Journal; War Stories, 418; 12th AAR – Jun 45.
13. ASHRAE Interview; Chapman Form 53-98; Chapman Form 100.

INDEX